A GRAPHIC SURVEY
of
PERCEPTION and BEHAVIOR for the Design Professions

A GRAPHIC SURVEY
of
PERCEPTION and BEHAVIOR for the Design Professions

Forrest Wilson

 VAN NOSTRAND REINHOLD COMPANY
NEW YORK   CINCINNATI   TORONTO   LONDON   MELBOURNE

Copyright © 1984 by Van Nostrand Reinhold Company Inc.

Library of Congress Catalog Card number: 82-13619
ISBN: 0-442-23891-6

Manufactured in the United States of America

Published by Van Nostrand Reinhold Company Inc.
135 West 50th Street, New York, N.Y. 10020

Van Nostrand Reinhold
480 Latrobe Street
Melbourne, Victoria 3000, Australia

Van Nostrand Reinhold Company Limited
Molly Millars Lane
Wokingham, Berkshire, England

15 14 13 12 11 10 9 8 7 6 5 4 3 2 1

Library of Congress Cataloging in Publication Data

Wilson, Forrest, 1918–
   A graphic survey of perception and behavior for the
design professions.

   Includes bibliographical references and index.
   1. Architecture—Human factors.   2. Visual perception.
I. Title.
NA2542.4.W55   1983   720′.1   82-13619
ISBN 0-442-23891-6

PREFACE

Architecture—art or science? The persistence of this frivolous debate exposes the recently fabricated dichotomy between the theoretical and the provable, the artistic and the scientific.

Architecture, as a word and idea as we know it today, did not come into being until some time after the middle of the sixteenth century. That is not very old as English words go. We can be sure that when it was coined there was little difference between art and science. Sixteenth-century architects prided themselves on their scientific knowledge, and natural philosophers of the period were often architectural designers of considerable knowledge and ability.

Several years ago the psychologist Robert Sommer lamented that the "bright future" of cooperation between behavioral scientists and the design professions projected during the 1960s had not materialized. It is true that behavioral scientists did not become an integral part of what was in those days termed the "architectural team," but neither did the "architectural team" itself materialize as projected.

Nevertheless, people such as anthropologist Edward T. Hall, the microbiologist Rene Dubos, J. E. Parr, Robert Gutman, and Sommer himself, to name but a very few, did have a vital influence on designers. We tend to forget that art historians, critics, artists, philosophers of art, and architects, such as Rudolf Arnheim, Steen Eiler Rasmussen, Walter Gropius, Wassily Kandinsky, and Paul Klee were vitally concerned with human behavior and the science of visual perception. Their concerns are in marked contrast to the present critical direction that interprets architecture as a linguistic/syntactical/semantic exercise.

Architect Philip Johnson's often quoted remark, "One cannot not know history," is obviously true, but it is equally obvious that history encompasses much more than architecture. The history of those who study and record how humankind works and lives in its environment is as vital as the history of the sequence of forms that the design professions have, over time, invented to house these functions. It was the desire to recall some of this rich design inspiration to the attention of students and young architects, and to do so by juxtaposing behavioral science and design, that prompted this book. It has been written in the belief that the ideas of the recent past, gathered together and graphically presented, might be of use to designers searching for values in an age of chaotic mannerism. It seeks to demonstrate the interdependent nature of art and science in the field of perception and behavior. We do not have to return to the sixteenth century to find a connection between the two; it is everywhere evident.

The thrill of Edward Hall's writings in the 1960s, which ran like an electric shock through the design professions, seems, on the surface, a thing of the past, but much of what we now take for granted in design conversations over drafting boards and 'crit' sessions in architectural schools was introduced to designers at this time. Hall and Sommer did not become fellows of the AIA, nor did Cesar Pelli, Louis Kahn, and I.M. Pei receive honorary Ph.D.s from colleges of psychiatric medicine. Nevertheless, there is, without doubt, more concern now for human beings in the built environment—their perceptions and response to it—than there has ever been before.

Midway in the preparation of this book, Dr. Arthur I. Rubin and Jacqueline Elder of the Environmental Design Research Division of the Center for Building Technology of the National Bureau of Standards published their work, *Building For People.* It is apparent from this encyclopedic compilation, liberally quoted in this text, that a great deal more interaction has been, and is, taking place than most people entering the design professions from design schools seem to realize.

It is difficult to believe that the science and technology of human action and perception in the built environment is a less valuable starting point to begin a search for meaning in architecture and design today than other starting points that may be accepted at the moment. Although it is true that one "cannot not know history," it should be remembered that the history of architecture as usually presented is a history of styles, technology, formal invention, or various revivals of these. In reality, history is merely a record of the zeitgeist of the time, and it should not be forgotten that designers think and design differently today then they did two decades ago because of the likes of Hall, Sommer, Gutman, Maslow, and many others. In sum, this book may be thought of as a miniature *Whole Earth Catalog*—"advertisements" for "the counter culture" of behavioral science in the design professions.

I would like to thank a great number of people, some for their direct help and others for their inspiration: Joseph Marzeki and Porter Driscoll, architects, and gentle but persistent critics of these efforts; Myron Goldsmith, for allowing me to include a fine lecture of his that establishes a rational basis for the perception of scale; Arthur I. Rubin, Jacqueline Elder, and all of those who assisted their efforts—Judy Cox, Tim White, and Stephen Kliment—to bring together a comprehensive survey of "what's happening" in the behavioral sciences. My appreciation also goes to W. H. Freeman and Co. and *Scientific American* for permission to quote from "Image, Illusion and Reality." Thanks to Pamela Waters for her many fine photographs, to Melvyn Kaufman, to Cesar Pelli and to Laurin B. Askew, architect and vice-president of the Rouse Company, for his help and photographs. Thanks as well to Skidmore Owings and Merrill, architects; Gunnar Birkerts, architect; Knoll International; and Zvi Hecker, architect. My gratitude to John Harbraken, Yonna Friedmann, Bruno Zevi, Oscar Newman, Edward Hall, Robert Sommer, and all of those discussed and quoted in the text; I can only hope that I have presented them in a way that will inspire students and young designers to pursue their work and ideas with renewed vigor.

FORREST WILSON

CONTENTS

A GRAPHIC SURVEY
of
PERCEPTION and BEHAVIOR for the Design Professions

"There is at the back of every artist's mind something like a pattern or a type of architecture. The original quality in any man of imagination is imagery. It is a thing like the landscape of his dreams; the sort of world he would like to make or in which he would wish to wander; the sort of thing he likes to think about. This general atmosphere, and pattern or structure of growth, governs all his creations, however varied."
G. K. Chesterton

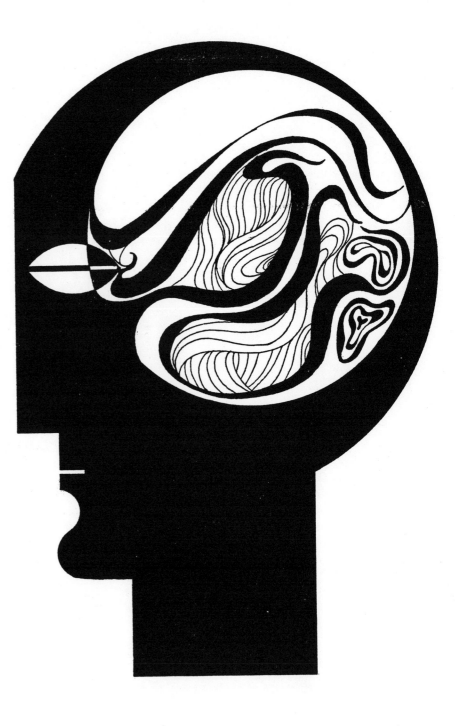

INTRODUCTION

"Each human being is unique, unprecedented, unrepeatable. The species Homo Sapiens can be described in the lifeless words of physics and chemistry, but not the man of flesh and bone. We recognize him as a unique person by his voice, his facial expressions, and the way he walks and even more by his creative response to surroundings and events. . . ." (Dubos 1968)

The irrepressible uniqueness of humans confounds those that would measure, quantify, and standardize their actions and fit them into 'building types.' We are reasonably sure that human action and decision is determined by environmental circumstance and genetic endowments. It would therefore seem possible, theoretically, to influence the human condition and human destiny through the medium of environmental design.

We have, it is true, accumulated a good deal of knowledge about matter and have developed powerful techniques to control and exploit the external world. Yet the goals of scientific enterprise, as presently conducted, are generally too lopsided to be of much assistance in the conduct of everyday human affairs, or in the design of everyday human surroundings.

We know a considerable amount about the body and have acquired certain skills in controlling its responses and correcting its mechanical defects, but our knowledge of it is only of the body as a machine. We know little, and seem little concerned, with the process by which humans convert experience and human potential into the unique individuality that is themselves. Without this knowledge our technical information is not as useful as it might be in helping us make ourselves comfortable in this world.

When scientific researchers and technicians justify their activities as 'relevant' they are often making judgments concerning the value of human life. This is unfortunately an area in which engineers and scientists have displayed no special competence.

It is becoming increasingly clear to all of us that the kind of life predicted for our future is unbelievable because it is incompatible with the fundamental needs of human nature, whatever that nature may be. Human perceptions, according to René Dubos, have not changed significantly since the late stone age and will probably not change appreciably in the near future. This fairly static state of affairs defines the limit beyond which any prediction of the future becomes literally unbelievable.

Despite the great variety and complexity of the inventions of scientific technology and wide ranging styles of art and architecture humans continue to use a narrow range of common senses to interpret and give meaning to the world.

This stability of humankind's fundamental sensing and perceiving apparatus affords a common ground on which the behavioral sciences and the design professions come together. Both are primarily concerned with how humans perceive and react to and in the world.

But unfortunately the experimental methods employed by scientists and designers to understand human actions leads them to focus their efforts on phenomena that are reproducible and measurable and, therefore, largely independent of human free will. Research is usually directed toward finding quantifiable answers to questions that are not necessarily the most important questions designers designing human environments must answer.

Humans seldom react passively to external forces. The most characteristic aspect of human behavior is its invariable active, unexpected, and creative response. Human vigor is reflected in the conversion of passive reaction to creative response. Mechanical definitions of human response miss the point because what is human is precisely that which is not mechanical and therefore measurable.

It is unlikely that a mechanical definition of life can be applied to either animal or human behavior. The unpredictability of animal behavior has been summed up in what has come to be known, among some researchers, as the 'Harvard Law Of Animal Behavior.' The law states: "Under precisely controlled conditions, an animal does as he damned pleases."

We believe life is conditioned by present and past experience, and hereditary and environmental influences. Yet human free will enables us to choose among ideas and possible courses of action and this may be the most important of all human attributes. This, contends René Dubos, is the critical determinant of human evolution. The most damning statement that can be made about the life sciences, and with them the design professions, as presently followed is that they deliberately ignore this most important phenomena of human life.

We might consider, Dubos has reminded us, that investigations concerning the mental processes involved in human choice and decision-making may reveal that it is impossible for the human brain to achieve complete understanding of itself and its workings, just as a computer could not completely predict the future of a universe of which it is a part.

The English geneticist J.B.S. Haldane expressed the extent to which the human choice is conditioned by the total environment. "That society enjoys the greatest amount of liberty," he wrote, "in which the greatest number of human genotypes can develop their peculiar abilities." It is not equally realized, Dubos adds, that it also demands a variety of opportunities.

Human values are quite often considered unchangeable, built into man's innate moral nature. In practice, Dubos points out, many of the values by which humans operate are based on prevailing social attitudes, as well as inclinations, prejudices, and common sense derived from daily life experiences. Scientific knowledge of itself cannot define or impose values to govern behavior. It can and does, however, provide facts upon which choice can be based and that is the reason for this book.

·The conflict between determinism and free will that Dubos has posed is the design dilemma of our time. A general revulsion against standardizing patterns imposed upon us appears to be the root cause of the almost universal feelings of alienation that permeate our society. Development of the ability to express free will by those who use the built environment, by breaking through the constraints imposed by design methodologies and behavioral standardizations that quantify, specify, collate, and mutilate the unique, unprecedented, unpredictable species, Homo Sapiens, is a worthy goal for both behavioral science and the design professions.

This objective requires that, in addition to the researcher and the artist, a third equal partner in the shaping of the built environment be included. This is the laboratory animal itself. As architect Yona Friedmann once wrote, any system that does not allow those who may be injured by the design a voice in its formulation is immoral.

This means we must find unique methods to incorporate the determinist-freedom polarity for each individual into the design. This book is a simple, perhaps somewhat egocentric, attempt to demystify behavioral and design information and thus help bring all parties of design activity together through a common understanding.

It should be apparent to all of us by now that our attitudes of designing ''for'' people, as presently formulated, have caused serious difficulties as long as they have been employed. It is possible that the attitudes and design problems are linked. It is true that people can be designed 'for' when activities are public, institutional, and communal. But designing 'for' now overwhelms us by extending to every facet of our lives. Almost all environmental decisions are made for us by others.

The areas that people rub against most intimately, home and the work-place, are where the knowledge of the behavioral scientist and designer is most urgently required. It is here that we must learn to apply it, and its most important application is perhaps knowing when to design and when not, and what to design and what not.

This is the major design challenge of our time. To accomplish this, knowledge and decisions concerning human behavior must be shared between those that design and those that will live and work in the spaces created. To do this, communication between the three participants is necessary. This book is presented as a beginning primer in this language—a tentative bridge between the exact knowledge of the researcher, the intuitive insights of the artist, and the ''I know what I like'' of the design user.

THE ENVIRONMENTAL IMAGE

Before men had power saws, automatic hammers, and all the machinery we now have to cut wood into boards and stone into blocks, they believed that rocks and trees had souls. Ancient builders worked their building material carefully, begged the stone's forgiveness when they removed him from the ground, and asked the tree's pardon for thinning her branches. When buildings were built by hand, cornerstones were laid with ceremony, thresholds were blessed, and the spirit of the building was revered.

Today we have a great deal of machinery to help us assemble buildings, huge cranes that lift entire sections into the air and trucks that carry enough concrete in one load to build a small house. But it takes more than putting building materials in place to create architecture. No one can explain exactly what that more is, except that architecture has a spirit that most of our building does not.

Architecture combines external form and internal space, structure and material into one essence. The structure of the building can be explained and the strength of the materials tested, but the spirit of the building, its form and spaces, lines, textures, openings, and solids must be felt in much the same way the ancients sensed spirits within the forms of rocks and trees.

This is a book about the built world around us. It is a gathering together of useful observations from many and varied sources. Some have been tested and proven by science and some can be proven by simple observation. No one knows for sure exactly why we put things together in our mind the way that we do. Science often obscures its exciting truths with dead language, and art often tries to make nonsense scientific. You will find both of these tendencies here, mixed about evenly.

Our search for meaning in the built environment is not an innocent game. It has a long history and is based on life and death necessity. During most of humankind's time on earth, as human perceptions were formed and trained, a correct interpretation of shape, color, and form of human surroundings was a matter of survival.

The original function of environmental knowledge and our image of where we are was to permit mobility in a world where mistaken identity was fatal. A correct mental map might, and often did, result in the life or death of primitive man. Kevin Lynch describes Australian aborigines driven from their territory by four years of drought. Their ability to survive depended upon the precise topographic memory of the oldest men. Through their experience, gained years before, and from descriptions of their grandfathers, they were able to locate the chain of tiny water holes that led the group out across the desert to safety.

The terror of being lost is as old as man. It is a reaction to the necessity that a mobile organism must be oriented to its surroundings. Finding one's way, says Lynch, is the original function of the environmental image and the basis on which its emotional associations may have been based. But it is not only valuable in the immediate sense as a map for directing movement, in a broader sense it serves as a general frame of reference within which the individual can act and to which he can attach his knowledge. It is an organizer, Lynch contends, of facts and possibilities. (Lynch 1960, p. 126)

"Our environmental image is still a fundamental part of our equipment for living, but for most people it is probably much less vivid and particular today." (Lynch 1960, p. 124)

Familiar parts of the environment can be given names, thus furnishing material for common memories—symbols which bind a group together and allow them to communicate with each other. In our world of rootlessness and continual agitated movement, each new environment we encounter must be examined carefully to find its implications for ourselves. Our atavistic memories of the danger of disorientation in strange surroundings add to the general feeling of social alienation. We all experience a pleasant sensation of rightness and familiarity in a recognized landscape.

It has been remarked by psychologists, and can be easily verified by casual observation, that people returning to a classroom, a restaurant, home, or any place they have been before will tend to select the same seat or location. The Netsilik Eskimo put this well-worn idea in their own way: "to be surrounded by the smell of one's own things." (Lynch 1960, p. 127)

The meanings in our surroundings, the significance of form, line, color, are consciously pursued by artists, but below the surface, in the atavistic stirrings of our subconscious, the meanings in the jumble of built form that surrounds us nags at our consciousness spurred by all the primordial fears that directed our senses in the first line of defense against lurking fang and claw.

The properties of nature are such that all things have meaning or are clues to meaning.

Man in a primitive state had to develop his perceptions to survive. Similarities, uniqueness, recurrent events, patterns, and alignments were vitally significant, for human survival depended upon their correct interpretation. To detect order amid the overwhelming chaos of nature meant life. Not to know the way back was to die.

Mythical purpose assigned to rocks, trees, wind, sun, and stars brought them into the realm of human control. To name a thing was to remember and have power over it. All forms had names and with their names significance.

Ordering the environment is as old as humankind and it is here that design begins. What scientists of human behavior can tell designers about how humans perceive things gives designers control over the environment. It brings human perception from unconscious instinctive action to conscious thought to become part of a framework of planned action.

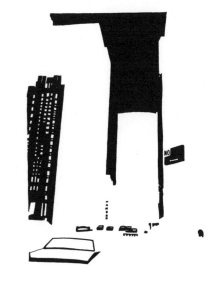

THE PLACE OF ART

A half century ago, Herbert Read laid down the premise upon which this book is based when he said: "Any general theory of art must begin with this supposition: that man responds to the shape and surface and mass of things present to his senses, and that certain arrangements in the proportion of the shape and surface and mass of things result in a pleasurable sensation, whilst the lack of such arrangement leads to indifference or even to positive discomfort and revulsion. The sense of pleasurable relationships is the sense of beauty; the opposite sense is the sense of ugliness. It is possible, of course, that some people are quite unaware of proportions in the physical aspect of things. Just as some people are color-blind, so others may be blind to shape and surface and mass. But just as people who are color-blind are comparatively rare, so there is every reason to believe that people wholly unaware of the other visible properties of objects are equally rare. They are more likely to be underdeveloped." (Read 1931, p. 16)

The work of art is in some sense a liberation of the personality, Read contended, for normally our feelings are inhibited and repressed. We can apply the same evaluation to a work of architecture, and to the combination of forms, shapes, colors, and smells that evokes reactions to our built environment. In fact, it is about the only certain means we have of evaluating the complex stimulations of the environment.

When we contemplate a work of art there is a release. But it is not only a release, for sympathy is a release of feeling, but there is a heightening, a tautening, a sublimation that takes place. Here, Read contends, lies the essential difference between art and sentimentality. Sentimentality is a release, but it is also a loosening, a relaxing of the emotions. Art is a release but also a bracing. Art is the economy of feeling; it is emotion cultivating good form. (Read 1931, p. 30–31)

This common, universal recognizable reaction of humans to art and their environment will have to be our measuring rod for the works of builder, designer, and architect, and for the findings of behaviorial scientists. If what they say and do does not cause a tautening of your sensibilities then you, the reader, are not obliged to take the word or the work seriously.

The permanent element in mankind, Read said, that corresponds to the element of form in art is man's aesthetic sensibility. It is this sensibility that is static. What is variable is the interpretation which men give to the forms of art, which are said to be 'expressive' when they correspond to his immediate feelings. But these same forms may have a different expressive value, not only for different people, but also for different periods of civilization. Expression is a very ambiguous word.

Expression is used to denote direct emotional reaction, but the very discipline of restraint by which the artist achieves form is itself a mode of expression. Form, though it can be analyzed into intellectual terms like measure, balance, rhythm, and harmony, is really intuitive in origin. It is not in the actual practice of artists an intellectual product. It is rather emotion directed and defined, and when we describe art as 'the will to form' we are not imagining any exclusively intellectual activity, but rather an exclusively instinctive one.

For this reason, Read says, "I do not think we can say that primitive art is a lower form of beauty than Greek art; although it may represent a lower kind of civilization, it may express an equal or even a finer instinct for form. The art of a period is a standard only so long as we learn to distinguish between the elements of form, which are universal, and the elements of expression, which are temporal. Still less can we say that in form Giotto is inferior to Michelangelo. He may be less complicated, but form is not valued for its degree of complexity. Frankly, I do not know how we are to judge form except by the same instinct that creates it." (Read 1931, p. 20, 21)

We have dwelt on these statements of Herbert Read because there have been few better descriptions of art that can be extrapolated to define the characteristics of good and bad environments. Both Read, the art historian, and Dubos, the scientist, dwelt on the unchanging nature of human perceptions, which would seem to indicate that the artist, architect, designer, scientist, and the occupants of the built environment are not separated as different kinds of people, but only differ in the development of common perceptions and sensibilities.

THE MYSTERY OF SEEING

Behaviorial scientists, artists, and architects all agree that sight is man's most important sense for gathering information about the world. But from the very beginnings of modern science natural philosophers have puzzled over how humans disentangle the mental images they form from how objects actually appear in the world.

If a clear cut relation did not exist between the perceived image and what was actually there the deception would be dangerous and sometimes fatal. Somehow, no matter how distorted things appear on our retina we manage to translate them correctly. But even if illusions deceive us about the world they do, at the same time, reveal important truths about the workings of the human mind. The relationship between the image and the object and the significance of illusion to the senses has and continues to fascinate scientists and artists alike. (Held 1971)

During the 17th century when investigators were seeking precise information concerning the relationship between objects and events in the physical world Johannes Kepler proposed a theory of lens formation of the optical image. He demonstrated that light reflected from an object forms an image on the retina of the observer's eye providing a model relating objects to sensed images. The retinal image was shown to be essentially an inverted replica of the object and it was assumed that the mental image would be a reinverted copy of the retinal image. This theory was sufficiently accurate to dominate ideas of perception until recent times.

But the theory contains a fallacy. If two identical circles equally distant from an observer are located on a drawing of converging lines, one would expect the observer to see them as circles of equal size. He does not. It is thus apparent that changing the surroundings of the circles changes their appearance. Observations of this kind forces us to recognize that we cannot assume that a simple correspondence exists between the local properties of the environment in which an object exists and those of an image. Such phenomena were apparently known to ancient Greek builders, for they compensated for optical illusion by distorting the true lines of their structures to make them appear level, horizontal, and vertical.

The recognition that the properties of an image cannot be identified in corresponding properties of the object or the sensory stimulation originating from it has led to a search by scientists, artists, and architects for those properties of stimulation which will produce the appropriate perception. Artists have been able to give the appearance of things being what they are not for several centuries, although unaware of the mechanisms of eye and mind that produced them.

Scientists see their problem as that of discovering the stimulus and matching it to the reaction. Both scientists and artists see illusion as at least as important as realistic images. This challenging scientific problem remains without general scientific solutions. When Purkinje, the renowned Czech physiologist said, "Deception of the senses are the truths of perception," he drew attention to the fact that illusions call to attention the workings of the visual system and are perhaps more fascinating to artists and scientists than the workings of normal perception. (Held 1971, Introduction)

The workings of the visual system expressed by researchers as rules or laws relate sense stimulation to perception. The physiology underlying some of these rules is known, others not. Once it was recognized that the perceptual system had laws of its own, the original premise was inverted. Instead of seeking to find images of the mind which correspond to simply physical descriptions of aspects of the world such as light intensity, wave length, measured distance, and motion the search changed to ways of partitioning the properties of the physical world to yield measures which can be related to perceptual descriptions.

The task, in short, becomes one of discovering the stimulus. It is an effort to discover how the stimulus influences the working of the perceptual system and is of great interest to both artists and scientists.

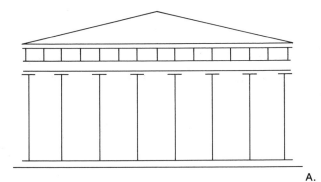

A.

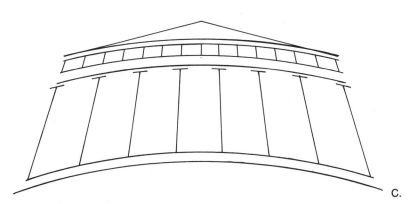

B.

C.

The effect of color or shadow on proportion.
With the background black, the columns appear sturdier, the architrave, triglyphs, and cornice have importance.
With a reversal of color or shadow the columns appear thinner and higher and the entablature loses something of its importance.
After Banister Fletcher

Diagram of the Parthenon, Athens, East Front
A. The temple as it appears
B. The temple as it would appear if built with parallel lines without optical correction.
C. The temple front with inclined vertical axis and convex stylobate, architectrave and entablature—as built so that it would appear as at A.
(Note: Distortions in B and C are exaggerated.)
After Banister Fletcher

Columns of National Gallery, Washington, D.C., Photo F. Wilson

Columns of National Gallery, Washington, D.C., Photo F. Wilson

THE EYE AND THE MEMORY IMAGE

"memory image" and viewed a second time. This suggests that the mechanism of visual memory is a natural extension of the mechanisms of vision. Although there is some truth in this proposition, claims Ulrich Nisser, it is not because perception and memory are copying processes but because neither perception nor memory is a copying process.

The fact is, he continues, that one does not see the retinal image, one sees with the aid of the retinal image. The incoming pattern of light provides information picked up by the nervous system. This information is used by the perceiver to guide his movements, to anticipate events, and to construct the internal representation of objects and of space called "conscious experience."

These internal representations are however, Nisser warns, not at all like the corresponding optical images on the back of the eye. The retinal images of specific objects are at the mercy of every irrelevant change of position, as the Futurists pointed out a half century ago. Size, shape, and location are seldom constant for a moment. Nevertheless perception is usually accurate, for real objects appear rigid and stable and appropriately located in three-dimensional space.

The first problem in the study of visual perception, says Nisser, is the discovery of the stimulus. What properties of the incoming optical array are informative for vision? What determines the way things look? How does light distribution over the retina for a period of time influence what we see?

Ecological optics—structuring light conveying information to the eye. Buckminster Fuller's dome at Expo '67, Montreal, Canada. Photo courtesy of Expo Corp.

Johannes Kepler was apparently the first to compare the eye to a "camera": a darkened chamber with an image in focus on its rear surface. He wrote, in 1604, that, "vision is brought about by pictures of the thing seen being formed on the white concave surface of the retina." A generation later René Descartes tried to clinch this argument by the direct observation of an experiment simulating the eyes action. He set the eye of an ox in a hole in a window shutter in the position it would have stood were it looking out. Looking at the back of the eye, which he had scraped to make transparent, he could see a small inverted image of the scene outside the window.

The eye camera analogy has been accepted and elaborated in numerous textbooks since the 17th century. As functional anatomy the analogy is partially accurate, but it carries some unfortunate implications for the study of vision according to Richard Held and Ulric Nisser. (Held 1971) It suggests that the perceiver is looking at pictures that appear on the back of his own retina. We use the same word, 'image,' for both the optical pattern thrown on the retina by an object and the mental experience of seeing the object. Although the 'camera' theory encounters numerous contradictions as soon as it is considered seriously, it has dominated philosophy and psychology for many years.

After having viewed the retinal image, the perceiver supposedly files it away as one might a photograph in an album. Later, if lucky, it can be retrieved as a

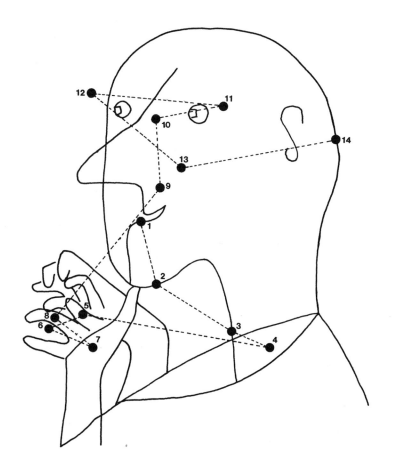

Eye Movements made by a subject viewing for the first time a drawing adapted from Paul Klee's "Old Man Figuring" appear as dotted lines. Numbers show the order of the subject's visual fixations on the picture during part of a 20-second viewing. (After *Image, Object and Illusion, Readings from Scientific American,* Freeman, 1963–1974)

We can consider, for example, the patterns of reflected light formed when objects and surfaces are illuminated by sunshine or lamplight. This results in a visual field. Most surfaces have some kind of texture, such as the grain of wood, individual stalks of grass, or the weave in fabric. These structure the light in a way that carries visual information to the eye.

The interrelation of textures, distances, and relative retinal sizes is but one example of ecological optics. The example just sited may be misleading, Nisser asserts, simply because it assumes a stationary eye fixed in space and oriented in a particular direction. This is not an ordinary characteristic of human vision. Eyes in normal use are rarely still. Apart from small tremors, their most common movement is a flick from one position to another called a "saccade." Saccades usually take less than a twentieth of a second, but occur several times each second. This means that there is a new retinal image every few hundred milliseconds when a picture or an actual scene is being inspected.

Such eye movements are necessary because the area of clear vision that the eye can encompass is very small. If one fixes their eyes on an unread printed page this will become apparent. Only a small region around the fixation point will be clear. Most of the page is seen peripherally and is hazily visible at best. Only in the fovea, the small central part of the retina, are the receptor cells packed closely enough together and organized appropriately to make a high degree of visual acuity possible.

This is the reason one must turn their eyes or head to look directly at objects in which they are particularly interested. It is also the reason why the eye must make several fixations on each line in reading, and why it roves widely over pictures.

It is difficult to reconcile the idea of saccadic movements with the idea that we are looking at an image on our retina. One sees the page as a whole or the scene in its entirety without any apparent discontinuity is space and time. People are usually unaware of their eye movements. Far from being a copy of the retinal display, the visual world is constructed of information taken in during many different fixations.

If the analogy between eye and camera were true the image would have to hold still like a photographer's model to be clearly seen. The opposite is true. Far from obscuring the shapes and spatial relations of things, movement generally clarifies them.

The perceiver experiences a rigid object on the basis of a fluidly changing retinal pattern. An interesting aspect of this is that the input information is ambiguous, Nisser points out. The same retinal changes could be produced by either a clockwise or counterclockwise rotation. As a result the perceiver may alternate between two perceptual experiences, one of which is illusory.

What one sees is a composite based on information accumulated over a period of time. The same is true in reading or in any instance where eye movements are involved. Information from past fixations is used together with current information and memory. How can we conceive of this storage? How is it organized? How long does it last? What other functions might it serve?

These questions, Nisser says, move us beyond the problem of specifying visual stimulus. In addition to identifying the sources of vision information we would like to know how that information is processed. Perhaps questions about this process should be answered by neurologists, but they are not prepared to supply these answers. We will have to be content, therefore, with a relatively abstract description of what appears to take place.

Although seeing requires the storage of information this memory cannot be thought of as a sequence of superposed retinal images. It seems that perceiving involves a memory that is not representational but schematic. During a series of fixations the perceiver synthesizes a model of schema of the scene before him, using information from each successive fixation to add detail or to extend the construction. This constructed whole is what directs his eye movements, including further scanning. In many cases it is what he or she describes when being introspective, in short this is what we see, says Nisser.

Even under these conditions, people are selective in their use of the information that reaches the eye. The choice may be made from material presented in a single brief exposure. But normally selection and construction take place over a series of glances. No iconic memory of individual "snapshots" can survive this rapid succession of images. The presentation of a second stimulus figure, shortly after the first, in a brief-exposure experiment tends to destroy the first iconic replica. The viewer may see a fusion of the two figures, only the second, or an apparent motion of the figures depending on their temporal and spatial relations. He does not see them separately.

The reaction of the nervous system to light stimulation is far from passive. The eye and brain do not act as a camera or a recording instrument. Neither in perceiving nor in remembering is there any enduring copy of the optical input. In perceiving, complex patterns are extracted from visual input and fed into the constructive process of vision. The movements and inner experience of the perceiver are usually in correspondence with his environment. Visual memory differs from perception because it is based primarily on stored rather than on current information, but it involves the same kind of synthesis. Although the eyes have been called the windows of the soul, they are not so much peepholes as entry ports, supplying raw material for the constructive activity of the visual system. (The foregoing capsulation of the seeing process is from *Image, object, and illusion,* Richard Held and Ulric Nisser, compiled from *Scientific American* articles published between 1968–1976, W.H. Freeman, San Francisco, 1971.)

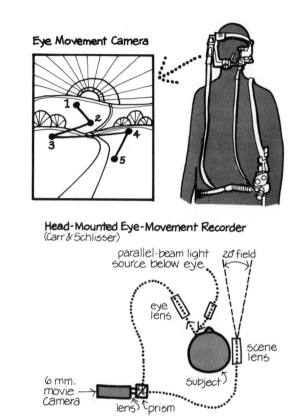

Eye Movement Camera

Head-Mounted Eye-Movement Recorder
(Carr & Schlisser)

parallel-beam light source below eye
20° field
eye lens
scene lens
6 mm. movie Camera
lens prism
subject

S. Carr, urban designer, and D. Schlisser, psychologist, examined individual impressions when entering a city on an elevated expressway by means of eye-movement recordings.
In their study, subjects took an automobile trip from the suburbs to the center of the city on an elevated expressway. An eye-movement recorder, which indicated where a subject was looking and for how long, was mounted on the subject's head. From the recorded data, the researchers evaluated interest in specific elements along the highway.
(Rubin, Elder 1980)

THE HERITAGE OF MODERN ART

Many of the artists at the beginning of this century were searching for meaning in form, line, and color to express the changing sensibilities and perceptions of modern industrial life.

They saw in the form of primitive artists an essential expression of abstract meanings embodied in line, space, and texture and became fascinated by the "abstract nature of form itself," by the science of color, and by how people perceived the world around them. These efforts to understand the world have more meaning for us today than when they were first proposed as theories. We have built the world they proposed and dreamed and it is probably, therefore, best explained in the terms of its theories.

Visual experience is the process of receiving fragmentary information, assigning form of these visual sensations, and arousing felt response, as we have just described. The light signals that bombard the retina are decoded clearly only over a very small area. To obtain adequate information the eye must move quickly around the entire visual field collecting a series of successively focused data.

After the eye has scanned the situation, the mind 'stitches together' the received messages into a visual image. The action is so fast that it appears to happen instantaneously calling upon all of our previous experience of the world of material form and space. How else can we account for the astonishing fact that the strange shape which the eye actually receives when looking at a table-top receding into the distance is immediately understood to be either a square or a rectangle? We therefore interpret the world of form, shape, color, line, light, and shadow by preexisting concepts. When faced with visual experiences for which we cannot supply such readily identifiable definitions as square, circle, rectangle, bottle, chair, we are often baffled.

As observers we are primarily concerned with making things agree with the labels formed for them in our minds. The interest is in the fact that red can describe fire, blood, or strawberries. The force of the color is of secondary importance, but for the artist and the architect both are important. The fact that the color evokes associations is significant, and the forces or energies or vectors contained in colors, shapes, lines, and forms are also significant, or they aid in analysis.

Artists at the turn of this century worked with pure dynamic forces in color, line, and form, and sought to create designs where the customary meanings of 'fire,' 'blood,' and 'strawberries' were secondary or nonexistent. Their search was to find and comprehend something of the rudimentary forces brought into being through dimensional relationships, juxtaposed shapes, and forms. The artist Ozenfant referred to these dynamic abstract forces as 'the geometry of sensation.' (Sausmarez 1964, p. 14)

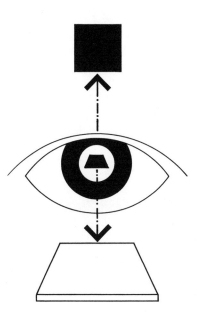

The eye receives – the mind interprets

Sausmarez defined the 'dynamics of visual form,' the title of his book, as: dynamics—the moving forces, and form—the mode in which a thing exists or manifests itself. To further define his meaning he quoted the Concise Oxford Dictionary definition of the French word 'form,' as the 'manner of acting or expressing oneself.' This could be combined with an engineering definition of form as 'a diagram of forces.' The 'diagram of forces' in line, form, and color was the objective of such artists as Kandinsky.

Finding such a visual coherence in the built world around us is related more to our psychophysiological being than to rational thought. It is therefore somewhat difficult to describe or define clearly. We can acknowlege visual coherence in feeling, and will find a remarkable degree of unanimity among observers. Human perceptions have not changed appreciably from the age of stone to the age of automation, as Dubos reminds us. The stone age cave paintings of Altamira and Lescaux in southern France, and paintings by Picasso were produced in cultures milleniums apart with entirely different cultural connotations, but the quality of line, form, and feeling appeals as well to our innate perceptions as it did to those of people over 5,000 years ago. As Read has said, the elements of form are universal; it is the elements of expression that are temporal.

Optical forces are continuously operative. We experience attraction and repulsion, expansion and contraction according to configurations of shapes and colors presented to our eye. Our sight is more than a stimulation of the retina by haphazard light rays organized into spatial unity. It is virtually impossible to perceive optical forces isolated and unaffected by the context in which they appear, and without organizing them into patterns in our head liberally mixed with associations and memories. The act of looking is inescapably the dynamic experience Sausmarez the artist and Nisser the scientist described.

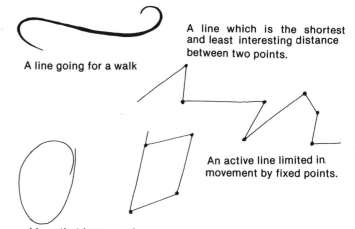

A line going for a walk

A line which is the shortest and least interesting distance between two points.

An active line limited in movement by fixed points.

Lines that become planes.

(Drawings from Paul Klee's *Pedagogical Sketch Book*)

Dancing Centaur With Black Background (Picasso 1948)

Passive angular lines and passive circular lines become active as planar constituents.

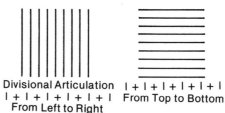

Divisional Articulation
I + I + I + I + I + I
From Left to Right

I + I + I + I + I + I
From Top to Bottom

Primitive structural rhythm in double motion. Top to Bottom Left to Right

(Drawing after Paul Klee's *Pedagogical Sketch Book*)

THE CONTRIBUTION OF THE FUTURISTS

The Futurists at the beginning of this century began to lay a groundwork of consciousness that will help us perceive the forms of the modern world. They sensed the dynamism and perceptual domination of the forms of an emerging technological society and strove to translate the kinetic rhythms and intense and confused sensations of the life they were experiencing into visual form, long before these technical manifestations dominated the urban world and became commonplace reality. The Futurists declared that no object, moving or still, can be seen in isolation. All objects 'absorb' their surroundings and in turn contribute to them. There is an interplay between object and environment, a continuous reciprocal activity. They emphasized this action by extending it to the forms of the objects themselves, and sought to add to this complex relationship and its surroundings the perceptual effect of forms in motion in space. These were remarkable insights, for much later research has shown that our perception of movement changes the shape of the object quite drastically.

The Futurists claimed all objects, static or moving, embodied two kinds of motion: one which tends to move in on itself suggesting centripetal force, and the other which moves outward into space mingling its rhythm with those of other objects and eventually merging into space itself. It followed in their thinking that no such thing as a definite isolated object can exist.

There are instead, they claimed, only intimations, hints, memories of objects within the continuous flux of perceived color, shade, shadow, and form. They sought to capture this shifting relationship between 'objectivity' and constant change by synthesizing images of both the object and motion.

The Futurists were attempting to picture the process of the mind in its constant admission, evaluation, and storage of new material. They were attempting to speak the mind's language by exploiting its capacity for association and sequential observation, and thus to create aesthetic satisfaction. We now know from controlled laboratory experiments that they may have intuitively sensed many working mechanisms of perception. These can now be used as tools.

These modern artists also contended that the impact of our various senses—touch, sound, and smell—cannot be isolated and that they mingle with sight to influence our emotional reactions. This mixture of our senses is contributed to by a powerful and uncontrollable 'image-giver.' "To perceive," said Savarini, "is after all nothing more than an opportunity to remember."

The images the Futurists evoked, although often derided at the time, were poetically vivid: "Our bodies enter into the divans on which we sit, the divans enter into us; just as the tram going by enters the house, and they in turn hurl themselves upon the tram and merge with it." "Distance either of time or space does not exist." "Sometimes on the cheek of the person to whom we are talking in the street we see the horse going by a long way off." These examples of Futurists descriptions of perception serve to suggest the wide scope of awareness which makes the world more real, and were intended by them to turn attention towards experience itself rather than focusing on external objects.

Today the glass curtain wall facades of high rise buildings in major cities fracture and multiply single images in kaleidoscope fashion hurling them back at the passersby in the street who merge with them as the houses merged with the tram. We can watch ourselves walk the pavement upside down in countless window mirrors. Instead of a horse reflected on our companion's cheek we see an entire world of motor cars, all swiftly rushing by.

The converging lines of perspective formed by buildings of the Futurists urban setting was horizontal as the lower building cornices moved down toward the horizon and the street moved upward to eye level. Today the high buildings overhead project lines of convergence into the sky that transfix the nature of space and disorient time. Building facades themselves disappear as they mirror each other across streets in the day in an endless chain of mirror reflections and become deep layered horizontal sandwiches of dark bands and lighted interiors as the cleaning crews work in them at night.

These vivid insights into the nature of perception in the modern world formed the base of a concept of dynamism. Their search was for equations that would explain and link the visual activity of the modern world and the workings of the mind and eye. These dynamic ideas were assimilated into the concepts of 'modern architecture.' The environments the Futurists dreamed and described but never saw are the commonplaces of our contemporary cities and compose the major portion of our urban world.

KANDINSKY

Kandinsky's description of the 'revelation' that turned his creative mind toward 'nonobjective' art may help us comprehend his creative step from the meaning of the object to a 'geometry of sensation.'

"Twilight was falling. I had just returned home with my box of colors after making a study. I was plunged in a reverie, still thinking over the work I had just finished, when suddenly I saw on the wall a picture of extraordinary beauty glowing with an inner light. I stood dumbfounded for a moment, then drew nearer to this cryptic picture, which I saw only in terms of forms and colors, since I could not make out what it represented. I soon solved the mystery—it was one of my own pictures that had been hung upside down. Next morning, by daylight, I tried to renew the impression of the night before, but with only partial success. Even when it was upside down, I could still distinguish the content and, of course, twilight was needed for the proper effect. It was then that I knew definitely that objects spoiled my painting.'' (Lassaigne 1964)

Kandinsky evolved an experimental system of concordances: The horizontal, flat and cold, is the plane on which man moves, and its color is black. The vertical stands for the right angle, the upright form, and corresponds to warmth. The diagonal, is an intermediary between the two and calls for color. The forms resulting from them are triangles, squares, and rectangles, and they have their own special tonal qualities which are characterized by different colors. The acute angle (triangle) is yellow, the right angle (square) is red, the obtuse angle (circle) is blue.

Kandinsky believed that the curve played a predominant part in the repertoire of forms. The curve is a straight line bent by constant pressure. The stronger the tension upon it the more it is inclined to close in on itself. Straight line and curve oppose and balance one another, as do triangle and circle, the straight line representing the negation of the surface, while the curve contains its nucleus.

Kandinsky adds his personal reflections to these observations. For example, the right angle has something young and unconsidered about it. The curve is an embodiment of maturity and conscious energy. The greater the number of forms acting on a point and the more varied their directions, the more complicated the surface will be. Curves can undergo an infinite number of variations and Kandinsky listed the most notable of these, particularly the various forms of undulation obtained by alternating tensions and realization, by active and passive pressures, in which the original geometrical aspect is soon left behind. Finally Kandinsky studied composite forms made up of geometrical and free-ranging elements, and the composition and organization of forces expressed in the tension between them. He achieved rhythm by the repetition and alternation of different types of lines of equal or unequal intervals. (Kandinsky 1926, p. 93)

The thin lines hold their own in the presence of the heavy point. (Kandinsky 1926)

14

Art imitates nature. Optical art by Jean Larcher, Dover Books.

Photo by Ezra Stoller Associates. Courtesy of TWA. Building reminiscent of the form of a bird.

The search for nonobjective forms is difficult, for almost all forms are reminiscent of objects; indeed, the term nonobjective appears to be a contradiction. Kandinsky sought to find forms that had meanings inherent in them in their shape, color, and place in space in relation to the environment of forms, shapes, lines, and colors; the geometry of sensation. He sought reds that were important for the force of their redness rather than for their association with blood or strawberries.

Architecture begins at the point Kandinsky arrived at with nonobjective painting. The image Kandinsky sought to discard and the forms that he searched for to express intrinsic meanings are the inherent nature of architectural form. Architectural form is abstract and has no natural counterpart. Efforts are sometimes made by architects to associate the abstract forms of architecture with natural or anthropomorphic forms, or even with human emotions. Buildings are said to look like birds, sit like frogs, stand or rest, or feel grand or grim. But architecture is essentially abstract, meanings such as these are human inventions tacked on.

Rasmussen put the case admirably: "For while the painting may fill a plane with its composition with continuously changing details, the architect is usually forced to create a regular method of subdivision in his composition on which so many building artisans will have to work together. The simplest method, for both the architect and artisans, is the absolute regular repetition of the same elements, for example, solid, void, solid, void, just as you count one, two, one, two.

It is a rhythm every one can grasp. Many people find it entirely too simple to mean anything at all. It says nothing to them and yet it is a classic example of man's special contribution to orderliness. It represents a regularity and precision found nowhere in Nature but only in the order man seeks to create." (Rasmussen 1959, p. 128–129)

It is precisely because the architect works so abstractly that he or she must know the meanings and associations people have with forms they create. And if there are 'universal' forms, as Read contends, they should know them. Research into human behavior and the insights of artists and those who write about art and architecture can, therefore, possibly be useful in understanding the problems of creating and living with the forms of the built environment. Even if the theories are later disproven, as scientific theories so often are, this does, at the very least, seem a good place to start.

Cadillac Assembly Line, Photo courtesy of GM.

Optical design by Jean Larcher, Dover Books.

PART I

DYNAMIC BASIS OF FORM

A form is a dynamic system or is based upon a dynamic system. Since the dynamic principles operate within the organism, a strong form is one which depends more upon the dynamic properties of the organism than upon the properties of the stimulus. (Fryer 1965)

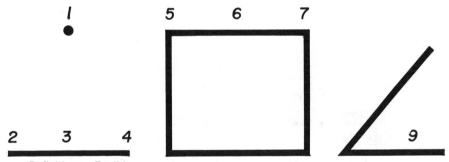

Definitions—Euclid

1. A point is that which has no parts, or which has no magnitude.
2. A line is length without breadth.
3. The extremities of a line are points.
4. A straight line is that which lies evenly between its extreme points.
5. A superficies is that which has only length and breadth. (superficies—a surface of a body or a region of space)
6. The extremities of a superficies are lines.
7. A plane superficies is that in which any two points being taken, the straight line between them lies wholly in that superficies.
8. A plane angle is the inclination of two lines to one another in a plane, which meet together, but are not in the same direction.
9. A plane rectilineal angle is the inclination of two straight lines to one another, which meet together, but are not in the same straight line.

Maurice de Sausmarez wrote in his book, *BASIC DESIGN: The Dynamics of Visual Form* that every configuration carries in its own nature an account of the forces, speed, and actions that created it. Every line he said, has an innate kinetic quality which is independent of its representational content. This is an essential part of its expressive content, for it is the visible path of the creative act. It is this, he says, added to the belief in 'significant' forms arising from a deeper stratum than consciousness can reach, that led many modern artists to use techniques which were as free as possible from the obstacles of deliberation, thereby allowing a free flow of organic image formation.

The following drawings are a development of some of Sausmarez' observations.

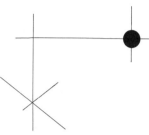

The simplest unit, a spot, not only indicates location but is felt to have within itself potential energies of expansion and contraction that activate the surrounding area.

A line can be thought of as a chain of spots joined together. It indicates position and direction and has within itself a certain energy; the energy appears to travel along its length and to be intensified at either end; speed is implied, and the space around it is activated.

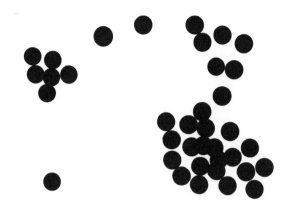

Freely used spots, in clusters or spread out, create a variety of energies and tensions activating the entire area in which they occur.

In a limited way the line is capable of expressing emotions. A thick line is associated with boldness, a straight line with strength and stability, a zig-zag line with excitement—although these are, of course, crude generalizations.

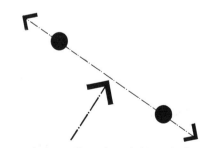

When two spots occur there is a statement of measurement and implied direction and the 'inner' energies create a specific tension between them which directly affects the intervening space.

All of these sensations are increased if differences in the sizes of the spots are allowed.

Straight lines of the same length and thickness in parallel groupings may introduce factors of proportional relationship and rhythmic interval; change the lengths and thicknesses and more complex rhythms and optical 'beat' are experienced. (Drawings after Sausmarez.)

Lobby of Sears Tower.
Photo Courtesy of Skidmore, Owings and Merrill, Chicago Office.

Wassily Kandinsky's course of analytical drawing at the Bauhaus was concerned with the extraction of inner lines of force. Objects were considered as energy tensions and the composition reduced to an arrangement of lines expressing these tensions. The eye, Sausmarez notes, is very readily forced into pursuit of linear directions and, as it follows the line, attributes to it the quality of movement. Such energy tensions operate also in the 'visual pull' of masses and colors and movement is achieved by deflecting the eye from concentration at any one point.

Sausmarez claims that we tend to see and interpret forms in reference to the stable norm of gravitation, and as a result whenever an object or form is placed in contradiction to the horizontal-vertical axes it seems to imply movement.

The following drawings and captions are after drawings in Kandinsky's book, *Point and Line to Plane (Punkt und Linie zu Fläche)* originally published in 1925 as the ninth in a series of fourteen Bauhaus books edited by Walter Gropius and L. Moholy-Nagy. Republished by Dover Books (New York) as *Point and Line to Plane.*

The point is the singular union of silence and speech. It signifies silence in the world of the practical-useful.

> Today I am going to the movies.
> Today I am going. To the movies
> Today I. Am going to the movies

Let the point be moved out of its practical-useful situation into an impractical, that is, an illogical, position. In the third sentence, the illogical, in pure form, is at work. This may be explained as a typographical error—the inner value of the point flashes forth for a moment and is immediately extinguished.

Let the point be moved so far out of its practical-useful situation that it loses its connection with the flow of the sentence.

> Today I am going to the movies

In this case, the point must have considerable open space around it, in order that its sound may have resonance. In spite of this, its sound remains delicate—overpowered by the sound of the print surrounding it.

●

As the surrounding space and the size of the point are increased, the sound of the print is reduced and the sound of the point becomes clearer and more powerful.

Thus arises a double sound, print-point, besides the practical-useful association. It is a balancing of two worlds which can never meet or agree. This is a useless, revolutionary state of affairs—the print is shaken by a foreign body which cannot be brought into any relation to it.

The point leaps from one world into another. It frees itself from dependency, from the practical-useful. It begins its life as an independent being. It is its own point. This is the world of painting and of architectural drawing.

The point may be defined as the smallest elementary form, but this definition is not exact. It is difficult to fix the exact limits of the concept "smallest form." The point can grow and cover the entire ground plane unnoticed—then, where would the boundary between point and plane be?

There are two considerations to be borne in mind here:

1. the relation of the size of the point to the size of the plane, and
2. the relative sizes of the point and of the other forms on this plane.

A form which, when on the otherwise empty basic plane, may still be considered to be a point, must be termed a plane when, for example, a very thin line appears with it upon the basic plane.

The relation of sizes in the first and second case determines the conception of the point, which, at present, can be tested on the basis of feeling only—since we lack an exact numerical expression for it.

Abstractly the point is thought of as ideally small, ideally round, an ideally small circle.

As in the case of its size, its limits are equally relative. In its material form, the point can assume an unlimited number of shapes. No boundaries can be fixed and the realm of points is unlimited.

The Point is the Innermost Concise Form.

It is turned inwards. It never completely loses this characteristic—even when it assumes, externally, an angular shape.

The point is a small world cut off more or less equally from all sides and almost torn out of its surroundings. Its fusion with the surroundings is minimal, and seems to be nonexistent in cases of perfected roundness. On the other hand, it maintains itself firmly in place and reveals not the slightest tendency to movement in any direction whatsoever, either horizontal or vertical. Furthermore, it neither advances nor recedes. Only its concentric tension discloses its inner kinship with the circle—while its further characteristics point to the square.

The Point is Temporarily the Briefest Form.

The point digs itself into the plane and asserts itself for all time. Thus it presents the briefest, constant, innermost assertion: short, fixed, and quickly created.

In theory, the point, which is:
1. a complex (size and form) and
2. a sharply-defined unit,
should constitute to some degree its relationship with the basic plane as a sufficient means of expression. Theoretically, a work of art can, in its final analysis, consist of a point. This should not be looked upon as an idle statement.

Is a point on a plane sufficient to create a work of art?

The simplest and briefest example of this condition is the centrally-placed point, the point lying in the center of a surface which is square in shape.

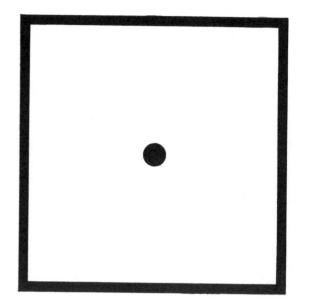

The restriction of the basic effect of the plane becomes intensified. As the double sound, point-plane, takes on the character of a single sound, the sound of the plane is relatively too slight to be noticeable. This, on the road to simplification, is the last stage in the progressive dissolution of multiple double sounds through elimination of all complicated elements. This reduces the composition to the single proto-element.

Kankinsky's definition of the concept, "composition" was: A composition is the inwardly-purposeful subordination
1. of the individual elements and
2. of the built-up (construction)
toward the goal of concrete pictoriality.

When a single sound completely embodies the pictorial aim, this single sound must be considered the equivalent of a composition. The single sound here is a composition.

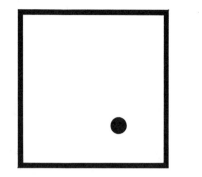

At the moment the point is moved from the center of the basic plane creating an eccentric structure, the double sound becomes audible:

1. absolute sound of the point,
2. sound of the given location in the basic plane.
   This second sound, which in the base of the centralized structure was almost silenced now becomes distinct. It transforms the sound of the point from the absolute to the relative.

TWO POINTS

Additional points will produce a still more complex result. Repetition is a potent means of heightening the inner vibration, and is, at the same time, a source of elementary rhythm which, in turn, is a means to the attainment of elementary harmony in every form of art.

We have to deal here with two double sounds: Every part of the basic plane has a sound peculiar to itself and an individual inner coloration. As a result, facts of apparently little importance produce consequences of unexpected complexity.

The inventory of this given example is:
Elements: two points + plane.
Result: 1. inner sound of a point,
           2. repetition of the sound,
           3. double sound of the first point,
           4. double sound of the second point,
           5. sound of the sum of all these sounds.

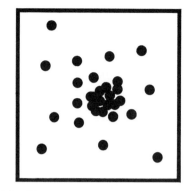

MANY POINTS

The point is a complex unit, size plus shape. It is therefore easy to imagine what a storm of sounds can develop from continuing accumulation of points on the basic plane. Even though these points are identical this turmoil develops and spreads out.

THE LINE

The Line

The geometric line is an invisible thing. It is the track made by the moving point; that is, its product. It is created by movement—specifically through the destruction of the self-contained repose of the point. Here, the leap from the static to the dynamic occurs.

The forces coming from without that transform the point into a line can be very diverse. The variation in lines depends upon the number of these forces and upon their combination.

In the final analysis, all line forms can be reduced to two cases:

1. application of one force, and
2. application of two forces:
   a) single or repeated, alternate action of both forces,
   b) simultaneous action of both forces.

Straight Line

When a single force, coming from without, moves the point in any direction the straight line results. The initial direction remains unchanged and the line has the tendency to run in a straight course to infinity.

This is the straight line whose tension represents the most concise form of the potentiality for endless movement.
vertical
diagonal
horizontal

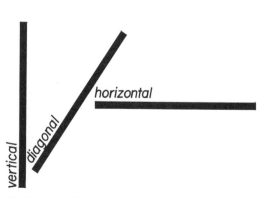

Basic types of geometric straight lines.

Diagram of basic types.

The simplest form of the straight line is the horizontal. In the human imagination, this corresponds to the line or the plane upon which the human being stands or moves. The horizontal line is also a cold supporting base which can be extended on the level in various directions. Coldness and flatness are the basic sounds of this line, and it can be designated as the most concise form of the potentiality for endless cold movement.

In complete contrast to this line in both an external and inner sense, is the vertical which stands at right angles to it, and in which flatness is supplanted by height, and coldness by warmth. Therefore, the vertical line is the most concise form of the potentiality for endless warm movement.

The third type of straight line is the diagonal which, in schematic form, diverges from both of the above to the same angle and, therefore, has the same inclination to both of them; a circumstance which determines its inner sound—equal union of coldness and warmth. Therefore, the diagonal line is the most concise form of the potentiality for endless cold-warm movement.

Straight lines organized about a common meeting point form a star. As the star becomes denser and denser the intersecting lines form a more compact center in which a point develops and seems to grow.

This is the axis about which the lines can move and, finally, flow into one another: A new form is born—a plane in the clear shape of a circle.

In this case we have to deal with a special characteristic of the line, its power to create a plane.

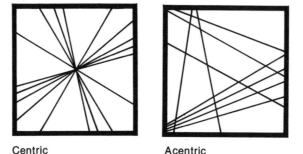

Centric   Acentric

The difference between diagonal lines and other diagonallike lines, which Kandinsky calls free straight lines, is a temperature difference. The free straight lines can never attain a balance between warmth and coldness (horizontal and vertical).

Free straight lines on a given plane can either possess a common center or lie outside the center. If they possess a common center they lie on the plane and exhibit no inclination to leave it. If they lie outside the center they are less completely fused to the plane and occasionally seem to pierce it. This is due to their appearance of perspective. These lines are the farthest removed from the point, which claws itself into the plane, since they have especially abandoned the element of rest.

The square consists of two horizontal elements of cold rest and two vertical elements of warm rest.

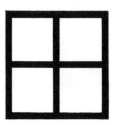

The point resting in the center of a square plane was defined as the harmonizing of the point and the plane. A horizontal and vertical in a central position on a square plane constitutes a similar prototypical expression.

These two straight lines (the horizontal and vertical) are, as has already been said, things living solitary and alone, since they know no repetition. They therefore develop a strong sound which can never be completely drowned out and, thereby, represent the protosound of straight lines.

This construction is, consequently, the prototype of linear expression or, of linear composition. It consists of a square divided into four squares, the most primitive form of the division of a schematic plane.

The sum of the tensions, consisting of 6 elements of cold rest and 6 elements of warm rest = 12. Therefore, the next step from the schematic point picture to the schematic line picture is reached through a surprisingly great increase of the means: A single sound is powerfully amplified to 12 sounds.

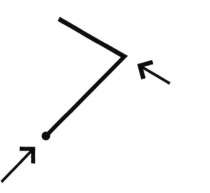

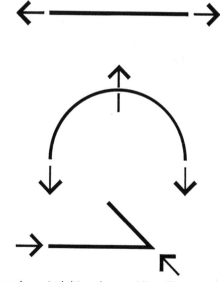

Angular lines are composed of straight lines and originate from the pressure of two forces. The simplest forms of angular lines consist of two parts. They are the result of two forces that have discontinued their action after a single thrust.

There is an important difference between straight and angular lines. The angular line is in much closer touch with the plane. It carries something planelike within it. The plane is in the process of creation and the angular line is a bridge.

The right angle is unchangeable in size but is able to change its direction. There can be only 4 right angles which touch each other—they either touch with their points and form a cross or, by the touching of their diverging sides, they form right-angle planes, in most instances creating a square.

The horizontal-vertical cross consists of one warm and one cold line—it is nothing other than the central position of the horizontal and vertical. This accounts for the cold-warm or warm-cold temperature of the right angle, depending on its direction.

The many-angled line can be composed of the most diverse parts-from the simpler to the more complex. The endless potentiality of straight lines for movement is always retained in these forms.

The differences between the countless angular lines depend entirely upon the sizes of the angles, in accordance with which they can be divided into three typical groups:
Acute angle, 45°
Right angle, 90°
Obtuse angle, 135°

The remainder are atypical acute or obtuse angles, and deviate from the typical in the number of their degrees.

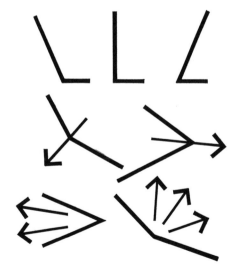

The absolute sound of the given forms of angles depends on three conditions:
1. the sound of the different lengths of their sides,
2. the sound of their inclination, and
3. the sound of their smaller or greater conquest of the plane.

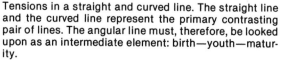

Tensions in a straight and curved line. The straight line and the curved line represent the primary contrasting pair of lines. The angular line must, therefore, be looked upon as an intermediate element: birth—youth—maturity.

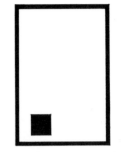

The straight line carries within it, with its other characteristics, the desire to give birth to a plane, to transform itself into a more compact, more self-contained thing. The straight line is capable of doing this, although, in contrast to the curved line, which can create a plane with two forces, it has need of three impulses in plane creation. In the case of this new plane, beginning and end cannot completely disappear; but are observable at three points. Complete absence of the straight and the angular on the one hand and, on the other, three straight lines with three angles—these are the signs of the two primary planes which stand in the greatest contrast to each other. Therefore these two planes confront each other as THE PRIMARY CONTRASTING PAIR OF PLANES.

Curve—Geometric wavelike:
Equal radius—uniform alternation of positive and negative pressure. Horizontal course with alternating tensions and release.

The closer one approaches the lower border of the BP, the denser the atmosphere becomes; the smallest individual areas lie nearer and nearer together and thereby sustain the larger and heavier forms with ever increasing ease. These forms lose weight and the note of heaviness decreases in sound. "Climbing" becomes more difficult —the forms seem to tear themselves loose by main force and something like the grating noise of friction is audible. (A straining upwards and arrested "falling" downwards.) Freedom of movement becomes more and more limited. The restraint attains its maximum.

Positive and negative pressure with irregular alternation, whereby the former gets much the upper hand of the latter.

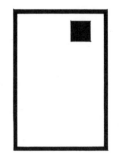

The more alternating forces there are acting on the point, the more diverse their directions, and the more different the individual segments of an angular line are in length, the more complex will be the planes created. The variations are inexhaustible.

Displacement increased. Especially temperamental struggle between the two forces. The positive pressure pushes to a very great height.

The 'above' gives the impression of a great looseness, a feeling of lightness, of emancipation, and, finally, of freedom. Each one of these related characteristics gives off an accompanying sound, which has in each case a slightly different color.

This "looseness" is a negation of density. The nearer to the upper border of the BP the smallest individual areas seem to be, the more disintegrated they appear.

The 'lightness' leads to further enhancement of this inner quality—the smallest individual areas are not only further removed from each other, but they themselves lose weight and, thereby, lose still more the capacity to support. Each weightier form thereby grows heavier in this upper position of the BP. The note of heaviness takes on a stronger sound.

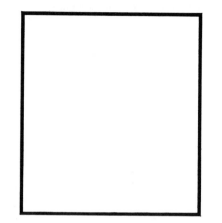

Every typical BP produced by 2 horizontal and 2 vertical lines has, correspondingly, 4 sides. Each of these 4 sides develops a sound peculiar to it alone, which passes beyond the boundaries of warm and cold rest. A second sound is, therefore, associated each time with the sound of warm or cold rest, which sound is unalterably and organically bound up with the position of the line-boundary.

The position of the two horizontal lines is above and below. The position of the two vertical lines is right and left.

THE BASIC PLANE

The term 'BASIC PLANE' is understood to mean the material plane which is called upon to receive the content of the work of art.

The schematic BP is bounded by 2 horizontal and 2 vertical lines, and is thereby set off as an individual thing in the realm of its surroundings.

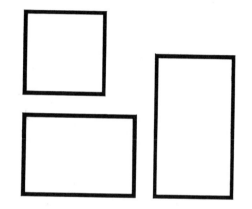

After the horizontal and the vertical have been characterized, the basic sound of the BP must of itself become clear: Two elements of cold rest and two elements of warm rest give two double sound of rest, which determine the tranquil-objective sound of the BP.

When the one or the other pair predominates, either in the width or height of the BP, this preponderance determines in any particular case the predominance of the cold or the warm in the objective sound.

This fact offers many possibilities in composition.

The most objective form of the typical BP is the square—both pairs of boundary lines possess an equally strong sound. Coldness and warmth are relatively balanced.

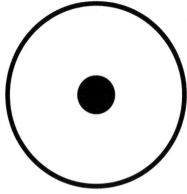

REST

Of all the forms of the plane, the circle tends most toward colorless rest as it is the result of two forces which always act uniformly and because it lacks the violence of the angle.

The point centered in the circle represents the most complete form of rest of the no longer isolated point.

RIGHT AND LEFT

The 'left' of the Basic Plane (the side opposite our right) produces the effect of great looseness, a feeling of lightness, of emancipation and, finally, of freedom. Thus, the characterization of 'above' is repeated here in every respect.

The 'right' is the continuation of 'below' (the side opposite our left). It is a continuation with the gradations of meaning from top to bottom.

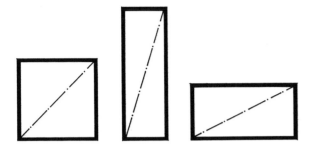

A DIAGONAL

If a diagonal is drawn through the square BP, this diagonal then stands at an angle of 45° to the horizontal. In the transition of the square BP to another right-angled plane the angle increases or decreases. This can therefore be looked upon as a measure of tension.

"Harmonious" diagonal.

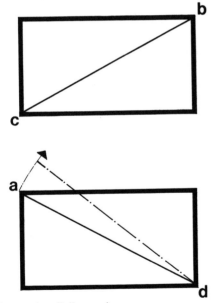

"Disharmonious" diagonal.

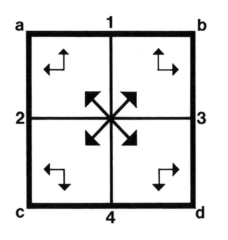

The point of intersection of the two diagonals determines the center of the BP. A horizontal and, subsequently, a vertical line drawn through the center divide the BP into four primary parts, each of which has its specific appearance. The corners of all of these touch at the 'indifferent' center, out of which tensions flow diagonally.

The numbers 1, 2, 3, 4 are the resistance forces of the borders. A, b, c, d are the designations of the four primary parts.

The diagram makes the following consequences possible:

Part a: tension toward 1, 2 = loosest combination,

Part d: tension toward 3, 4 = greatest resistance.

Parts a and d stand, therefore, in the greatest contrast to each other.

Part b: tension toward 1, 3 = moderate resistance upwards,

Part c: tension toward 2, 4 = moderate resistance downwards.

Parts b and c stand, therefore, in moderate contrast to each other, and their relationship can readily be recognized.

Vetical Position
"warm rest"

Horizontal Position
"cold rest"

Diagonal Position
"disharmonious"

Diagonal Position
"harmonious"

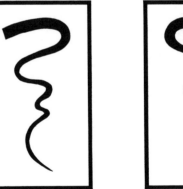

Obstinancy with Forebearance.
   The bends are loose.
Resistance from the left, weak.
At the right, compressed layer

Obstinancy in stiff tension.
   The bends harder.
Resistance from the right
strongly restraining. At
the left, loose "air."

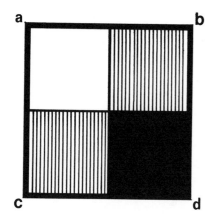

In combination with the forces of resistance in the plane's borderlines, a weight pattern results.

A combination of the two factors is conclusive and answers the question as to which of the two diagonals, bc or ad, should be called the "harmonious" and which the "disharmonious."

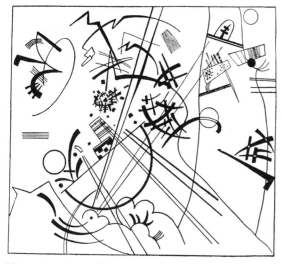

Linear structure of the picture *Little Dream in Red* (**Kandinsky** 1925).

Free wavelike line with accent-horizontal position.

The same wavelike line accompanied by geometric lines.

In nature, the dot in space is a moving object. On the painter's canvas it is located on a field bounded by the edges of the picture. But in architecture, being what it is, the dot is anchored to the ground. On the architect's plan the dot is usually a column and the line a wall and these are only seen in ruins or imaginary situations of sections hypothetically cut through the elevation of the structure.

All of the perceptual phenomenon of the built environment have one unescapable characteristic that differs markedly from the painter's canvas. All the forms have meanings in relation to the physical forces exerted on the structure anchored to the ground. The pull of gravity on the horizontal and the vertical are the basic characteristics of all building elements and therefore influence our perception of them.

The plan of the abbey of Monte Cassino appears after repeated bombardment in WWII.

Photo courtesy of the U. S. Air Force

A *dot* on the painter's canvas is fixed in the field established by the edges of the picture.

A distant airplane.

An approaching cannon ball.

A dot in space
is a spaced out dot.

The Dot.

The Dot in space.

A close gnat—gnaturally.

The Sun   The Moon

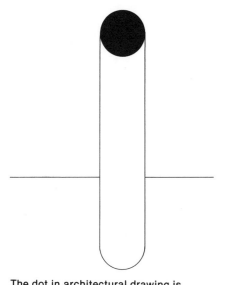

The dot in architectural drawing is fixed in space—a column.

● Paul Klee said that all forms began from the dot.

● The dot extended becomes a line.

The line extended becomes a plane.

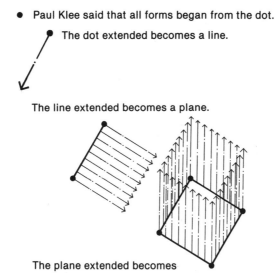

The plane extended becomes a volume.

We can, if we like, extend Paul Klee's dot and line one more step to carry us into the three-dimensional realm of architecture.

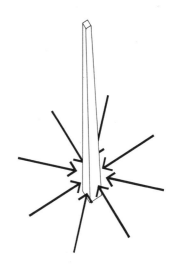

The point extended vertically to become a single spatial landmark is nondirectional. Any number of lines can pass through it, from any one or part of 360°.

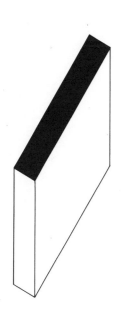

The line in plan is a wall.

The point in space is nondirectional. The circle on a sheet of paper is nondirectional. Any number of lines can pass through it from any one or part of 360°.

Bunker Hill Monument, Charlestown, MA.
Photo courtesy of Massachusetts Dept. of Commerce and Development, Div. of Tourism.

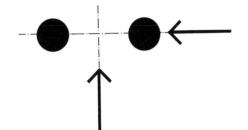

Two points establish two directions, through their centers or between them.

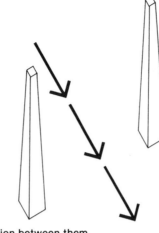

The direction between them.

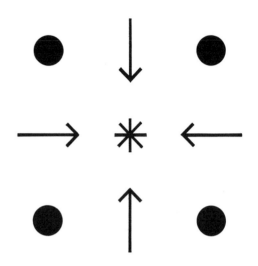

Bridge of Robert Maillart.
Photo courtesy of Swiss National Tourist Office.

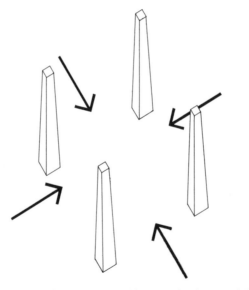

Four points, if equally spaced from each other, establish a center and four directions, through their centers and through their diagonals. If the points vary in size or spacing, they can give either greater or lesser importance to the directions and the faces and sides they present.

Calder Sculpture, Montreal Expo '67.
Photo courtesy of Expo Corp.

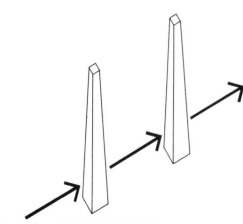

A direction through their centers.

Lines and forms on architectural drawings differ from those of the artist, for they are diagrams of three-dimensional solids and hollows. Architectural drawings may have the dynamic quality of the artist's drawings, but this is a property of the drawing itself, and may or may not describe the quality of space and structure that is to be or has been built.

When we look at the plans of buildings and cities, we must translate them into structures and spaces in the mind's eye, which is a special talent that must be developed to see architectural plans as diagrams of real buildings and cityscapes rather than dynamic representations of the draftsman's art.

Selby Public Library, Sarasota, Florida. Architects—Skidmore Owings and Merrill Chicago, Ill. Photo by Hedrick Blessing. Courtesy of Skidmore Owings and Merrill.

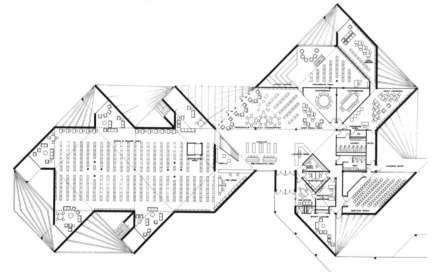

Plan: Main level, Selby Public Library, Sarasota, Florida. Architects—Skidmore Owings and Merrill, Chicago

A Kandinsky-like diagram of the sculptures and the Eifel Tower.

Palace de Chaillot and the Eifel Tower.

Photo courtesy of French Government Tourist Office.

There is probably no satisfactory classification of visual illusions, but to cover the subject, divisions are necessary. We have chosen to arrange them alphabetically to make recall easier.

We begin by discussing the effects of the presence of angles on illusions. There are a number of types of illusions presented here, but the reason for this grouping is that angles play such an important part directly and indirectly in the production of illusions. What might be a somewhat confusing classification for social scientists is a very handy one for designers since angles are an inherent, ever present, condition of architectural design. Right angles in perspective are the most prevalent characteristic of the man-made environment.

New York City Building.

Photo by F. Wilson.

ANGLES—THE INFLUENCE OF ANGLES

A characteristic of the buildings of industrial societies is the use of angles in their construction. The basis of building is the joining of surface to surface and the most convenient and consistent method of joining lasting materials such as stone and brick is to join flat right angled surfaces to each other; the 90° angle.

The vertical or 90° angle is also the most efficient position for humans standing upright on the earth's surface for it brings the lines of force straight through their bodies, reducing the moments of cantilevers. For example, place a book on your head then hold it at arms length to feel the difference of muscular strain in the two positions.

The other primary direction, associated with the vertical, is the horizontal. This is the direction in which people can move along with the least exertion. It is also the "ground plane" and "plane of reference." Combined, the two, the horizontal and the vertical, join at an angle of 90°. It is this angle that allows us to build vertically into the air joining the surfaces of building materials to assure equal distribution over their surfaces of the pull of gravity toward the center of the earth.

But a 90° angle between horizontal and vertical is seen only in very small artifacts. When objects assume the size of buildings they recede from our eyes in all directions, horizontally, vertically, and the directions in between. We learn to judge angles as if they were 90° in perspective. This is the secret of angles and how we perceive them.

Our tendency is to see, even as simple an arrangement as two crossed lines, as right angles in perspective as two different spatial arrangements of one or both lines.

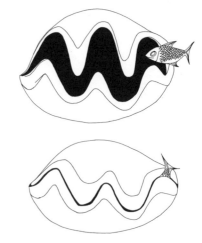

The irregular edges of a giant clam shell can only close in one position.

We are not sure whether it is the ability of angles to generate optical illusions that explains the eyes' fascination with them, or whether the eyes' fascination generates the optical illusions. But we do know that fascinating illusions occur.

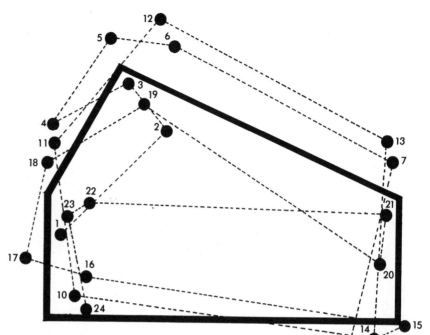

Importance of Angles—Angles are features that the brain employs in memorizing and recognizing an object. This was apparent in experiments conducted by Leonard Zusne and Kenneth M. Michels at Purdue University. The sequence of eye fixation of one subject in an eight-second viewing appears in this drawing. After diagram *Image, Object, and Illusion*, Scientific American 1963–74.

Fascinating illusions—East Wing, National Gallery, Washington, D.C.
Photo by F. Wilson.

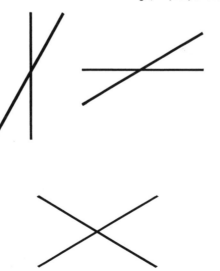

Crossed lines can be perceived as right angles in perspective

Photo by Jim Rankin.

Courtesy of Armco Steel Corp.

There are no 90° angles in this photograph, except the edges of the photograph itself, yet all the spatial divisions pictured are perceived as right angles.

Digital clock at 127 John Street, NYC. Design by Melvyn Kaufmann of the William Kaufmann Organization.

Photo courtesy of Kaufmann Organization.

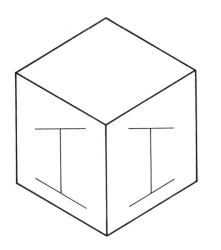

Which of the angles on the face of this cube are actually 90 degrees?

Zollner's illusion of direction.

According to Luckiesh, Zollner accidentally noticed the illusion on a pattern designed for a print for dress goods. The long parallel lines appear to diverge in the direction in which the crossing lines converge.

Zollner established that the illusion is greatest when the long parallel lines are inclined about 45 degrees to the horizontal. This may be accomplished by turning the page held in a vertical plane through an angle of 45 degrees from normal. The illusion vanishes when held too far from the eye to distinguish the short crossing lines, and its strength varies with the inclination of the oblique lines to the main parallels. The most effective angle between the short crossing lines and the main parallels appears to be approximately 30 degrees. In this figure there are two illusions of direction. The parallel vertical strips appear unparallel and the right and left portions of the oblique cross-lines appear to be shifted vertically. It is interesting to note that steady fixation diminishes and even destroys the illusion. (Luckiesh 1965, p. 76, 77)

The three horizontal lines are of equal length but can be made to appear unequal.

If lines are added to their ends they will be made to appear longer or shorter by varying the angles.

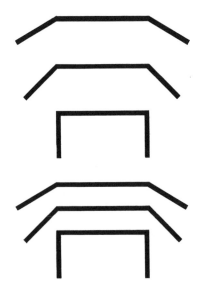

Within certain limits, the greater the angle the greater is the apparent elongation of the central horizontal portion.

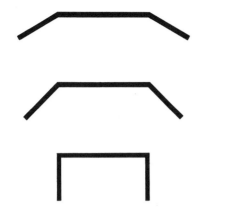

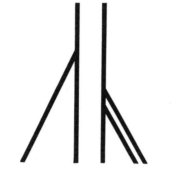

When oblique lines are extended across vertical lines the illusion is striking. The line on the right, if extended, would meet the line on the left.

Other factors that contribute to the extent of the illusion are the positions of the figures and the distance between them.

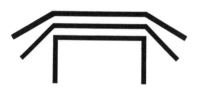

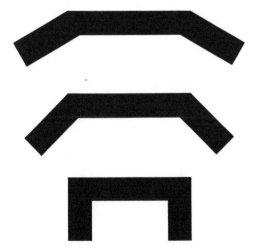

The second line on the right has been drawn to appear to meet the line on the left if extended. In reality, it would be above it.

A theory of the Muller-Lyer illusion suggests that the eye unconsciously interprets the arrowlike figures as three-dimensional structures, resembling either an outside (left) or inside corner (right) of a physical structure. A perceptual mechanism evidently shrinks the former and enlarges the latter to compensate for distortion caused by perspective.

Seemingly oblique lines meeting across vertical lines.

At Labyrinth building, Expo '67 Montreal.

Photo courtesy of Expo Corp.

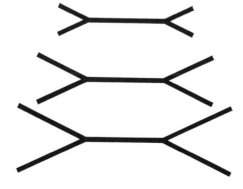

By increasing the size of the angles at the end of the horizontal line and illusion of perspective is created. The top horizontal line appears longer than the bottom. The distance between the top and middle figure appears greater than that between the middle and bottom figure.

The amount of distortion varies with the angles

Muller-Lyer illusion in office partitions.
Photo courtesy of Knoll International.

The obtuse angle tends to tilt the left and right sides of the horizontal line downward.

The horizontal line is continued by our imagination forming an obtuse angle so that the real horizontal line appears to tilt downward.

Muller-Lyer illusion at interior corner of office partition.

Photo by Scott Hyde.

Courtesy of Knoll International.

When two straight lines are separated it is usually possible to connect them visually and to determine that if connected they would be on a straight line.

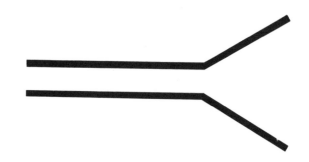

The angle at the left appears to tilt the straight line downward while the angle at the right appears to tilt it upward.

If another line is connected to one, thus forming an angle, the lines which appear to be continuous no longer appear so. The angle bends the line downward.

Conversely lines that are not on the same straight line may be made to appear to be by a line attached to one forming the proper angle.

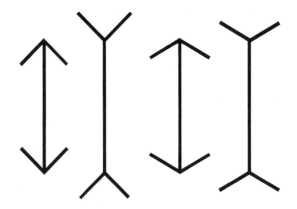

Obtuse angles arranged so that their effects are additive. The horizontal lines appear to have a maximum deviation.

The horizontal straight line seems to sag at its end titlting upward towards the center.

The horizontal line appears to tilt upward toward its extremities and sag in the middle.

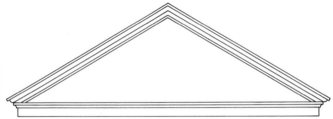

Wood framing, note wall plate under gable end.

Photo courtesy of Western Wood Products Association.

Pediment of church in Tallahassee, Florida.
Photo by F. Wilson.

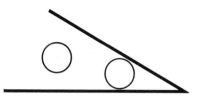

Which circle is larger?

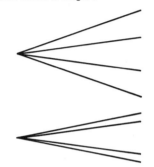

Which interior angle is larger?

Gallery, Iowa School of Architecture Building, Ames, Iowa.
Photo by F. Wilson.

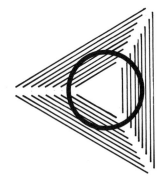

Distortions of a circle contour by the imposition of oblique lines and angles.

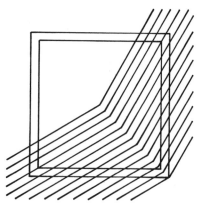

Distortion of the contour of a square by the imposition of oblique angles

Note the difference in appearance of the ring elements below and between the windows. The vertical columns (or mullions) between the windows seem to pass through the continuous circular sill interrupting its smooth flow. The sill below the first tier of windows appears continuous.
Hirshhorn Museum, Washington D.C. (Inner Court). Architects—Skidmore Owings and Merrill.
Photo by F. Wilson.

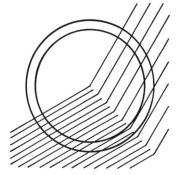

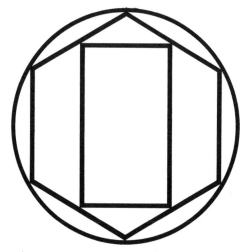

Distortion of Contour
The bounding figure is a true circle but it appears to be distorted or dented inward where the angles of the hexagon meet it. Similarly, the sides of the hexagon appear to sag inward where the corners of the rectangle meet them.

I. M. Pei National Gallery, Washington, D. C.

Is the ceiling grid composed of real triangles or are we reading 90° angles as triangles?
Photo by F. Wilson.

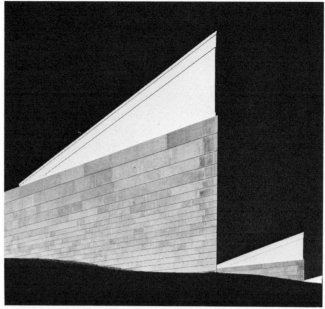

Art Center, Miami University, Oxford Ohio.
Photo by Sadin/Karant. Courtesy of Skidmore Owings
and Merrill.

Isometric drawing of Art Center, Miami University, Oxford, Ohio. Skidmore Owings and Merrill, Chicago Office
Photo Courtesy of Skidmore Owings and Merrill.

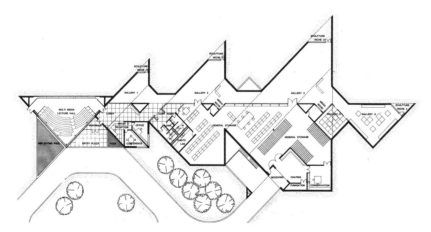

Floor Plan—Art Center, Miami University, Oxford, Ohio.
Courtesy of Skidmore Owings and Merrill.

Art Center, Miami University, Oxford, Ohio.
Photo by Sadin/Karant. Courtesy of Skidmore Owings
and Merrill.

ARTICULATION

"Forms vary from simple to complex in the degree of articulation or differentiation that they possess." (Fryer 1965, p. 85, 86)

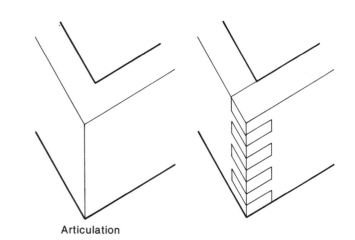

Articulation

Articulation can be a function of distance—the closer we approach an object the more clearly we can see its parts.

The corner implied.

The corner realized.

The corner emphasized. As the lines that create the corner go on to do other things they emphasize it more strongly than either of the other two conditions. An adjacent mirroring of the corner's shape occurs as the lines cross.

ARTICULATION

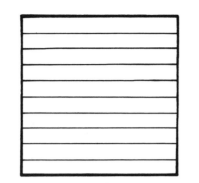

Articulation—the act or manner of joining.

Articulation as a function of distance. Foreground structure is clearly defined while the structural members of the pavilion in the distance fuse into one form.

Theme Pavilions Expo '67.

Photo by Expo '67.

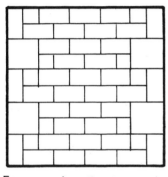
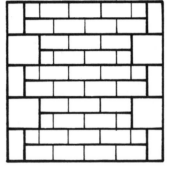

Forms vary from the simple to the complex to the degree that they display the joinery of their parts.

Masonry corner of Racquet Club, Park Avenue, Manhattan.
Photo by F. Wilson.

The articulation of materials in an Atlanta, Georgia doorway.
Photo by F. Wilson.

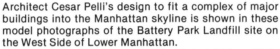

Architect Cesar Pelli's design to fit a complex of major buildings into the Manhattan skyline is shown in these model photographs of the Battery Park Landfill site on the West Side of Lower Manhattan.

Four major office towers ranging in height from 33 to 50 stories adjacent to the World Trade Center and adjacent buildings are fit into and unify the city context.

The buildings are designed of granite and reflective glass with the base granite sheeting articulating the transition to reflective glass at various levels. The towers set back where the transition occurs to correspond to the heights of surrounding buildings. Setbacks, similarity of material, and the complimentary forms of the distinctive tops provide a perceptual unity with the great variety of shapes of the Manhattan skyline.

Battery Park Landfill Site.
Architect—Cesar Pelli.
Photo by Kenneth Champlin. Courtesy of Cesar Pelli.

Articulation of materials as a function of distance. Looking through an arched opening into the 'nunnery quadrangle' at Uxmal, Yucatan.
Photo by F. Wilson.

Mosaic sculptured relief over doorway in 'nunnery quadrangle,' Uxmal, Yucatan.
Photo by F. Wilson.

Battery Park Landfill Site, Manhattan.
Architect—Cesar Pelli.
Photo by Kenneth Champlin. Courtesy of Cesar Pelli.

Plan view of Battery Park Landfill model.
Photo courtesy of Cesar Pelli.

BALANCE

Balance in architecture is subject to illusions and might be considered an illusion itself. For example, our judgment of balance is based largely upon mechanical laws. A composition must appear to be stable; that is, a large component such as a tower must not be situated so far from what we take as a center of gravity as to appear capable of tipping the remainder of the structure. In physics we would apply the term "moment." Each mass must be multiplied by its distance from the center of gravity, thus determining its moment. For a building or other composition to appear stable the sum of these moments must be zero; that is, those tending to turn the figure in one direction must be counterbalanced by those tending to turn it in another direction. In appraising a composition our intellect sums the effects of different parts somewhat in this manner, if satisfactory balance is considered to have been attained. The colors of the various components exert an influence in this respect, so it is seen that illusions may have much to do with the satisfactoriness of architectural compositions.

This is similar to the balance we seek in structure. We instinctively seek the balance of forces and the correct weight and size of structural members. Part of this may be visually instinctive, gained from our experience in the physical world since childhood. When we are faced with the illusion of instability or incongruity we feel a distinct unease.

Yet there is a difference in that how we perceive things is not always as exact as the forces at work on a structure. Things appear larger or smaller, less and greater in bulk according to color, shadow, markings, or texture. (Luckiesh 1965, p. 201)

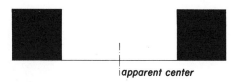
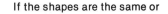

If the shapes are the same or

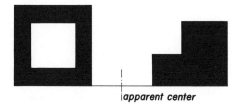

appear equal the balance will be in the center.

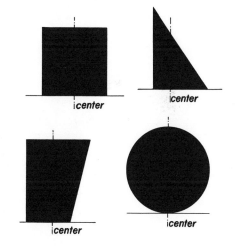

A mass viewed by itself has its own center of gravity.

Center of Gravity   *Mass*

Distance

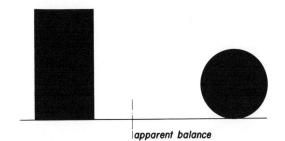

apparent balance

Two shapes seen together will appear to have a center of gravity—a point of balance—between them.

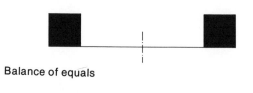

Balance of equals

The smaller the mass the more leverage (distance) it needs to balance itself against the larger mass.

If shapes are not the same or equal the apparent center between them will be a function of mass times distance.

A mass appears to rotate around a center of gravity

A symmetrical balance in which each roadway weights equally on either side of the supporting column. Photo courtesy of Bethelehem Steel Co.

An asymmetrical balance. The various complex elements weigh against each other to create a center where the downward stairway leaves the platform. This is also almost on the exact center line of the photograph.
Photo: Interior of U.S. Pavilion, Expo '67.
Photo courtesy of Expo Corp.

The pedimented portico of the central building on the campus of the University of Maryland is balanced by two pavilions.
Photo by F. Wilson

...administration.
Photo by F. Wilson

Balance achieved by the repetition of similar forms and voids. The forms are symmetrical around a vertical line through the center of the cow's skull.
Photo by F. Wilson

Balanced by columns, centered on the frieze of the entablature, is the building's function. . .
Photo by F. Wilson

Administration balances the pediment, the portico, the pavilions, and the world.
Photo by F. Wilson

CHANGE IN STIMULUS

"Any change in the stimulus situation is likely to gain attention such as loud to soft, red to green, hot to cold, going to stopping, stopped to going, large to small, smooth to rough, etc." (Fryer 1965, p. 62)

SIZE—MAGNITUDE—INTENSITY
"Other things equal, stimuli of greater magnitude are more likely to gain attention than are stimuli of lesser magnitude." (Fryer 1965, p. 62)

UNEXPECTED
"The unexpected is effective in gaining attention. The white cow stands out in a herd of otherwise black ones." (Fryer 1965, p. 62)

"Another way to make a strong impression is to employ familiar forms that have been given an eccentric turn which will take the spectator by surprise and force him to regard the work more closely.

An architect who is interested in construction for construction's sake, or in cavity for cavity's sake, will not employ such contrasts or mannerisms. It is difficult to imagine anyone trying to emphasize the effect of a large iron bridge by using contrasting detail. But the artist who wishes to create a sensational visual effect can employ such means to accentuate certain parts of the work. . . .

At all times there can be found Mannerists of this kind with a predilection for the visually effective. But there are also entire periods which are wholly dominated by such aesthetic tendencies. . . . ." (Rasmussen 1964, p. 59)

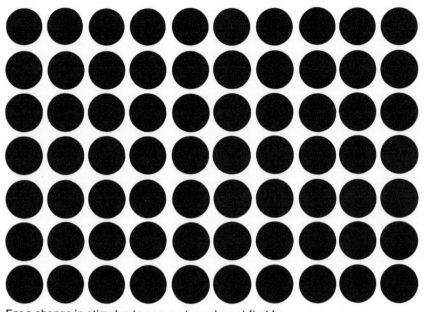

For a change in stimulus to occur a 'norm' must first be established. Here the 'norm' is a succession of circles, all of the same size and consistently spaced.

Sculpture at Expo '67.
Photo courtesy of Expo Corp.

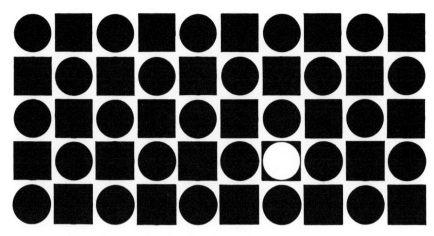

Here the 'norm' of alternating black circles and squares is violated by a white circle in a black square.

The 'norm' violated by a larger and a smaller circle and a square.

Photo courtesy of Expo '67 Corp.

During the Renaissance a 'norm' was established of classic details. Courtesy of the University of Virginia Library.

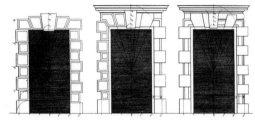

During the Baroque period that followed the Renaissance the 'norm' of classic details was violated by 'rustic' treatment, where masonry units were made to alternate in size to achieve aesthetic affect by the violation of Renaissance 'norms.'
Drawings courtesy of the University of Virginia Library.

We do not expect 'architectural surprises', changes of stimulus, in such structures as bridges.
Golden Gate Bridge, San Francisco, California.

We are surrounded by 'changes of stimulus' in our everyday life. Many are technical contrasts. A change of stimulus occurs when things seem out of place or out of context, contrast with their surroundings, or are other than we expect.

The following are examples.

A television antenna on an 18th century roof in New Orleans and the head of Michelangelo's David on a shelf behind a wire grating in a New Orleans novelty shop.
Photo by F. Wilson.

A Volkswagon 'beetle' converted to a mobile home parked on a San Diego street.
Photo by F. Wilson.

The Sydney Opera House opening in October of 1973, in which the Opera House, inspired by the appearance of billowing sails, is surrounded by a celebration of motor boats.
Photo courtesy of Australian Information Service.

CLEARNESS

"Objects with sharp outlines appear nearer than objects with hazy outlines. Color plays an important part in this connection. The brightness of colors dissipates with increasing distance." (Fryer 1965, p. 83)

Clearness

The buildings behind the grave yard appear closer because their forms are distinct. They are also recognizable forms (rectangles).

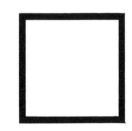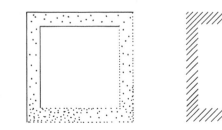

Three squares of equal size—which appears nearest?

Clearness due to sharp outlines. The boy whose outline we can see clearly seems closer than the child whose indistinct outlines are in reality in the foreground.
Photo by F. Wilson.

The building toward the center of the photo appears closer than the one to its left whose outlines are blurred by the tree's shadow. (Cuernevaca, Mexico)
Photo by F. Wilson.

Photograph of early German Albatross of World War I photographed looking up the tower of a ruined cathedral. The planes seem closer or as close as the bombed out building shell.
Photo Courtesy of the U. S. Air Force.

The diffused lines of this transparent telephone bubble in Helsinki, Finland make the sharp lines of the telephone appear closer than the bubble opening.
Photo by F. Wilson.

CLOSURE

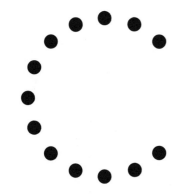

OPEN AND CLOSED FORMS—An open form tends to change toward a certain good form (strong form such as a square, circle or rectangle). When a form has assumed stable equilibrium, it has achieved closure. Thus a series of dots which almost make a circle are perceived as a circle but with a part missing rather than as part circle.

CLOSURE—Incomplete objects which suggest complete organizations tend to complete themselves.

C

Incomplete objects suggest complete organizations. We do not see them as partial groupings complete in themselves. Our eye treats them as if they were actually complete even though parts are missing. (Fryer 1965, p. 64)

Stonehenge from the air appears to be a complete circle even though stones near the entrance road are missing. Photo courtesy of CBS News Service.

The grouping of bollards at the National Gallery designed by I. M. Pei imply closure. Photo by F. Wilson.

In a closer view in which neither the outer nor the inner circle is seen completely, our perception continues to be that of completed circles. Photo courtesy of CBS News Service.

Arched form of 'Theme Building' at Expo '67 in Montreal completes itself as a triangle.
Photo courtesy of Expo Corp.

Alignment creates a center triangle.
(after Kanzsa 1976)

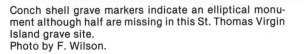

Conch shell grave markers indicate an elliptical monument although half are missing in this St. Thomas Virgin Island grave site.
Photo by F. Wilson.

The brain seeks to tie the subjective contours, the components of an incomplete picture, together by creating the perception of contours that complete the picture.

CONSTANCY

CONSTANCY PHENOMENA

"An object is perceived correctly as to size or intensity within a wide range of actual stimulus variations. An automobile seen at a distance of 100 yards does not appear smaller than one seen at 20 yards, even though there is a greater disparity in the size of the retinal image. A shout heard from afar is still recognized as a shout instead of a whisper, even though the actual stimulus intensity may be quite low by the time the auditory mechanism is stimulated. A lawn is seen as the same shade of green, even though part of it lies in bright sunshine and part in shadow." (Fryer 1965, p. 64)

"A form tends to preserve its proper shape, size, and color." (Fryer 1965 p. 85, 86)

GESTALT

Gestalt advocates argue that the proper subject of study is the unified whole incapable of further analysis. People are said to experience the whole inherently as an innate experience which is not the result of learning. As an example, a table is perceived as a table and not something which has a top and a number of legs. People, the gestaltists argue, look for phenomena—unbiased free experiences which emerge instantaneously.

To live and move we must perceive objects in space. A notable aspect of perception is that objects retain their identity despite how they are viewed. When we see an object in a room such as a chair, it does not appear to increase in size as we approach; the size appears constant. When a person wearing a dark colored shirt moves from a shady area to the sunlight the shirt still appears to be of the same color, if there are no direct reflections. Features of objects remain approximately constant despite environmental orientation changes which do, in reality, alter their appearance.

An example of the constancy phenomenon can be demonstrated by the 'afterimage.' This is an image that persists after the original stimulus has been removed.

If you will stare at the dot in the center of the black square for about a minute than hold a piece of paper about ten inches from your eyes you will see the afterimage of the square. If you now move the paper about twice the distance it was held originally the afterimage square will appear to be twice the size. If you then induce another afterimage square and look at a still more distant surface, such as a white wall, the afterimage will appear even larger.

The size of the afterimage has not changed since it is based on our original perception of the square. The change is in our perceived image of the square. As our eyes focus at greater distances our brain interprets the afterimage as representing a larger object.
(Braun 1979)

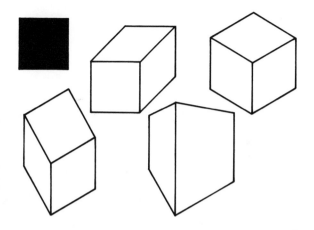

Constant cube.

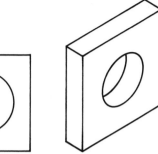

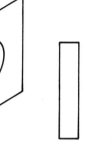

Objects retain their identity despite how they are viewed.

Front View

Isometric view

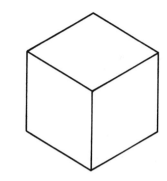

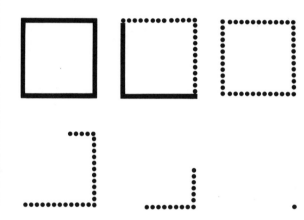

Memory of a square.

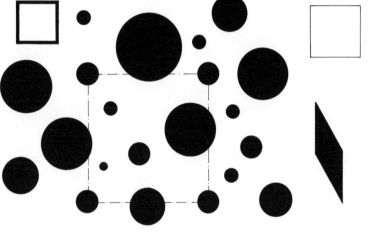

Memory of a square.

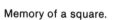

Memory of constant cubes.

FAMILIAR FIGURES

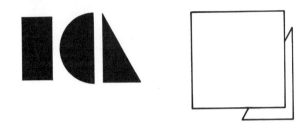

Given this figure....

....we tend to see a square overlapping a triangle....

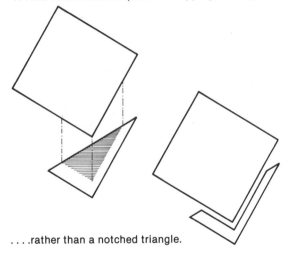

....rather than a notched triangle.

PERCEPTUAL CONSTANCY

When we move toward a tree, the image that it casts on the retina becomes larger, its color grows more distinct, and the details of the branches and trunk become sharper. Yet we know that the tree has not in fact become larger, more colorful, or sprouted more details. In the same way, the image cast by a car that is moving away becomes smaller, but we do not perceive the car as actually changing size. Even when there are larger changes in the sensory information received from objects in the environment, the moment to moment changes tend to be ignored in favor of a constant predictable view of the world. This tendency to perceive objects as having properties that are stable is known as the constancy phenomena.

It has a number of characteristics which can be grouped into types such as that of size. The farther away an object is the smaller the size of the image it projects on the retina. Yet if we have information that the object is far away, we automatically take this into account and translate the object's projected size into its real size.

This happens when we identify objects in the distance as to size in relation to objects whose size we know. For example, the only means we have of knowing the size of the nodes (round balls to which the truss members are attached) of this huge space frame truss is by seeing them in relation to the men on the ground.

The relationship between an object's projected size and its distance is the same for both eye and camera. An inverse relationship exists between distance and projected image. The greater the distance, the smaller the image projected. When an object's distance from the eye or camera is doubled its projected size is halved. Thus if we take a photograph of a tree from 100 feet and another photograph from 200 feet, the tree will be twice as high in the first photograph as in the second. Our brain seems to process this data only if distance can be inferred taking into account the relationship between size and known distance, or known size and estimated distance.

Truss nodes for 'Festival Plaza' by architect Kenzo Tange at Expo '70, Osaka. Their size can be compared to that of the engineers standing next to them.
Photo by Ogawa. Courtesy of Expo '70 Osaka.

Truss of 'Festival Plaza' in place. We tend to see the nodes as 'huge' almost man-sized although their image on our retina is not much larger than the head of a straight pin.
Photo courtesy of Expo Osaka.

Pigeon and Young (Picasso 1947).

The constancy phenomena is evident in these two Picasso lithographs. They show the movement of objects in space and the eye's movement as it seeks to determine the form of objects in space by viewing them from different lines of sight.

Picasso's use of this device is particularly evident in the pigeon's head and stylized skull which are viewed both frontally and in profile. A study of these drawings will reveal aspects of the objects turned in space.

Black Pitcher and Death's Head (Picasso 1946).

Constancy of image is the result of mentally combining all of the eye's quick motions and images and memories of the object into a complete vision of the whole.

The ability to 'see,' that is, to visualize and interpret images of great difference in size, color, and outline in their true forms, is an editing performance of incredible complexity.

An attempt to disassemble these images into the various impressions one receives when viewing architecture at various distances, walking through and around its structure and spaces, is an effort to understand the dynamic experience of the eye composing the completed image. It is an effort to see what seeing is.

Training the eye to appreciate and assess relationships is a necessity today to place ourself in space. In the earlier development of humans, survival depended upon this ability.

The State Capital Building in Honolulu.
Photo by F. Wilson.

The State Capital Building viewed from a distance is seen in the context of its surroundings. . .
Photo by F. Wilson.

but is visualized as the impressive building we first saw.
Photo by F. Wilson.

CO-OPERATION OF THE SENSES

"Different sensitivities are integrated, particularly from past experience. A steel ball is perceived as heavy, whereas a rubber one is "seen" as relatively light. Velvet is "seen" as soft, smooth, or even sensual. All of this occurs even though the immediate stimulus is merely the energy change involved in the reflected light stimulating the receptor cells of the retina." (Fryer 1965, p. 64)

The black desk front appears hard and black; the chairs appear soft; and the black ceiling tiles are an unknown quality, either hard or soft. The white paneling in the background is hard white; the white rug is soft. In reality, if we did not know the nature of these materials from previous experience we would be hard put to identify them. The hard edges of the soft upholstery are very similar to the precise edge of the marble table. The white rug does not appear much different than the back of the paneled cabinet or the white wall in the background or the column covering. The ceiling could be hard marble or soft upholstery. The plants could be plastic, hard, soft, or poisoned.

The facade of Alto's auditorium at Otaniemi, Finland is 'seen' as brick masonry although it actually appears as a wool fabric.
Photo by F. Wilson.

The children are supported by a cushioned transparent fabric filled with vacancy. We assume it to be filled with air and soft.

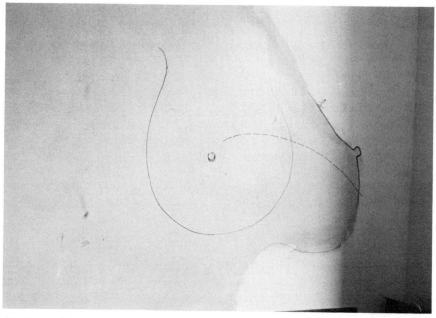

Plaster patch converted to erotic graffitti. Plaster becomes 'sensual,' fleshlike.
Photo by F. Wilson

Photo by F. Wilson.

DIRECTING ATTENTION

Directing attention as a means of controlling human action can be accomplished by the use of most of the perceptual phenomena we have discussed thus far. For example the center of balance directs attention to itself. Making things clear attracts our notice to them. The introduction of an inconsistent element makes it conspicuous. However when the objective is to consciously direct attention, to control, the perceptual phenomenon used to do so this may be viewed as a unique phenomenon in itself.

The most effective means of directing attention is the arrow that simply points out what is to be noticed.

There are however other means of controlling action and telling people what is expected of them, such as furniture arrangements. This is an effective means. Classroom seating indicates that a mass of people are to be entertained by one person. They sit passively in rows while the teacher faces them in the opposite direction and has freedom of movement. Ropes and chains attached to stanchions indicate people are to queue for service in banks and supermarkets. Street signs use shape, words, and graphic symbols to direct attention.

The arrows at this Metro stop at Catholic University in Washington, D.C. seem to be directing toward heaven and hell rather than the direction of a two-way street. Photo by F. Wilson.

Sculptures outside the entrance of the railway station in Helsinki direct the passengers' attention to the entrance. Photo by F. Wilson.

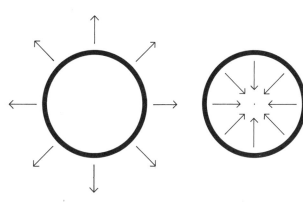

An effect of diverting or directing attention by suggestion is demonstrated. Attention is directed toward two contrasting and expanding circles of equal area. Which appears larger?

Although the larger circle is the most prominent, the arrow directs our attention to the smaller.

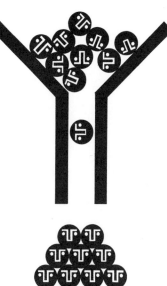

Objects seem to direct human activity by the implication of physical placement.

Chairs arranged in orderly rows at New York State University at Buffalo direct attention to the students in how they are to sit as disciplined learners.
Photo by F. Wilson.

The Council Chamber of the Boston City Hall directs attention to itself, and the main entrance of the building, by location and increase in scale.
Photo courtesy of the Massachusetts Dept. of Commerce and Development, Division of Tourism.

Directed attention undirected. The spire of the "Old South Meetinghouse in Boston" no longer towers above surrounding buildings to direct attention to its importance.
Photo courtesy of the Massachusetts Dept. of Commerce and Development, Division of Tourism.

EQUIVOCAL FIGURES

ILLUSIONS

"Illusions of the senses have for us the same appeal as a magician's trick. They contradict our everyday experience; they defy, and yet demand, rational explanation. For some thinkers they have raised questions about reality itself.

How can the observer be sure that everything he senses is not illusory? Of course, even if it were, we would still have the problem of why some aspects of perception are called illusions, in the narrow sense, although others are not. Why do we consider that some perceived images truthfully represent external objects but that others do not?

The answer depends upon what we assume is the necessary correspondence between certain of the properties of the object—such as wavelength of reflected light, measured size, and geometric shape—and those of its perceived image, color, apparent size, form. In many instances the assumed correspondence may hold and we regard the perceptions as true. If, however one or more of these assumed correspondences proves incorrect, we term the perception an illusion. Accordingly, the illusion simply indicates the inadequacies of the assumed correspondences. They can be likened to the visible tops of icebergs; they indicate hidden regions of ignorance about the works of perceptual processes.

Some illusions are fascinating because they show us in a particularly clear way the workings of our own perceptual processes. The works of certain artists, such as Escher, play on such themes, but most compelling in this respect are the reversible figures. A cube appearing to extend toward the observer may suddenly switch its orientation and appear to extend away from him. The observer need not have performed any particular action and certainly the cube did not change. Then to what must this change be attributed? Obviously, some alteration in the observer himself has occurred, implicating a perceptual process that has at least two states, each corresponding to a different appearance of the figure. We expect that such a perceptual process is, in turn, the expression of an underlying neural mechanism. An understanding of such mechanisms, which is still quite remote, can be expected to yield the ultimate explanation of sensory illusions. In the meantime they serve as fascinating challenges." (Held 1974)

The visual illusions that we discuss here can be divided into two kinds. First those that Mr. Held describes as changing due to some underlying neutral mechanism, cubes that advance and recede, stairs that reverse their direction, and the like. Although these may occasionally occur in architecture it is the second kind that is the most common, where what we see appears differently than it is actually built.

ARCHITECTURAL ILLUSIONS

Many illusions are found in architecture. These were recognized long before they were recognized in the graphic arts. The architecture of classic Greece displays a highly developed knowledge of many geometrical illusions and the architects of these centuries carefully worked out details for counteracting them.

The architects drawings may reveal illusions to the architect, but many are not predicted by them. The ever-changing relations of lines and forms in architecture as our point of view varies introduce many illusions which may appear and disappear.

No view of a group of buildings or of the components of a single structure can be free from optical illusions. We never see in reality the same relations of lines, forms, colors, and brightnesses as indicated by the drawings or blueprints. Perhaps this is one of the best reasons for justifying the construction of expensive models of our more ambitious structures. Other devices are also used, such as a series of lenses that allow the designer to look inside the model for interior relationships. TV cameras have been adjusted to picture the building as it might appear when completed.

In architecture the eye is not satisfied by such tools as the level, the square, and the plumb line. The eye is satisfied only when the appearance is satisfactory. For the purpose of showing the extent of certain architectural illusions the compensatory measures applied by the Greeks are excellent examples. They also reveal the remarkable application of science to architecture as compared with the scanty application to painting of the same period.

The Parthenon of Athens affords an excellent example of the magnitude of the corrections which the designer thought necessary in order to satisfy the eye. The long lines of the architrave (the beam which surmounts the columns or extends from column to column) would appear to sag if it were actually straight. This is also true of the stylobate (substructure of the colonnade) and of pediments and other features. These lines were constructed convex instead of straight so that they would appear straight to the eye.

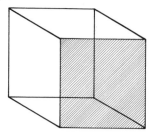

The 'Necker Cube' is a much publicized example of equivocation. The shaded surface sometimes appears as the top and sometimes as the bottom surface of the cube.

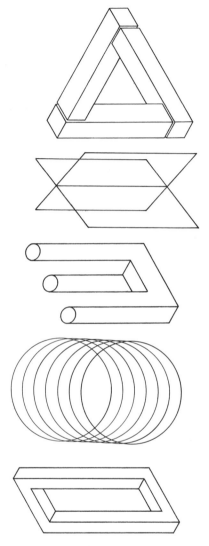

A series of figures that appear to reverse themselves.

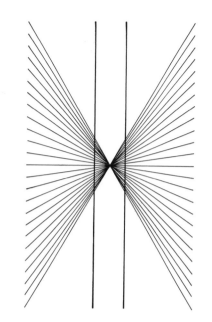

Parallel lines that appear to bulge outward at the center.

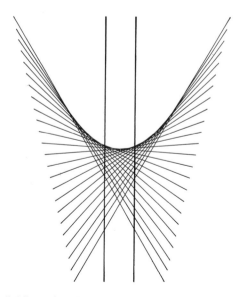

Parallel lines that do not appear parallel.

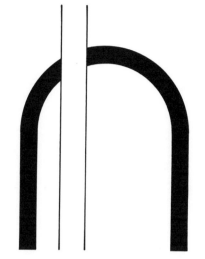

Parallel lines disrupt the curve of the arch.

A more common occurrence of the same phenomena where a street light standard interrupts our view of the arched building walkway in the background.
Photo by F. Wilson.

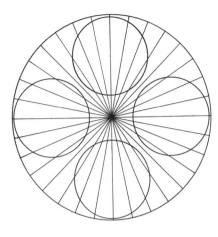

Circles distorted by radiating lines.

The white square in a black area appears larger than the black square surrounded by white. Both are the same size.

An optical illusion of alternating star and cubes

The phenomena of irradiation causes apparent changes in the size of architectural elements.

The stacks of Alto's power plant at Otaniemi, Finland appear smaller in shadow than they would in full light. (See introduction.)
Photo by F. Wilson.

Width and spacing of parallel lines cause them to appear curving and receding.

Transformation of the square.

Dark spots appear at the intersection of white lines.

Corbusier's 'hand' if viewed upside down or rotated at a 45° angle will appear convex instead of incised as a concave sculpture.

Transformation of the square.

Light and Shade
Patterns of highlights and shadows suggest the character of the object. If the shadow is cast on the lower portion of the image, the object is considered as convex; if the shadow is on the upper portion, the object is considered concave. In addition, shadows falling laterally on the object viewed frontally give further indications of the form and the depth.

An abrupt shift in brightness will be interpreted as an edge. Gradual transitions in brightness are a means of perceiving roundness.

The circular lighting fixture casts a shadow on the ceiling that makes the ceiling appear to curve downward.
Photo courtesy of Knoll International.

The highlights rather than the shadows of the fabric covering of the inflated structure make them appear convex in the foreground and the white fabric to the rear appears to curve upward.
Photo courtesy of Birdair Structures.

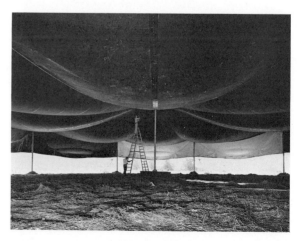

FIGURE GROUND

The figure-ground phenomena is one of the most important or at least one of the most used of the Gestalt laws of form.

"Figure and Ground: A form tends to be a figure set upon a ground, and a figure-ground dichotomy is fundamental to all perception." (Fryer 1965, p. 85, 86)

"Perception can be changed from the object to the space around the object (the ground). When this is done the figure becomes the ground and the ground the figure. This is most common in optical illusions." (Fryer 1965, p. 64)

"The elementary impressions of a visual world are those of surface and edge . . . the impression of a continuous surface may account for visual space conceived as a background. The impressions of an edge may account for an outline or figure against the background—the 'figure ground phenomenon'— and together with the surface enclosure may account for the perception of an object." (Gibson 1950)

To characterize the fundamental difference between figure and ground it is useful to consider the contour which is defined as the common boundary of the two fields. One can then state as a fundamental principle: When two fields have a common border, and one is seen as figure and the other as ground, the immediate perceptual experience is characterized by a shaping effect which emerges from the common border of the fields and which operates only on one field, or operates more strongly on one than on the other. E. Rubin (Danish psychologist)

Steen Eiler Rasmussen in his book "Experiencing Architecture" says: "If you paint a black vase on a white ground, you consider all the black as "figure" and all the white as that which it really is—as background which lies behind the figure and stretches out on both sides with no definite form. If we try to fix the figure in our minds we will note that at the bottom the foot spreads out on both sides and above it a number of convexities also project on to the white ground.

But if we consider the white as figure and the black as ground—for example, a hole in the figure opening into a black space—then we see something quite different. Gone is the vase and in its stead are two faces in profile. Now the white becomes the convexities projecting out onto the black ground and forming nose, lips and chin.

We can shift our perception at will from one to the other, alternately seeing vase and profiles. But each time there must be an absolute change in perception. We cannot see both vase and profiles at the same time.

The strange thing is that we do not conceive the two figures as complementing each other. If you try to draw them you will involuntarily exaggerate the size of the area which at the moment appears as convexities. Ordinarily convex forms are seen as figure, concave as ground. This can be seen on the figure (black vase). The outline being a wavy line it is possible to see either black or white convexities, as you choose. . . ."

Rasmussen maintains that some architects are "structure-minded" and others "cavity-minded," and that some architectural periods work preferably with solids and others with cavities. This perference, he maintained, had much to do with our figure ground perception of buildings.

Gothic architecture, Rasmussen says, was constructional. All bodies were convex with more and more material added to them. The architect and sculptor were so enamored of spiky excrescences of all kinds that no human being could possibly conceive of the shape of the space, the ground, around them.

The transition from Gothic to Renaissance was not only a change from dominating vertical elements to dominating horizontal ones, Rasmussen points out, but above all a complete transformation from an architecture of sharp and pointed structures to an architecture of well-shaped cavities. (Rasmussen 1959, p. 50)

The concept of "Contextualism" seems to have begun some time during the early 1960s, at least this is what Charles Jencks claims to be the case. The technique of figure-ground became an important perceptual device for "seeing" the way that cities formed various patterns.

". . . .By definition the design must fit with, respond to, mediate its surroundings, perhaps completing a pattern implicit in the street layout or introducing a new one. Crucial to this appreciation of the urban patterns is the double image of the figure-ground. The pattern that could be read either way, solid or void, black or white was the key to the contextualist approach to urban space. (Grahame Shane, "Contextualism," *Architectural Design,* No. 11, 1976, pp. 676–9.) (Jencks 1977)

Ambiguous figure—Black on White or White on Black? (Figure-ground reversal)

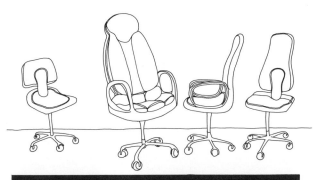

Picasso's *The Large Owl,* 1948 lithograph, is a study in figure-ground perch and flight. The eye moves from the bird at rest in white figure and black ground to the reversal of bird in flight when black becomes figure and white ground.

Is there a visual connection?
Note: Small objects on a large field tend to become figures on a ground.

Large objects on a small field can become either figure or ground.

GESTALT PRINCIPLES

According to Gestalt psychologists we are constantly organizing bits and pieces of information into meaningful patterns. These patterns are called gestalts, after the German word for "pattern" or whole. Because of the organization of black forms, for example, we can perceive a warrior's face, a slight rearrangement of these forms would obscure this perception. The head is a gestalt, a perceptual whole. Although we can perceive each of the elements in the pattern, more than just these elements is perceived. We recognize the whole form of the head. Therefore, the gestalt is said to be greater than the sum of its parts.

Gestalt psychology originated in Germany early in the 20th century with psychologists such as Max Wertheimer, Kurt Koffa, and Wolfgang Kohler, and its influence extends to present-day psychology. In their research, the early gestalt psychologists presented people with various patterns, often consisting of dots or musical tones, and simply asked the people what they saw or heard. From this data they formulated a number of principles to explain how sensory stimuli are structured so as to lead to the perception of gestalts. Two of the major concepts they came up with are groupings and figure-ground.

Try turning the page upside down to see if the groupings of the warrior's head still compose a face.

A reversal of the figure-ground relationship in which the building exists as figure and the spaces around it as ground occurs in this passageway through and between buildings in Helsinki, Finland. The vaulted opening is the figure that the pedestrian enters on the street above. It continues as a figural spatial configuration opening and closing as one walks in the passageway between buildings, down stairs, and at last enters the courtyard of a building on the lower level preparatory to entering the vaulted exit to a street on the lower level.

Throughout the varied spatial happenings, the walker experiences the space as form or figure and the buildings as background.

A

B

Photos by F. Wilson (Helsinki, Finland).

Midblock passage from higher to lower street in Helsinki.

C

E

G

D

F

H

69

FUSION

Fusion of Forms—Two forms may fuse, giving rise to a new form; or, in combination, the stronger one may persist, eliminating the weaker.

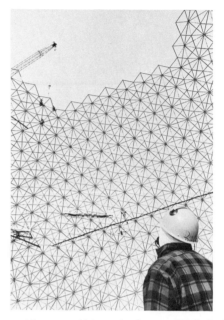

Hexagonal forms and triangular forms of Fuller's dome. Photo courtesy of Expo Corp.

Triangular form fusing into hexagon which becomes the dominant figure. If you rotate this photograph the dominance of the hexagon will disappear.
Photo courtesy of Expo Corp.

Hexagonal and triangular forms fuse and merge with spherical form of the dome itself.
Photo courtesy of Expo Corp.

Fusion of building and bamboo forms.

Fine Arts Building, University of Hawaii at Manoa.
Photo by F. Wilson.

North and South America and the West Coast of Africa are fused into the dominant form of 'the big blue marble' in this NASA Environmental Satellite photograph. Photo courtesy of NASA.

FIGURE GROUPINGS

GROUPING

"Objects relatively close together are seen as a group." (Fryer 1965, p. 64)

"Objects of the same color, shape, or other dimensional characteristic are seen as a group." (Fryer 1965, p. 64)

"Objects moving simultaneously in the same direction are seen as a group." (Fryer 1965, p. 64)

We tend to group units on the basis of proximity or of similarity. Two shapes situated close to each other or seen together as a visual 'whole' even though they may be dissimilar. But more insistent is the linking together of similar units, shapes or colors, event though they may be placed far apart from each other in the visual field.

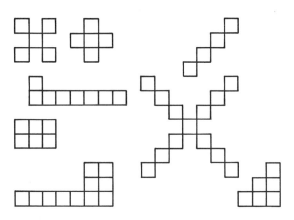

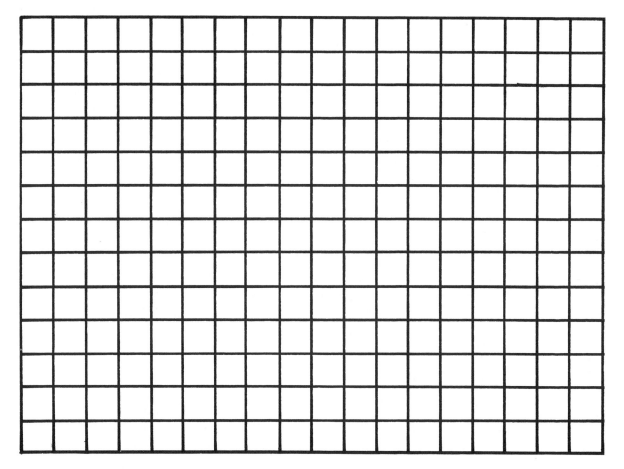

Figure groupings occur when one stares at a matrix of squares. The simple figures organize themselves spontaneously, and with effort more complex figures can be perceived. Some figures, however, are so complex that they are difficult to maintain.
(Held, p, 97)

Fusion of window forms. World Bank Building, Washington, D.C.
Photo by F. Wilson.

Figure grouping of forms in background casket wall in graveyard in lower Mexico.
Photo by F. Wilson.

Fusion of window forms. FBI Building, Washington, D.C.
Photo by F. Wilson.

Figure groupings of barrels and windows at Fiorio de Ischia.
Photo by F. Wilson.

Grouping by nearness.

Grouping by size.

Grouping by similarity.

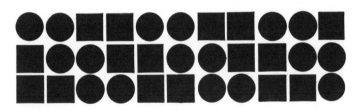

Groupings appear diagonally.

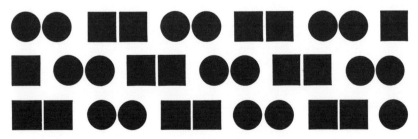

Groupings appear both diagonally and horizontally.

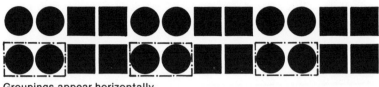

Groupings appear horizontally.

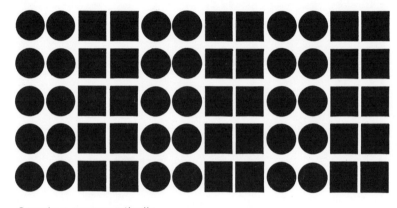

Groupings appear vertically.

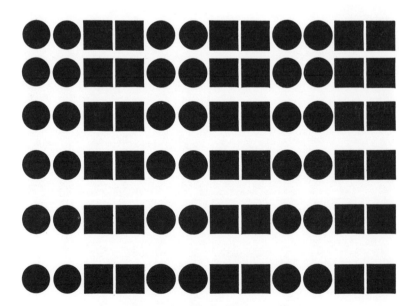

Groupings appear to change from horizontal to vertical as the spaces between lines decreases.

Vertical and horizontal groupings of windows at Fiorio de Ischia.

The Arched window of the Norman tower in the background groups with the arched window of the apartment facade below it while the rectangular windows group together horizontally.
Photo by F. Wilson.

Groupings of dormer windows.
Photo by F. Wilson.

Assembly line chaos organized by grouping of windows in Cadillac bodies.
Photo courtesy of Cadillac (General Motors).

Spontaneous grouping of building elements—Taxco, Mexico.
Photo by F. Wilson.

HORIZONTAL-VERTICAL-OBLIQUE

The vertical and the horizontal have marked influences on perception, as proven by both scientific research and the concurring observations of artists and architects.

The primary angle is the angle that people make standing upright on the surface of the earth. In the many directions that a person can move, one, the vertical is distinguished by the pull of gravity. The vertical acts as an axis, a frame of reference for all other directions. (Arnheim 1977, p. 32)

Verticals do not run parallel but converge toward the center of the earth due to the pull of gravity. One particular vertical can be seen as the spoke of a wheel pushing toward the hub, the center of gravity.

Arnheim claims, and it is born out by laboratory experiment, that the vertical direction defines the horizontal plane as the only one for which the vertical serves as an axis of symmetry.

He claims that it therefore follows that no direction along the ground plane is spatially distinguished. Christian Norberg Shultz has written that, "the horizontal directions represent man's concrete world of action. In a certain sense, all horizontal directions are equal and form a plane of infinite extension. The simplest model of man's existential space is therefore horizontal plane pierced by a vertical axis." Frank Lloyd Wright pointed out that the automobile opened to Americans the unlimited freedom of the horizontal plane.

The column, from ancient times, has been a symbol of the upright integrity of the vertical. Alberti emphasized that the column was the principle ornament of all of architecture. Although he saw it as an ornament, as part of a wall, he and others also saw it as a symbol of the striving of humankind standing upright upon the earth.

Mondrian, is said to have felt so strongly about the vertical and the horizontal that Van Doesburg's adoption of the diagonal element in his paintings was one of the reasons that he disassociated himself finally from the De Stijl movement in 1925. (Overy 1969)

We find that Sausmarez claims that horizontals and verticals operating together introduce the principle of balanced oppositions of tensions. The vertical expresses a force which is of primary significance—gravitational pull, the horizontal again contributes a primary sensation—a supporting flatness; the two together produce a deeply satisfying resolved feeling, perhaps because, he speculates, together they symbolize the human experience of absolute balance, of standing erect on level ground. (Sausmarez 1964, p. 21, 22)

Visual fields expand vertically. The architectural setting induces a definite ceiling to the sky above it. An impression of a definite height of the sky is caused by the interplay of the height of the surrounding buildings and the expansion and width and length of the street. The height of the sky is strongly influenced by the contours of eaves and gables, chimneys and towers.

Generally the height above a closed square is imagined as three or four times the height of the tallest building on the square Arnheim tells us. (Arnheim 1977, p. 25). Over wide open squares such as the Place de la Concorde in Paris the visual distance of the sky is only vaguely perceived. The height of the skies is the limit of the field of forces that issues from the ground architecture.

Here the World Trade Center towers belie this rule for it is so high that the sky seems to rest on their top. In Lenningrad, the street car trolly lines make a ceiling to the street. The height of the buildings, the width of the street, and the long vistas in Lenningrad generally dwarf the people in the street. A regiment of Peter the Great's Imperial Guards could walk down this street quite comfortably and not overly obstruct traffic in doing so.

The sky in this street in Fiorio de Ischia rests quite comfortably on the shoulder of the hill in the background. The street is made for walking people who, passing each other, can distinguish each others features, and pass a greeting without stopping, and be understood. The sky forms a comfortable top to the building enclosures.

Street in Fiorio de Ischia.
Photo by F. Wilson.

World Trade Center.
Photo by F. Wilson.

The vertical, horizontal and oblique have been an innate part of man's perceptual understanding from the beginning of history, according to Siegfried Giedion.

There are three space conceptions discernable in the history of architecture according to Giedion, and they have one thing in common. Despite other major differences, all accept the dominance of the vertical.

The prehistoric, prearchitectural space conception was not dominated by the vertical, for in the cave paintings of the Magdalenian Age the animals never stand on a precisely horizontal base, Giedion notes. They stand at various angles on the sloping rock walls of the caverns; sometimes they are tilted to such a degree that to our eyes they appear to be falling. But in the eyes of primitive men, such as the Eskimo, Giedion contends, they are simply standing near one another.

The beginning of architecture is closely linked with the development of a sense of order, a sense of the vertical and its corollary, the horizontal plane.
(Giedion 1971, p. 3)

Artists of much later date than primitive man, particularly those of the early modern movement, have taken the horizontal, the vertical, and the oblique quite seriously. Van Doesburg's adoption of the diagonal element in his paintings was one of the reasons that led Mondrian to disassociate himself finally from De Stijl in 1925.
(Overy 1969, p. 95)

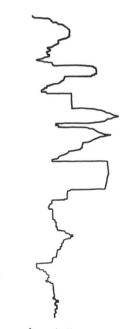

"...the 'height of the sky' as the limit of the field of forces that issues from the architecture on the ground but cannot reach beyond a certain distance. With increasing distance the field peters out into the empty sky...the architecture diffuses gradually into the sky...." (Arnheim, p. 26)

Leningrad Street.
Photo by F. Wilson.

New York City Skyline.

"If one turns the shape of a skyline by 90° one is reminded that a similar gradual diffusion into the surrounding space is much less appropriate for the vertical boundaries of buildings. This is due to a basic difference between the vertical and the horizontal dimensions..."
(Arnheim, p. 26)

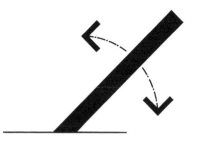

Diagonals introduce powerful directional impulses, a dynamism which is the outcome of the unresolved tendencies towards vertical and horizontal which are held in balanced suspension.
(Sausmarez, p. 21–22)

Deering Milleken office, N.Y.C.
The oblique line introduced by the escalator in the background.
Photos courtesy of Knoll International.

Escalator in Helsinki, Finland Shopping Center.
Photo by F. Wilson.

The vertical line appears longer than the horizontal line of the same length. The distance between the vertical circles appears greater than that between the horizontal. A pole or a tree is generally appraised as of greater length when it is standing than when it lies down upon the ground. An explanation offered by some is that more effort is required to raise the eyes, or point of sight, through a certain vertical distance than through an equal horizontal distance.

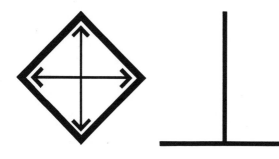

The vertical axis of a diamond appears longer than the horizontal.

Other explanations for the difference in apparent length of the vertical and horizontal lines are that the vertical lines often represent lines extending away from the observer, who sees them foreshortened, and therefore appear longer than horizontal lines of equal length, which are not subject to foreshortening.

A vertical line may also suggest a resistance against gravitational force, with the result that the line appears longer than a horizontal one resting in peace.

IMPRESSION OF SYMMETRY is spontaneous only when a figure is symmetrical around a vertical axis. Subjects were asked to indicate which of two figures (middle and right) was most like the left figure. The figure at right was selected most frequently, presumably because it is symmetrical around its vertical axis. If the page is tilted 90 degrees, the figure in the middle will now be selected as being more similar to the figure on the left. This suggests that it is not the symmetry around the egocentric vertical axis on the retina but rather the symmetry around the environmental axis of the figure that determines perceived symmetry.
(From *Image, Object, and Illusion:* "The Perception of Disoriented Figures" by Irving Rock, 1974 *Scientific American*)

Arnheim says about this phenomena: "...In daily visual experience, a thing or creature shows up by rising above the ground, and a vertical axis is a particularly characteristic aspect of its shape. Around the central stem of such an axis the mass of the object tends to arrange itself symmetrically, in accordance with the fact that in the horizontal plane all directions are equivalent."
(Arnheim 1977, p. 35)

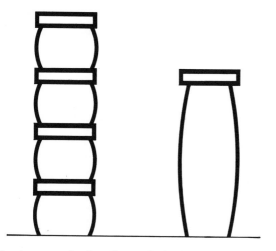

"...In a predominantly vertical shape we see any horizontal element first of all at its place within the vertical order. Only in that context can it be compared with a similar detail in a neighboring object. For example, when details in two neighboring objects are located objectively at the same height, they cannot be appropriately perceived as so located if they occupy different places within each object's vertical pattern."
(Arnheim 1977, p. 36)

Building addition, University of Maryland (note Arnheim comments).
Photo by F. Wilson.

INTERPOSITION

"If one object partially covers another, it is perceived as nearer." (Fryer 1965, p. 83)

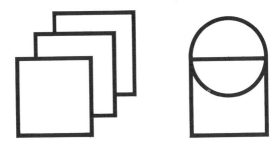

Overlapping figures that appear to be in back of the square

Ambiguous overlapping figure-is the square in front of the circle?

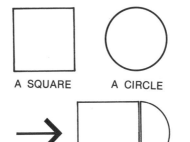

A SQUARE   A CIRCLE

THE SQUARE APPEARS TO BE IN FRONT OF THE CIRCLE

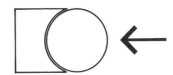

THE CIRCLE APPEARS TO BE IN FRONT OF THE SQUARE

If One object partially covers another, it is perceived as nearer.

.....as do the columns of Le Corbusier's Carpenter Center at Harvard.
Photo courtesy of Harvard University.

Stainless steel tubes of Ken Snelson's sculpture establish depth by overlapping interposition....
Photo by F. Wilson.

MEANINGFULNESS OF FORMS

Meaningfulness of Forms—A form tends to be meaningful and to have objectivity.

Forms can have meanings that are sometimes a combination of their perceptual qualities and other meanings assigned to them by association or given to them aside from their natural attributes. For example we have come to associate the star with the badge of a sheriff or "the law."

In architecture, the triangular form of the pediment and the colonnade resting on a pedestal has come to be associated with important civic or institutional buildings.

"Although we may not be aware of it consciously, because we tend to relate what we see to our own bodily reactions to situations in space, shapes appear to fall or be pulled by gravitational factors, appear to lean over, to fly, to move fast or slow, to be trapped to be free." (Sausmarez 1964, p. 28)

We find that Filarete (1400–1465), architect and sculptor, wrote in his "Trattato di Architecture" concerning the soothing effect of the circle: "in looking at a circle the glance sweeps round instantaneously without interruption or obstacle." (Wittkower 1942, p. 10)

Rudolf Wittkower tells us that the first architectural treatise of the Renaissance, Alberti's *De re Aedificatoria,* written about 1450, contains the first full program of the ideal church of the Renaissance. Alberti's survey of desirable shapes for temples, his synonym for churches, begins with an eulogy of the circle. Nature herself, Alberti declares, enjoys the round form above all others, as is proved by her own creations such as the globe, the stars, the trees, animals and their nests, and many other things.

Alberti, according to Wittkower, recommends nine basic geometrical figures in all for churches; including the circle. He lists the square, the hexagon, the octagon, the decagon, and dodecagon (six, eight, ten and twelve sided polygons). All of these figures are deteremined by the circle and Alberti explains how to derive the lengths of their sides from the radius of the circle into which they are inscribed. In addition to these six figures he mentions three developments from the square, namely the square plus one-half, the square plus one-third, and the square doubled.

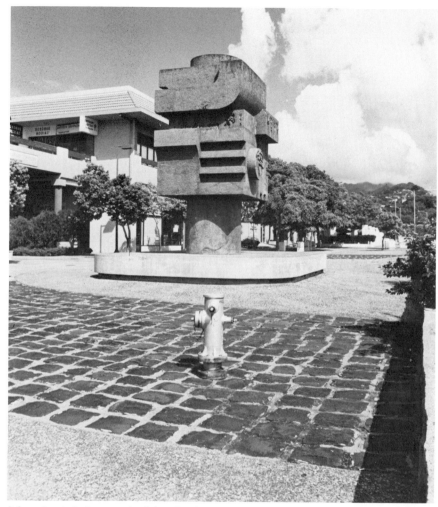

A form tends to be meaningful and to have objectivity.
Honolulu, Hawaii, 1980.
Photo by F. Wilson.

circle square hexagon

octagon decagon dodecagon

square + one-third square + one-half

two squares

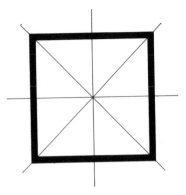

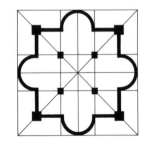

Development of centralized temple after Da Vinci.

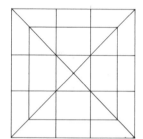

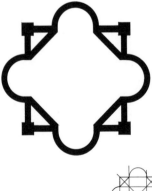

A form tends to be meaningful and to have objectivity, but how do we interpret the object of the form? We may return to the remarks of Maurice de Sausmarez previously mentioned for a beginning. Every configuration carries in its own nature an account of the forces, the speed, the actions which created it.

An essential part of its expressive content is the fact that it is the visible path of the creative act. If we add this to a belief in 'significant' forms that arises from a deeper stratum than consciousness can reach, we will find this conviction running through art and architecture from expressions of Renaissance artists to modern artists and undoubtedly from the beginning of art and architecture as an activity.

The gestalt psychologists say that a form is a dynamic system or is based upon a dynamic system. Since the dynamic principles operate within the organism, a strong form is one which depends more upon the dynamic properties of the organism than upon the properties of the stimulus. (Fryer 1976, p. 85, 86)

An important criteria for determining whether phenomena, objects, etc. are readily perceived is the idea of the 'good figure.' But how can 'good' be defined in a way that is meaningful to researchers and designers.

Good form or quality depends upon several features. Among the most important of them are symmetry, closure, and simplicity. M. Mowaft, psychologist, conducted a study to determine how subjects judged a variety of material viewed in terms of these parameters. His tests show that closure and symmetry were considered by those tested to be good properties of a figure.

Good and poor forms are distinguished by the fact that good form is well articulated and as such tends to impress itself upon the observer, to persist and recur. A circle is a good form, as is a square and a rectangle. Alberti's description of the nine basic geometrical figures appropriate for a sacred building test out in Mowaft's study as being considered 'good' properties by the majority of those tested.

SET AND SUGGESTION
"Apparently the tendency and desire to perceive 'good' figures is quite deep rooted. The momentary set of the individual may greatly influence perception. This situation is furthered by the individual's use of symbols in describing perceptions. An ambiguous figure described as resembling some familiar object will later be recalled in imagery to resemble the object much more nearly than did the original ambiguous figure." (Fryer 1965, p. 64)

STRONG AND WEAK FORMS
"A strong form hangs together and resists attempts to analyze it into parts or fuse it with another form." (Fryer 1965, p. 85, 86)

GOOD FORMS
Good and Poor Forms. A good form is well articulated and as such tends to impress itself upon the observer, to persist and recur. A circle is a good form.

Good figure is an important criterion for determining whether phenomena, objects, etc., are readily perceived. But, how can 'good' be defined in a way that is meaningful to researchers and designers?

Wertheimer says that 'good form' or quality depends upon several features. Among the most important of them are symmetry, closure, and simplicity, something Alberti could have told him five centuries before the invention of gestalt.

Subjective Meaning of Form
People sitting underneath a huge digital clock as above them the light flashes on number after number indicating the spent seconds of one of the last days of their lives while the garbage can of the 'grim reaper' stands by? Photo by Dirck Halstead.
Courtesy of the Kaufman Organization.

The headlight imbedded in this Georgia gravestone was a tribute to some event in the life of the person buried here? What happened?

Beyond the meanings that Kandinsky tried to find in form itself there are meanings that we all attribute to forms in our search for 'what does that mean?'
Georgia Gravetone.
Photo by John Shepard.

Why the lids of pots imbedded in this Mexican gravestone? A tribute to a cook, someone who liked to eat, or a decorative touch?
Mexican Graveyard.
Photo by F. Wilson.

A circle....

....we tend to see things in the simplest possible way.

A SQUARE.... ho hum

A DIAMOND WOW!

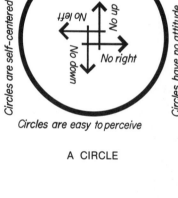

A CIRCLE

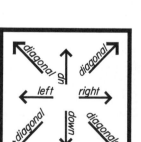

A SQUARE

A TRIANGLE

Triangles indicate three elements.

A DIAMOND

A rotated square becomes such a unique figure that it is given a special name—diamond.

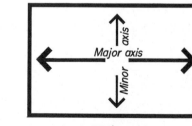

A RECTANGLE

Rectangles have a sense of direction.

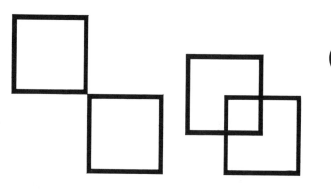

Figures may touch or overlap.

Overlapping figures do not have to be complete for us to recognize their formal origins. We visualize the closure of the form.

MORPH—FORM; relating to form; one having (such) a form

A square as form.

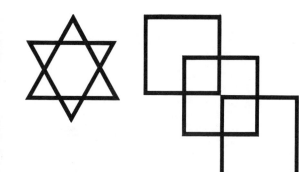

Overlapping figures create different configurations and meanings.

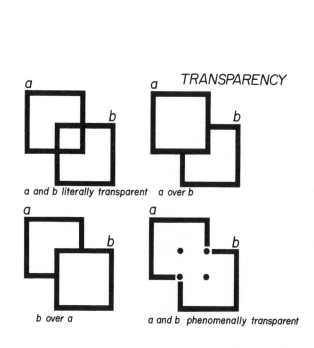

a and *b* literally transparent

a over *b*

b over *a*

a and *b* phenomenally transparent

TRANSPARENCY

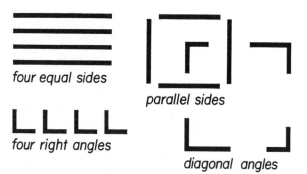

four equal sides

parallel sides

four right angles

diagonal angles

The morphology of the square.

MORPHOLOGY—the form and structure of an organism or any of its parts

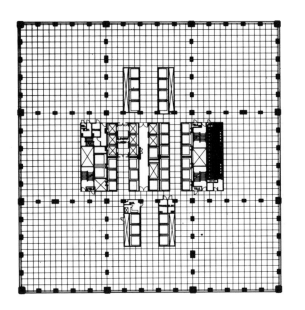

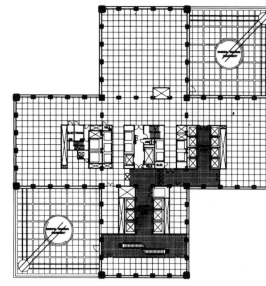

Transformation of the square as the building rises in height.

Transformation of the square by Zvi Hecker in partnership with A. Neumann in the proposal for Ashdod City Center (1965). From Zvi Hecker Exhibition, The Israel Museum, Jerusalem.

TYPICAL LOWER FLOOR ⬡

TYPICAL SKY LOBBY ⬡

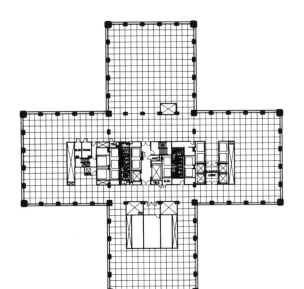

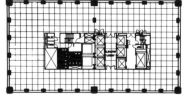

TYPICAL INTERMEDIATE FLOOR ⬡

TYPICAL UPPER FLOOR ⬡

Sears Tower by Skidmore Owings and Merrill Architects.

Photo by Ezra Stoller. Courtesy of Skidmore Owings and Merrill.

86

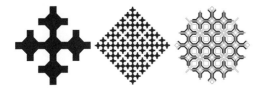

The basic geometric unit and its multiplication—urban planning—Zvi Hecker

1966 desert synagogue, interior space, drawing—Zvi Hecker

1965 Ashdod City Center proposal, by Zvi Hecker in partnership with A. Neumann.

A FORM WITH THREE POSSIBLE READINGS; a G, an Arrow with a circular tail, or a figure ground reversal.

Detail from a periodical heading by Hans Richter, 1927-. (Neumann 1967, p. 55)

A white arrow pointing up or a black arrow pointing down?

An arrow pointing at a star?

A turtle ambiguity.
Photo by F. Wilson.

Stairs have traditionally had very strong meanings in architecture. Narrow stairs with high steps (risers) were designed in the back of houses for the use of servants. They were made steep to hurry the user and to conserve space in the building.

Trash receptacle.
University of Maryland.
Photo by F. Wilson.

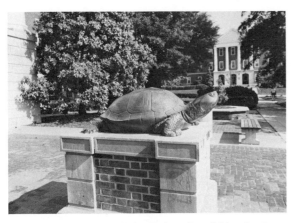

The Terrapin totum of the University of Maryland occupies a conspicuous position of honor.
Photo by F. Wilson.

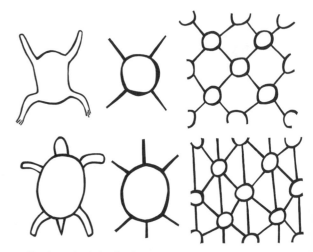

Wide, low, stately stairs were designed for the front of the house. These were often designed for ceremonial entrance and ascent or descent. The important people, owners and guests in the house, were expected to enter spaces leisurely in a stately fashion. In short the two kinds of stairs indicated use by entirely different 'animals.'

"...'an aboriginal's design may be crude, but his imagination is nevertheless, wonderful; we see the line, but he sees the life; we behold the image, he the form'.
...in the sketches above we see the normal conventional frog and tortoise becoming emblematic patterns.'' (Moorehead 1966)

The unique form of this silhouette is to architecture what red is to strawberries and blood.

Mendelsohn's rough sketch has the quality of 'good form.' It is symmetrical around a vertical axis and the figure closes. Although we are not sure of its 'meaning' (unless we have seen a photograph or the completed building) the form of the drawing stays in our mind.

Einstein Tower, Potsdam, 1919.

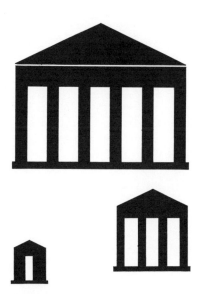

It says, Greek temple, and like white on rice it can be endlessly abstracted.

Einstein tower after Mendelsohn.

MOVEMENT

Movement as it is discussed here is part of the constancy phenomenon, for it deals with the retention of image as we envision a building in three dimensions. It is how we piece the three dimensional reality of a building together by assembling and remembering a number of 'flat' views with our flickering eyes.

One interesting aspect of this phenomena is that we retain our original impression of the building and impose it on subsequent views. What we then have is an impression like the cubist paintings of Picasso and Braque.

What possibilities are presented if form in movement is accepted? This is the experience of the observer moving around the object or the object moving around the observer, as one walks around or through a building. We are concerned, when we do this, with the diagrams of perceptual forces, in most instances these are forces which are intuitively felt to be present in the changing sequences of movement. If one sets a three-dimensional form in motion and then notes in drawing fragments of the significant 'phases' of movement, a new image, a synthetic image compounded of these fragments of retained information emerges.

This was a technique used by the 'Futurists' in picturing movement. It was also employed by the 'Cubists' and was part of a general interest in portraying or capturing movement in both art and in industry. It is also a useful device for understanding the successive views of architecture as we move through and around buildings.

Cubist analytical drawing attempted to achieve a synthesis of different aspects of the forms represented into one compounded image (a universal view of the many views encountered when moving around an object). These were aspects ordinarily associated with the 'seen' form combined with the 'known' form. In architecture this would be a fusing of plan, section, and facade. How deliberate this was as a method is perhaps arguable but the drawings themselves suggest it as a possible aim.

Interest in 'dynamism' characterized the period. The Futurists attempted to make drawings which would be virtual diagrams of 'felt' energies in the passage of a moving form.

Severini, an able spokesman, wrote, "Movement becomes what it is in reality, a continuity, a synthesis of matter and energy. This aesthetic reality is indefinable and infinite, it neither belongs integrally to the reality of vision or that of knowledge but participates in both." He suggests that a symbolizing of form in movement is the outcome of the complex influences of vision, memory, emotion, and what he calls 'ambience,' the sense of totality which we experience, including smells, sounds, and other sensations, all of which Savarini believed could be expressed plastically.

The human ability to see the three dimensional quality of form is due to the ability to combine into a coherent whole the succession of a number of views.

We must be capable of seeing around the building to understand it. If the building faces the observer 'frontally', Arnheim says, it is looking him squarely in the face. A kind of "eye to eye" contact is established. The building monumentalizes the scene and overpowers the observer. This is somewhat like standing in the path of a locomotive. (Arnheim 1977)

Despite the powerful impact of the experience, nothing is seen but the face of the building. The difference is between what one sees looking at the front of a cube compared to an isometric projection of it in which front, side, and top are revealed. But an isometric is a distortion, a convention used to represent objects in three dimensions. They do not appear as they would in three dimensions. A perspective view is a more accurate representation although it shows the object from but one point in space.

A three dimensional quality in a building can be expressed by certain architectural devices even though the building is seen head on. Octagonal and hexagonal towers, bay windows, and oblique corner openings are all means designers use to indicate the three dimensional quality of their designs from a frontal view.

The sides of a cube would become visible if we changed position or walked around it as we do buildings. A flat roof on a building makes the facade seem flat, but a pitched or hipped roof indicates an interior volume behind the facade. Setbacks let us see that the building has volume.

Actually buildings do not face their viewers frontally except when seen far in the distance. Usually their size is such that they recede toward the top in perspective. The sides diminish, the bottom rising and the top declining toward the viewers eye level. As we may remember from our discussion of angles, the predominant indication of building form in an urban industrial environment is largely an interpretation of 90° angles in perspective.

Buildings are almost never seen in one stationary view, from one viewpoint. Our impressions of them are made up of a number of views by moving our heads, and by walking around and through them. The visible properties of building are interpreted by those viewing them. Their meanings are deciphered as we give meaning to the lines, planes, angles, and curves of a Kandinsky drawing or painting. We try to understand them in relation to the building's practical functions and the expressive choices made by its designer.

Another means of perceiving depth is called motion parallax. This is the apparent differences in the relative movements of retinal images that seem to occur when we move or change our position. This disparity between near and far is a means of perceiving depth. When we ride in a train the telephone poles seem to zip by and the distant houses or mountains stand almost motionless. If we move our head, near objects are displaced, but those in the distance seem almost stationary.

"We choose to concentrate our attention on things in motion," Saverini wrote circa 1910, "because our modern sensibility is particularly qualified to grasp the idea of speed. Heavy powerful motorcars rushing through the streets of our cities, dancers reflected in the fairy ambience of light and color, airplanes flying above the heads of the excited throng. . . These sources of emotion satisfy our sense of a lyric and dramatic universe, better than do two pears and an apple."

". . . .we are the primitives of a new completely transformed sensibility," the Futurists claimed, and this sensibility accorded emotional value to a mechanized world.
(Taylor 1961)

Passing people, motorcars, and buildings compose animated collages on the glass walls of the Seagrams Building, NYC.
Photo by F. Wilson.

The cube seen frontally

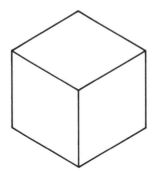

The cube in isometric

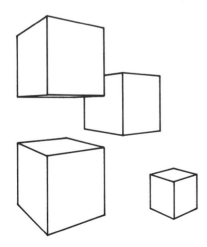

Cubes in perspective.

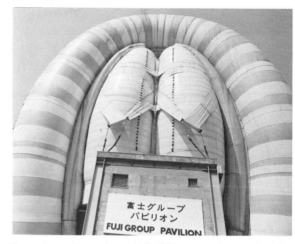

'Sometimes front views of buildings can be awe inspiring.'
Fuji Group Pavilion, Expo Osaka, Japan. Courtesy of Osaka Expo.

Building set backs give some idea of their volume.
Photo by J. Alex Langley.
Courtesy of Emery Roth Architects.

A corner view of a building allows us to see something of its whole form. Building in San Francisco.
Photo by F. Wilson.

A three dimensional caboose.
Photo by F. Wilson.

A

The movement of this building around an acute angled corner has something of the quality of Picasso's early cubist lithographs. We watch it turn from profile to full face in a series of movements.

The designer's problem was to conform to the siting of buildings on two streets bordering a corner lot (g). This is a comparatively simple problem if the streets form a 90 degree corner. In this instance they do not. We therefore have an ingenious shifting from profile to full face in a series of moves. The result is 'doing right' by both streets.

As Arnheim previously pointed out, a full face facade is fearsome and flat. The facade of this building seen from directly across the main street (e) and even beginning to turn the corner (d) gives little indication of the volume of the building in contrast to the adjoining faces (a), (b), (c), which seem to belong to a building of much greater girth than (e) and (d) would lead us to suspect. The effect would have been quite different if the corner had been obtuse as you may observe in an octagonal building or the accompanying photo of a bay window on a caboose.

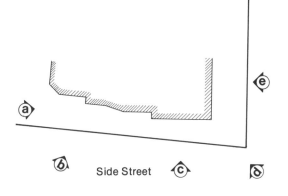

Side Street

D

Picasso stylized face, 1948

B

E

C

93

Octagon House, Washington, D.C.
Photo by F. Wilson.

The Hirshhorn Museum, Washington, D.C.
Photo by F. Wilson.

East Wing, National Gallery, Washington, D.C.
Photo by F. Wilson.

NATURAL ORGANIZATION

Naturalness of form—A field tends to become organized and to take on form. Groups tend to form structures, and disconnected units tend to become connected.

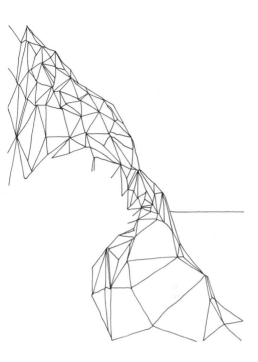

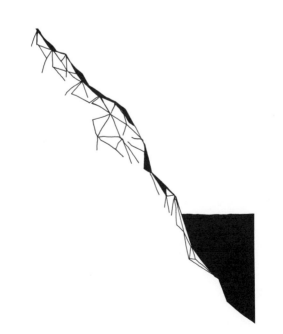

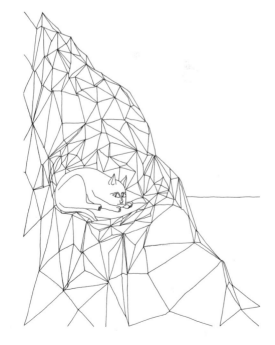

The mind proceeds in a scale of increasing complexity when interpreting spatial images. Major divisions appear first, then the outlines of larger forms, followed by increasing detail.

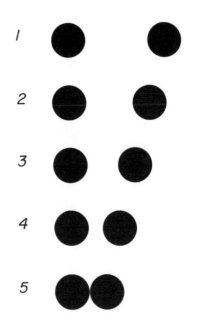

Attitude is the figure to figure property found in the spaces between figures.

INTEGRATION OF SIMILARS AND ADJACENTS. Units similar in size, shape, and color tend to combine to make better articulated forms.

When do the two circles become visually connected?

Individual figures can be organized into a single, larger, more complex figure.

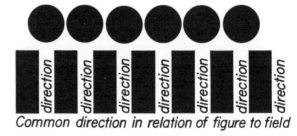

Common direction in relation of figure to field

Interval is the space between figures. Interval is the property most characteristic of the field.

The apartments of 'Habitat'—each an individual 'box'—fuse into one pyramidial form.
Photo courtesy of Expo Corp.

Natural Organization

Elements that are aligned tend to be read together and to form larger figures

Four forms with parts removed. The former rectangle and former triangle may be associated since parts of them are aligned. The former square and former circle do not seem related.

The four forms related in a figure-ground closure of a circle.

The alignment of the four forms indicates that they are related and we tend to associate them as related.

The four forms placed randomly. Their commonality is their color, black, and that they are basic forms.

The 'streets in the air' (the enclosed horizontal elements) tend to organize the apartment 'boxes.'

The assembly line with its procession of automobiles of similar shape organizes the jumble of machinery in this Ford automotive assembly factory. Photo courtesy of Ford Motor Co.

Elevated railway organizes the confusion of architectural forms at Expo '70 in Osaka.

Photo courtesy of Osaka Expo.

THE STREET AS ORGANIZER

One strong dominating form such as a street will tend to organize the jumble of city forms. This occurs even around the jumble of waiting and discarded material of a construction site.
Photo by F. Wilson.

Three elementary forms in squares of space.

Every possible combination of the three forms (6 combinations).

Arranged in a 3 x 3 square.

Two rows of three 3 x 3 squares each. Figure groupings tend to move diagonally combining similar shapes in a natural diagonal organization.

A sphere organized of countless panels.
Photo courtesy of Expo Corp.

PERSISTENCE OF FORM AND FORM REMEMBERED

Persistence of Form—A form once perceived tends to persist, and to recur when the stimulus situation recurs. The recurrence of part of a previously perceived form tends to reinstate the whole.

Forms Remembered—A portion of the originally effective stimulus pattern may come to be quite as effective as the total. Sight of a man's hand means that the whole man is present. The barking of a dog in the next room is sufficient for identification of the entire dog.

These two phenomenon seem inseparable in the realm of human building and architecture. The persistence of form and forms remembered seem entwined as perceptual response to the building works of humans. One of the oldest and most persistent of building forms is the 'megaron' which existed before the Hittites and is found in Roman building.

Rasmussen has described the act of remembering or 'reintegration' quite clearly. Seeing, he says, demands a certain activity on the part of the spectator. It is not enough passively to let a picture form itself on the retina of the eye. The retina is like a movie screen on which a continuously changing stream of pictures appear. The mind behind the eye concerns itself with only a very few of them. But in contrast to this seeming disregard only a very faint visual impression is necessary for us to think that we have seen a thing. A tiny detail of it is enough to evoke a recall mechanism.

Rasmussen uses the example of a man walking along the street with his head bent. He has an impression of blue jeans and his mind tells him that he has seen a man though actually all he saw was the characteristic seam running down the side of the leg of a pair of blue trousers. From this small observation he concludes that a man has passed because where there is that sort of seam there must be a man inside of them. For some reason our man decides to have a closer look at the person and finds to his surprise that it is a young girl. He will then probably observe her and add detail to detail until he assembles a 'correct' picture. (Rasmussen 1959)

This activity, Rasmussen reminds us, is common to all observers. It is the activity necessary to experience the thing seen. This experience can vary enormously for there is no objectively correct idea of a thing's appearance, only an infinite number of subjective impressions of it.

It is usually easier to perceive a thing when we know something about it beforehand. We will then see what is familiar and disregard the rest. That is to say we recreate the observed into something intimate and comprehensible even if what we observe is a mere part of the whole like the seam of the jeans in Rasmussen's description.

The two phenomena are often intertwined; we may interpret a detail of a persistent form thereby recreating an entire picture of the thing in our mind.

When we approach someone we know on the street we recognize them long before we can distinguish their individual features. We know that it is them by the shape of the head and the way they walk and carry themselves. The same formal recognition occurs in architectural form.

To return to the 'megaron' form. The Hittites, although the best known of the ancient peoples of Anatolia were not the earliest inhabitants. They inherited on their arrival in Mesopotamia about 2,000 B.C., a building which seems to have been Anatolian in origin. It was the 'megaron,' a rectangular room with central hearth and door at one end, set in a deep porch formed by the prolongation of the side walls to make 'antae.' This unit is too simple not to have been evolved independently in different regions, though it was suited to the extremes of the Anatolian climate. Examples have been found in Troy from the first settlement about 3250 to 2600 B.C.

We find three megaron forms in the ruins of the palace of Tiryns. They are repeated again in temple plans by Vitruvius in the first century B.C. and Thomas Jefferson borrowed the form of the Maison Carree at Nimes for the design of the State Capitol at Richmond, Virginia 1789–98.

Animal tracks will stimulate a perception of the animal if we have seen the animal before.

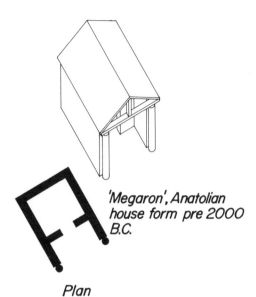

'Megaron', Anatolian house form pre 2000 B.C.

Plan

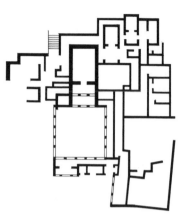

The Citadel of Tiryns (c. 1300 B.C.) part-plan showing the plans of three megarons.

Broken pediment over Board of Education building entrance, Plainfield, New Jersey.

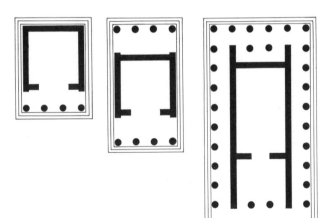

Temple plans—after Vitruvius (first century B.C.).

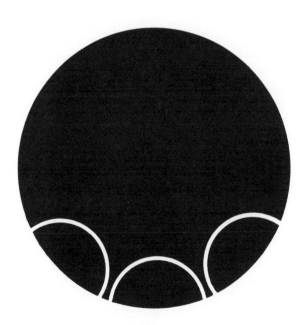

"And what, pray tell, is this?"

100

Wall of 'masks' Kabah, Yucatan.
Photo by F. Wilson.

Theme and variation of the broken pediment.

Broken pediment on a corner. Kenebunkport, Maine.
Photo by F. Wilson.

Broken pediment abstraction over entrance to Fraternity House, University of Maryland.
Photo by F. Wilson.

Remnant of 'mask' is reminiscent of entire wall at Kabah.
Photo by F. Wilson.

Broken pediment. Townhouse entrance, College Park, Maryland.
Photo by F. Wilson.

What does this remind you of? Where did you see it before?
Can you picture the entire structure from this fragment?
Photo courtesy of CBS Broadcasting.

REPETITION AND CONTINUITY

CONTINUITY

"Objects organized for continuity of pattern take precedence." (Fryer 1965, p. 64)

REPETITION; RECURRING STIMULUS—

"A recurring stimulus has more attention getting value than a constant stimulus of the same magnitude. However, if the repetition continues over a long period of time it may develop a continuity of its own and lose effectiveness." (Fryer 1965, p. 62)

Auto body forms organize the space.
Photo courtesy of Volkswagon.

Gable ends and porches repeated in this row of abandoned New Mexico miners' cabins.
Photo by F. Wilson.

Endless repetition of curtain wall facade makes it appear as a texture.
Photo by F. Wilson.

Repetition of language study carrels.
Photo by F. Wilson.

Continuity and repetition of window frames symbolizes identical government functions contrasted with enlarged, emphasized Mayor's office and Council Chamber enclosures.
Photo courtesy of the Massachusetts Dept. of Commerce and Development, Division of Tourism.

Lockers endlessly repeated in a school corridor make it difficult to distinguish ownership.
Photo by F. Wilson.

Continuity of facade pattern of Corbusier's Carpenter Center at Harvard University.
Photo courtesy of Harvard University.

Faneuil Hall Boston.

Renewed and revitalized by Ben Thompson Associated and The Rouse Co.
Photo courtesy of The Rouse Co.

PERSPECTIVE CONVERGING LINES AND TEXTURE VARIATIONS

PERSPECTIVE—CONVERGING LINES

Size Perspective—A decrease in the size of the shapes or figures in the visual field.

Linear Perspective—This is size perspective when contours are rectilinear. It is a gradual decrease in the spacing as the size or dimension between outlines or inlines in the visual field decreases. This occurs primarily with man-made objects.

Motion Perspective—A gradual change in the rate of displacement of texture elements or contours in the visual field. The change is from motion in one direction through zero to motion in the other direction.

A suggestion of augmented height is often given by decreasing the size of successive portions more rapidly than demanded by perspective alone. This occurs with transmission towers. It is most commonly observed in engineering structures that follow structural logic. Lower elements must carry the load of those above and must therefore be sturdier.

Dimensions between columns are sometimes deliberately gradually reduced to heighten the sense of depth of a space. A roof can be made to appear larger by gradually decreasing the weather exposure of its shingles.

The following is a summary of James Gibson's thirteen varieties of perspective as abstracted from *The Perception of the Visual World* and mentioned by Hall in *The Hidden Dimension*.

There is, says Gibson, no such thing as a perception of space without a continuous background surface (see illustration of circles). Perception is dependent upon the memory of past stimulation.

Thirteen varieties of perspective or 'sensory shifts' that are the visual impressions which accompany the perception of depth over a continuous surface and depth at a contour are listed here. They constitute the basic structural categories of experience into which the more specific varieties of vision fit, Gibson claims.

Scenes contain information built from a variety of elements. Gibson analyzes and describes the system and the component 'stimulus variable' which combine to furnish the information man needs to move about the earth more effectively.

Gibson's analysis can be divided into four classifications:

1–perspective of position
2–perspective of parallax
3–perspective independent of position or motion
4–depth of contour

Perspective of Position

1–Texture perspective, which is the gradual increase in the density of the tex-

ture of a surface as it recedes in the distance. (See Moscow subway scenes.)

2–Size perspective is apparent; as the objects one views get further away they decrease in size.

3–Linear perspective is when parallel lines such as railroad tracks or separate lines of a highway join in a single vanishing point on the horizon.

Perspective of Parallax

4–Binocular perspective is dependent on awareness. Due to the separation of the eyes it is sensed through the projection of different images by each eye. Difference is more apparent at close distances than at greater. Closing and opening one eye and then the other will reveal this difference in image.

5–Moving forward in space; approaching a stationary object, movement is apparent. The closer one approaches the faster it appears to move. Objects moving at uniform speeds appear to move more slowly at greater distances.

Perspective Independent of the Position
or Motion of the Observer

6–Aerial perspective is derived from the increased haziness and changes in color caused by the intervening atmosphere. This is an indicator of distance that becomes confusing in very clear atmospheres and is not as reliable as some of the other forms of perspective.

7–Objects in a visual plane other than the one which the eyes have focused may appear less distinct and blurred.

8–The horizon is seen as a line at eye level. The further from the ground the observer is, the more pronounced this effect. In the context of every day experience the observer looks down at objects close at hand, and up at objects in the far distance.

9–Shifts in texture or linear spacing. A valley seen over the edge of a cliff will be perceived as more distant because of the break or rapid increase in texture density. Blades of grass seen on a hillside against a village in the distance may appear as wide as the houses.

10–Shift in the amount of double imagery. If one looks at a distant point the objects are to the viewer the greater the doubling that occurs. The more distant the point, the less doubling. The gradient in the shift is a cue to distance. A steep gradient is read as close, a gradual gradient as far.

11–Shift in the rate of motion is one of the most dependable and consistent means of sensing depth. Close objects move much more quickly than distant ones. If two objects are seen as overlapping and do not shift position relative to each other when the viewer changes positions they are either on the same plane or so far distant that the shift is inperceptible.

12–Camouflage is deceptive because it breaks the completeness or continuity of outline. Even if there is no texture difference, no shift in double imagery and no shift in the rate of motion, the manner in which one object obscures (eclipses) another determines whether the one is interpreted as behind the other or not.

Depth of Contour

13–Transitions between light and shade. An abrupt shift or change in the texture of an object in the visual field will signal a cliff or an edge.

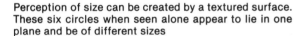

Moscow Subway.
Photo by F. Wilson.

Perspective Texture

Perception of size can be created by a textured surface. These six circles when seen alone appear to lie in one plane and be of different sizes

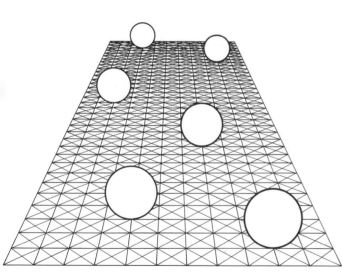

Forced perspective due to gradual lessening of size of structural members makes pyramid appear higher than it actually is.

Textured perspective, Connecticut General Bldg.
Photo courtesy of Knoll International.

Placed on an apparently receding surface they appear to lie in six different planes. Since each circle covers the same ratio of surface texture, there is a tendency to see them as of equal size. (Illustration after work of J. J. Gibson of Cornell, from *Image, Object, and Illusion*, 1974, p. 5.)

Identical sized pattern of lower triangular members contradict their reduction in size. Structural members without filling texture (above) appear in perspective, those below appear as an overall texture.

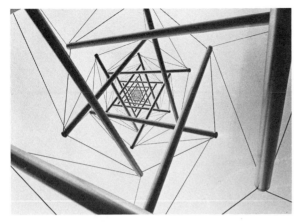

Forced perspective in tensegrity structure by Ken Snelson.

Horizontal perspective of converging lines.
Photo by Dirck Halstead. Courtesy of Kaufman Organization

Vetical, converging lines.

Seagrams Office Building, NYC.
Photo by F. Wilson.

Distortion of figures between converging lines. Converging lines make the upper figure appear larger than the lower figure, since we read it as more distant.

Photo by F. Wilson.

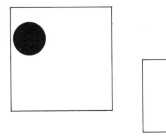

A dot in the distance.

Which is the largest, which the smallest?

Which is the closest and which is the farthest in the distance?

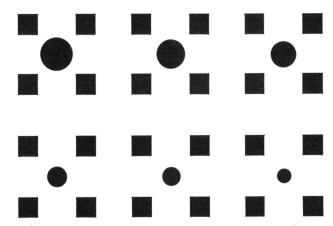

A circle between four squares that remain the same size; as the circle grows smaller, it seems to be moving away into the distance, due to the illusion of perspective.

Converging lines of this Ford assembly line approach the patterns of op art.
Photo courtesy of Ford Motor Co.

Converging lines as an art form
From *Geometrical Designs and Optical Art* by Jean Larcher, Dover Books, 1974.

Some comments on perspective by Robert Hughes in his book *The Shock of the New,* p. 16–17:

"Since the Renaissance, almost all painting had obeyed a convention: that of one-point perspective. It was a geometrical system for depicting the illusion of reality, based on the fact that things seem to get smaller as they go further from one's eye. Once the construction for setting up a perspective scene is known, things can be represented on a flat sheet of paper as though they were in space, in their right sizes and positions. To fifteenth-century artists, perspective was the philosopher's stone of art; one can hardly exaggerate the excitement they felt in the face of its ability to conjure up a measurable, precise illusion of the world. . .no powerful tool for the ordering of visual experience in terms of illusion had even been invented; indeed, perspective in the fifteenth century was sometimes seen not only as a branch of mathematics but as an almost magical process, having something of the surprise that our grandparents got from their Kodaks. Apply the method and the illusion unfolds; you press the button, we do the rest.

Nevertheless, there are conventions in perspective. It presupposes a certain way of seeing things, and this way does not always accord with the way we actually see. Essentially, perspective is a form of abstraction. It simplifies the relationship between eye, brain, and object. It is an ideal view, imagined as being seen by a one-eyed, motionless person who is clearly detached from what he sees. It makes a god of the spectator, who becomes the person on whom the whole world converges, the unmoved onlooker. Perspective gathers the visual facts and stabilizes them; it makes of them a unified field. The eye is clearly distinct from that field, as the brain is separate from the world it contemplates.

Despite its apparent precision, perspective is a generalization about experience. It schematizes but does not really represent the way that we see. Look at any object: Your eye is never still. It flickers, involuntarily restless, from side to side. Nor is your head still in relation to the object; every moment brings a fractional shift in its position, which results in a minuscule difference of aspect. The more you move, the bigger the shifts and differences become. If asked to, the brain can isolate a given view, frozen in perspective setup, a mosaic of multiple relationships, one of them (as far as vision is concerned) wholly fixed. Any sight is a sum of different glimpses. And so reality includes the painter's efforts to perceive it. Both the viewer and the view are part of the same field. Reality, in short, is interaction."

SPACE

SPACE "Space is the given that percedes the objects in it, the setting in which everything takes its place." Rudolph Arnheim.

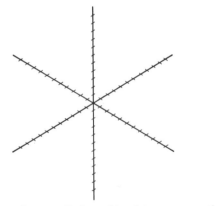

A concept of space that would exist even were there nothing in it must assume an absolute base of reference, which implies a system of cartesian coordinates to indicate the distance from the frame of reference. (after Arnheim 1977, p. 9–13)

No three-dimensional framework exists for the solitary ball suspended in emptiness. No up, down, left or right, neither size nor velocity; a single ball, a sad sphere in infinite expanse.

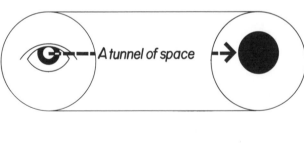

A tunnel of space

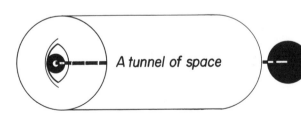

A tunnel of space

A linear connection is formed.

We therefore adopt the idea that space perception occurs only in the presence of perceivable things. Space is experienced through the interrelation of objects.

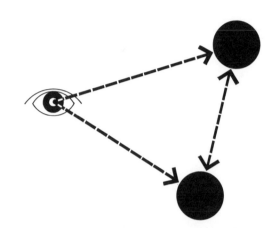

When there are two points in space and an observer we experience a flat triangle, the simplest structure in a two-dimensional world.

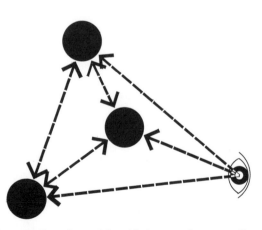

When another element is added, space becomes three-dimensional; a four cornered polyhedron.

108

INTERSPACE

Interspace establishes a particular ratio of remoteness and connectedness affecting architectural complexes as a whole. Considered dynamically interspaces depend on forces of attraction and repulsion. Objects that appear too close display mutual repulsion through the space between them; they appear to want to be moved apart. A greater interval between forms may appear just right or the objects may seem to attract each other. (Rudolf Arnheim 1977, pp.16–21)

These forces operate wherever objects are related across space and determine the spacing of pictures on a wall, our placement of furniture in a room and, supposedly, the proper distances between buildings. But these are perceptual judgments that determine the correct spacing determined intuitively, or by our sense of sight, and are not necessarily influenced by actual setback laws or the floor area ratio of land coverage that makes it profitable to develop.

Strains and stresses in the placement of objects are activated in the brain by the particular constellation of stimuli they encounter. Spatial distances between people in daily intercourse, 'proxemic norms,' are more within our control and we exercise them to ease or eliminate strains and stresses. We can watch this behavior exercised by the visual distances judged by the behavior of the perceptual forces generated by them.

Balancing applies always to the forces generated by buildings or people across the interspaces between them. When distances between objects increase, the density of the interval lessens and eventually disappears entirely. We no longer experience relationships between the buildings or between the people.

Lack of attraction and repulsion, excessively undefined distances, can cause terror or the social equivalent in people. They feel totally abandoned, the environment is complete without them and nothing refers to them. The lack of external definition destroys their internal sense of identity, nothing needs them, calls to them, or responds to them.

People define the nature of their own being largely by their place in a network of personal relations and these relations include the nature of the built world around them.

The architect Portoghesi said that we speak of matter when the concentration of energy is high and of fields when the concentration is weaker.

He described buildings as islands in space that create patterns of force in concentric circles like those that appear on the surface of a pond when a stone is dropped in it.

It needs to be recognized, he said, that buildings of any shape create fields of forces around themselves. The particular configuration of such fields depends in every case on the form of the generating structure.

What then can we know of the design of space, the interspace between the enclosure of the buildings' structure and the space between buildings themselves, and how this affects human beings?

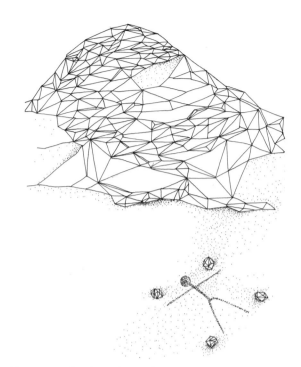

Humans and animals have always sought to arrange the world around them to establish a sense of place in space.

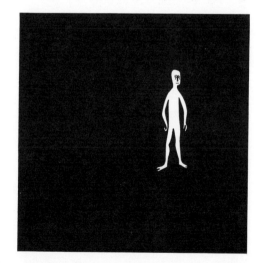

Perceptual emptiness can be described as a quality of an area whose spatial characteristics are not controlled by surrounding objects. Extreme emptiness is where there are no objects at all, in darkness or on the oceans or in outer space. There is an absence of all points of reference or orientation.

The anthropologist Edward T. Hall has warned us against the error of transposing spatial arrangements of the past to present day perceptions of space and its human implications. If the artist is very successful, Hall says, and the viewer shares the artist's culture, the viewer can replace what is missing in the painting. Both the painter and the writer know that the essence of their craft is to provide the reader, the listener, or the viewer with properly selected cues that are not only congruent with the events depicted but consistent with the unspoken culture of the audience.

It is, says Hall, the artist's task to remove obstacles that stand between his audience and the events he describes. In so doing he abstracts from nature those parts which, if properly organized, can stand for the whole and constitute a more forceful, uncluttered statement than the layman might make for himself. In other words, one of the principal functions of the artist is to help the layman order his cultural universe.

Art and architecture have been interpreted and reinterpreted in terms of the contemporary scene. A most important point to remember, Hall warns, is that modern man is forever barred from the full experience of the many sensory worlds of his ancestors. These worlds were inevitably integrated and deeply rooted in an organized context that could be fully understood only by the people of the times.

Modern man must guard against jumping to conclusions too quickly when he looks at architecture of other periods. By studying art of the past it is possible to learn something from our own responses about the nature and organization of our visual systems and expectations, and to get some notion of what the perceptual world of early man may have been like. However our present day picture of their world will always be incomplete and only an approximation of the original. The greatest criticism that one can make of many attempts to interpret man's past is that they project into the visual world of the past the structure of the visual world of the present.

Therefore neither the cave paintings at Altamira nor the temples at Luxor can be counted on to evoke the same cultural images today as when they were created. However this does not prevent our perceptual enjoyment of them in terms of form, line, figure, and ground.

Temples like Amen-Ra at Karnak are full of columns, many more were used than was required to support them structurally. We may feel when entering them that it is like walking into a forest of standing beautifully proportioned petrified logs, although the spatial experience of the closeness of the columns may be disturbing to modern man.

The early Egyptian experience of space was very different from our own. Their preoccupation was apparently more with the appropriate orientation and alignment of their religious and ceremonial structures in the cosmos than with the space they enclosed. The same is true of the buildings of the ancient Maya and other of the pre-Columbian civilizations.

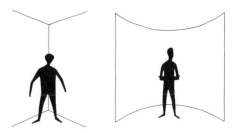

We instinctively respond to spatial configurations.

People reared in contemporary Western culture can be disturbed by the absence of interior space of those Greek temples that are sufficiently preserved to give some sense of their original form. The Western idea of a religious edifice is that it communicate spatially. Chapels are small and intimate while cathedrals are awe inspiring and remind one of the cosmos by virtue of the space they enclose.

Although Western man at the time of ancient Greece had developed highly sophisticated sculptural and architectural forms and even the structural capacity to create great spaces, the awareness, the desire to relate man to larger enclosed spaces was not there. Man, only gradually began to fully experience himself in space on the level of everyday life using all of his senses and this sense of space continues to change.

Bruno Zevi has claimed that to grasp space, to know how to see it, is the key to the understanding of building. Until, he says, we have learned not only to understand space theoretically, but also to apply this understanding as a central factor in the criticism of architecture, our history, and thus our enjoyment, of architecture will remain haphazard. (Zevi 1974, p. 24)

What does Zevi mean when he discusses 'architectural space'? The facade and walls of a building, house, church, or palace, no matter how beautiful they may be are only the container, the box formed by the walls; the content is the internal space. We find buildings which show a clear discrepancy between container and contained, Zevi says, and analysis will often show that the box formed by the walls was the object of more thought and labor than the architectural space itself.

Every architectural volume, every structure of walls, constitutes a boundary, a pause in the continuity of space. It is clear that every building functions in the creation of two kinds of space. This is its internal space, defined by the building itself, and its external or urban space defined by the building and the other buildings and objects around it.

Perhaps one of the most important things that Zevi can do for us is to describe the characteristics of spaces of other times, as he sees them.

The fundamental characteristic of Roman space, as Zevi sees it, is that it was conceived statically. In both circular and rectangular spaces the rule is sym-

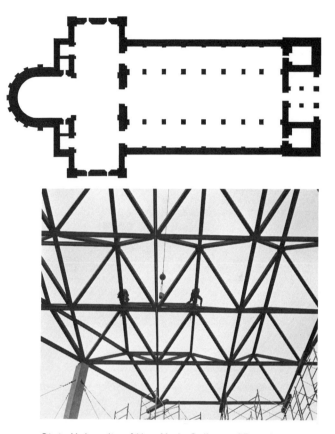

State University of New York, College at Potsdam.
Photo courtesy of P. Gugliotta.
Space Frame Designer.

metry, an absolute autonomy with respect to neighboring spaces emphasized by thick dividing walls and a biaxial grandiosity on an inhuman and monumental scale. It is a space essentially self-contained and independent of the observer.

Essentially, Zevi concludes from this that official Roman building is an affirmation of authority, a symbol dominating the mass of citizens and announcing that the Empire is and embodies the force and meaning of their whole lives. The scale of Roman building was the scale of that mythos, and it neither is, nor was it intended to be, the scale of man.

Zevi notes that when the 'Roman Style' was used in recent times it was used for the interiors of great American banks, for the immense marble halls of railroad stations, for works which impress us with their size but do not move us with their inspiration. These are structures, Zevi notes, which are always cold and where we do not feel comfortably at home.

Roman buildings have also been imitated by academia whenever it has had a program of architecture as a symbol. These vain attempts at revival of myths of imperial military and political supremacy have resulted in buildings of static spaces, rapt in the bombast of meglomania and rhetoric.

The Christians, in contrast to the Romans, had a human direction to their space, in Zevi's opinion. They selected the forms of their churches from the lexicon of Hellenistic and Roman architecture. From these two preceding styles they chose the elements that were the most vitally important to them. They sought to marry in their churches the human scale of the Greeks and the awareness of interior space of the Romans.

The Christian church had to be a place of congregation. They chose the bascilica form because it represented the social, congregational theme of the building. They reduced its proportions to adjust to those it was designed to receive and elevate spiritually. This was a quantitative and dimensional revolution in architecture, Zevi maintains. The spatial revolution involved consisted in ordering all the elements of the church in terms of man's path inside it.

The Greeks, Zevi says, had achieved their 'human scale' through a static proportion or ratio between the column and the height of man. The Christian

world accepted and exalted the dynamic character of man. It oriented the entire building according to his path by constructing and enclosing space in the direction he was to walk. (Zevi 1974, p. 84)

When it comes to modern space Zevi has this to say: It is based on the open plan. Social needs no longer set grandiose and monumental themes for architecture. The problem is rather homes for middle-class families or dwellings for workers and farmers who until now have lived in suffocating little row-cubicles. These needs plus new techniques of construction in steel and reinforced concrete will generate the form of modern space.

Internal wall partitions which no longer serve static bearing wall functions may now be thin, curved, and freely movable. This creates the possibility of linking up interior spaces, of joining together the numerous cubicles of the 19th century. We may pass from the static plan of the traditional house to the free, open, and elastic plan of modern building.

GOTCHA!

The space between objects influences the degree of mutual dependence and independence. With the interspace eliminated the two tend to coalesce into one with the smaller one appearing as a small appendage of the larger. At the other extreme, the greater distance extinguishes the relations between the two.

1

2

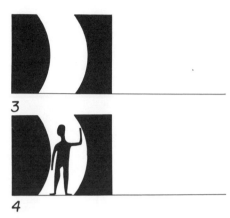

3

4

The Spoiler

The design of spatial relationships between objects is changed by the introduction of people.

UNFILLED SPACE—Filled areas appear greater in size than unfilled areas of equal size.

Space created as the relationship between objects.

There are aspects of experience of which we are not explicitly conscious that influence our awareness in important ways. Space between objects turns out not to look simply empty with the reversal of the figure ground. (b)

Two objects, one large, the other small, standing at a moderate distance from each other can be seen independently. This derives from our tunnel vision enabling us to see the objects of the continuous environment in isolation from their context. (a)

Unimpaired vision will perceive the two objects as elements of one image with a large mass contrasting with the smaller one. Looking at the two can be an eminently dynamic experience as the space between them becomes an inseparable part of the image. Far from empty, the space between is pervaded by gradients.

If the width of the interval changes and the two objects come closer, the gradients of the space between changes concomitantly, as does the contrast between the objects. We see from this that space has a perceptual presence of its own.

As the two figures draw closer together their relationships change, as does the space between them. At a certain point they seem to attract each other (1, 2); at another they seem to repel (4, 5). At 3 they form an implied square by closure and the distance between them is the same as the width of the smaller figure at top and its height at bottom. At 6 they become one figure enclosing a space which is the same in size as the smaller figure.

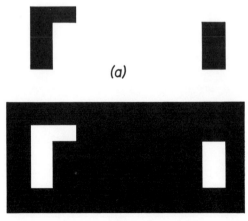

(a)

(b)

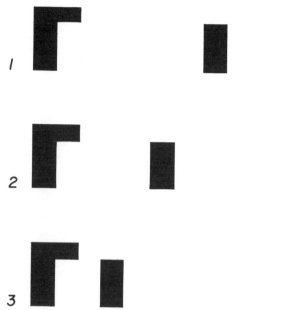

1

2

3

4

5

6

Arnheim contends that one could chart the forces each object generates around itself by its size, mass, location, and direction, which he likens to vectors, and thus show how its local field is supported or not supported by that of its neighbors.

Disorientation is created from a chaos of forces impinging on one another in a disorderly fashion, which makes it impossible to determine the place and spatial functioning of any object within the perceptual field, as we see here in this aerial photograph of the U. S. pavilion at Expo '70 in Osaka, Japan.

The huge air enfloated roof of the U.S. building is complete in itself and bears no relationship to any of the surrounding structures nor do they relate to each other. It is a Tower of Babel in which each building talks to itself in its own language, which is characteristic of world exhibitions in which each nation or each group seeks to express its unique individuality and attract by its difference. The result is such overwhelming chaos that nothing is noted individually at a distance at which they can be seen together.

THE PERCEPTION OF STRUCTURE

The relationship of structure and space may be described through the analogy of words and silence. To learn the grammar of silence is to learn the meaning of language, Ivan Illich once said. Much more is relayed from one person to another through silence than in words.

Words and sentences are composed of silences more meaningful than sounds. The pauses between sounds become luminous points in an incredible void; as electrons in the atom, as planets in the solar system. Language is a chord of silence with sounds the knots, as nodes in a Peruvian quipu, in which the empty spaces speak.

It is thus not so much the other person's words as their silences which we must learn to understand them. It is not the sounds which give meaning, but through the pauses that we make ourselves understood. Learning a language is as much the learning of its silences as its sounds.

It requires more time, effort, and delicacy, Illich maintained, to learn the silences of a people than to learn their sounds. Some people have a special gift for this, others, despite great effort and good will, never learn to speak properly. They never learn to communicate in silence. To learn the grammar of silence is an art much more difficult to learn than the grammar of sounds.

The relationship between silence and sound in the spoken language described by Illich is analogous to space and structure in the comprehension of the language of architecture. Space is to structure what silence is to language. We may perceive structure as a frame for space as words are used to build silences.

To learn the meaning of building structure is to learn the meaning of the spaces inherent in structural systems. The rhythm of a structure is denoted by the spatial pauses it generates. The significance of structure can be perceived as that of creating pauses. The unfilled voids distinguish architecture from sculpture.

It requires, perhaps, as much time and delicacy to learn the meaning of the spaces structure creates as it does to learn the meaning of structures themselves.

An essential difference between how engineers and architects perceive and design buildings is in the difference between science and art. Engineers see building structure as an evolution through history, a march toward optimization which is the using of more powerful words to create greater silences, of fewer words to say more. Engineering books describe the progress of structure as the advancement from smaller to greater span, from small to greater heights, from weaker to stronger material. This is a language, often of beauty and eloquence and spaces, the silences it creates can be magnificent but they differ from those of architecture.

The architect is intrigued with words and shades of meaning. An architect may well find inspiration in an arrangement of spaces discovered by Palladio

Maillart Bridge Switzerland.
Photo by John Pile.

Federal Reserve Bank by architect Gunnar Birkerts and associates.
Photo by Balthazar Korab, Ltd.
Courtesy of Gunnar Birkerts.

Drawings after Hawaiian petroglyphs.
(after Emory Lanai 1924).

Female head, Linoleum cut, Matisse 1938.

and use them in a contemporary design. An engineer finds little present day inspiration in the beam theory of Galileo. It is here that we find the difference between the science of engineering and the art of architecture and the spaces they create, although often the interest of the two overlap and at one time in history were the same, when engineer and architect were the same designer.

Modern science, progresses from triumph to triumph discarding superseded truths. But in art, only fools argue that the drawings of Picasso, Braque, and Matisse are greater or lesser art than stone age painting.

We may differ in opinion concerning styles of art and architecture but in absolute terms we award them equality, much the same as we recognize the unique differences of languages such as French, Italian, German, Chinese, Persian, and English—all are quite different with different arrangements of sounds and silences. All are capable of saying beautiful and vulgar things; poetry and swear words are found in every language. The language of engineering is written in formulas. We cannot write either poetry or swear words with numbers but they do reveal universal truths like Kandinsky sought in his analysis of point, line, and plane.

Our interest here is in the perception of structure and spaces in the language of architecture. Each arrangement whether ancient or modern, dominantly engineering or architecture, has unique perceptual meaning in the language of structure and space.

MEANINGS AND CONTRADICTIONS

There can be a multiplicity of perceptual meanings in a facade. Even though the modern movement in architecture sought to simplify form and present it in the elementary shapes of great primary forms—the cube, the sphere, the cone, distinct and without ambiguity—a typical 'modern' facade is full of perceptual meanings.

As the architect Robert Venturi wrote, "Ambiguity and tension are everywhere in an architecture of complexity and contradiction. Architecture is form and substance, abstract and concrete, and its meaning derives from its interior characteristics and its particular context. An architectural element is perceived as form and structure, texture and material. These oscillating relationships, complex and contradictory, are the source of the ambiguity and tension characteristic of the medium of architecture." (Venturi 1966)

Venturi points out that the conjunction "or" with a question mark can usually describe ambiguous relationships. He asks whether the plan is round or square, open or closed, and other such questions. It is the most practical for our purposes to study the perceptual meanings in a building singly in their simplest definitions and then to combine them; for example, figure ground, the combining patterns of repetitious openings, the structural logic of thick and thin, and heavy and light. We can then combine them after single analysis.

It will be found that in even the simplest of "modern" buildings without decoration, complexity and contradiction runs rampant. Is the thin line a column or a plumbing pipe, are they pilasters or ducts? The game of guess what can continue indefinitely.

One figure in black and white on a page is designed to concentrate the reader's interest upon a single phenomenon. In the world of buildings, where these phenomenon are encountered, they are never met singly. There are a great number of intruding circumstances. Any one phenomenon must be separated from others and other kinds of perceptual stimulation such as light, color, the third dimension of depth, and even sound and scent, that may influence the viewer but that we cannot present or control on a flat page.

While we isolate and analyze the particular phenomenon to understand it and concentrate upon it, as we do upon one aspect of an optical illusion, it is the total effect, the combination, the hierarchy, the totality of the built environment that gives us the dominant impression of a building.

What we study here is a kit of parts, tools, and even though we may analyze them and arrive at the means the craftsman and the designer used to accomplish his or her task, the ability to duplicate may elude us. For craftsmanship and design are things that people learn but cannot be taught. The purpose of these pages is to make the elements of design comprehensible. Their combination is what makes them unique.

ON GROWTH AND FORM

Why are things the size and shape that they are? If gravity affects most living things, and the composition of their structure and form is somewhat similar, then there might be laws, and perhaps simple ones at that, that will help us understand the nature of the world we see around us every day and have observed from earliest childhood. Perhaps we understand more than we believe we do, and if we can bring it to the level of our consciousness it can become part of our perception of the world.

D'Arcy Thompson insisted that, no matter how great the variety of living things, their growth and form obeys simple, easily comprehended relationships. This comprehension is part of our perception of the world around us and, although sometimes filed away in some subconscious notation, is a vital element of our perception of the structure of the world around us.

We must assume that people have had experience with forces and the forms they influence by the mere fact of living in a world composed of physical objects shaped and moving or held in place by physical forces. The observer, the one looking, therefore possesses a certain amount of rudimentary education in the physical sciences. We may assume then that this education and experience influences human perception of both form and forces.

In the language of elementary physics, force is described as an action causing

Forces of compression.

Forces of tension.

World Trade Center New York City.
Photo courtesy of Aluminum Co. of America.

116

Photo by F. Wilson.

or changing motion, preventing change in motion, or maintaining a state of rest. Force, unlike matter has no independent objective existence. It is known or unknown energy in its various forms acting upon matter. But when we abstract the form of a material, or the thing moving and its motions, we are dealing with the subjective conceptions of form, movement, or the movement that change in form implies. Force then is an appropriate term to use. It is essential for a conception of the causes by which these forms and changes of form are brought about.

The form of a portion of matter, living or dead, and the changes of form which are apparent in its movements and in its growth, may be described as due to the action of force. In this sense, the form of an object, is a 'diagram of forces.' We can deduce from the form the forces that are acting, or have acted upon it. In this particular sense, Thompson states, it is therefore a diagram of forces impressed upon it when it was formed combined with those that enable it to retain its present conformation.

The form of a liquid or a gas is a diagram of the forces that, for the moment, are acting on it to restrain or balance its inherent mobility. A soap bubble is perhaps one of the most eloquent of delicate forms held in balance momentarily by internal and external forces.

In organisms, great and small, we must interpret the nature of the motions of living substance in terms of force combined with the conformation of the organism itself. The performance or equilibrium of the organism can be explained by the interaction or a balance of forces solved by statics. If we can view living, breathing, moving growing things in the way that D'Arcy Thompson explains so clearly, then the innate forms of buildings are simple to comprehend.

The state, including the shape or form, of a portion of matter is the result of a number of forces representing or symbolizing the manifestations of various kinds of energy.

It was Galileo, Thompson reminds us, who first laid out a general principle of similitude. He did so using a great wealth of illustration drawn from structures both living and dead. Galileo said that if we were to attempt to build ships, palaces, and temples of enormous size, their beams, bolts, and columns would cease to hold together. Nature cannot, Galileo observed, grow a tree nor an animal beyond a certain size employing the proportions and materials that serve the purpose of smaller forms and structures. Structures that have grown beyond a certain size simply fall to pieces, brought to destruction by their own weight.

If we change the relative proportions within a given structural and growth system, the system becomes monstrous, clumsy, and inefficient. We might instead find new material that is harder and stronger than that used before, or we may introduce new configurations. There is evidence of both of these processes in nature. They are also found in the practical application of engineering and architecture, which today builds structures in cement and steel undreamed of even in the mind of as great a scientist as Galileo.

Thompson puts this point very succinctly when he says that body size is no mere accident. Man, respiring as he does, cannot be as small as an insect, nor vice versa. Only now and then, as in the case of the Goliath beetle, do the sizes of insect and mammal, mouse and beetle, meet and overlap. The descending scale of mammals stops short at a weight of about 5 grams, that of beetles at a length of about half a millimeter. Every group of animals has its upper and lower limitations of size. And not far from the lower limit of our vision, does the long series of bacteria come to an end.

In fact, Thompson observes, each main group of animals has its mean and characteristic size, and a range on either side of it, sometimes greater and sometimes less. A certain range, and a narrow one, contains mouse and elephant and all whose business it is to walk and run. This is our world, the world of man, with whose dimensions our lives, our limbs, and are senses are in tune.

The great whales, Thompson observes, grow out of this range by throwing the burden of their bulk upon the waters. The dinosaurs that wallowed in the swamp, and the hippopotamus, the sea-elephant and Steller's great sea-cow pass or passed their lives in the rivers or the sea.

The things which fly are smaller than the things which walk and run. The flying birds are never as large as the largest mammals, the lesser birds and mammals are much of a muchness, but insects come down a step in the scale and more. The lessening infuence of gravity facilitates flight, but makes it less easy to walk and to run. First there are claws, then hooks and suckers and glandular hairs help to secure a foothold. Until to creep upon wall or ceiling becomes as easy as to walk upon the ground. Fishes, by evading gravity, increase their range of magnitude both above and below that of terrestrial animals. Smaller than all of these, passing out of our range of vision and going down to the least dimensions of living things are protozoa, rotifers, spores, pollen-grains, and bacteria. All save the largest of these float rather than swim. They are buoyed up by air or water and fall, as Stoke's law explains, with exceeding slowness.

Thompson says that we can observe a great deal about the forces forming organisms from the organisms speed and size. The strength of a muscle and the resistance to crushing stress of a bone vary, like a rope or girder, with their cross sections. But in terrestial animals the weight that tends to crush their limbs, or that its muscles have to move, varies as the cube of its linear dimensions. There is a limit of the possible magnitude, therefore of an animal, living under the direct action of gravity.

The dimensions of the elephant's limb bones show a tendency toward disproportionate thickness when compared with the smaller mammals. The elephant's agility is diminished and its movements are in many ways hampered. It tends towards the maximal limit of size which the physical forces permit. On the other hand the daddy-long legs must have its own factor of safety conditional on the creature's excessively scanty bulk and weight. After their own

Photo by F. Wilson.

Photo by F. Wilson.

Photo by F. Wilson.

fashion even these small creatures tend towards an inevitable limitation of natural size.

But as Galileo also saw, if the animal be wholly immersed in water, like the whale, or if partly so, as was probably the case with the largest of the giant reptiles of the mesozoic age, then the weight is counterpoised if the density of the animal's body including air, is identical, as the whale's very nearly is, with that of the water around.

Under these circumstances there is no longer the same physical barrier to the indefinite growth of the animal. Indeed, in the case of the aquatic animal, there is, as Herbert Spencer pointed out, a distinct advantage, in that the larger it grows the greater is its speed. For its available energy depends on the mass of its muscles, while its motion through the water is opposed, not by gravity, but by 'skin-friction,' which increases only as the square of the linear dimensions. Other things being equal, the bigger the ship or the bigger the fish the faster it tends to go.

The tapering pine-tree is a special case of a wider problem. The oak does not grow as tall as the pine-tree but it carries a heavier load and its boll, broad-based upon its sprouting roots, shows a different contour. Smeaton took it for the pattern of his lighthouse, and Eiffel built his great tree of steel, a thousand feet high, to a similar but stricter plan. Here the profile of tower or tree follows, or tends to follow, a logarithmic curve, giving equal strength throughout.

Besides the question of stress and strain in the strength of muscles to lift increasing weight or of bones to resist crushing stress there is the most essential question of bending moments. These to greater or lesser extent enter into an entire range of problems affecting the form of skeletons. They set limits to the height of trees, determine the form of animals, and are the governing principle of architectural configurations like trusses and space frames that seek to circumvent them.

Among animals we see how small birds and beasts are quick and agile, and observe the slower, more sedate movements that come with larger size. Exaggerated bulk brings with it a certain clumsiness, inefficiency, and element of risk and danger.

In elementary mechanics, in the simple case of two similar beams supported at both ends and carrying only their own weight they will, within the limts of their elasticity tend to be deflected, or sag downwards, in proportion to the square of their linear dimensions. For example, if a match stick is 2 inches long and a beam similar in configuration is 6 feet long, 36 times the length of the match stick, the beam will sag under its own weight thirteen hundred times as much as the match stick.

To counteract this tendency, as the size of an animal increases the limbs tend to become thicker and shorter and the entire skeleton bulkier and heavier. Bones make up some 8 percent (by weight) of the body of the mouse or wren, 13 or 14 percent of goose or dog, and 17 or 18 percent of the body of man.

Elephant and hippopotamus have grown clumsier, as well as bigger, and the elk, of necessity is less graceful than the gazelle.

In contrast, a small porpoise and a great whale display little difference in skeletal proportions for the influence of gravity has become nearly negligible in both of these sea creatures. (The foregoing is capsulated from D'Arcy Thompson's wonderful book, *On Growth and Form,* Cambridge University Press, 1971.)

SIZE IS NO ACCIDENT

There is a correct size, or correct range of sizes, for every living thing according to its form and its environment, D'Arcy Thompson so clearly described.

A spider monkey cannot be as large as a man, nor a man the same size as a house. The horse and the elephant although built on relatively similar principles are quite different animals through a very modest doubling in size.

Eifel Tower.
Courtesy of French Government Tourist Office.

There is a correct size for structural members as there is for animals, humans, and every living thing. A stone bridge four inches thick may well span a small stream of six or eight feet. However, if we increase its size but ten times to a depth of 40 inches and a length of 80 feet it would easily break from its own weight if we attempted to lift it from the ground.

The important thing to observe in the realm of structures built by man is this, the changes in geometry or materials with extreme change in size. A stone lintel in classic construction had approximately a maximum span of 15 feet. If a larger distance were to be reached in stone then the form would have to be changed. A form that took advantage of the compressive strength of stone and minimized the tensil stresses was that of the arch. Large spaces in classic and renaissance structures are characterized by the curvilinear form of arch, vault and dome.

We can easily see the relation of form and span in beam, truss, arch, and cable. Each horizontal structural member spans space but a certain distance until the form must be changed if the distance is to be increased. The rectangular form of the beam, the triangular patterns of the truss, the upward curve of the arch, and the downward curve of the cable are geometric responses to stress.

We have learned that the increase in size to double the size of a creature or structure increases area four times the number squared but the volume is increased eight times, the number cubed. A man the size of a spider monkey unless designed as a spider monkey would tear himself apart if he attempted to scratch his neck and a man twelve feet tall would break himself apart if he tripped over a doorstep.

Humans have an empathetic feeling for structure and the proof of this is how it has crept into our language. We tend to feel the heavy burden of the column which was immortalized in the caryatids and atlases. The entasis of the column makes it appear bulging with muscles. We describe portals as gaping, houses and buildings sit, stand, and lie. The human body can be conceived and thought of as a structural system in itself. The bone structure is a skeleton, the muscles are pneumatic structures, and the tensile structure is the sinews. And even in the most clumsy of us, the body is marvelously coordinated.

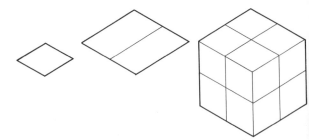

Doubling size increases area four times and volume eight times.

Photo by Del Ankers.
Courtesy of Weyerhauser Corp.

Drawing by Andreas Vesalius.

Wiring service core for Instant Rehap.
Photo courtesy of HUD.

Drawing by Andreas Vesalius.

The act of recreation, says Rasmussen, is often carried out by identifying ourselves with the object, imagining ourselves in its stead. In such instances, our activity is like that of an actor getting the feel of a role. When we look at a portrait of someone laughing or smiling we become cheerful ourselves. If, on the other hand, the face is tragic, we feel sad. People looking at pictures have a remarkable ability to enter a role that seems very foreign to them. A weak little man swells with heroism and zest for life when he sees a Hercules performing daring deeds. Commercial artists and producers of comic strips are aware of this tendency and make use of it in their work. Men's clothes sell more readily when they are displayed on athletic figures. The observer identifies himself with the handsomely built model and believes he will resemble him simply by donning the same apparel. A middle-aged woman uncritically buys the costume she sees in an advertisement on a shapely glamour girl. The boy with glowing cheeks who sits spellbound over the adventures in a comic strip imagines himself in Tarzan's or Superman's stead. (Rasmussen 1959)

PERCEPTION OF STRUCTURE IN MODERN ARCHITECTURE

One of the beliefs of modern architects was that their expression of structural forces were beautiful in themselves. Building techniques have always influenced building forms and those that view buildings have derived inspiration from them. The Parthenon and a Gothic cathedral are refinements of particular building techniques.

The ideals of modern architecture dictated that structural framing was an essential part of all construction and this technique emerged as a design factor that must be considered seriously if modern architecture is to be understood. Modern architects felt that it was a violation of the principles of modern architecture to 'humanize' the structural expression of their buildings with decoration although, paradoxically, they have used structural members as decoratively as classic architects. Mies van der Rohe used bronze 'H' sections as window mullions on the facade of one of the most famous of the buildings of modern architecture, the Seagram's building.

An understanding of technical form presupposes technical knowledge, intuition is not sufficient. Architectural forms dominated by technology are not entirely intelligible without some technical initiation, although, as we have just discussed, we have acquired a good deal of this knowledge through the simple expedient of living in a world dominated by physical forces, unless we have made a conscious effort to ignore them.

The fact that technical knowledge is required to understand the world of architectural forms indicates an intrusion of 'reason' into the sphere of 'aesthetics.' (Siegel, 1962)

If technical considerations are part of our perceptual values, then an engineering idea, that of 'economy' or optimization, must be considered. Optimization or economy was considered an intellectual principle verging on moral law. It demanded the maximum return in a spiritual, aesthetic, and material sense for minimal outlay, Siegel claims.

From the beginning of the modern movement the question of function was oversimplified and keenly debated. Van de Velde defined the essence of architectural beauty as the perfect harmony of means and ends. Mies van der Rohe said function was an art. Misinterpreted, such statements can be made to seem ridiculous. However when seriously understood and applied, they express a unity of art and technology that upon occasion has been a redeeming characteristic of modern architecture.

The features of forms derived from this union, using contemporary techniques of construction, are termed 'structural forms.' Although the term often becomes a 'cliche,' in its original sense it suggests an order imposed on built and assembled artifacts. But structural forms are not the result of computation alone, they must be designed. The relationship between structure and form is too complex to be expressible in numbers alone.

The basic structural forms in architecture recur and outlast individual styles. The elementary stone lintel resting on two pillars appears at Stonehenge and in prehistoric temples and is resurrected in the architecture of almost all succeeding cultures. Although there are differences in cultural context, differences in materials and differences in treatment, they prove to be variations on the basic form. But the essential form remains constant. It is destroyed most commonly as the result of frivolous modifications, in Siegel's opinion.

The simple column symbolizes the ability to support loads. It is found all over the world, wherever the art of building is practiced. Whereas the capital and the base, being points of transition, can be made to suggest the transfer of forces in a hundred different ways, apart from ornamentation, the shaft of the column remains a closed, mainly cylindrical or prismatic form, in which the emphasis is laid on the vertical. A pillar made up of an intertwining cluster of columns is as unreasonable, as a single shaft twisted into a helix. In both cases the structural context has been sacrificed for theatrical effect.

The prominent vault ribs of the great Gothic cathedrals are not just decorative trimming. They are part of the structure and splendid examples of structural form. The decorative rib patterns of late Gothic pseudo-vaulting no longer reflect the actual distribution of forces. They have no load-bearing function. They are graphic patterns rather than structural forms.

In the 1920s, we find that technical ideas begin to be considered as formal inspiration, and a corresponding application begins in architecture. It was architects and not engineers that started the movement. The Bauhaus and Le Corbusier introduced the concept that technology could motivate a 'style' in architecture. They anticipated a new world of technological forms and shaped it

Arcway in village designed by Hassen Fathy, appears smaller in shadow.

Stone walls, street and arch. Taxco, Mexico.

Steel framing.
Photo by Jim Rankin. Courtesy of Bethlehem Steel Co.

Frei Otto tensile structure at Expo Montreal.
Photo courtesy of Expo Corp.

by pure intuition. The results of their work were recognized as architectural 'landmarks' which influenced later technical developments. The final clarification and general recognition of the forms of technological structure did not come until later. In the decade that followed, ideas about building underwent a complete transformation and the concept of technology as a motivating cause and aesthetic triumphed. In the early 1930s, Hitchcock and Johnson published their book *The International Style,* which recognized the emergence of this style.

The recognition of technical facility also resulted in the removal of previous limitations on the arbitrariness in design. It now seemed that everything had become technically feasible. The corrective that had previously limited certain 'nonsensical' forms was withdrawn. In the ferment that followed, technical and structural virtuosity became as stylistic in its application as any of the previous 'styles.' The purifying influence of technical logic and its 'moral force' were forgotten, Siegel laments, and finally the artistic failure was paradoxically laid at the door of technology.

In this situation it would seem fitting, Siegel proposed, to broach the question of the 'correctness' of seemingly technological forms in architecture and to attempt a logical and simple answer. If the rightness and wrongness of form generated by structural logic can attain the importance of a 'moral force,' as Siegel felt it did, then there must obviously be a correct and incorrect application of these principles. Our interest in them is in our perception of them and if we do indeed distinguish their 'correctness' perceptually.

The difficulty, says Siegel, is that the bases of architectural appreciation are never established by purely rational means. A range of standards is admitted that is both broad and difficult to define. Logical deductions are easy to challenge 'on architectural grounds,' Siegel complains. Whoever questions 'artistic' or architectural pronouncements and opposes them with equally valid but purely technical arguments immediately runs the risk of being declared a philistine, to whom the doors of art are barred. This is why, Siegel states with some justification, that in discussions about architecture logical arguments carry so little weight compared with reasoning that, however tenuous, champions the 'human element,' at the expense of the rational. "As if reason and logic were not themselves human characteristics!"

It is hard not to agree with Siegels's somewhat petulant remarks, for probably more has been done in architecture to harm humans through the justification of catering to the 'human element' than technology unaided has ever accomplished.

We now proceed to discuss the heart of Siegel's argument. Since architecture of necessity must include a technological component, it should be possible to comprehend this aspect rationally.

Modern architecture as the architecture of a technological age displayed the technical problems that determined form and from these sought to fashion an aesthetic. Since modern architecture rests heavily on technology, it is most properly understood along with a knowledge of construction. We are encouraged to penetrate far more extensively and systematically than hitherto customary into the mechanical and physical relationships upon which the development of structural forms are based. Previously, building technology seemed universally intelligible whether it was or not; today, we are obliged to seek ways of speaking and understanding the complicated engineering and scientific language which has become part of architecture.

An effort to grasp the contemporary significance of technology, the importance of which does not seem to have been questioned in past ages, and see it in its position as a form-determining element is rooted in natural laws which were a powerful impetus to modern architecture.

The importance of the arguments put forth by Siegel at this time in favor of a rational structural logic, a perception and an aesthetic based on the 'logic' of structure, is that they provide a marvelous opportunity to test and find important facts about human perception.

The urban clusters of buildings designed to follow the 'modern' philosophy, whether fashioned to 'morally correct' principles or not, have resulted in environmental clusters of form in which the concepts of gestalt perception can be observed and tested on a gigantic scale.

What remains for the human eye is the significance of angles, countless parallel lines converging in all directions toward the horizon on into the sky. Instead of the eye seeking symmetry and harmony and the ordered 'good form' of square and circle, it is seduced by fleeting natural organizations of figure groupings or equivocal figures.

Despite protests to the contrary that define the constant repetition and simplicity of forms as sterile sameness, it is and can be a stimulating perceptual world harking back to the natural world that so fascinated D'Arcy Thompson, if we choose to look at it.

Siegel provided some clues for seeing, for perceiving the built environment around us. We will have to seek out the remainder ourselves.

These model photographs of Gunnar Birkerts Federal Reserve Bank contrast compressive, tensile, and bending forces as handsomely as an accomplished athelete 'pumping iron'.

The design was proposed by Birkerts in two stages. In the first the suspension structure is held in equilibrium by the strong horizontal of the top section; like a stout beam post tensioned by the horizontal components of the cable sag. The vertical components are held by two stout columns; the end walls. The second stage would add the compressive force of the arch balancing the suspension cables below and adding additional tension to counter the bending of what now has become an interior beam.

This design has, for me at least, a delight reminiscent of Gaudi's delicate balancing of corbel and arch, but on a grand scale.

The clear statement of forces at work add to and combine with the stimulation of texture, pattern, and proportion. The result is a synthesis of appreciation, a tautening of sensibilities satisfying our perception of 'how things work.'

It is this sense of structure added to the other sensual satisfactions of building form that distinguishes architecture from the other arts.

Photos by Balthazar Korab. Courtesy of Gunnar Birkerts.

Seagrams Building NYC.
Photo by F. Wilson.

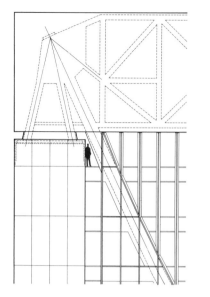

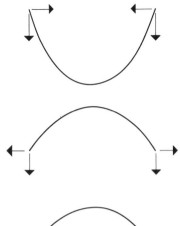

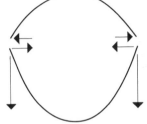

THE EFFECTS OF SCALE

By Myron Goldsmith, ASCE, FAIA

The following talk was given by Mr. Goldsmith at the American Society of Civil Engineers at their National Convention in Dallas Texas in 1977. It is presented here as a clear statement of the relation between structure size and perception. Text and illustrations courtesy of Mr. Goldsmith.

INTRODUCTION

In the seventeenth century the prevailing opinion on the relation of size to structure was expressed by Sagredo in the *Dialogues Concerning Two New Sciences,* reported by Galileo in 1638 as follows: "If a large machine be constructed in such a way that its parts bear to one another the same ratios as in a smaller one and if the smaller is sufficiently strong for its purpose, I do not see why the larger is not."(5)

Galileo refuted this proposition by saying that the size of an organism or artifact has a decisive influence on its structure and its function. He proved his theory with the utmost possible clearness, and with a great wealth of illustration drawn from animate and inanimate structures. He said: "You can plainly see the impossibility of increasing the size of structures to vast dimensions either in art or in nature, likewise the impossibility of building ships, palaces or temples of enormous size in such a way that their oars, yardbeams, iron-bolts and in short all their parts can hold together; nor can nature produce trees of extraordinary size because their branches would break down under their own weight; so also it would be impossible to build up the bony structures of men, horses or other animals so as to hold together and perform their normal function if these animals were to be increased enormously in height, for this increase in height can be accomplished only by employing a material which is harder and stronger than usual, or by enlarging the size of bones thus changing their shape until the form and appearance of the animals suggest a monstrosity.

To illustrate briefly I have sketched a bone whose natural length has been increased three times and whose thickness has been multiplied until, for a correspondingly large animal, it would perform the same function which the smaller bone performs for its small animal. From these figures . . . you can see how out of proportion the large bone appears (Fig. 1). Clearly then, if one wishes to maintain in a great giant the same proportion of limb as that found in an ordinary man, he must either find a harder and stronger material for making the bones or he must admit a diminution of strength."(5)

In this remarkable work Galileo formulates the idea of an ultimate size for structures. He says: "Among heavy prisms or cylinders of similar figure there is one and only one which under the stress of its own weight lies just on the limit between breaking and not breaking so that every larger one is unable to carry the load of its own weight and breaks while every smaller one is able to withstand some additional force tending to break it."(5)

The principles dealing with the effects of magnitude, laid down by Galileo, have since been extended and elaborated in many fields, such as biology, mathematics, philosophy, and engineering. Sir D'Arcy Wentworth Thompson in his work *On Growth and Form* cites many examples from these fields. He says: "We learn in elementary mechanics the simple case of two similar beams supported at both ends and carrying no other weight than their own. Within the limits of their elasticity they tend to be deflected, or to sag downwards, in proportion to the squares of their linear dimensions; if a match stick be 2″ (0.05 m) and a similar beam 6′ (1.8 m) (or thirty-six times as long), the latter will sag under its own weight thirteen-hundred times as much as the other. To counteract this tendency, as the size of an animal increases the limbs tend to become thicker and shorter and the whole skeleton bulkier and heavier; bones make up some 8 per cent of the body of mouse or wren, 13 or 14 per cent of goose or dog and 17 or 18 per cent of the body of a man. Elephant and hippopotamus have grown clumsy as well as big, and the elk is of necessity less graceful than the gazelle. It is of high interest, on the other hand to observe how little the skeletal proportions differ in a little porpoise and a great whale, even in the limbs and limb bones; for the whole influence of gravity has become negligible, or nearly so, in both of these."(10)

Concerning limitations on height Thompson observes that the tall tree tends to bend under its own weight and mentions how Greenhill showed that a British Columbian pine tree 221′ (67.4 m) high and 21″ (0.55 m) in diameter at the base could not have grown beyond 300′ (91.5 m), the very limitation on growth for trees anticipated by Galileo.

Analogies to the tapering pine tree are to be found in Smeaton's lighthouse and the Eiffel tower, whose profiles follow a logarithmic curve so that the structural strength is uniform throughout their height.

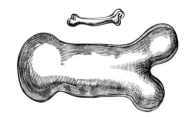

Fig. 1 Sketch of bone structures by Galileo.

"From the examples cited so far, it would seem that every increase in size is accompanied by a decrease in efficiency. This is not always true, and there are many structures whose increasing efficiency due to increasing volume with proportionately decreasing surface continues up to the limits of the strength of the materials. If we consider the case of two similar obelisks of different size it can be shown that as long as the strength of the material is not exceeded the larger will resist winds that will blow down the smaller, and in the case of similar chimneys the larger may be expected to be capable of standing a greater storm than the smaller. In these cases the overturning forces are proportional to the areas exposed to the wind, while the stabilizing forces are proportional to the volumes, since every increase in size is accompanied by a disproportionately higher increase in volume than in area, these structures become more stable as they increase in size."(10) Then there is a series of structures whose performance does not change over wide ranges of size. The tank for containing fluid is one such structure, and the chart shows the weight per gallon contained as the capacity increases. The weight is constant over a wide range (Fig. 2). (2) There are also structures whose performances follow typical optimization curves with their greatest efficiency occurring neither at their largest nor smallest sizes.

In 1947, after studying *On Growth & Form,* I became convinced that different scales required different structures. A study was made of how these principles are found to be applicable to modern engineering structures. The first study shows a comparison of the spans of different types of bridge structures (Fig. 3).(9) Each type has an upper and lower limit. The longest plate girder span is 860′ (262.3 m) while the simple truss has been used up to spans of 720′ (219.6 m) and continuous truss has been carried to a span of 1,000′ (305 m). Thereafter the span increases rapidly, the arch spanning 1,600′ (488 m), the cantilever bridge 1,800′ (549 m), and finally the suspension bridge reaching a present maximum of 4,200′ (1,281 m) with predictable limits in the region of

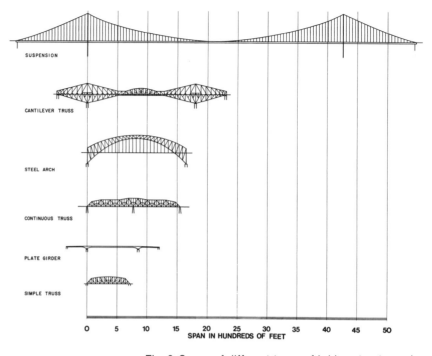

Fig. 3 Spans of different types of bridge structures, by Myron Goldsmith

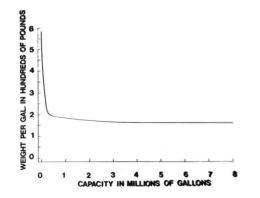

Fig. 2. Chart showing the decrease in weight per gallon of fluid contained in tank as the capacity increases.

10,000′ (3,050 m). So it is seen that at certain limits the structural system has to be changed. The reason for the upper limit of structural systems becomes clear by comparing the weights of railroad bridges of different span (Fig. 4). It is seen that a 150′ (45.75 m) span structure weighs 400,000 pounds (181,200 kg) whereas a 600′ (183 m) structure weighs 4,500,000 pounds (2,038,500 kg), thus representing an increase of four times in span and eleven times in weight. The curve of the graph shows that at 600′ (183 m) span the increments of weight increase rapidly for every increase in span and it can be expected that the maximum span for this type of construction will be reached not far beyond 700′ (213.5 m).(8) The steel skeletons of multistory buildings exhibit similar behavior. An 8-story building requires 10 pounds (4.53 kg) of steel per square foot (3) while a 100-story building requires 30 pounds (13.59 kg).

In summing up it can be said that every structure has a maximum and minimum size. For example in the bridge structures there is a region between 400′ (122 m) and 700′ (213.5 m) where now one and then another type is used but above 2,000′ (610 m) the suspension system reigns supreme, while below 400′ (122 m) the suspension bridge is reaching a minimum efficiency. In the final analysis an optimum size may be found somewhere between these extremes and its exact determination will be at its point of maximum efficiency.

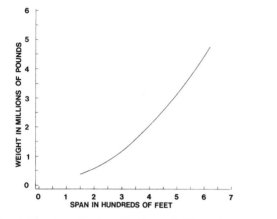

Fig. 4 Weights of railroad bridges of different spans.

Fig. 5 Oil supertanker

SCALE AND ENVIRONMENT

Large scale construction can have positive and negative effects environmentally and aesthetically. These effects are often complex and difficult to assess in advance. The problems can be seen in the study of the oil supertankers (Fig. 5). Advocates claim that the larger the size of the tanker, the less the cost of transporting oil, and consequently, the price of petroleum products will decrease. The large-tanker critics, on the other hand, say that as size increases so will problems such as oil spillage and water pollution. In 1959, the first 100,000 ton tanker (49 foot (14.9 m) draft) was built, and since then we have progressed rapidly to 200,000 ton and 300,000 ton ships. Plans for a 500,000 ton tanker are on the drawing board and it is rumored that an oil company has considered tankers of 800,000 tons. It is believed technically feasible to build 1,000,000 ton tankers. In the language of economics, the reduction in cost as a result of increasing size (scale) of the plant is called an economy of scale. In the tankership industry there are economies of scale at both the construction and the operating stages. The table shows the reduction in oil transport cost as the size of tanker increases.

Tanker Size (Tons)	Draft (Feet) (m)	Relative of Cost of Oil Transport
19,000	30 (9.5 m)	100
45,000	39 (11.5 m)	57
70,000	42 (12.8 m)	48
100,000	49 (14.9 m)	42
200,000	61 (18.6 m)	37
300,000	72 (21.9 m)	36
500,000	85 (25.9 m)	34

It is clear from the table that the rate of reduction in transport cost decreases as the tanker's size increase. One of the reasons for these diminishing returns is that the tanker owners limit the tanker's draft as the size is increased in order to increase the tanker's operating flexibility. Naturally, the shorter the draft, the greater the number of ports that can accommodate the tanker.(11)

Mining machinery has similar economies of scale. Enormous excavating machines weighing thousands of tons, moving earth thousands of feet, now make it economical to reshape land, to create lakes and canals, and to remove overburden hundreds of feet thick from coal and ores. The walking dragline (Fig. 6) weighs 15,000 tons, has a bucket capacity of 220 cubic yards (168.3 m³), has a boom length of 310 feet (94.5 m), and it can move material over 1000 feet (305 m) in a single cycle. It is the world's largest, and its yearly capacity is 60,000,000 cubic yards (45,900,000 m³). It moves earth for about 1/20 the cost of moving it with a small machine.(1) The wheel excavator used for mining coal stands 200 feet (61 m) high and has a capacity of over 25,000 cubic yards (19,125 m³) per day (Fig. 7).(1) The large excavators resulted in the manufacturing of enormous trucks, which can haul hundred of tons of material in a single load. This truck (Fig. 8) for mining operations has a capacity of 350 tons and is over 50 feet (15.2 m) long; with the body at raised position, it soars to the height of a six story building.(6) This enormous size machinery can be justified also because of a reduction in operational and construction cost.

Electrical utilities have been building bigger and bigger power plants in a quest for economies of scale, but a report recently released by the U.S. Federal Energy Administration (FEA) indicates the strategy may be backfiring. According to FEA, such plants are available for service only 70 percent of the time, meaning utilities must build three of them to get the service of two. Improved efficiency means not only more power, but reducing forced shutdowns by a percentage point could mean saving in construction cost to utilities of $1.8 billion by 1980.(4)

Amid all the pros and cons of today's search for alternate sources of energy, a new and controversial energy-related issue has emerged: whether or not to build 765 kilovolt transmission lines. Some drawbacks: Aside from the visual problems of 140 foot to 200 foot (42.6 to 60.9 m) towers crisscrossing the landscape, the lines may produce noise pollution, generate ozone, cause electric shocks from induced currents, and also create strong electrostatic and electromagnetic fields that could have adverse effects on living organisms including plants, animals, and humans. Such high voltage networks as the 765 kv will make it possible to transmit more energy over greater distances at lower cost. For example, five 345 kv lines would be needed to transmit the same power as one 765 line. But at the same time, it can have the above-mentioned disadvantages. High concentrations of ozone probably cause more injury to vegetation than any other air pollutant and it can have harmful effects on human health.(12)

Ecologically, the aforementioned examples can be very destructive, or lead to great benefits when their use is carefully controlled. Large constructions can produce large scale changes of the environment. When building gigantic oil tankers, the danger of oil spillage as well as destruction from accidents must be carefully weighed. In our built environment we must weigh the land use, energy use, and cost of building low density versus high density, multifunctional complexes in urban centers. The protection of human health from noise, water, and air pollution should be foremost in our minds.

Fig. 6 Walking dragline, 220 yards, Bucyrus Erie Co.

Fig. 7 Wheel excavator, Bucyrus Erie Co.

Fig. 8 Earthmoving truck, 350 tons. Courtesy of General Motors.

SCALE AND AESTHETICS

The large engineering structures and machinery have had an enormous influence on a certain area of contemporary art. There are many examples; an obvious one is the Solar Telescope at Kitt Peak's influence on Minimal Sculpture (Fig. 9)—its unconventional appearance is a result of its enormous focal length of 300 feet (91.5 m). The best machines are also works of art, and those interested in art ought to go to see these colossal machines, especially in motion, in the same way they would go to museums.

There has been a great deal of debate on the effects of colossal structures on cities and landscapes. The most famous debate occurred when the Eiffel Tower was built in 1891. At that time it was considered by many to be a monstrosity and out of scale with the city. Today it is considered by many to symbolize Paris (Fig. 11). The beautiful Bosporous Bridge, with a span of 3,500 feet (1067.5 m) and towers 540 feet (164.7 m) high, with a deck 206 feet (62.8 m) above the water, so startling in its size in relation to Istanbul, is rapidly becoming its symbol (Fig. 12). There is a similar debate going on in Chicago. The giant buildings like Sears Tower and John Hancock are rapidly becoming the symbol of the city (Fig. 13).

The aforementioned colossuses are unusual examples. A city can have only a limited number of these before it becomes a problem how to make them relate well to each other and their surroundings. Some other structures can be out of scale and foreign to existing conditions. For example, the American expressways when built in urban areas usually have negative attributes: noise and air pollution as well as disastrous aesthetic intrusion on the surroundings.

So there is the general problem of how to place new structures in harmony with their surroundings. One such problem was the competition for the Garibaldi Bridge in Rome, Italy, 1954. In our entry proposal we carefully adjusted the scale and form of the structure to the site and the character and surroundings of the city (Fig. 14). The project was designed with James Ferris, Bruno Zevi, and Carlo Cestelli - Guidi.(7) A similar bridge project designed in 1958 was an adaptation of the previous design, but for long spans (Fig. 15). It was designed by Myron Goldsmith and James Ferris, with T.Y. Lin as consultant.

In a similar way the Ruck-A-Chucky bridge in California (1976) was fitted to a unique rural site. The bridge is located about half way up from the bottom of a steep valley. The horizontal arc allows the bridge to flow into the hillside, minimizing cuts. The slopes are turned into an asset by being utilized to suspend the entire span. The engineers for the bridge were T.Y. Lin International and Hansen Engineers, and I was the consultant on architectural and environmental design (Figs. 16 and 17).

Fig. 9 Solar telescope at Kitt Peak, Arizona, USA, by Skidmore, Owings and Merrill, Myron Goldsmith and William Dunlap. Photo by Ezra Stoller. Courtesy of Skidmore, Owings and Merrill

Fig. 11 Eiffel Tower in Paris.

Fig. 12 Bosphorous Bridge, Istanbul, Turkey.

130

Fig. 13 Chicago skyline.

Fig. 14. Competition entry for the Garibaldi Bridge, Rome, Italy, by Myron Goldsmith, James Ferris, Bruno Zevi, and Carlo Cestelli-Guidi.

Fig. 15 Bridge project for Universal Atlas Cement Co., by Myron Goldsmith and James D. Ferris and T.Y. Lin, consultant.

Fig. 16 Ruck-A-Chucky Bridge, for the Bureau of Reclamation, California.

Fig. 17. Ruck-A-Chucky Bridge.

PROBLEMS OF THE TALL BUILDING

The effects of magnitude as stated in the preceding part will now be examined in relation to the tall building.

Masonry structures are at their greatest efficiency in low buildings where the thickness of wall required for protection against the elements is sufficiently strong to carry the floors and roof. The maximum height of masonry office structures was reached in the sixteen story Monadnock building (Figs. 18 and 19), build in Chicago in 1891 by Burnham and Root. It has walls 6 feet (1.83 m) at the base decreasing gradually through the upper stories to 30 inches (0.76 m) in thickness. The internal columns are of cast iron; the external walls are of masonry acting as bearing walls and stabilizing the structure by their mass.

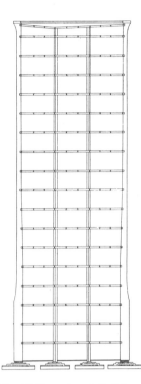

Fig. 19 Monadnock Building.

Fig. 18 Monadnock Building, Chicago Illinois, USA by Burnham and Root.

A reinforced concrete skeleton is a monolithic structure in which all the vertical loads are carried by means of columns, while the horizontal loads are resisted by the columns stiffened by the beams and girders. It is characteristic of this structural type, of which the Promontory Apartment Building, built in Chicago in 1948 by Mies Van der Rohe, is a good example, that the thickness of the floor construction may remain constant for every story (Figs. 20 and 21), whereas the columns and girders must increase in the lower stories due to the increase of vertical and horizontal loads. The skeleton type permits great flexibility in internal planning, since the vertical members are relatively small and isolated; but the increasing size of the principal members in the lower stories of tall buildings tends to interfere with the use and flexibility of the interior space, and as a consequence, the practical limit on height for this structural type has been about twenty-five stories.

The limitations inherent in the pure concrete frame were rapidly overcome by the introduction of a whole new series of concrete structures: the frame and shear wall combination; the concrete tube (where the exterior resists lateral forces); and various combinations of these. This clarification came about through the work of Fazlur Khan during the fifties and sixties. One project

Fig. 20 Promotory Apartment Building, Chicago, Illinois, USA, by Mies van der Rohe.

showing this development of the concrete tube is the Chestnut De Witt Apartment Building (Fig. 22), designed by Skidmore, Owings & Merrill with Bruce Graham—Design Partner, Myron Goldsmith—Senior Designer, and Fazlur Kahn—Chief Structural Engineer. Another such project is the 116-story, braced tube office building designed as a Masters Thesis at Illinois Institute of Technology, in 1968 by Robert C. Hodgkinson with Myron Goldsmith, Fazlur Khan, and David Sharpe as main advisors (Fig. 23).

Simultaneously, there was a similar development of steel structures for tall buildings, also by Fazlur Khan. He identified the heights at which various structural systems in steel were economical (Fig. 24).

There have been recent developments in elevatoring of high-rise buildings that recognize the scale effects. The double deck elevators and sky lobbies in the World Trade Center and Sears Tower are two such examples.

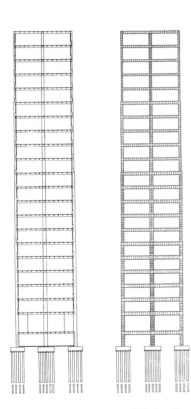

Fig. 21 Promontory Apartment Building (section).

Fig. 23 116-story concrete high-rise building for Illinois Center, Chicago Illinois, USA, by Robert L. Hodgkinson, with advisors M. Goldsmith, F. Kahn, and D. Sharpe. Photo by Bill Engdahl, Hedrick-Blessing. Courtesy of Skidmore, Owings and Merrill.

Fig. 22 Chestnut-De Witt Apartment Building, by Skidmore, Owings and Merrill, Bruce J. Graham and Myron Goldsmith.

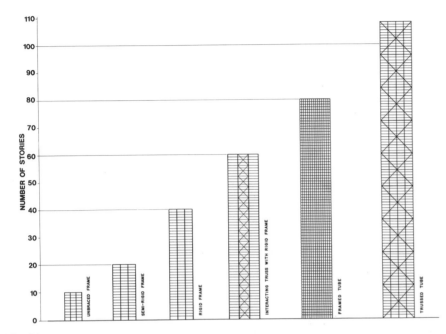

Fig. 24
Structural systems for high-rise buildings in steel by
Fazlur Khan.

Fig. 25 Sears Tower by Skidmore, Owings and Merrill,
Photo by Ezra Stoller. Courtesy of Skidmore, Owings and
Merrill.

Fig. 26 John Hancock Building by Skidmore, Owings and
Merrill. Photo by Ezra Stoller. Courtesy of Skidmore, Owings and Merrill.

The proliferation of new structures has led to a corresponding development in the architectural expression of these structures, as diverse as in the Sears Tower (Fig. 25) and the John Hancock Building (Fig. 26).
small scale. The printing press, painted bright yellow, sits immediately behind the glass perimeter and appears as much a sculpture as a machine.

Just as with high-rise buildings, we must change structural systems in low-rise buildings as the spans increase and the functional requirements change. The Republic Newspaper building had very fixed functional requirements, while the UAL building required maximum flexibility and therefore large span with a logical solution.

PROBLEMS OF THE LOW-RISE BUILDING

A similar refinement of low-rise structures can be seen in several Skidmore, Owings & Merrill buildings. For the United Airlines Maintenance and Wash Hangars in San Francisco (Figs. 27 and 28), with their 160 feet (48.8 m) cantilever, several schemes of approximately the same economy were investigated (Fig. 29), but the choice was finally for the architectural and aesthetic reasons. The architect can usually control the visual aspect of a project, even within stringent economic limitations.

The United Airlines Executive Office Building, near O'Hare Airport in Illinois, and the Republic Newspaper Plant in Columbus, Indiana, are two low-rise buildings of vastly different scale. UAL is a very large building on a suburban site, and with 60 x 66 feet (18.3 m x 20.1 m) bays (in prestressed concrete) it gives maximum flexibility for the interior functional activities. The elegant exposed steel structure of the Republic gives the building a sense of detail and

The scale of the structural systems and detailing relate directly to the size of the buildings and the functional requirements and the need for flexibility.

The effects of scale on urban settlements should be systematically studied. This photo of Chicago (Fig. 32) shows some of the extensive rail and highway network that connects the city with its center. The city center of a large metropolitan area is the focal point for the transportation network and for the political and cultural institutions. The extremely high density at the center surrounded by a sea of lower density construction is the logical result of the above facts.

Fig. 27 United Air Lines Hangar, San Francisco, California, USA, by Skidmore, Owings and Merrill, Myron Goldsmith, Chief Structural Engineer.

Fig. 28 United Air Lines Wash Hangar, San Francisco, California, by Skidmore, Owings and Merrill, Myron Goldsmith, Chief Structural Engineer.

SUSPENDED STEEL TRUSS
A

CANTILEVER STEEL TRUSS
B

CANTILEVER PRESTRESSED CONCRETE GIRDER
C

Fig. 29 Alternate schemes for hangars.

Fig. 30 UAL Executive Office Building, Illinois, USA, by Skidmore, Owings and Merrill, Bruce Graham, Myron Goldsmith, and James Ferris.

Fig. 31 The Republic Newspaper Building, Columbus, Indiana, USA, by Skidmore, Owings and Merrill, Myron Goldsmith and Jim Kim. Photo by Ezra Stoller. Courtesy of Skidmore, Owings and Merrill.

Fig. 32 City of Chicago.

APPENDIX 1—REFERENCES

1. Bucyrus Erie, Manufacturer's Data
2. Chicago Bridge and Iron Company, Manufacturer's Data.
3. Clark, W.C., and Kingston, J.C., *The Skyscraper: A Study in the Economic Height of Modern Office Buildings,* New York, New York, 1930, p. 50.
4. Federal Energy Administration, "Study points out bigger power plants as uneconomical and unreliable," *Engineering News Record,* March 13, 1975, p. 16.
5. Galilei, Galileo, *Dialogues Concerning Two New Sciences,* Henry Crew and Alfonse De Salvio. trans., Chicago, Ill., 1914.
6. General Motors, Manufacturer's Data.
7. Goldsmith, Myron and Ferris, James, "Five Projects," *Arts and Architecture,* Los Angeles, November, 1956.
8. Ketchum, Milo S., *Structural Engineerings' Handbook,* New York, New York, 1924, p. 204.
9. Steinmann, David B., "The World's Most Notable Bridges," *Engineering News Record,* revised by Myron Goldsmith, Dec. 9, 1948, pp. 92–94.
10. Thompson, Sir D'Arcy Wentworth, *On Growth and Form,* Cambridge: Cambridge University Press, 1948.
11. Tourk, Chairy A., "Supertankers: A Bird's-Eye View," *I.I.T. Technology and Human Affairs,* Vol. 5, No. 3, Fall 1973, Chicago, Ill, pp. 11–14.
12. No author, "Engineering News: High Voltage Power Lines; Some Doubts are Raised," *Civic Engineering-ASCE,* March, 1975, p. 16.

SYMMETRY

Man the Measure of All Things—Measured Man

Man as the measure and man measured provides the most revealing comparison between the postures and attitudes of designers and behavioral scientists and their approaches to the creation of the man-made environment.

The two are compared here beginning with classic, Renaissance, and then recent notions of symmetry and harmony in which man is the measure juxtaposed to the science of measuring man, anthropometry and human factors.

Symmetry of form—A form tends toward symmetry, balance, and proportion. Integration of similars and adjacents, units similar in size and shape, and color tend to combine to make better articulated forms. (Fryer 1965, p. 85, 86) Symmetry, to the architect, is much more than the balancing of forms. In the past the notion of symmetry and beauty were inseparable.

Symmetry, as defined in Webster's New Collegiate dictionary, is: "**1:** balanced proportions; *also:* beauty of form arising from balanced proportions **2:** the property of being symmetrical; *esp:* correspondence in size, shape, and relative position of parts on opposite sides of a dividing line or median plane or about a center or axis. . ."

In the first century B.C., the Roman architect Vitruvius, in his *On Symmetry: In Temples And In The Human Body,* wrote,

The design of a temple depends on symmetry, the principles of which must be most carefully observed by the architect. They are due to proportion. . .Proportion is a correspondence among the measures of the members of an entire work, and of the whole to a certain part selected as a standard. . .as in the case of those of a well shaped man.

For the human body is so designed by nature that the face, from the chin to the top of the forehead and the lowest roots of the hair, is a tenth part of the whole height; the open hand from the wrist to the tip of the middle finger is just the same; the head from the chin to the crown is an eighth, and with the neck and shoulder from the top of the breast to the lowest roots of the hair is a sixth; from the middle of the breast to the summit of the crown is a fourth. If we take the height of the face itself, the distance from the bottom of the chin to the underside of the nostrils is one third of it; the nose from the underside of the nostrils to a line between the eyebrows is the same; from there to the lowest roots of the hair is also a third, comprising the forehead.

The length of the foot is one sixth of the height of the body; of the forearm one-fourth; and the breadth of the breast is also one-fourth. The other members, too have their own symmetrical proportions, and it was by employing them that the famous painters and sculptors of antiquity attained to great and endless renown.

. . .Then again, in the human body the central point is naturally the navel. For if a man be placed flat on his back, with his hands and feet extended, and a pair of compasses centered at his navel, the fingers and toes of his two hands and feet will touch the circumference of a circle described therefrom. And just as the human body yields

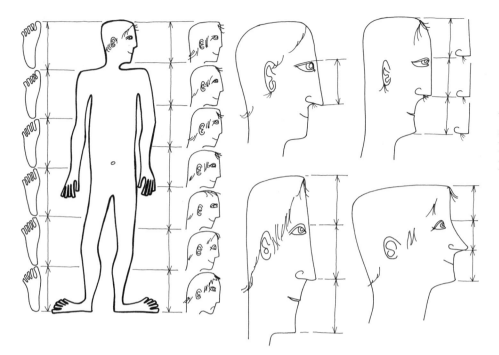

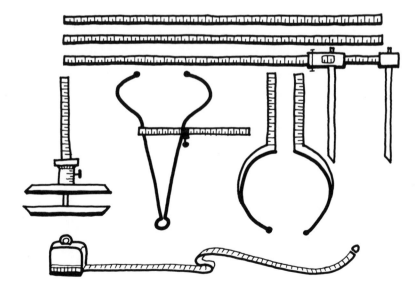

A common set of anthropometric instruments.
(Rubin, Elder 1980)

a circular outline, so too a square figure may be found from it. For if we measure the distance from the soles of the feet to the top of the head, and then apply that measure to the outstretched arms, the breadth will be found to be the same as the height, as in the case of plane surfaces which are perfectly square.

Symmetry, said Vitruvius, "is a proper agreement between the members of a work itself, and relation between the different parts and the whole general scheme in accordance with a certain part selected as a standard. Thus in the human body there is a kind of symmetrical harmony between forearm, foot, palm, finger, and other small parts; and so it is with perfect buildings. . ."

Leone Battista Alberti, Italian architect, musician, painter, and humanist, was explicit concerning the character of the 'ideal church' and his definition of how it should be designed was based on Vitruvian ideals of 'symmetry' as these were conceived during the Renaissance.

"It (the church) should be the noblest ornament of a city and its beauty should surpass imagination. It is this staggering beauty which awakens sublime sensations and arouses piety in the people. It has purifying effect and produces the state of innocence which is pleasing to God." What is this staggering beauty that has so powerful an effect?

According to Alberti's well known mathematical definition, based on Vitruvius, beauty consists of a rational integration of the proportions of all the parts of a building in such a way that every part has its absolutely fixed size and shape and nothing could be added or taken away without destroying the harmony of the whole. This conformity of ratios and correspondence of all the parts, this organic geometry, should be observed in every building, but above all in churches. (Wittkower 1942)

Alberti concluded that no geometrical form was more apt to fulfill this demand that the circle or forms derived from it. (See Section I–17 on Meaningfulness of Forms) In such centralized plans the geometrical pattern will appear absolute, immutable, static, and entirely lucid. Without that organic geometrical equilibrium where all the parts are harmonically related like the members of a body, divinity cannot reveal itself, Alberti said.

Not only has Alberti told us that architectural form will influence human behavior but he has told us in no uncertain terms how to achieve this result.

We know that since the early days of Greek philosophy men have tried to find in art geometrical laws. For if art, which they have defined and identified as beauty, is harmony and harmony is the due observance of proportions, it seems reasonable to assume that these proportions are fixed. The geometrical proportion known as the Golden Section has for centuries been regarded as such a key to the mysteries of art. So universal is its application, not only in art but also in nature, that this proportion has at times been treated with religious veneration. Several writers during the sixteenth century related the three parts of the Golden Section to the Trinity.

Herbert Read in discussing this wrote that "We can assume either that the good artist consciously applies the section in the structure of his work, or that he inevitably comes to it by his instinctive sense of form. se is often made of the Golden Section to secure the right proportion between the length and breadth in the rectangles made by windows and doors, by picture-frames and by the page of a book or a journal. . ."

Read went on to say that not only the Golden Section, but other geometrical ratios, such as the square within the rectangle of the width of the rectangle are employed in almost endless combination to secure a perfect harmony. But, Read said, it is the relative endlessness of such combinations which precludes any mechanistic explanation of the total harmony of a work of art; for although the counters in the game are rigid, it requires instinct and sensibility to use them for a fine effect. (Read 1931, p. 23–25)

In more recent times, the French architect Le Corbusier applied the measurements of man to the problem of creating a harmonious built environment and he did so with an ingenious scheme to incorporte the pleasing harmonies of the Golden Section into mass industrial production.

In his books *Modulor I and II,* Le Corbusier prefaces his undertaking with a discussion of space:

> To take possession of space is the first gesture of the living, men and beasts, plants and clouds, the fundamental manifestation of equilibrium and permanence. The first proof of existence is to occupy space.
>
> The flower, the plant, the tree, the mountain, all these are upright, living in an environment. If the true greatness of their aspect draws attention to itself, it is because they seem contained in themselves, yet producing resonances all round. We stop short, conscious of as much natural harmony; and we look, moved by so much unity commanding so much space; and then we measure what we see.
>
> Without wishing to put forward any ambitious claims, I have something to say about the 'magnification' of space first attempted by the artists of my generation during the marvelously creative early days of cubism, around 1910.
>
> They spoke of a fourth dimension, some with a little more intuition and insight, some with a little less, no matter. A life devoted to art, and most particularly the quest for harmony, has enabled me, through the practice of three arts—architecture, sculpture, and painting—to learn something about it in my turn.
>
> The fourth dimension is, I believe, the moment of boundless freedom brought about by an exceptionally happy consonance of the plastic means employed in a work of art. In other words its harmonious attributes which are pleasing to human perceptions.
>
> "It is not the effect of the subject chosen by the artist, but a triumph of proportioning in all things—the physical properties of the work as well as the fulfillment of the artist's intention, controlled or uncontrolled, tangible or intangible, but existing in any case, and owing its being to intuition, that miraculous catalyst of knowledge, acquired, assimilated, perhaps even forgotten. . .I have not experienced the miracle of faith, but I have often known the miracle of inexpressible space, the apotheosis of plastic emotion.

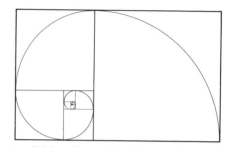

How to divide a line so that the smaller part is to the larger as the larger is to the whole, eb:ae = ae:ab.

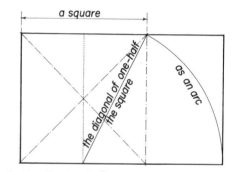

A "Golden Rectangle."

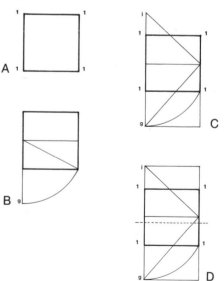

A. A square.
B. Its golden section.
C. Right angle set on the axis of the original square gives point 'i.'
D. The line g-i is divided into two equal parts.

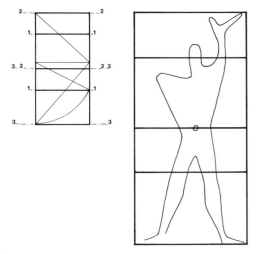

Two continguous squares each equal to the initial square.

Dominican Monastery of La Tourette.

by Le Corbusier.

Photo courtesy of French Cultural Services.

From this poetic description of the perceptual attributes of harmony and symmetry, not unlike the writings of Alberti, although as an agnostic Le Corbusier worships harmoniously proportioned space rather than God, he goes on to state a faith, if not in the almighty, in the ability of standardization to achieve an ideal world.

"We must strive towards the establishment of a standard in order to face the problem of perfection."

"The Parthenon is the product of selection applied to a standard."

"Standards are the products of logic, of analysis and painstaking study; they are evolved on the basis of a problem well stated, in the final analysis, however, a standard is established by experimentation."

And experiment Le Corbusier did, converting his atelier into a laboratory and recording his progress in his two books *Modulor I and II* written as scientific notes documenting his research. These investigations formed the perceptual basis of a number of his buildings.

Corbusier proposed that the dimensions of the Modulor be adopted by manufacturers as standardized measurement to take the place of the jumble of sizes that had developed with industrialization. He claimed this to be a more rational solution to measurement than either the metric system or feet and inches and would eliminate the problem and controversy over conversion from one to the other.

His proposal did not meet with success. Standardization took other less harmonious courses.

During the course of his researches, Le Corbusier had a tape made based on the dimensions of his standardized 'Modulor' man of 1.75 m in height. By using this tape he found that the dimensions of many objects considered pleasing coincided with the graduations on his modulor tape. This same experiment has been conducted countless times by teachers of art and architecture. Pleasing proportioned objects, man-made and natural, often fall within the ratio of parts of the 'golden mean' or Golden Section, which comes to 1:0.618 (see drawings).

Corbusier then proceeded to pin down the human body at the decisive points of its occupation of space using a red and blue series of numbers coinciding with critical human dimensions: knees, navel, elbows, top of head, and tip of fingers with arm upraised. How now had a harmonious system of measurement in which the dimensions of the human body were 'standardized' to his satisfaction.

This invention, Le Corbusier and his fellow researchers named the 'Modulor,' the module of gold. When it was shown to the great scientist Einstein, he commented, "It is a scale of proportions which makes the bad difficult and the good easy." (Le Corbusier 1954)

Corbusier's genius lay in conceiving the possibility of marrying harmony and perception to standardized mass production. If each part was harmonious, related to every other part, then harmony would prevail eliminating cacophony no matter how haphazardly they were combined.

This most recent attempt to impose a classic harmony on the man-made environment occurred midway in this century. It was a last ditch battle to forestall the rule of the statistically averaged automated man. The machine that conceivably was capable of classifying and serving man's unique individuality was instead devoted to finding even more sophisticated realms of measuring and imposing statistical averages.

Le Corbusier's dream of mass-produced perceptually pleasing environments for everyman was a grandiose concept that not even Vitruvius or Alberti dared entertain; a mass man renaissance with everyman's palazzo.

Corbusier's idealism was matched by an equally fervid conviction of the scientists that if man's every moving part could be recorded an ideal world would ensue. Man the measure of all things slipped quite easily and logically into measured man. It proved easier and much more practical to fit man to his machines than to retool machines to harmoniously encircle man. (Corbusier 1954, 1955)

MEASURED MAN

Anthropometry has been defined as the science of measuring the human body—its parts and functional capacities. Anthropometric studies therefore encompass measurements of the body at rest, as well as the space and other attributes, such as shape, necessary for a person to carry out a required task.

As in other areas of man-environment research, the greatest demand for information has been made by the military for the design of clothing and equipment. The design of jobs, machines, and equipment to be used in manufacturing and commercial settings also requires anthropometric information. More recently man-environmental problems have provided an important impetus to the collection of anthropometric data for building design purposes.

The discipline or practice of anthropometry is traceable to the 19th century work of Sir Francis Galton (British anthropologist), who was the first investigator to conduct extensive studies to determine how physical, sensory, and other characteristics were distributed among the general population. Galton developed many measurement techniques to acquire the necessary data, and statistical procedures to analyze them, once collected. In all anthropometric studies, statistical considerations are of primary importance. To be accurate, anthropometric measures must be taken on a group of people representative of the population being studied. For example, studies have been made to determine the range of sizes of people who are pilots of military aircraft to ensure that the dimensions of the equipment and the aircraft itself are compatible with the user population. Investigations of this type are conducted using actual pilots and those training to fly airplanes. Much of the research in anthropometrics is conducted by means of surveys of the user population. Since it

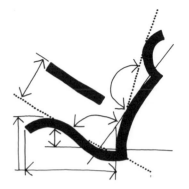

Design for Experimental Chair.
(Grandjean)

Preferred Armchair Dimensions and Adjustments
Based on Activities of Reading, Television Viewing
(Le Carpentier)

Construction detail	n (Subjects)	Average	Standard Deviation	Recommendation for two positions		only one position
Front height of seat, unloaded (cm)	20	40	±3.8	38	38	42
Depth of seat (cm)	20	48	±3.2	47	47	47
Angle of seat (°)	20	10.3	±3.4	10.5	9	12
Angle between seat and backrest (°)	20	109.1	±5.5	110	113	105
Armrests, height above seat when occupied (cm)	12	16	±1.6	16.5	16.5	16.5
Head rest in front of back surface	12	3.8	±5.7	6.4	6.4	6.4
Angle between headrest and backrest (°)	12	7.9	±3.3	8	8	8

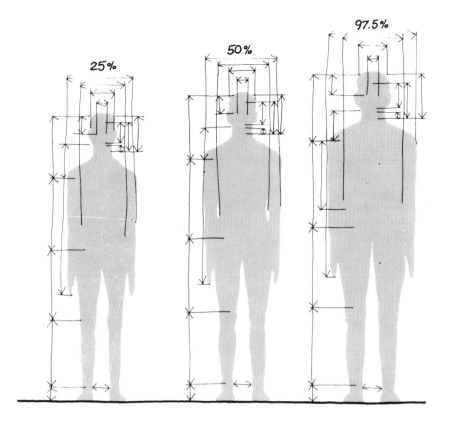

25% 50% 97.5%

Anthropometric Data-Standing Adult Male

Henry Dreyfuss Associates, industrial designers, have been leaders in the compilation of anthropometric data. They published 32 anthropometric charts and two life-sized charts of the average adult male and female with anthropometric measurements indicated. The first charts published in 1955 have since been redone several times with new data added. The charts cover 95% of the adult population. Each chart has three figures—one representing the mean percentile, 50; one representing the small extreme percentile, 2.5; and one representing the large extreme percentile, 97.5.
(Rubin, Elder 1980)

is often impractical to survey the entire population, statistical procedures are used to derive judgments from sample studies, which may then be extended to the entire user population.

Two types of basic anthropometric measures are employed, static and dynamic. Static measurements are taken with the body at rest. They define the minimum requirements necessary to accommodate the person while engaging in sedentary activity such as reading. Static measurements are a major source of data for industrial designers who must dimension furniture and furniture products used in buildings.

Activities performed in buildings require that people move. Researchers have identified major causes of movement which basically accompany activities. They measure people performing basic movements and distribute the data. While the study of basic movements is termed anthropometry, the investigation of the actual performance of activities requires another discipline, and this is termed 'human facors' or ergonomics.

The procedures used to collect anthropometric data date from the early methods of 100 years ago to sophisticated contemporary systems designed to simplify measurement and recording operations. The tape measure and caliper remain the most widely used working tools. They are employed to make virtually every required bodily measurement. Reliance on them makes the task of measurement of large groups time-consuming and costly.

Alternative approaches have been developed in recent years to quicken data collection. One popular procedure employs a two-way grid system as a means for taking rapid measurements. A photographic system is used in conjunction with the grids to record dimensions and determine dimensional requirements.
Special Groups—Aged and Handicapped

Many people in the general population have disabilities which make it difficult, sometimes impossible, to use buildings designed for those without handicaps. Possibly the most apparent design response to these needs is seen in the presence of ramps in government buildings to facilitate the movement of people confined to wheelchairs. Many existing restroom facilities are being modified and new ones are being designed.

Some research efforts have been directed toward a better understanding of how well people with impaired abilities, due to age and handicap, are able to carry out their desired activities in buildings. Other studies have focused on overcoming handicaps by providing alternative means of adjusting to the environment by substituting one sense for another.

L.A. Pastalan sought to duplicate environmental experiences of the elderly by simulating normal sensory loss of a person in his late seventies. Mechanical devices were developed, based on age-related sensory loss data, to reproduce the effects of sensory loss. The devices allowed for such simulation in the following sensory areas.

- Visual: The increased opaqueness and decreased elasticity of the eye were simulated by specially coated lenses.
- Auditory: A material in the form of earplugs simulated auditory loss above the 2,000 Hz range, and decible loss of around 30.
- Olfactory: Diminished sensitivity to odors as approximated by placing cotton wadding in the nasal passages.
- Tactile: The finger tips were coated with a liquid fixative which simulated a certain degree of touch desensitivity.

A research team of four architectural students under Pastalan at the University of Michigan experienced three specified settings an hour each day for 6 months, in this artifically 'aged' condition. The settings were a dwelling unit, a senior center, and a shopping center. Each person kept a daily record of his experiences and from time to time met with other researchers to compare notes.

In the visual area, glare from uncontrolled natural light and from unbalanced artificial light sources was the greatest problem. A single intense artificial light source increased the likelihood of uncomfortable glare.

Colors also tended to fade fast, and it was difficult to distinguish the boundary between two contrasting surfaces. With sufficiently similar surfaces, boundaries tended to disappear altogether. Depth perception was affected and adaption between dark and light areas was difficult as was the ability to discriminate fine visual detail.

In the auditory area, background noise interfered with conversation. Parts of words were often unintelligible, it was difficult to locate and identify sounds, and some combinations of carpeting, acoustical tile, and draperies absorbed too much sound and made comprehension difficult.

The simulation of odor loss caused a lessening of appetite. The tactile losses led to difficulty with fine muscle control in eye-hand coordination tasks and with temperature discrimination.

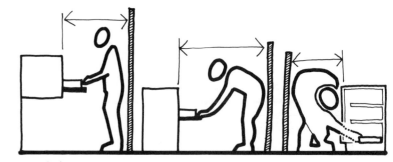

Screen technique.
(Swedish Researchers)

Recommended Table Heights for Standing Work
(Ward and Kirk)

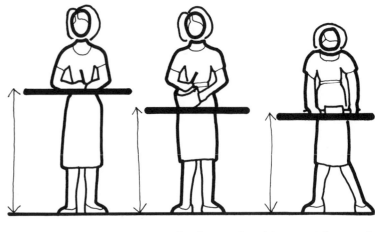

Delicate Work
100-110 cm (men)
95-105 cm (wm.)

Light Manual
90-95 cm.(men)
85-90 cm. (wm.)

Heavy Manual
75-90 cm. (men)
70-85 cm. (wm.)

Measurement device.

(Dempsey)

A procedure employed to determine the dimensions of a reaching task is illustrated in a study by C. Dempsey, who wanted to determine space requirements—maximum, minimum, and optimum—for Air Force pilots. In order to obtain this information he designed a device consisting of 10 horizontal and 5 vertical arms. When the subject adjusts the sliding arms, the actual vertical and horizontal distance from that point can be measured directly by means of a scale on the side of each arm.
(Rubin, Elder)

New York Apartment Buildings.
Photo by F. Wilson.

Space age technology has made it possible for blind people to obtain information in new ways. One development is the conversion of optical images into vibrations. The optacon (for optical-to-tactile converter) is one such device, developed at the Stanford University Electronics Laboratories. It consists of an optical camera connected to a vibrating tactile simulator. An array of 144 phototransistors controls the activation of 144 corresponding vibrating pins which reproduces the visual images. The pins can be sensed by one fingertip. The optacon has been employed in reading tasks, with moderate success. Although reading speed is considerably below that achieved with braille, it has enabled blind people to read conventional printing.

Another system relying on tactile stimulation was developed termed the Tactile Vision Substitution System. It enables blind observers to 'see' objects in the environment using a pair of 'seeing eyeglasses' which transmits images to a lightweight camera by way of a flexible fiber-optic bundle. The camera then converts the image into corresponding electronic pulses by an array of small electrodes which are in contact with the skin.

From the foregoing capsulation of the work of behaviorial scientists and researchers in the field of anthropometry, it can be seen that either man or the square and the circle must be stretched considerably to obtain a fit.

Human Factors includes problem areas ranging from the "macro" to the "micro" scale. At the macro scale is how human performance relates to an overall system. For example a problem faced by both equipment and building designers is the need to integrate manually operated controls for the best system performance. Ample, effective lighting depends upon the ability to control the quantity and quality of light where it is needed and in areas only where it is required. Consequently, area control of lighting is more desirable than a single control for a partially occupied large area. The architect or designer must determine where to place controls.

At the micro scale one major concern is the proper design of products such as furniture. Between the macro and micro scales, researchers have addressed problems of permanent and temporary features of buildings, such as determining the proper dimensions for shelves and kitchen work surfaces. The common feature in such investigations is the focus on the performance of a given activity.

Body Position and Performance

A major concern for those responsible for designing a work area is the typical position of the body when an activity is being performed either seated or standing. Methods have been employed to investigate the relationship of body position and task performance.

A Swedish report (*Anatomy for Planners*) discusses various experimental procedures used to correlate body measurements, working heights, and space measurements.

Four techniques were used to measure research height. The first involved the use of a pedometer, which placed contact plates on the hands of the experimental subject. These plates recorded the change in the distribution of body weight. The subject's task was to place both hands with the palms down on a shelf of adjustable height.

The second technique involved the use of electromyography (EMG) which measured the degree of activity in a muscle, and this in turn indicated the extent of the load on that muscle. In the case of reach height, EMG was used to measure the distribution of load on the subject's leg muscles.

In the third test, researchers asked subjects to indicate what they felt would be the most comfortable reach height. Finally, the experimenters employed stereophotography. This enabled them to photograph movement simultaneously from side, front, and rear. From these photographs it was possible to determine which joints a person used when stretching to reach high shelves and also to indicate the sequence in which the joints were active.

The results from these four measurement techniques were used to develop the following criteria set up by the experimenters: When the person tested lays the entire palm of a hand on the shelf, his or her weight should be borne equally by both feet, as it is when one stands upright in a symmetrical and relaxed posture; the person tested must not lean against the worktop; distribution of

Photo Courtesy Sikorsky Aircraft.

weight on the leg muscles must be the same as when a person stands in a symmetrical and relaxed posture; the person tested should feel that he or she reaches the shelf height being tested. The shelf height at which all these conditions are fulfilled was designated "vertical reach."

Chair design has received considerable research attention. E. Grandjean (Swiss researcher) and U. Burandt developed a sitting machine to study seating comfort. The machine allowed a great deal of variation in the shape of the seat and back rest, the height of the seat, and the height of the armrests. Instruments in the chair recorded body movements and the variations these movements produced in the pressures of the body on the seat and back rest. A questionnaire asked for an assessment of seven body postures as "uncomfortable," "indifferent," or "comfortable." Then questions asked for an assessment of individual components such as seat depth. The results indicated that the latter questioning provided a better assessment of seat comfort.

N. Diffrient (industrial designer) applied the techniques used to develop the design of aircraft seats. Physiological data on seating posture were collected by x-rays. An extremely flexible sitting-machine was developed allowing research subjects to change seat bottom and back cushions and also allowing for adjustment of recline angles, armrest positions, and seat heights. A system was devised in which small probes were placed in the seat cushions and when the cushion was depressed the probes protuded a distance comparable to the depression. A grid diagram of the body's interaction with the cushion was obtained.

To determine the desirable chair characteristics for leisure activities, Le Carpentier studied twenty subjects, 10 male and 10 female. They were required to read or watch television for several 3-hour sessions. Each subject could adjust the characteristics of the chair as desired in terms of angles and dimensions by means of manual controls. The results indicated that while subjects preferred chair settings which permitted their legs to be outstretched, female subjects were more apt to keep their legs in a vertical position.

The foregoing are but a few of the experiments and researches conducted by those involved in 'human factors' research. (Rubin and Elder 1980)

Photo by F. Wilson.

PART II

INTRODUCTION

Animals design their homes instinctively. We depend on product research. The beaver winters in the lodge he has built and the fox in the burrow he has dug. We sleep in cubicles designed and built by others. Humans, the masters of the beasts, are measured and fit into spaces as sardines in a tin. Lesser creatures, the baboon and the fish, create the structures that they wish.

People are expected to dutifully sit two feet on centers, fill rooms in an orderly fashion, and depart in sequence. Humans are fit equally in the democracy of the square and cubic foot. We are allowed so many cubic feet of air per minute to breathe, so many lumens to see, and so many square and cubic feet to sit, stand, walk, or run to the nearest exit.

People and animals are neither conceived nor born at right angles. People insist on growing two unmatched feet, a right and a left. These usually differ in size and always point in different directions. We have two hands and each acquires different skills. We have two eyes in the front of our head, both of which we do not need in this location, and no eye in the back, which would be very useful.

Our inexact haphazard measurements are fit to spaces manufactured to exact repetitive dimensions. People, in contrast to standardized modules, are made in a great many unpredictable and interesting ways. As a result no two of us are alike in any detail. We are dimensional nightmares.

If this were not bad enough we even refuse to stack efficiently. We like to be close to each other, but like porcupines, not close enough to stick or be stuck. We surround ourselves with invisible spatial boundaries and are pricked when they are invaded by others and prick back when the same is done to us. Within pricking perimeters we close our eyes as we do on crowded subways or making love.

Where do the designers exact dimensions and the very inexact people sizes meet? They certainly do not in design products called living spaces. Product design does not take into consideration the essential element of how people act in space. Designers dimension tables and chairs by averaging the height of stationary buttocks and knee caps. But our porcupine personalities are seldom considered.

The design of living space ignores how people and animals invariably have made, and do make, themselves comfortable in the world. People and creatures adjust their surroundings to fit their preferences, superstitions, taboos, scents, and customs. Such environmental adaption is part of what we have termed

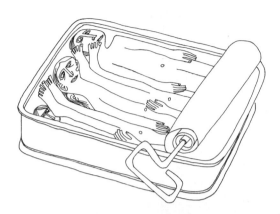

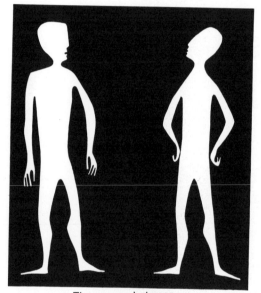

The spaces between

PERSONAL SPACE

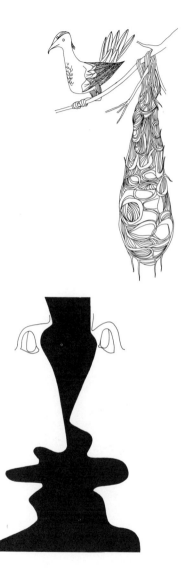

evolution, and some say that the exercise of this ability is what has made man the prime primate of the vertebrates.

The slogan that ''man'' (meaning designers) shapes buildings, then buildings shape him, is hardly accurate. Shaping to the building is the occupant's and not the building's decision. People in prison and animals in cages are not shaped by their surroundings; they escape by going out of their minds instead. We do not survive through design, as the architect Richard Neutra once claimed, but quite often survive in spite of it.

Living spaces designed as consumer products omit an essential design ingredient. The missing element is how people will choose to react in space due to their invisible boundaries and other personal, social, and cultural needs. They will not act as the designer believes they ought to act to square themselves with the square foot. Of this we can be sure.

The wealth of instinctive, conscious, and subconscious observations and decisions concerning the limits of personal, communal, and territorial space, and all of the other myriad invisible directives set for reasons we only partially comprehend are seldom part of official design decisions. Human personalities are much too complex for even an instrument as marvelous as the computer to solve, for even it can only make decisions based on a simple binary yes or no. The computer, for all of its complexity cannot program a simple maybe, which is after all, the most common of all human decisions. The only successful fit designed that users do not change is the coffin.

What follows is a tool to aid users and designers, which is all of us, to think about porcupines in space. It is an assemblage of what we have learned about customs, taboos, rituals, preferences, and spatial happenings. Information has been gathered wherever it could be found. Ideas have been assembled with a pack rat's lack of discrimination. Some might be immediately useful, others, bright shiny ideas that catch the mind's eye, may not really prove that valuable at all. All the answers are not here. This is only the beginning of putting such ideas together in a form that will be accessible to designers and those designed upon. Once we think of spaces built around us in terms of how they are actually used, we will construct other patterns from personal experience and observation and will correct the ones illustrated here. We may even find that we cannot design one kind of space but must design spaces that do not obstruct and that encourage instead of direct, and this is an entirely different kind of idea from those we have pursued before.

Most of what follows is presented graphically because drawings and photographs combined with words cover a wider range of ideas, interpretations, and associations. They are meant to jog and stimulate your imagination. Robert Ardrey once wrote that man is only an animal with a very thin layer of veneer between him and the animals he dominates. This may be true, for no one can deny the similarity between man's and animals' assertions of territoriality and their use of personal and communal space. The two are much too consistently similar to ignore.

Creature nests, cacoons, burrows, and dens fit their occupants very well. Living spaces when designed for us by others seldom do. We should not be too proud therefore to learn from dogs, rats, humming birds, and each other. We need all of the help we can get in the painful task of making ourselves comfortable in this world and it does not matter where it comes from, whether it be from a master mason or a mongoose.

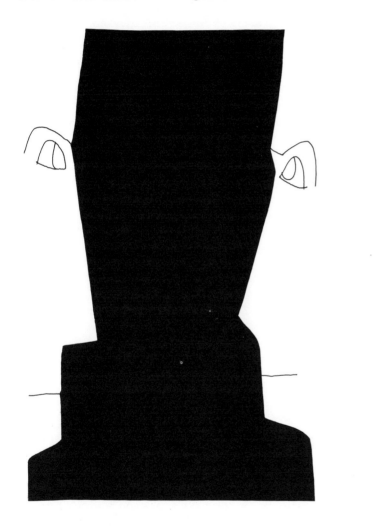

HISTORIC PERSPECTIVE

The discipline of psychology was developed to respond to questions such as:

- why do people perceive the world as they do,
- what role does experience play in our lives,
- what influences people to make favorable or unfavorable judgments about their environment?

The procedures developed by those researching these questions consist of a variety of measurement methods traceable to work first performed in the 18th and 19th centuries.

Both social scientists and architects work with problems difficult to categorize because they both seek to satisfy human requirements that respond to environments consciously and subconsciously. Some of these responses are tangible, readily defined, such as protection from fire, clean water, pure air, and protection from contagion. But others are based in the emotions and aesthetic responses that resist exact definition.

The diverse origins of present day psychology can be traced to the approaches used in the past to study psychological phenomena. They ranged from philosophical speculation to classical scientific analytical experiments. Recently, new techniques have been developed to augment traditional methods, as the traditional approaches have proved inadequate to explain many phenomena.

Some of the issues that have interested psychology since its origins and have also influenced architectural design are:

- how do humans become aware of their environment,
- what are the relationships between thought and emotion,
- in what ways are individuals similar, and what ways different,
- what commonalities exist among species, including man?

To seek answers to these questions psychological researchers have followed two major approaches. One is the traditional scientific approach based on analytic experimental procedures and the other is a 'unitary' approach that treats humans as complete entities.

The classical scientific approach is analytic. It controls all variables except the one being examined. The 'independent' variable is then systematically manipulated and measurements made on another variable termed the 'dependent' variable. After sufficient experiments have been made a mathematical model of the phenomena is developed to enable predictions to be made regarding the nature and extent of the influence of the independent variable on the dependent variable.

Physiological research, using this classical approach, has been and continues to be an important contributor to the discipline of psychology. Physiological research seeks a biological basis to explain environmental response. It measures the relationship between the structure of the body and the way that it functions. Psychology has been closely associated with the classical physiological tradition investigating how the sensory processes of man operate.

Psychophysical research was developed to explore the relationships between physical stimuli, such as the intensity of light, and the sensory perception of them, such as brightness, by the individual. The goal has been to find objective, quantitative information regarding sensory experiences. This research uses experimental subjects controlled to function as pure measuring devices, untainted by subjective judgments and opinions.

The validity of classical research methods and its findings were challenged when problems arose and responses were discovered that could not be solved or explained using classical analytic methods. Researchers in both physiological and psychophysical 'sensory' studies challenged classical research procedures and the assumptions associated with the research approaches.

Rene Descartes (1596-1650) was concerned with the relationship of the mind and the body. He speculated that the mind and body interacted at the pineal gland at the base of the brain. Descartes relied on the empirical approach used by scientists. He dissected parts of the body to observe them in detail in an effort to learn how the nervous system operated.

Gottfried Wilhelm von Leibnitz (1646-1716) held that the human body was born with a system of complex and interrelated elements termed "monads," fundamental activities which appeared while the person matured. In a sense, the monad can be termed a perceptual element incapable of further analysis. Leibnitz addressed two problems of psychological research: the importance of innate characteristics and the limitations of the traditional analytic approach to research.

Immanual Kant (1724-1804) speculated that the human 'mind' is predisposed to perceive in a certain way. For example, spatial relationships are perceived as they are because perceptual ordering is a psychological necessity. This view point, elaborated by later researchers, constituted a major alternative to the analytic procedures of classical scientific research. The rationale for phenomenological, Gestalt, and other present day perceptual researches can be traced to the work of Kant.

Sigmund Freud (1856-1939) was trained as a neurophysiologist, but could not explain behavioral symptoms for ailments, such as hysteria, on the basis of physiological findings alone. He consequently developed alternative methods of interpreting behavior. These interpretations considered the patient's entire life experience and were qualitative and subjective.

The phenomenological and gestalt movements in psychology rejected the analytic approach as unapplicable to behavioral research. The pioneer gestalt scientists developed research methods quite different from those traditionally used. They emphasized qualitative rather than quantitative findings and relied on demonstrations which everyone could experience.

The two approaches were often closely interrelated and exercised influence on each other. When one predominated, the other developed alternatives. For example, the Gestalt emphasis on an integrated approach based on immediate and naive perceptions was evolved as a reaction to the analytic procedures developed by psychophysicists seeking to analyze the elements of sensation and perception.

Current behavioral research is traced to traditions in both philosophy and science, which until quite recently were one and the same activity.

Traditionally, philosophical research has asked how does the inner world of man interact with the outside world? There have always been two major, opposing viewpoints. The first is that people are basically programmed in a way that ensures their ability to live effectively in the world. The other is that people are born with the potential for learning, and life experiences provide the learning process for survival and accomplishment.

Rudolph Herman Lotze (1817-1881) indicated that the mind has an inherent capacity to arrange sensory content spatially, even though that content is not inherently spatial. Or if this idea were phrased differently, perceived space is derived from conscious data which is itself not spatial. This concept had a direct important influence on the Gestalt movement.

Thomas Hobbes (1588-1679) postulated that people learn by association, that is, by associated sense impressions when two conditions come together either in space or time. The association is strengthened when the conditions are repeated. For example, when we say grass we think the color green because we repeatedly experience the visual sensation of green grass.

John Locke (1632-1704) carried Hobbes position further. He claimed a newborn infant's mind was blank; and it therefore followed that all knowledge is gained from experience. Ideas, Locke said, are the elements of experience, which an analysis of the mind reveals. The mind can be analyzed in terms of elements called ideas.

James Mill (1773-1836) claimed that ideas and sensations are the raw material of the mind. Knowledge begins with sensations and is then transformed into larger units capable of analysis into elements. For example, a brick is a complex idea, mortar another complex idea. These ideas together with ideas of position and quantity compose the idea of the wall.

John Stuart Mill (1806-1873) argued that many elements may generate complex ideas, but that these are more than the sum of individual parts. For example, if we add blue and yellow pigments together we obtain green which would not be predicted from each of the constituent elements. Stuart Mill stressed the need for direct experimentation rather than speculation to learn man's characteristics.

Present day psychology is also related to that branch of physiology that sought to understand the functioning of the brain, nervous system, and sensory modalities, and their interaction. Some of the early researchers and their method of findings are recorded here.

THE HARD ON DOGS SCHOOL

Marshall Hall (1790-1857) is said to be the forerunner of physiological psychology. He observed animals after decapitation and recorded that their movements continued when appropriate stimulation was provided. Hall concluded that there are several layers of behavior; voluntary, brain (cerebrum); reflex, spinal cord; involuntary, muscles; respiratory, brain (medulla).

Pierre Fluorens (1794-1870) continued the work of Hall but concentrated on the brain still connected to the body. He removed areas of the animal's brain to determine the effects on behavior. One major area at a time was removed assuming that each part had separate and independent functions. He found that brain structures were closely related to particular sensory and motor functions.

G. Fritsche (1838-1927) and I. Hitzig (1838-1907) applied electrical stimulation to the cerebral cortex of a dog as an independent variable to identify the motor areas within the brain. Movements of the body and limbs were considered the dependent variables. This work led to further studies resulting in the detailed mapping of the motor centers of a variety of animals.

Charles Bell (1774-1842) and Francois Magendle (1783-1855) contributed to the tradition of psychology by systematically severing the nerves of experimental animals to determine the effects on motor movement. They discovered that sensory and motor nerves are both anatomically and functionally separate in the spinal cord.

Paul Broca (1824-1880) has been identified historically as the originator of clinical 'symptomatic' study of brain functioning. Dr. Broca treated a patient for many years who could not speak but was normal in every other respect. When the patient died an autopsy revealed a brain lesion which was the cause of the speech impairment.

M. Sechenov (1829-1905), studying reflex behavior, demonstrated that when salt was placed on the cut end of the spinal cord, spinal reflexes were inhibited. He also identified an inhibitory center in the brain and argued that all thinking and intelligence depended on stimulation and that all acts of conscious and unconscious life are reflexes.

Ivan Pavlov (1849-1936) was influenced by the earlier work of Sechenov in his studies of reflexes. Pavlov operated on dogs to bring the digestive secretion ducts to the surface of their bodies so that secretions could be seen and measured. He observed that digestive juices flow when an animal anticipates food. From this grew the technique of conditioned reflex from the observation of the flow of gastric and intestinal juices.

Wilhelm Wundt (1832-1920) is considered the founder of experimental psychology because he was the first to introduce the idea of psychology as an independent science. Wundt's research was a logical extension of the philosophy of John Stuart Mill. He declared the problem of psychology to be:

- the analysis of conscious processes into elements,
- determination of the manner of connection of these elements, and
- determination of their laws of connection.

The goal of analytic psychology is the analysis of mind into simple qualities and the determination of the form of their ordered multiplicity. Wundt explored the areas of sensation and perception with special emphasis on vision. He studied color, form, size perception, optical illusions, binocular vision, and perceived movement.

GESTALT

The study of complex visual phenomena is attributed to the gestalt movement in psychology. These psychologists supported the argument that an analytic approach was not applicable to the study of human behavior, as had been proposed by Leibnitz and Kant.

Gestalt psychologists favored a dynamic interpretation of behavior. People, they contended, respond to their environments as entities. If analytical methods are used that isolate one facet of this, response then both the study and the reaction are deformed. They argued that people respond to the environment in an integrated way and that an integrated, 'global,' 'holistic' study of behavior was therefore necessary.

The Gestalt movement concentrated its observations on the naive everyday response of people. For example, a range of visual phenomena such as optical illusions were and still are known and recognized by laymen and researchers. However, sensory psychologists could neither measure nor quantify these phenomena with the analytic tools at their disposal.

The origins of Gestalt psychology are therefore similar to that of psychoanalysis. Researchers were faced with a problem that could not be solved using the methods available at that time. They therefore formulated an alternative hypothesis and research approach. The Gestalt psychologists initiated and carried on the first systematic investigation of such phenomena as optical illusions and proposed theoretical formulations to account for them.

Max Wertheimer (1880-1943) is generally credited as the founder of Gestalt psychology. He broke with the past because his findings in perceptual organization and apparent movement involved an insight which questioned the very research framework assumed by his predecessors. The study of apparent movements led him and other Gestaltists to reject the classical analytic research approach to perceptual phenomena. The methodology Wertheimer employed followed classical principles, but the findings could not be explained by this theoretical framework.

Franz Brentano (1836–1917) provided a philosophical explanation for the appearance of illusions. He argued that physical phenomena are 'acts.' When one sees a color, the color itself is not mental. It is the act of seeing that is mental. There is no meaning to seeing unless something is seen. The act always implies an object, that is refers to a content.

Erich Jaensch (1883–1940) addressed the problem of depth perception. He discussed phenomenology in terms of empty space and its "psychic" representation. Jaensch was interested in constancy phenomena, that is, when characteristics of objects such as size and color do not appear to change when there are changes in the physical world that 'should' lead to such perceptual changes. (Rubin and Elder 1980)

REVOLUTIONS IN BEHAVIORAL THINKING AND MODERN ARCHITECTURE

Sigmund Freud's psychoanalytic theory appears as the first formal theory of personality, and has been by far the most influential since its proposal. It has been as authoritative as the theories of truth to material and functionalism have been to modern architecture.

Briefly Freud's theories dealt with a concept of the unconscious mind based on the study of memories, wishes, and fears revealed through free association. Psychoanalysis, a method of analyzing psychic phenomena is a therapeutic process that attempts to raise material that affect behavior from the subconscious to the conscious mind of the patient.

Freud used the technique of free association, remembered dreams, jokes, and accidents to identify unconscious conflicts. He proposed a universal theory of personality. This in its all embracing concept is similar to the attempts of modern artists such as Kandinsky to create nonobjective symbols from which a universally comprehensible art could be fashioned.

Freud's theory held that human personality consisted of three interacting agencies: the id, the ego and the superego. The id was a pool of biological drives, or instincts born with the infant divided between Eros, the life instinct generated by the libido, and Thanatos, the death instinct. The id's devotion to the immediate reduction of tension was termed the pleasure principle. The id also served as energy source for the ego and superego.

The ego, Freud held, developed in the child after six months and acted as the executive agency of personality mediating at first between the id and reality and later, when it was developed, between the id and superego. The ego controlled the individual's actions and manipulated the environment according to reality based on the organism's concern for safety.

The superego, Freud claimed, acted as the personality's conscience and was concerned with the pursuit of moral goals. It emerges as the child internalizes the moral standards of the parent of its own sex. Superego impels the individual, not toward realistic goals, but toward the ego ideal of moral perfection.

Freud believed nearly all human behavior was directed toward resolving inner conflicts and restoring equilibrium to the personality. He conceived instincts as possessing characteristic features, a source, an aim, an object, and an impetus which remained constant throughout the person's life.

Repression, fixation, regression, projection, and the decisive role of infancy and childhood in determining a person's basic personality structure were Freud's contribution to this first formal theory of personality.

Those that agreed with and worked with Freud and later diverging from his original formulations built upon them and contributed to and enlarged the Freudian heritage. Alfred Adler's individual psychology emphasized the drive toward perfection as the highest motivation of human beings. Karen Horney believed that motivation and conflict were based on social factors. Eric Fromm evolved a theory of personality based on interpersonal relationships set in a historical context. Erik Erickson's theory was that personality development was a lifelong process. All these enlarged the first formal theory of personality.

Accompanying the Freudian development was the Gestalt school of psychology that interpreted phenomena as organized wholes rather than as aggregates of distinct parts maintaining that the whole is more than the sum of its parts. The movement was begun in Germany and later transferred to the United States in the 1930s. The term Gestalt was coined by Charles von Ehrenfelds in 1890, and after 1895 investigation was carried out along lines suggested by him. In 1912, the movement was given further impetus by Max Wertheimer, Wolfgang Kohler, and Kurt Koffka.

Two basic laws were derived from early experimentation: that of membership character, which states that each element of a pattern, through a dynamic participation, alters its individuality in becoming a constituent of the whole; and that concerning the dynamic attribute of self-fulfillment in all structured wholes, which allows, for instance, small gaps in a drawn figure to be disregarded (closure). The body-mind problem is solved by proposing a structural correspondence between the sensory process and the corresponding extrasensory mental process.

The theories of Freud and Gestalt have become as much a part of our accepted stock of behavioral ideas as the ideas of the Bauhaus, Le Corbusier, and De Stijl which we lump together and call the modern movement in architecture. Both were developed during roughly the same period of time and the modern movement has become the folklore of architects and designers. Both are today either accepted or reacted against. But either, for or against, they occupy firm places in historic dogma.

At the time that Freud broke with traditional psychological experimentation and theories and he and his associates were developing the concepts of the subconscious mind, and Wertheimer and his associates were arriving at a holistic approach to phenomena, architects and artists were proclaiming seemingly analogous goals. They also proposed a universal design theory that they hoped would be universally comprehensible.

Walter Gropius stated in 1919 in the founding manifesto of the Bauhaus goals not unlike Wertheimer's 'holistic approach':

"The ultimate aim of all visual arts in the complete building! To embellish buildings was once the noblest function of the fine arts; they were the indispensible components of great architecture. Today the arts exist in isolation, from which they can be rescued only through the conscious co-operative effort of all craftsmen. Architects, painters, and sculptors must recognize anew and learn to grasp the composite character of a building both as an entity and in its separate parts. Only then will their work be imbued with the artistic spirit which is lost as 'salon art'." (Conrads 1964, p. 49)

Gropius claimed that the schools of art could not produce this unity since art cannot be taught. Art must be merged once more with the workshop, just as Freud wanted the unconscious processes to merge into self-conscious action in free association. As Freud claimed the primitive biological urges cannot be suppressed, Gropius declared that the irrepressible creativity of the crafts must merge into a work of architecture.

Wertheimer developed a theory of critical phenomena to demonstrate general principles of perceptual comprehension at the same time Kandinsky was teaching at the Bauhaus and writing *The Point, Line, and Plane*. Many of their findings are strikingly similar, as you have seen in the first section of this book.

The stimuli studied by Wertheimer are not limited in terms of scale, the groupings might be buildings, objects in a room, people, or abstract symbols. Kandinsky used concepts of engineering force, heat, cold, and sound to explain his formal nonobjective theories.

"The Bauhaus strives to bring together all creative effort into one whole, to reunify all the disciplines of practical art, sculpture, paintings, handicrafts, and the crafts, as inseparable components of a new architecture. The ultimate, if distinct, aim of the Bauhaus is the unified work of art, the great structure, in which there is no distinction between monumental and decorative art," said Gropius in his manifesto. (Conrads 1964)

Art and the subconscious motivations of a people cannot be taught, but the crafts can, just as one can, through analysis, understand and direct one's self. Architects, painters, and sculptors are craftsmen, said Gropius. He therefore required a thorough training in the crafts be acquired in workshops and on experimental and practical sites by all students as the indispensible basis for all artistic production. Gropius saw the crafts as the subconscious energy of Freud's id to be managed by the architect's superego.

The De Stijl manifesto V of 1923 declared, "By breaking up enclosing elements (walls, etc.) we have eliminated the duality of interior and exterior." Freudians were at the time bringing the interior subconscious and exterior conscious into a harmonic equilibrium.

Although there is now a good deal of doubt about the wisdom of Corbusier's city planning, as there is about Freud's sexual theories, Corbusier held that the plan, as the diagram of human action, was the essence of the building.

The plan, declared Corbusier, was the generating principle of architecture, at least this is what he declared it to be in 1920.

"The plan is the generator.

Without a plan, you have lack of order and willfulness.

The plan holds in itself the essence of sensation.

The great problems of tomorrow, dictated by collective necessities, put the question of 'plan' in new form.

Modern life demands, and is waiting for, a new kind of plan, both for the house and for the city." (Conrads 1964, p. 60)

Theo Van Doesberg agreed with this idea he wrote in *Towards a Plastic Architecture* in 1924 that the ground plan of the new architecture "has opened the walls and so done away with the separation of inside and outside. The walls themselves no longer support; they merely provide supporting points. The result is a new, open ground plan entirely different from the classical one, since inside and outside now pass over into one another."

This striving for equilibrium between inside and outside space occurred at the time the Freudians were analyzing the conflict between life and death instincts, love and hate, creativity and destructiveness, and the urge to satisfy primitive instincts and yet obey the rules of society which insist that our instinctual desires be restrained and rechanneled in socially acceptable ways.

To determine whether a case can be made for a linkage between the revolution of the study of the personality and behavioral studies and modern art and architecture needs much more examination than this cursory bringing together and perhaps stretching for similarities. However both occurred at the same time in history as part of the 'zeitgeist' of the time and must therefore have influenced each other. Freud, Gestalt, Gropius, De Stijl, and Corbusier are names associated with vital ideas lasting from the turn of the century well through World War II and beyond; even though these proud beginnings of the study of the human mind and a desire to reshape the world into 'radiant cities' more often than not ended in aberrations such as industrial psychology and bleak housing projects.

WHERE WE ARE NOW

"Very few architects stand a real chance of becoming successful free-lance practitioners. . . .it means that the employed architect in the big office will become increasingly specialized, seeing less and less of the entire field of practice and of the clients themselves. Second it implies that more and more of his clients are themselves corporate entities—big business, big institutions, big government." These words of James Marston Fitch appeared in *The Architectural Manipulation of Space, Time, and Gravity* (Fitch 1970). They surprised very few poeple. He had said them before and the same message had been published in a number of architectural periodicals from the 1960s onward.

The implications were that the architect's legal client was less and less his real client. The white collar worker in the big skyscraper, the blue collar worker in the large manufacturing plant, the housewife in the housing project, and the child in the consolidated school are the people ultimately affected by the architect's design. And it has been said that it is to them that the architect is ultimately responsible. Buildings should be sensitively designed for human perception and response. Yet the architect today seldom sees those who will live in, respond to, and use the spaces the architect designs.

"It cannot be assumed that these corporate or institutional clients, acting though they may be as legal agents for the consuming public, are always to be relied upon to represent its best interests or optimal requirements. In a profit-motivated society, criteria for architectural projects are all too apt to approach the minimal permitted by building codes or the law of supply and demand. Of course, this tendency will vary from field to field," Fitch declared.

It is obvious that under these conditions the building consumer is unable to effectively express his or her demands, requirements, and expectations. The condition is further complicated by the fact that the architect's isolation from the real users of the design leads inevitably to the abstract, the formal, and the platitudinous in architectural and urban design.

The architect's cultural orientation, by the very nature of his work has always been associated more with the rich than with the common folk. His services are admittedly less imperative for ordinary people than the services of his fellow professionals, the doctor and the lawyer.

There was a tradition, a very short tradition, of the socially conscious, intellectually committed architect in the United States. It was apparent during the great depression of the 1930s and was resurrected again, briefly, during the years of the "counter culture." However the main thrust of architectural education and architectural practice is directed toward satisfying corporate, institutional, and government clients with as high as 80 to 90 percent of architectural commissions awarded by speculative entrepreneurial developers.

Mountainside squatter houses overlooking Rio De Janeiro.
Photo courtesy of Gilda and Vic Bonardi.

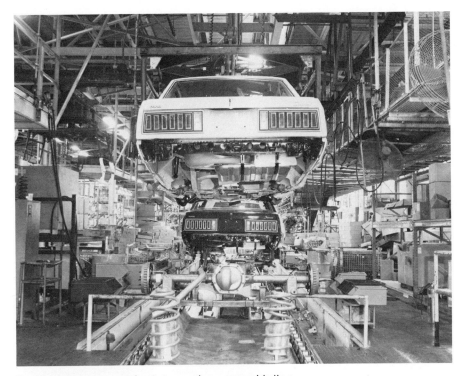

Ford body being lowered onto rear axle on assembly line.
Photo courtesy of Ford Motor Co.

From *Geometrical Design* by Jean Larcher, Dover Books, 1974.

There are some notable exceptions. Men like John Turner who worked in the barriadas of South America, John Habraken who sought to find a way to satisfy human choice within the matrix of architectural and industrial production, Yona Friedmann who proposed a 'scientific architecture' of choice, Martin Pawley, Gernot Minke, Michael Reynolds, Shiu Kay Kan, and Whitold Rybczynski whose proposal for a "Garbage Architecture" would place the tools and the means of building into the hands of the users. There are others of this persuasion, but they are seldom mentioned in the mainstream of 'architectural activity,' the ironically termed 'cutting edge' of architectural art. The major thrust of architectural practice is toward spaces for anonymous users as demanded by institutional and corporate clients.

The behavioral scientists fare little better. Their researches are subsidized by the same institutional and corporate clients that retain architects. Behavioral information is uneven in respect to quality or accessibility. Studies are generally performed to respond to specific problems. As a consequence they have little general applicability. Furthermore, in all too many instances, the information developed in behavioral studies is difficult to evaluate because the research procedures, according to the scientists themselves, have not been adequately documented. Since these very procedures distinguish scientific research from casual observation the questionable quality of much of behavioral data is not surprising.

If we can assume that agreement exists among architects and behavioral scientists that the crucial problem of our time is the adaption of humankind to their built environment, we have at least the beginning of a solution for we know for certain from past experience what does not work.

The most striking feature of the information sought is the breadth of its interest. Relevant information can come from the physiological, psychological, cultural, and social attributes of the interaction of people and their surroundings. This encompasses almost the whole wide world and fairly outlines the requirements of building users.

Many disciplines can contribute toward a better understanding of these relationships. The design problem being investigated will dictate the proper approach. The one major attribute that the disciplines share is the employment of scientific methods in collecting data, but this is only part of the problem. We must learn to search in a larger realm, to include and take seriously much that is not presently considered scientific, such as the intuition and insights of artists. But perhaps the most important is to respect the great store of information and that is provided by the reactions of the users themselves. This is an effort to combine the insights of behavioral researcher, the designer, and that ultimate receiver, the anonymous person who uses the world specified by researcher and designer.

THE METHODS

Design professionals retain consultants such as engineers and other specialists to ensure the adequacy of a building from the standpoint of safety and health. The availability of appropriate data may be traced to the ability of researchers to identify and measure the important parameters of materials, built elements, and building subsystems, and relate them to building performance. While these measurable elements of the built environment have received considerable attention, human behavior in relation to them has not. We know very little about how people act in emergency although we are fairly certain about the attributes of flame spread of various materials.

The quality of scientific information depends on the consistency and relevance of observations made by researchers in the study area. Researchers who employ standard methods, observing similar phenomena will obtain equivalent data. "Hard" sciences can be differentiated from "soft" sciences in terms of their ability to obtain such reproducible findings.

Moreover hard sciences, because of the objectivity inherent in most observations, can make quantitative statements about their observations, i.e., they use sophisticated measurements which enable scientists to employ mathematical techniques to develop conceptual models of the phenomena. These models are an integral part of the research process of formulating hypotheses which are then tested by collecting experimental data.

There remains one problem. Things that can be quantified and put into mathematical models are not necessarily the most important in terms of humankind's relation to the built world around it. The hard sciences perhaps have the most sure methods, but the "soft" sciences become involved with the most important questions, in terms of human behavior in the built environment.

Researchers do not conduct their studies in a theoretical vacuum. Even researchers who conduct studies for the most pragmatic purposes, such as solving a particular design problem, make assumptions about the likely effect of design features on the way people act. These assumptions, when taken together, constitute a conceptual or theoretical model.

PARAMETRIC MODELS

The elusive search for objectivity in behavioral studies has led some researchers to develop Stimulus-Response models, which eliminate in their minds the need to be concerned about differences among people. Behavior (response, R) is explained solely in terms of environmental (stimulus, S) conditions. This model, if successful, would be ideal for architects. It infers that the behavior of people is determined by the nature of their surroundings.

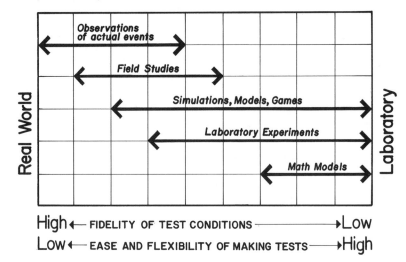

Fidelity and flexibility of test techniques
(after Van Cott)

A very convenient concept says that if the architect wants people to act in a particular way all that is necessary is to design a building appropriately. Unfortunately, the stimulus-response model has proven to be far too simplistic to deal with the behavior of people because it fails to account for the characteristics which make people differ from one another. It further implies that people have no control over their destinies. The history of the world should have put this myth to rest long before the R/S methodology arrived in a laboratory.

A classical behavioral research model which attempts to deal with differences among individuals is termed the stimulus (S), organism (O), and response (R) approach. Briefly, the behavior of organisms such as people or animals is explained in terms of characteristics of the outside world.

Behavior (R) is explained in terms of an environmental feature (S) which affects a person (O) in a particular way. Although the model was developed to explore individual behavior, it readily lends itself to categorizing many of the variables in the relationships between humans and their environment. Assuming, of course, that (O) is sufficiently simple to justify the conclusion.

The stimulus/response and stimulus/organism/response models of behavior are basically analytic in that the research goal is to determine cause/effect relationships between independent stimulus and dependent response variables, while controlling differences among individuals (O) by means of the design of the experiment.

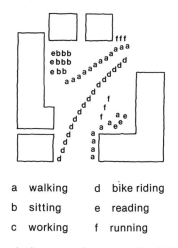

a walking   d bike riding

b sitting   e reading

c working   f running

An activity analysis approach was used by R. Hester (architect) in several studies. In one study, members of his design team observed and recorded behaviors taking place in a schoolyard. A form was developed as a means of recording the frequency with which activities occurred, and the people participating in them. The data were then analyzed by developing a map which indicated the intensity of use in the various schoolyard locations.

Site plan of courtyard—after Hester drawing.
(Rubin 1980, p. 31)

At this point one is reminded of the famous 'Harvard Law of Animal Response,' which says that, "in precisely controlled laboratory conditions an animal will do as it 'damned' pleases."

THE STIMULUS (ENVIRONMENTAL)

S. Stevens (psychophysicist) examined the problem with another approach. He postulated that, in a sense, only one problem must be solved in psychology and that was to define the stimulus. He expressed the reason: "The complete definition of the stimulus to a given response involves the specification of all the transformations of the environment, both internal and external, that leave the response invariant. This specification of the condition of invariance would entail, of course, a complete understanding of the factors that produce and alter response. It is easy enough, of course, to decide upon arbitrary definitions of "stimulus objects" (e.g., a given pattern of lines, a quantity of luminous flux, an acoustic waveform, etc.), but the question is: What properties of these objects do the stimulating? Viewed in this fashion, it is evident that for no response have we yet given a complete definition of stimulus. At best we have

only partially determined the conditions and limits of invariance." In an attempt to disentangle this multitude of double negatives we might say simply that we could solve the problem if we knew the answer, which we do not.

Stevens illustrated the point by examining the well researched area of hearing. Under what conditions do people perceive a particular pitch? Can the frequency of a sound be changed without any change in pitch perception? (Yes, within limits.) Can the phase be changed with similar lack of results? (Yes, also within limits). Stevens then goes on to state that the effects on pitch perception of many other parameters having potential importance, such as waveform power spectrum and duration, are simply not known. We therefore know very little about the "stimulus" which produces pitch sensations. Moreover, when we examine complex responses such as attitudes and preferences or a sense of privacy and territoriality, even less is known about the conditions which produce these responses.

The not very helpful Stevens then notes that in one way or another we are constantly guessing the physical values of relations of stimuli. That is, we know a subjective impression which is used to predict the result expected if objective measurements are made. For example, we may try to judge the size of objects within a room or the length of a corridor, rather than actually measure them.

Stevens concluded that if we had sufficient information about environmental stimulus and its relationships to the person, then the work of psychologists and researchers generally would be completed. Unfortunately, the "if" is prodigious. Stevens has rather ingeniously told us what we already suspected: We can measure only very simple things in environmental response, and most of the time a good guess is sufficient.

CORRELATION MODEL

It is not surprising to find that many researchers have concluded that the complex problems that concern them cannot be solved using the traditional analytic approaches. Instead, an alternative method has been advanced. This is to find the degree of relationship between the variables being examined without making cause and effect statements.

For example, if we wish to test the hypothesis that library design should maximize window area we would determine if the tables near the windows are used more than others. We would, by observing existing library usage, determine the relationship between proximity to windows and usage. If we assume that usage and nearness to windows are highly correlated, that is, the closer to the window, the more likely the table was to be occupied, we might conclude that library seating arrangements should take this factor into account. This recommendation might be plausible even though we had no idea as to why people were seated as they were. The reason might be due to one or more window characteristics, but other explanations are possible such as territoriality, privacy, lighting levels, or other factors. Explaining why these results occurred may or may not be important depending on the reason for conducting the study. For the designer the fact that it did occur, is sufficient. The researcher would want a more complete explanation.

The psychologist R. Barker has been involved in developing a theoretical method of dealing with the psychological environment, i.e., the world as it is perceived by a person as related to the ecological environment. The latter he defines as the real life setting within which people behave. He has been the major proponent of ecological psychology, which emphasizes the need to study human behavior in a realistic setting with all of its complexities. By describing the environment in which behavior takes place, Barker hopes to better understand the relationship between a specific environment or setting and the behavior occurring in it.

In defining the subject matter of ecological psychology he claims it is necessary to identify the natural units of the phenomenon studied. The nature of the units with which ecology deals is the same whether they are physical, social biological, or behavior units. That is they occur without feedback from the investigator; they are self-generated. Each unit has a time-space locus and an unbroken boundary separates an internal pattern from a different external pattern.

Such units are towns, schools, class meetings, and baseball games; and Barker uses the term behavior setting to describe them. These settings provided a basis for describing and measuring the extent, the variety, and the behavior output of the environment, and the relations between its extent and its output. Behavior settings were recorded as entities with a variety of properties that can be directly observed and measured.

Apparently Barker conceded the impossibility of measuring the complexities and variations of one individual in relation to the environment or the nuances of meaning and differences of the environment in relation to the individual; if both stimulus (S) and organism (O) were too complex to measure then perhaps by measuring a great number of O's under S conditions that could not be influenced by the presence of the researcher, something might be learned.

The following are some of the 'behavior setting attributes' studied by Barker:

1 . Geographical locus (location in space)
2. Occurrence (number of days a year)
3. Duration (numbers of hours a year)
4. Population (total number of different persons involved in a year)
5. Functional position of inhabitants (level of involvement by participants)

6 . Action patterns (arbitrary, such as, aesthetic, governmental, educational, social, religious, etc.)
7. Behavior mechanisms (affective, gross motor, manipulation, verbal, thinking)
8. Pressure (degree to which population subgroups are encouraged to enter and participate)
9. Autonomy (degree to which behavior setting is subject to external influence)
10. Welfare (degree to which needs of various groups are met)

Barker conducted a field study to validate and further explore his theoretical concepts. The researchers documented behavior settings and their characteristics for an agricultural town in Kansas. The town with a population of 11,000 was studied for one year and various data obtained to further Barker's development of his theory. (Barker 1968)

A Norwegian researcher, D. Aas, said this in relation to the practical application of Barker's work: "The insight provided by the theory makes it possible to better grasp the meaning of activity. The theory stresses that the environment is part of the activities and that activity is a vital part of the environment. Furthermore, stress is put on the dimension of time: Behavior and activity are segments of time and can be seen as sequences and strings of related actions."

Mr. Aas states that S and O are related on a large scale and these relationships can be studied over time. He conducted behavior setting research in a Norwegian town which looked at sociocultural activities and attempted to identify the types of facilities needed for these activities. From his research Aas was able to determine: (1) the number of organizations sponsoring activities; (2) the number of general types of activities throughout the year; (3) the total number of events taking place; and (4) the average duration of the events. Not much more in all than would have been collected by assembling the programs and newspaper accounts. (Aas 1975)

From this data Aas then calculated the average time per person spent on sociocultural activities. With all of this information it was possible to draw several conclusions concerning the activity studies. Recommendations could be made on the adequacy of existing facilities, on the scheduling of events, and on the population's interest in these events. In Barker's terms, Aas looked at the occurrence, duration, population, and occupancy time associated with a behavior setting (sociocultural event) within a particular millieu (the Norwegian town studied). The end result was that changes in the environment, buildings, could be then specified safely and surely.

OTHER BEHAVIORAL DESIGN MODELS

Other sets of models applicable to and used in behavioral research are briefly described here in terms of their function.

Descriptive models—The prime function is to portray the relationships that are seen to exist. For instance, models of circulation movement showing the relationship of corridor and elevator dimensions to flow capacity, or structural equations showing the relationship of shape and dimension of members to stress and deflection. Most research findings produce descriptive models of this kind. The two mentioned examples are of course normal procedure in building design and have been for a number of years, since elevators were invented and since the practice of mathematical calculation was introduced into building.

Predictive models—Given a set of relationships such as the descriptive models recounted above, if one variable can be predicted and the relationship is proven, then the other variable(s) can be predicted. For example, given an elevator size and speed, the waiting time, under specified arrival patterns, can be predicted. Air-conditioning loads have been predicted in this way for various configurations of buildings for some time.

Decision models—From a set of predictive models or alternate solutions a solution must be chosen. This requires the use of a criterion. When this is done analytically, to derive an optimum, by such tendencies as linear programming for instance, the optimization procedure involves building a decision model.

With the description of decision-making models, which have been common procedure in building for some time, we will now return to the major concern, that of observing and measuring the building user, for which we have not found many workable answers to up to this juncture.

OBSERVATIONAL APPROACHES

We might ask ourself at this point, what is meant by observation in behavioral studies? The word covers characteristics and measurements of the environment and the activities of the individual, whether recorded by an experimenter, a subject, or by instruments. "Observation" used in the broadest sense applies to what is being examined in any form.

The environment under study must be described and/or measured in 'usable terms' if we are to make progress in determining its effects on the behavior of building occupants. The big if is 'usable terms.' This may be very different for the behavioral scientist, the engineer, and the artist or architect.

However, since this description is posed for psychologists, not physical scientists or engineers, its emphasis is on people, the raw material of their work. Since their main concern is the person, psychologists feel that physical scientists should not be the only ones to decide which physical attributes of the environment are to be observed and measured. For example in noise research, acoustic measurements are often made because the state-of-the-art makes such measurements possible and not because people respond to the attributes being measured. The behavioral scientist should be capable of deciding the importance of behavioral research on a general comparative scale. But if one will recall, the behavioral scientists themselves have been accused of only measuring that which is measurable and leaving harder to quantify but more important aspects of human behavior unexamined. The question of who should make this decision—engineer, behavioral researcher, or architect—lies very close to the heart of the problem.

Methods of making observations can be decided from the viewpoint of the level of disturbance of natural behaviors being examined, for example, the extent to which an activity in an environment is disrupted by the presence of the researchers and their recording and measuring instruments. Observational approaches need highly trained and sensitized experimenters who can make relatively unbiased observations and measurements as inconspicuously as possible.

At the beginning of a study, while defining the problem, the researcher may want to play the role of a passive observer striving not to intrude and thus alter or disturb the environment.

In a classroom, for example, the presence of the observer might affect the performance of the teacher and the students. As a passive observer, the researcher might record data on natural, undisturbed behaviors from behind a one way mirror in a wall of the room. This would probably be effective for one class session. The second time they would know the mirror was there and its function.

Behaviors observed are likely to be complex and difficult to define. For example, the teacher could be observed 'speaking of the class,' 'moving about the room' and the students could be 'attentive' or 'restless.' In most instances, a limited number of subjects or activities is watched for relatively long periods of time. Since many events occur during an experimentation, it is difficult to find agreement among researchers as to what should be observed and what records should be made of observations, and perhaps what to make of both records and observations. Standardized procedures are developed to counteract this using careful selection and training of observers. Observations are generally made of public, natural, and therefore highly visible events rather than personal or private ones. After making a number of observations, particular activities and environmental characteristics might be examined, such as the effects of sunlight glare on reading activities.

Modification of the passive observer technique is advocated by some researchers using another approach. They select a setting for observation and then introduce a logical, natural modification into the environment. Observations are made and compared under both conditions. A round table might be substituted in place of a rectangular one. The number of times people speak to each other would be recorded. The rectangular table might be replaced to see if people then behaved as they did before the first change.

An extension of this approach is for the researcher to be part of the environment examined. This introduces a dynamic element into an experiment. The experimenter can move, or talk to subjects in a predetermined way, thereby studying behaviors in controlled social situations. For example, researchers have seated themselves next to subjects on public benches to determine the separation distance typically desired by people (personal space). The researchers moved closer and closer to the person until the subject either moved away or punched them in the nose. Information gained in this way might be applied to determine the appropriate length of public benches to accommodate a given number of people or the ducking reflexes of researchers, which might appear an equally valuable smidgen of information given the provocative nature of this type of research.

Finally, researchers have extended observational methods of collecting data to include information on what the subjects themselves observe as they participate in experiments. Devices recording eye movements, unobtrusive techniques such as television and film cameras are used, and maps are drawn by subjects traveling along a prescribed route. The subject is treated as an experimental animal using more sophisticated measuring devices. These do not include consulting the subjects opinions but rather what the subject does. The subjects opinions are an entirely separate area of research involving entirely different techniques and perhaps attitudes.

SIMULATION APPROACH

If we want to determine how people respond to a building there does not seem to be a satisfactory substitute for studying the building and how people use it. Often, this is not feasible. When a new building is to be designed it cannot be observed because it does not exist. One option is to examine an existing building having features of the one designed.

It is also possible to simulate important characteristics of the environment assessed. Architects have used these techniques—such as drawings, scale models, and more recently photographs—for centuries, although the latter have been extended to include television and movie cameras. These procedures are designed to be highly realistic, that is to closely resemble the physical appearance of the environment being simulated. Other, highly abstract, simulations are also used such as mathematical models.

The philosophy underlying simulation is quite simple. If some part of the actual environment is simulated—for example, a scale model is used to represent an actual building—the researcher has the ability to control, manipulate, study, and measure the conceptual model without waiting to verify conjectures by actual conditions. Under ideal conditions the experimental findings obtained from simulation are applicable to building design problems generally.

CONCEPTUAL MODEL OF BEHAVIORAL REQUIREMENTS

In recent years a number of designers and researchers have developed conceptual models for defining requirements. One of the most comprehensive and widely used was developed by the psychologist, A. Maslow.

Maslow treated human needs as an ever-changing process, rather than as a fixed set of requirements that apply to all people. Maslow's conceptual model is termed the 'need hierarchy system.' (See diagram.) It assumes that complete satisfaction of need is not possible because when one set of needs is satisfied, another set emerges.

The need hierarchy starts with the basic physiological requirements to sustain life and health. Without being able to satisfy these needs, the individual cannot survive for any length of time. When these basic requirements are met, usually associated with food, clothing, and shelter, safety needs emerge. The individual becomes concerned about security, the avoidance of harm, and the need for protection. These needs are still oriented toward survival in a hostile environment. After some measure of safety has been assured, a need to belong becomes apparent. The individual strives to be a member of a group. As a group member, one strives for maximum acceptance by peers. This need is demonstrated by a reluctance to be a standout, either by excelling or failing in group activities.

When a person has achieved the goal of being accepted by a group, ego status needs come into play. The individual tries to excel and thereby achieve status within an organization, and/or among professional peers. Ego-status needs are satisfied in tangible ways such as a larger office, carpeting, and an expensive desk, and in intangible ways, such as being treated with deference and respect. Finally, Maslow says recognition by others is inherently limited and one strives to fulfill one's own highest needs by what he calls, self-actualization, the need of a person to strive for the fullest potential as a human being.

Maslow pointed out the conceptual and theoretical nature of his system, which should be applied figuratively, not literally. People do not move from one level to another in any precise fashion and many of the needs are seldom completely satisfied. For example, a professional who wants to satisfy a need for ego-status may, if he loses his job, find he is trying to satisfy basic needs. Many people, such as artists and writers, ignore the intermediate levels of Maslow's system and work toward self-actualization.

Maslow's system shows that most of the industrialized nations have advanced to the higher level needs above the physiological and safety requirements.

The research literature dealing with the subject of user requirements in buildings has a very narrow base. It is almost uniformly produced by and for professionals who work and live in highly industrialized societies, with relatively high standards of living. Coming from this cultural background, requirements reflect the affluence of these cultures. Consequently, the research community thinks primarily in terms of requirements of belonging, ego-status, and self-actualization. (Maslow 1954)

HIERARCHY OF NEEDS

(After Maslow)

Maslow's conceptual model (parti) is termed the "need hierarchy system." It assumes that complete satisfaction of needs is not possible because when one set of needs is satisfied, another set emerges.

self-actualization
FULFILLING ONE'S OWN HIGHEST NEEDS—Striving for the fullest potential as a human being.

self-esteem
EGO STATUS—Achieve status within an organization.

belonging
NEED TO BELONG—Striving for membership in a group.

safety
SECURITY—Avoidance of harm, need for protection.

physiological needs
SUSTAIN LIFE AND HEALTH—Food, clothing, shelter, health.

Survival in a hostile environment.

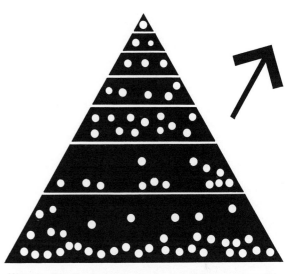

Wassily Kandinsky had a somewhat different view of the triangle than did Maslow. He was concerned only with that small top segment, self-actualization, as he expressed his views in his book, *Concerning the Spiritual in Art*.

"The life of the spirit may be fairly represented in diagram as a large acute-angled triangle divided horizontally into unequal parts with the narrowest segment uppermost. The lower the segment the greater it is in breadth, depth, and area.

The whole triangle is moving slowly, almost invisibly forwards and upwards. Where the apex was today the second segment is tomorrow; what today can be understood only by the apex and to the rest of the triangle is an incomprehensible gibberish, forms tomorrow the true thought and feeling of the second segment.

At the apex of the top segment stands often one man, and only one. His joyful vision cloaks a vast sorrow. Even those who are nearest to him in sympathy do not understand him..."
(Kandinsky 1926)

163

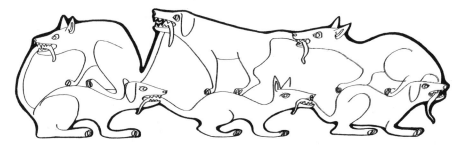

HALLS "THE VOCABULARY OF CULTURE"

One of the most important and influential thinkers, and the most lucid in description in the realm of human action and perception is the anthropologist Edward Hall. In his book *The Silent Language* he discusses 'the vocabulary of culture,' which is about as clear a blueprint to human action as was ever furnished to architects who ignore it at their peril.

Words hide much more than they reveal. The interest and the importance of architecture is in what it reveals. Although we communicate or describe what architecture is or does in words, the words are the only means we have, a very inadequate means, of describing things difficult to characterize, and are often of as little use or consequence as are the usual program notes for a symphony. It is for this reason that architects use drawings and photographs.

They also attempt to use form, line, mass, and the elements of the built environment to communicate in what Edward T. Hall has termed Primary Message Systems (PMC).

Only one of Hall's systems involves language, the first of his listing of 10 PMC. The remaining 9 are nonlinguistic. The question for the architect and builder is can he or she manipulate the elements of their craft to communicate the contents of primary message systems. Since each of the following is enmeshed in the others, we might begin with any one of them in our study of a culture and eventually include the others.

Hall's designations of PMC are:

1. Interaction
2. Association
3. Subsistence
4. Biosexuality
5. Territoriality
6. Temporality
7. Learning
8. Play
9. Defense
10. Exploitation

We will discuss them in this order and relate them to our investigation of man's actions in his built environment.

Interaction

This message system, Hall says, is based in the underlying irritability of all living substance. Irritability is assumed to mean the property of protoplasm or a living organism that permits it to react to stimuli. To interact with the environment is to be alive, to fail to do so is to be dead, Hall reminds us. Interaction patterns become more complex as we ascend the scale of organisms growing in complexity.

Speech is the most highly elaborated form of interaction. It is reinforced by tone, silence, and gesture. Writing, a special form of interaction, uses a particular set of symbols and specially developed forms. Humans react with others because they live in groups in time and space. Ultimately, Hall says everything man does involves an interaction is the hub of culture. Everything grows from it. Humankind's building is one form of interaction between people and things and we will attempt to link building and human behavior according to the PMC that Hall has defined.

Association

Association begins in basic joining. Complex organisms are in reality societies of cells, most of which have highly specialized functions. The first association was between cells when they banded together into colonies. Association begins when two cells are joined. The history of human housing from the primitive to highly industrialized cultures can or could be described as a joining of cells. An African compound is an association of cells loosely held together. As societies become more organized, the cells of their buildings become more complex in organization.

Status, dominance, and compatibility are all forms of association or attitudes that influence association. All living things arrange their lives in a recognizable pattern of association.

Associations change through environmental pressures, if exerted, otherwise they persist and do so over long periods of time. Environmental pressures appear to act, as do forces in physics, to either move, change, or hold in place forms of association.

Forms of association are seen in flocks of sheep, herds of deer or cattle, schools of fish, and paired relationships of birds and mammals. Hall quotes an account of the anthropologist Ralph Linton, who described the hunting procedures of lions in Kenya who sought their prey either singly or in pairs. When game became scarce they hunted in packs. The interesting feature of their cooperative hunting was that each lion had a functional association with a role in the group. They formed a large circle, leaving one of their number in the center. By roaring and moving toward the center they herded the game to where it could be killed by the single lion. This, Hall notes, anticipates the kind of adaptive behavior man exhibits.

Subsistence

The nature of living things can be understood by what they eat and how they get their food. Humans have elaborated the process of feeding and making a living. There is little consistency in how they do so however. Different groups of people eat differently, prefer different food, and there are innumerable ways of earning a living. These variations exist across nations, regions, and within small personal groups.

There are also strict taboos and customs concerning eating habits and behavior governing how people eat together and the status of work. There are table and poolroom manners; and in some cultures hand work is considered menial while in others the hand craftsman is highly respected.

Biosexuality

There is an agreeable difference between male and female in any species of animal, and all cultures differentiate between men and women. Hall notes that there are usually different behavior patterns and when one becomes associated with one sex it will usually be abandoned by the other. However, Hall reminds us that much of this behavior is "learned," and the concept of masculinity and femininity may vary from one culture to another.

Places in the built environment where the behavior of the sexes toward each other is prescribed such as the parlor, kitchen, or bedroom are examples of environmental primary message systems, Hall claims. There is also a mingling of sex and territory. In the culture of the ancient Maya the cooking stones are the woman's and the shrine the man's and the house is divided in an imaginary line between these two realms. At the present time there are men's and women's clubs and activities.

Territoriality

When we speak of territoriality we usually mean the taking possession of or the use or the defense of a space by a living organism. Birds establish recognizable territories in which they feed and nest; this has been studied and described by Konrad Lorenz, Robert Ardrey, and a host of others. Carnivorous animals mark out areas which they consider theirs; the grizzly bear will claw a tree standing on his forelegs and the wolf will urinate on bushes as territorial markers. Bees have places in which they search for honey. Man uses space for all of the activities in which he engages. The balance of life in the use of space, Hall says, is one of the most delicate of nature. Territoriality reaches into every nook and cranny of life. In the extreme case of the fighting bulls of Spain, Hall notes that even they are likely to establish safe territories from which it is difficult to get them to move.

Temporality

Time cannot be ignored in its relationship to life, Hall says. Life is full of cycles and rhythms. Some are related directly to nature, such as the respiratory rate, heartbeat, and menstrual cycle. There are other divisions which are man-made, such as age-grading in schools, senior citizens, and retirement, and are a combination of real time and association. There are mealtimes, and sleeping times which vary with cultures and individuals and are evident in the plans of our dwellings. We tend to isolate the noisy or eating and service functions of a house from the sleeping. Houses are designed to greet the morning sun in the kitchen and generally take into account activities and when they occur.

Learning

Learning as we know, Hall says, is an adaptive mechanism, and dates from the time that an unknown common ancestor of birds and mammals became warm-blooded, either late in the Permian or early Triassiac periods, over 100,000,000 years ago.

The tempo of life of cold blooded creatures slows with lowering temperature. As movement slowed before warm blooded creatures it slowed for all living things universally, Hall notes. It therefore caused no startling changes when both hunter and hunted slowed their pace. With the internalization of temperature controls the warm-blooded animals were freed from the restrictions imposed upon them by fluctuations in external temperature, but they also had to adapt to survive. They were endowed with improved survival capabilities, but they had to develop their sensory perceptions to do so. Learning is necessary for survival, Hall reminds us, and continues to be of prime importance. We must continue to learn in changing social, economic, and environmental conditions to survive, and we must often learn the different learning techniques of other cultures if we are to design for and with them.

Play

We do not know what role play occupies in the course of evolution, Hall states. It seems well developed in mammals, but does not appear as evident in birds, and is perhaps unknown in reptiles. Humans have developed times and places for play. In the Primary Message System if you can learn the humor of a people and control it, you can control just about everything else. There seem few better examples of this statement of Hall than Disney World and Disney Land where people are controlled in a designed environment very much like the animated cartoon characters that are provided to entertain them. There is a category of relationship known as the "playmate." Playing and learning seem intimately intwined and it is not too difficult to demonstrate a relationship between intelligence and play. Some games like chess are almost entirely a function of a specified type of intellectual development. Poker and bridge are two entirely different kinds of games and attract entirely different kinds of people to play them.

Play and defense are also closely related. Animals play at fighting and defending themselves. Some of the most graceful oriental dances or exercises are ritualized fighting. Humor is used to protect or hide vulnerabilities and is often used quite aggressively. A further example of the close relationship between play and defense, Hall reminds us, is the practice exercises and maneuvers of the military entitled "war games."

Defense

All life forms have defensive mechanisms, and a researcher may learn these before he discovers the details of an animal's diet. The opossum plays dead, the chameleon changes color, the skunk deploys an odor, the turtle pulls in its head, and the squid releases a fluid in the water to confuse its pursuers.

The ability of man to develop defensive and offensive techniques is astounding. He defends himself not only against potentially hostile forces in nature, but also against those within human society. He must also cope with the destructive forces of his own nature. Religion is concerned with warding off both the dangers in nature and those within the individual. Law enforcement agencies deal with offenders against society, and armies are used against other societies. Medicine is a form of defense against disease.

Humankind's building for defense extends from the fortified castle to the chain link fence to subtle territorial markers. Interior spaces are arranged to assure defense against outside intruders and a defense of the inhabitant's privacy.

Exploitation

To exploit the environment all organisms adapt their bodies to meet specialized environmental conditions. Witness the long neck of the giraffe, the teeth of the saber toothed tiger, the toes of the tree sloth, the hoof of the horse, and the opposing thumb of the human. Occasionally organisms develop specialized extensions of their bodies to take the place of what the body itself might do and thereby free the body for other things. This is exhibited in the web of the spider, cocoons, and nests of birds and fish, Hall reminds us.

Animals developed fang and claw and then, as men, weapons as an extension of fangs and claws. As men, they extended their muscles with wind, water, steam, and gasoline machines. They extended their senses—hearing with sonar and the telephone, and sight with radar and television—and continue to reach for extensions beyond the surface of the earth with satellites.

Each PMS has a material aspect closely associated with it. Men and women dress differently. Time and space are measured with instruments. Toys are used for play; books are used for learning, and there are material signs of status. The relationship between materials and language is particularly close. Not only does each material thing have a name, but language and materials are often handled by men in much the same way. It is impossible to think of culture without the language of materials.

It is thought, Hall says, that language arose at about the same time as tool making, which is some 500,000 to 2,000,000 years ago. It is the particular talent of Hall to bring the peculiarities of humans as they have developed during their evolution to the attention of the design professions to help them see their task in a new light. Association and defense are functions of each other, Hall says, for people form protective associations. Work and play are also related. Bisexuality and learning, space and time must also be associated as part of the unique bundle of drives, compulsions, perceptions.

Summary

In conclusion, Hall reminds us that culture is a complex series of interrelated activities deeply buried in the past. The development of language and technology, an interrelated pair, make possible the storing of knowledge giving man a lever to pry out the secrets of nature.

None of this would have been possible, Hall contends, if it had not been for the highly evolved infracultural system elaborated by lower organisms. By the time man arrived on the scene a good deal of evolution basic to culture had taken place in the development of the very systems that are considered to be, ironically, the most characteristically human.

The last generalization is that culture has not only great breadth and depth in the historical sense, but it also has other dimensions of equal importance. Culture, Hall says, is saturated with emotion and intelligence. Many things men do are not even experienced, Hall contends, for they are accomplished out-of-awareness. But a great part of human activity is the direct result of conscious thought, or suffused with emotion and feeling. After Freud, man can no longer be considered rational and ruled by logic. Humankind can no longer be conceived as an elegantly tooled machine operated from the higher centers of the brain. Humans, Hall says, become, as a result, less predictable but more interesting when they are viewed as a battleground of conflicting drives and emotions; many of which are hidden, as man is conceived of a being existing on a number of different levels at once. (Hall 1966)

THE ARENA OF HUMAN BEHAVIOR

The building plan is the arena of human behavior, Arnheim says. Unfortunately the plan is not revealed when the building is standing. Only when it is demolished, burned, bombed, or rotted away is the foundation, which traces the outline of the plan, exposed. Those that design buildings, and archaeologists that dig them up, are the only ones in a position to study the behavioral arena as an entire diagram.

Once the building is completed, the plan is converted to the converging lines of perspective. It is obscured by furniture and divided by partitions; and its outlines are distracted by human use. The simultaneity of the overall pattern seen on the drawing board is replaced by a sequence of vistas.

But we must, and inevitably do, attempt to reconstruct the plan in our minds from the message of the building facade and the clues that partial glimpses of the interior reveal. Not to know the plan is to be lost in interior space, which is almost as frightening as being disoriented in the chaos of nature. Only when we know the plan can we feel that we know where we are.

There is a fundamental difference between the world of human action, the horizontal surface, and the world of vision, which is primarily the vertical. What is relevant to human action, as Arnheim has expressed so well, tends to be revealed by the plan.

Only a small segment of the world around us can be surveyed in a downward glance unless we are very high in the air, on the upper floor of a tall building or riding in a helicopter, for example.

Entrance to 'Nunnery Quadrangle' at ♀1.

Elevation of building to the left of entrance at ♀3.
Photo by F. Wilson.

Facade of building seen from the entrance at ♀1 from the side and above at ♀2.

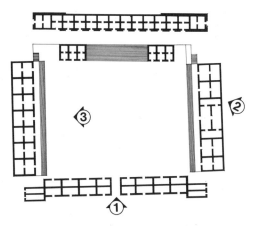

Plan of the 'Nunnery quadrangle' at Uxmal, Yucatan.

Fixed-feature space.
Photo courtesy of Cadillac Motor Co.

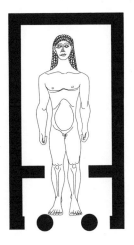

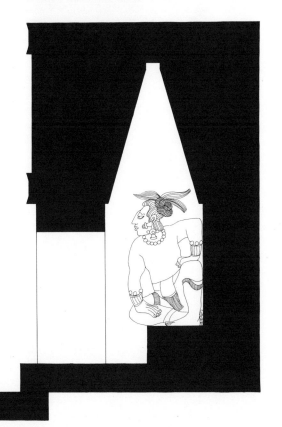

The building as organizer of human activities—see plan

If we wish to see large objects without constraint and excessive distortion we must look at them in a position where they meet our line of sight perpendicularly.

This is revealed in the horizontal and vertical form of buildings. A cathedral towers above us reducing our stature and reminding us of our insignificance while humans prefer living on a horizontal surface close to the earth. We are consequently faced with a paradox. Our perception of buildings is vertical while our behavior within them is horizontal. The plan is therefore the diagram of human behavior, and the vertical the diagram of human perceptions.

We expect a building facade to reveal to us the plan of the building inside. If we can visualize the plan in our mind, then we can judge how the building serves as an organizer of human acitivity. The plan tells us where to go and what we can and cannot do, thereby indicating the parameters of human behavior.

The plan is an indication of how people arrange space as their culture filtered through their personal idiosyncrasies dictates. Corbusier once said that "the plan is the generator," meaning that the plan generated the building form; but the plan is generated by the culture, as anthropologist Edward Hall has pointed out.

FIXED FEATURE SPACE

The anthropologist Hall used the term 'proxemics' to describe and define the interrelated observations and theories of man's use of space. Hall claimed that scientists must inevitably refer to a precultural sensory base when making comparisons of two cultures. Hall defined three levels of 'proxemics.' One is the infracultural behavior that is rooted in man's biological past. The second is the precultural, and is physiological and in the present. The third, the microcultural level, is the one in which most proxemic observations are made. Proxemics was discussed by Hall as a manifestation of microculture fixed-feature, semifixed-feature, and informal spatial relations.

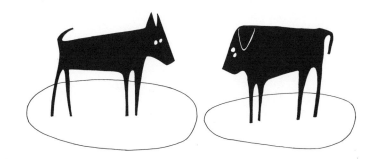

Fixed-feature space is a basic way of organizing activities of individuals and groups. Buildings are one expression of fixed-feature patterns because they are grouped together in characteristic ways and divide external space and are divided internally according to culturally determined patterns. The layout of villages, towns, cities, and the intervening countryside is not left to chance nor is it haphazard. It follows instead a plan which changes with time and culture.

The inside of the Western house is organized spatially so that there are special rooms for special functions such as food preparation, eating, entertaining, socializing, rest, recuperation, and procreation, and for sanitation as well. If artifacts or activities associated with one space are transferred to another the fact is immediately obvious. People who fail to classify activities and artifacts according to uniform, consistent, or predictable spatial plans are said to live in a mess. At the opposite end of the scale from the mass is the assembly line, a precise organization of objects in time and space.

This designation of room function is a comparatively recent development, for rooms had no fixed functions in European houses until the 18th century. Members of the family had no privacy as we know of it today. Spaces were not specialized and strangers came and went at will. Beds and tables were set up and taken down according to moods and appetites of the occupants.

Children, Hall states, were treated as adults. Childhood and the nuclear family were not formed until the specialization of rooms according to function and the separation of rooms from each other occurred.

In the 18th century, the house altered its form; the room was distinguished from the hall, and the function of the room indicated by its name, e.g., bedroom, living room, dining room. Rooms were arranged to open into a corridor or hall, like houses into a street. Occupants no longer passed through one room into another. Family patterns began to stabilize and were expressed in the house form. There was a facade that people presented to the world and a self that they hid behind it. The facade of a house recognizes that there are levels to be penetrated and hits at the function performed by the architectural features of the plan. It presents a screen behind which the occupants can retire from time to time. The strain of maintaining a social facade is great and architecture assumes this burden for people. It provides a refuge where individuals can relax and be themselves. The plan usually indicates levels of penetration of the families and the individual's privacy behind the facade. The fixed feature space of the house gives people a place to function and live. Mostly, women work best in their own kitchens as do men in their own workshops.

ORIENTATION IN SPACE

The fixed feature of the grid plan of cities makes any stranger as much at home as the oldest resident. When a person cannot find their way around a city they feel it is a personal affront.

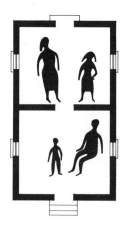

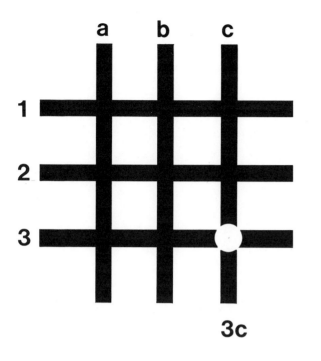

a b c

1

2

3

3c

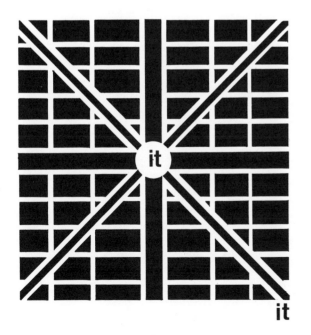

it

it

The radiating star of the French, Roman, and Greek grid made centers to be recognized. The European system of identifying place in city space is to stress and name lines. The Japanese treat the intersecting points technically and forget about the lines. In Japan, the intersections are named and not the streets. Homes instead of being related in space are related in time, Hall notes, and numbered in the order in which they were built. This Japanese pattern emphasizes hierarchies that grow around centers.

The American plan finds its ultimate development in the sameness of suburbia, one number along a line is the same as any other. In a Japanese neighborhood, the house numbers are a constant reminder to the residents of house = 20 that = 1 was built first.

Some aspects of fixed feature space are not visible until one observes the human behavior associated with it. The separate dining room is vanishing from American houses, but the line separating dining area from the remainder of the living room is maintained as real. The invisible boundaries that separate one yard from another in suburbia is also a fixed-feature of American culture, or at least of a middle-class subculture.

Hall capsulizes his discussion of fixed feature space with this statement. People have implanted within them ideals of fixed-feature space, such as high ceilings, views, and room configurations, put there by cultural influences and through their own past experience, which they seek and use to reinforce ideas they have of themselves. Fixed-feature space is the mold into which a great deal of behavior is cast. (Hall 1959, p. 98)

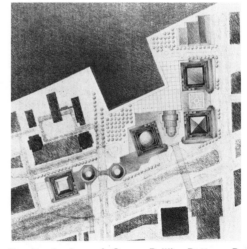

Rendered plan of Cesar Pelli's Battery Park City-Commercial Center.
Photo by K. Champlin.
Courtesy of Cesar Pelli and Associates.

HALL—THE HIDDEN DIMENSION

Language, Benjamin Lee Whorf said, is more than just a medium for expressing thought. It is, in fact, a major element in the formation of thought . . . Man's very perception of the world around him is programmed by the language he speaks, just as a computer is programmed. (Hall 1966, p. 1) Like the computer, man's mind will register and structure external reality only in accordance with the program, as Dr. Edward De Bono describes in his book *The Mechanism of the Mind.*

This is a strike at the doctrine of free will, for it indicates that all men are captive of the language they speak as long as they take their language for granted.

These principles apply to the rest of human behavior as well, in fact, to all culture. It has long been believed that experience is what all men share, that it is always possible somehow to bypass language and culture and refer back to experience in order to reach another human being. This belief concerning man's relation to experience was based on the assumption that, when two human beings are subject to the same "experience," virtually the same data are being fed to the two central nervous systems and that the two brains record similarly.

Proxemic research casts serious doubt on the validity of this assumption, in Hall's view, particularly when the cultures are different. People who speak different languages perhaps inhabit different sensory worlds. Selective screening of sensory data admits some things while filtering out others, so that experience as it is perceived through one set of culturally patterned sensory screens is quite different from experience perceived through another. The architectural and urban environments that people create are expressions of this filtering-screening process. In fact, from these man-altered environments, it is possible to learn how different people use their senses. Experience, therefore, cannot be counted on as a stable point of reference, because it occurs in a setting that has been molded by man.

In light of what is known of ethology, it may be profitable in the long run if man is viewed as an organism that has elaborated and specialized his extensions to such a degree that they have taken over and are rapidly replacing nature. In other words, man has created a new dimension, the cultural dimension, of which Hall's proxemics is only a part. The relationship between man and the cultural dimension is one in which both man and his environment participate in molding each other. Man is now in the position of actually creating the total world in which he lives, what ethologists refer to as his biotope. In creating this world he is actually determining what kind of an organism he will be. This is a frightening thought, in view of how very little is known about man. It also means that, in a very deep sense, our cities are creating different types of people in their slums, mental hospitals, prisons, and suburbs. (Hall 1966, p. 4)

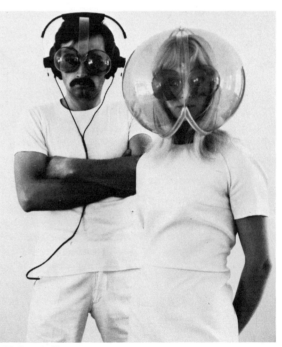

biotope

"Flyheads."

Haus-Rucker Co.

Facet-like helmets with color glasses and stereo headsets, intensifying the optical and acoustical experience.
Photo courtesy of Haus-Rucker.

"The loveliness of San Marco Square in Venice is due not only to the excitement of the place, but because its size and proportions are such that every inch of it can be traversed on foot."
(Hall)
Photo by F. Wilson.

San Marco.
Photo by F. Wilson.

Although there are great individual and cultural differences in spatial needs, as Hall reminds us, there are still certain generalizations that can be made about what it is that differentiates one space from another.

Briefly, Hall reminds us what you can do in it determines how you experience a given space, and this is about as practical a yardstick as one will find. A room that can be traversed in one or two steps gives an entirely different experience from one that requires fifteen or twenty steps to go from wall to wall. A room with a ceiling you can touch is quite different from one with a ceiling eleven or twelve feet high. In large outdoor spaces, the sense of spaciousness actually experienced depends on whether or not you can walk around. The loveliness of San Marco Square in Venice is due not only to the excitement of the place, but because its size and proportions are such that every inch of it can be traversed on foot. (Hall, p. 52)

Space also has perceptual qualities that are difficult to describe, as Giedion explains. There was a medieval comfort, he insists, despite the harshness of the age. It must be sought in another than those we look for because it cannot be measured on the material scale. The satisfaction and delight that were medieval comfort have their source in the configuration of space. Comfort is the atmosphere with which man surrounds himself and in which he lives. Like the medieval Kingdom of God, medieval space is something that eludes the grasp of hands. Medieval comfort is the comfort of space.

Notre Dame of Paris from the Seine.
Photo courtesy of the French Government Tourist Office.

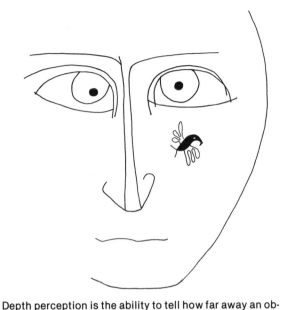

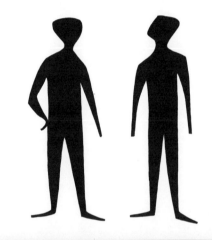

The space between people is filled with meaning.

The space between inanimate objects can have formal meaning as we have just seen. But the animated space between people is more highly charged with implications because it is kinetic. We also associate personal, social, and cultural experience and prejudices with distances between people and the attitudes of their bodies that tell us something about their feelings towards each other. We read the amount of space between them and how it is arranged. It becomes charged as it does with objects. But body language speaks more clearly than building language. Our interest here is in how the two influence each other.

Depth perception is the ability to tell how far away an object is. The eyes, like the ears, are set apart, so that the retinal image that each eye receives is slightly different. The difference is called binocular disparity.

As we look at things with both eyes, the information from the two eyes combines to give a perception of depth.

It is not necessary to have two eyes to perceive depth. There are a number of monocular cues, that is cues to one eye, that augment depth perception. In fact, motion parallax provides both monocular and binocular cues about depth. Another aid to monocular depth perception is interposition, in which one subject partially blocks the view of another object, creating the illusion that the second object is further away.

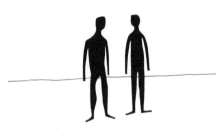

People are aware of spatial confines......

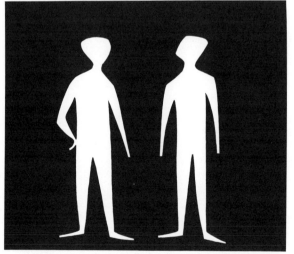

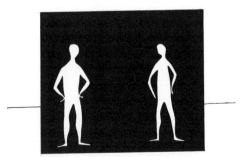

......and arrange themselves differently indoors than outdoors.

ATTENTION

Attention is a crucial concept for understanding why only some information enters into memory storage. Our senses are constantly being bombarded by the environment. Sights, sounds, odors, tactile sensations are all simultaneously present. There are limitations on the amount of information that can be attended to at one time. For example while listening to music a person may be unaware of the discomfort of a tight pair of shoes. If the irritation were to grow more intense, however, it would probably become difficult to concentrate on the music. Likewise, if you were instructed to count and remember the number of vowels from a passage in this book, you would probably recall very little of the meaning conveyed in that passage. Conversely, when you read for content you are unlikely to notice the number of vowels in the passage.

Past experience can also direct attention to environmental information. We will be more attentive to information about driving safety if we recall a previous automobile accident. If we are devoting attention to a situation, such as an exam or a problem solving task that demands information, we tend to put other sensory data on hold. One of the goals of psychologists is to determine how attention operates in selecting information, storing it, and recalling it from memory.

The brain monitors incoming sensory information directing attention to one type of sensory input while putting a damper on information that is less important. For example, while attending to a visual stimulus, the brain reduces the volume of information coming from other sensory channels. Thus when examining a painting, a person may be less aware of surrounding sounds and odors. The selective tuning in on a particular sensory input while reducing others is called sensory gating. It cuts down extraneous environmental cues permitting attention to be focused in one place. Sensory selection does not completely eliminate information from the damped-down senses. If a strange sound, or an unexpected silence, is detected while looking, attention may shift from what is being seen to what is being heard. This indicates that information in the tuned-down sensory system is still processed to some extent, thus enabling us to know when to shift our attention. People will, for example, detect their own name in a conversation that is otherwise meaningless to them.

A complex form of information selection can occur within a single sensory channel. Where we carry on a conversation at a crowded cocktail party, for example, our ears receive a great deal of extraneous information. In addition to hearing the person we are speaking with, we may also hear the din of other conversations, the clink of glasses, the sound of music, smell food and perfumes, feel the texture of utensils, and taste food. Despite the confusion of sounds, smells, and tactile impressions we somehow manage to follow our partners conversation.

We do not completely ignore all other impressions. Research indicates that the other stimulations seemingly unattended are awarded an elementary form of attention. Information is not completely eliminated from reaching the other senses. Selective attention permits some processing of information that is not the focus of attention within the same sensory channel.

We cannot, therefore, be unaware of all the other happenings in the environment when experiencing architecture and the forms of our built environment.

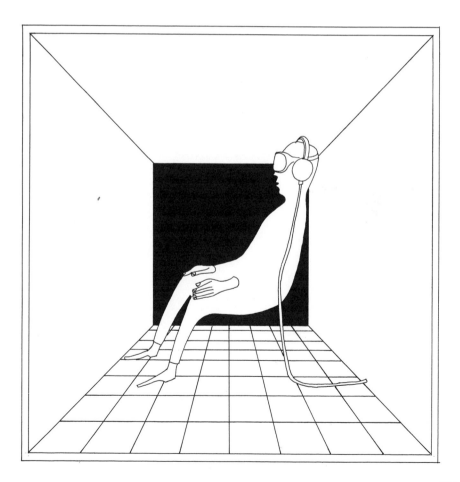

AUDITORY SPACE

HEARING AND SIZE

The scale of noise in the creature world was expressed quite beautifully by D'Arcy Thompson in his book *On Growth and Form*. "We know," he said, "by common experience of fiddle, drum, or organ, that pitch rises, or the frequency of vibration increases, as the dimensions of pipe or membrane or string diminish; and in like manner we expect to hear a bass note from the great beasts and a piping treble from the small. The rate of vibration of a stretched string depends on its tension and its density; these being equal it varies inversely as its own length and as its diameter.

We then associate sound with size for if we suppose one animal to be fifty times less than another, vocal cords and all, then one's voice will be pitched 2500 times as many beats, or some ten or eleven octaves, above the other's, D'Arcy reminds us. The same comparison or the same contrast will apply to the tympanic membranes by which the vibrations are received.

But the perception humans have of musical notes only reaches to 4,000 vibrations per second or thereabouts. When bats squeak or mice scream they are heard by few and to vibrations of 10,000 per second all of us are stone-deaf."

For this reason, D'Arcy says, ". . . . .mere size is enough to give the lesser birds and beasts a music quite different to our own; the humming-bird, for aught we know, may be singing all day long. A minute insect may utter and receive vibrations of prodigious rapidity; even its little wings may beat hundreds of times a second. For more things happen to it in a second than to us; a thousandth part of a second is no longer negligible, and time itself seems to run a different course to ours." (Thompson 1971, p. 34)

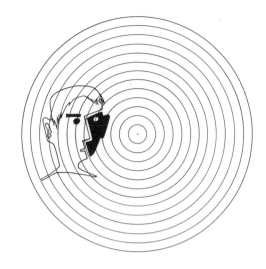

The fact that the human ears are located on either side of our head allows us to locate the origin of a sound. The difference between the time sound reaches one ear and the time it reaches the other, sometimes a difference of as little as one-thirty millionth of a second, is apparent to us. This amazing sensitivity helps us tell where sound originates.

SOUND

"The sense of hearing is based on the ability of the ear to transmit to the brain a range of airborne vibrations. The brain processes simultaneous or successive information cues and assigns them mental significance.

Hearing is decisive when visual signals are poor, and it may also affect spatial orientation. There may be a desire to identify and locate the source of sonic signals. There may also be sensations of spatial hardness and softness communicated through hearing.

The human ear detects sound over a broad range of intensities. In terms of time separation, two clicks as near in sequence as 0.001 second can be detected by the ear as separate signals. The ear, however, is incapable of sending to the brain the entire range of vibration frequencies. For example, a tuning fork vibrating at a rate of 15 cps (cycles per second) arouses no sensation of hearing. Most people do not perceive sound until approximately 30 cps is reached.

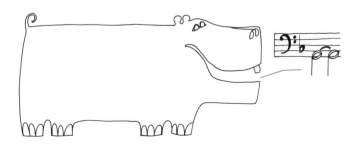

Photo by F. Wilson.

AN AUDITORY ENVIRONMENT

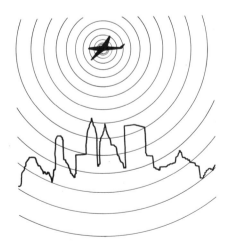

AUDITORY ENVIRONMENT

The full range of human response to sound involves a frequency spectrum that ranges from approximately 30 cps at the low end to approximately 10,000 cps at the upper end. For some individuals the range of sensitivity extends as low as 20 or as high as 20,000 cps. Optimum sensitivity occurs in the frequency range between 500 and 6,000 cps. This includes the range of most principal speech.'' (Flynn 1970, p. 48)

VISUAL AND AUDITORY SPACE

The amount of information gathered by the eye contrasted with the ears has not been precisely calculated. Calculations would involve a translation process. Scientists are handicapped in making such measurements for they do not know what to measure.

A general notation of relative complexities of the two systems can be obtained by comparing the size of the nerves connecting the eyes and the ears to the brain centers. Since the optic nerve contains roughly eighteen times as many neurons as the cochlear nerve, we assume it transmits at least that much more information.

Actually, in normally alert subjects, it is probable that the eyes may be as much as a thousand times as effective as the ears in sweeping up information.

Up to 20 feet the ear is very efficient. At about one hundred feet, one way vocal communication is possible, but slower than at conversational distance. Two-way conversation is considerably altered. Beyond this distance, the auditory cues with which man works begin to break down rapidly.

The unaided eye, on the other hand, sweeps up an extraordinary amount of information within a hundred-yard radius and is still quite efficient for human interaction at a mile.

Impulses that activate the ear and eye differ in speed as well as in quality. At 0° C at sea level sound waves travel 1100 feet a second and can be heard at frequencies of 50 to 15,000 Hz. Light rays travel 186,000 miles a second and are visible at frequencies of 10^{15} Hz.

The type and complexity of the instruments used to extend the eye and the ear indicate the amount of information handled by the two systems. Radio is much simpler to build, developed long before television and there is still a great difference between the quality of the reproduction of sound and vision. It is possible to produce a level of audio fidelity that exceeds the ability of the ear to detect distortion. The visual image is a little more than a moving reminder system that has to be translated before it can be interpreted by the brain.

There is not only a difference in the amount and type of information that the two receptor systems can process, but also in the amount of space that can be efficiently probed. (Hall 1966, p. 40)

Visual space has an entirely different character than auditory space. Visual information tends to be less ambiguous and more focused than auditory information.

Sound in architecture today is usually considered as noise to be suppressed. In a concert hall or other room designed for music or sound as entertainment, sound properties are studied and prescribed by acoustic experts who control one set of sound levels and find means of amplifying others; all unwanted or unplanned sound is noise.

Vitruvius wrote concerning the design of a theater: "The curved cross-aisles should be constructed in proportionate relation, it is thought, to the height of the theater, but not higher than the footway of the passage is broad. If they are loftier, they will throw back the voice and drive it away from the upper portion, thus preventing the case-endings of words from reaching with distinct meaning the ears of those who are in the uppermost seats above the cross-aisles..." (Vitruvius 1960, p. 138)

Particular pains must also be taken that the site be not a "deaf" one, but one through which the voice can range with the greatest clearness. This can be brought about if a site is selected where there is no obstruction due to echo.

Voice is a flowing breath of air, perceptible to the hearing by contact. It moves in an endless number of circular rounds, like the innumerable increasing circular waves which appear when a stone is thrown into smooth water, and which keep on spreading indefinitely from the center unless interrupted by narrow limits, or by some obstruction which prevents such waves from reaching their end in due formation. When they are interrupted by obstructions, the first waves, flowing back, break up the formation of those which follow.

In the same manner the voice executes its movements in concentric circles; but while in the case of water the circles move horizontally on a plane surface, the voice not only proceeds horizontally, but also ascends vertically by regular stages. Therefore, as in the case of waves formed in the water, so it is in the case of the voice; the first wave, when there is no obstruction to interrupt it, does not break up the second or the following waves, but they all reach the ears of the lowest and highest spectators without an echo.

Hence the ancient architects, following in the footsteps of nature perfected the ascending rows of seats in theaters from their investigations of the ascending voice, and by means of the canonical theory of the musicians, endeavored to make every voice uttered on the stage come with greater clearness and sweetness to the ears of the audience..."

HEARING ARCHITECTURE

Perhaps one of the best descriptions of the sound of space was written by Rasmussen in his wonderful little book *Experiencing Architecture*.

We may think, he says, that a room is cold and formal, and we seldom mean that the temperature is low. Our reaction is most probably a natural antipathy

Executive Reception Area, Columbia Broadcasting System, NYC.
Photo courtesy of Knoll International.

Photo courtesy of The Metropolitan Museum of Art—Fletcher Fund 1956.

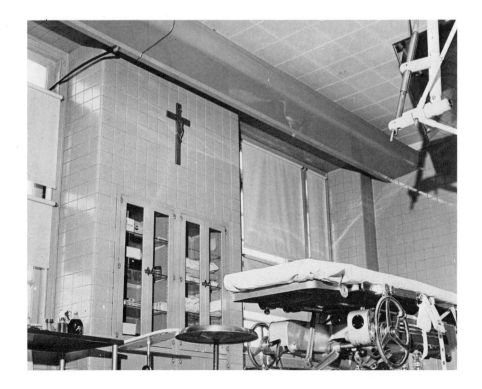

to the materials found in the room. The colors may be cold or it may be the acoustics, something we hear. If it were in warm colors, and furnished with rugs and draperies to soften the acoustics, we would probably find it warm and cosy, although the temperature remained unchanged.

Rasmussen describes experiencing structures acoustically from his childhood experiences in a barrel-vaulted passage leading to Copenhagen's old citadel. The effect of soldiers marching through with fife and drum was 'terrific' he recalls. Even a small boy such as himself could fill it with a tremendous and fascinating din, that is, when the sentry was out of sight.

He also speaks of a movie in which all that he heard was the splashing of water and the echoes of men hunting each other in a tunnel. He speaks of the sound reverberating qualities of a stone museum, home of statues, which because of the sound of the marble floor and marble walls is more like Rome. One is transported from the provincial capital in which the museum was built.

In a similar way, when one dons earphones one is transported to the space in which the music was played, rather than staying in the room in which one sits while listening. Sound creates space and one can experience it by listening to music and closing one's eyes so that only the sense of hearing is conveying information to the brain.

The chants created for the early Christian church in Rome would have sounded very well in the stone hall that Rasmussen described. Although the Roman bascillicas were not vaulted they had the same hard character of surface from the tile floors and stone walls.

The acoustical conditions of such a church must by their very nature lead to a certain, definite kind of music. When the priest wished to address the congregation he could not use his ordinary speaking voice. If it were powerful enough to be heard throughout the church, each syllable would reverberate for so long that an overlapping of whole words would occur and the sermon would become a confused and meaningless jumble. It therefore became necessary to employ a more rhythmic manner of speaking to recite or intone. In large churches with a marked reverberation there is frequently what is termed a sympathetic note, that is to say a region of pitch in which tone is apparently reinforced. If the reciting note of the priest was close to this sympathetic note the sonorous Latin vowels would be carried full-toned to the entire congregation. The reverberation would be reinforced.

The priest began on the reciting note and then let his voice fall away in a cadence, going up and down so that the main syllables were distinctly heard and then died away while the others followed them as modulations. In this way, the confusion caused by overlapping was eliminated. The text became a song which lived in the church, and in a soul-stirring manner turned the great edifice into a musical experience. The Gregorian chants were especially composed for the old basilica of St. Peter in Rome.

Polyphonic music as heard today in Westminster Cathedral, says Hope Bagenal, was directly produced by a building form and by the open vowels of the Latin language.

Rasmussen describes the domes of St. Marks in Venice and how Giovanni Gabrieli used them as mighty resonators. The music was heard from both sides of the gallery, and the congregation not only heard two orchestras, it heard two domed rooms, one speaking with silver tones, the other responding in resounding brass.

Every large church interior has its own voice, its special possibilities. After the reformation, Bagenal says, the church for which Johann Sebastian Bach composed his music, a large Gothic church, was paneled with wood over the naked stone and the wood absorbed a great deal of sound and greatly reduced the period of reverberation. Side walls were lined with tiers of wooden galleries and numerous private boxes. This allowed Bach to write his works in a variety of keys.

Rasmussen described the Rococo houses with their variously shaped rooms each with a different acoustic characteristic: The entrance, which resounded with the rattle of side arms and the clatter of high heels as the guest followed the major domo across the stone floor and entered the door held open for him; a dining room acoustically adapted for table music; a salon with silk or damask paneled walls which absorbed sound and shortened reverberations and wooden dadoes which gave the right resonance to chamber music; a smaller room in which the fragile tones of a spinet might be enjoyed; and, finally, madam's boudoir, like a satin-lined jewel box where intimate friends could converse together whispering the latest scandals.

With the eclectic style, the architect and the user lost the thought of the acoustic functions of each room, and later, with the talking picture, the space became a receptacle for any sound the screened drama demanded.

The characteristic of modern buildings is remarkable, with glass walls and smooth shiny resonant material that is acoustically dampened so that they all sound alike.

Sound is killed as noise and then fed back electronically and controlled as are natural light, natural odors, and the natural thermal environment.

What was the effect of Handel's water music played on barges in the Thames carried across the water? We still sing in the bathtub. We make marble bathrooms and kill the sound with acoustic tile. It is in this context that we approach the sensory environment. It is, in fact, an ideal approach for our scientists and technicians. All sound is eliminated and then reintroduced in measured increments that can be counted and calculated. (Rasmussen 1959, p. 225)

NOISE

Noise has often been defined as unwanted sound. Noise if defined in these terms is a highly personal subjective reaction to, and interpretation of, per-

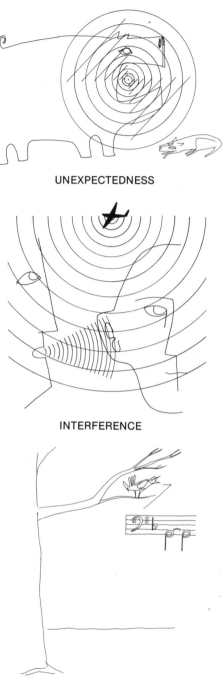

UNEXPECTEDNESS

INTERFERENCE

INAPPROPRIATENESS

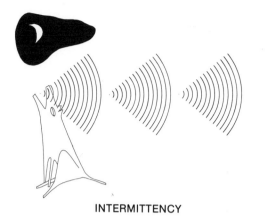

INTERMITTENCY

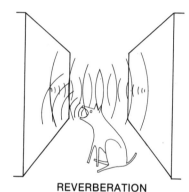

REVERBERATION

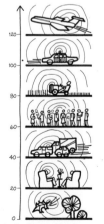

Decibel scale for sounds.
Noise criteria (NC) curves.

ceived sound. Noise, as a quality of sound, must not be confused with loudness. In general, a loud, sharp sound will have all of the attributes of noise, since it is usually, particularly if unexpected, intrusive because of its intensity. It therefore has a high annoyance value. Under most circumstances sounds of high intensity are less easily ignored, day or night, than sounds of low intensity. (Farr 1972, p. 206)

We are thus dealing with the annoyance value of sound. Kryter has characterized this under five qualities.

1. unexpectedness
2. interference
3. inappropriateness
4. intermittency
5. reverberation

Farr adds one other additional important quality of sound, its origin. For he points out that self-generated sound commands a very high tolerance in the individual generating it. Yet it may have two or more of Kryter's annoyance values. Sound generated by another person or an impersonal sound, such as a sonic boom, has a very high annoyance value, for external sound generally seems to amplify each of the qualities responsible for annoyance.

Most people at advanced age suffer a loss of hearing acuity. This gradual loss of hearing increases the likelihood of extraneous sounds causing interference in communication with greater frequency, and at lower intensities of the extraneous sound. This may lead to social embarrassment, leading to changing patterns of behavior.

Farr suggests that in some instances these changed patterns appear to have been incorporated into "status symbols of success." During the previous era most executives were older people. The older executive may compensate, in part, for loss of hearing acuity by reducing background noise. It was customary a few years ago to provide quiet, noise controlled offices for senior executives. In contrast today we find younger senior executives working in open office plans.

The converse picture of this loss of discriminating ability is optimized by a teenager studying in front of the television or radio set at near full volume, Farr points out. If a telephone call is anticipated it will be heard with astonishing perception out of a varied mixture of high-intensity sounds.

The difference in these two extremes may explain why certain background sound may be annoying to some and a matter of indifference to others. (Rubin and Elder 1980)

NOISE IS A NUISANCE

Noise has a number of characteristics in common with other environmental polutants such as solid and liquid waste and particulate matter in the air. Its effects are biological, psychological, and sociological. Another shared feature is the difficulty in establishing simple cause-and-effect relationships between the pollutant and its consequences. For example as we do not know the effects of long-term exposure to minute quantities of toxic chemicals found in our drinking water supply, the long-range consequences of low level (below 85 dBA) noises are unknown. Finally, a broad range of effects has been attributed to noise. A loud explosion can destroy the sensory perception of the ears and cause total deafness. Temporary physiological changes, such as changes in heart rate and blood chemistry, often accompany exposure to moderate levels of noise. Most available findings fall between these extremes.

To complicate the situation, the quality of information concerning noise effects is not uniform, it differs from discipline to discipline. Physiological consequences, such as causes of permanent hearing damage are better understood than psychological ones, and both of these disciplines are further advanced than sociological research in their studies of noise effects.

Noise can cause permanent hearing impairment under some circumstances. The industrial setting is the most likely locale for this to occur though in few environments are people completely protected from levels of noise which can cause deafness. This hazard is very real, yet in most design situations noise poses a psychological rather than a medical problem. The most typical reaction of laymen is that noise is a nuisance; it interferes with many activities.

The development of a general methodology which adequately relates, in quantitative terms, the physical characteristics of sound with psychological responses to them has been very difficult.

The Auditory Evaluation of Buildings

In designing an auditory environment today, the architect has a number of guides, developed primarily by accousticians. For the most part these criteria describe the acoustic environment of spaces, on the one hand, and the noise transmission characteristics of building components such as walls, floors, and ceiling assemblies, on the other. The adequacy of these working tools depends on their relatedness to the behavior and activities performed in a building. For example, a given noise criterion (NC) curve is associated with a noise level appropriate for an activity such as sleeping. The curve is therefore an appropriate design tool if adequate data exist demonstrating that, at the selected level, people can sleep; whereas sleeping is difficult at the highest NC level. In a similar fashion, sound transmission class (STC) ratings have been developed to enable the architect to design a space using built elements having predetermined sound transmission loss characteristics. For example, if a room housing quiet activities, such as reading, is to adjoin one which is likely to be noisy, such as a kitchen, then the wall between these rooms should have good sound insulation properties.

If both instances, NC and STC ratings, the adequacy of criteria depend on the quality of the research data used to formulate them.

Noise Criterion (NC) Curves

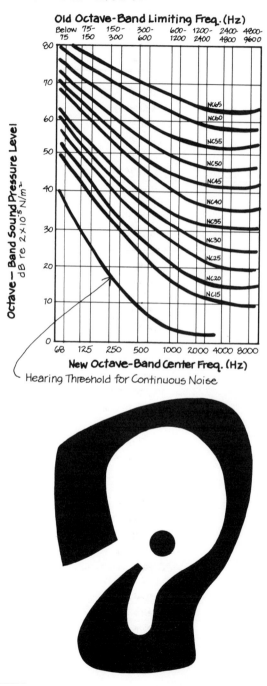

Noise Criteria (NC) Curves

Hearing Threshold for Continuous Noise

The "Walk-Away" Noise Test (HUD)

speaker   listener

DIMENSIONS OF AUDITORY SPACE-After Hall

The following shifts in voice are associated with specific ranges of distance for north Americans: (H1–163)

1-Very close (3 in. to 6 in.)...........................Soft whisper; top secret
2-Close (8 in. to 12 in.)..............................Audible whisper; very confidential
3-Near (12 in. to 20 in .).............................Indoors, soft voices; outdoors, full voices; confidential.
4-Neutral (20 in. to 36 in.)...........................Soft voice, low volume; personal subject matter.
5-Neutral (4½ ft. to 5 ft.)............................Full voice; information of nonpersonal nature.
6-Public Distance (5½ ft. to 8 ft.)....................Full voice with slight overloudness; public information for others to hear
7-Across the room (8 ft. to 20 ft.)....................Loud voice; talking to a group
8-Stretching the limits of distance....................Hailing distance, departures
(20 ft. to 24 ft. indoors; up to 100 ft. outdoors)

The original purpose of the NC curves was to lower the number of complaints by those being disturbed by noise. They were intended to specify the maximum noise levels which can be present in an environment without eliciting complaints. The levels were analyzed in terms of octave bands and the noise was assumed to have a continuous noise spectrum. The NC curves were developed by L. Beranek (acoustician) on the basis of opinion/attitude surveys of office workers. The researchers questioned the workers regarding the effects of noise on their ability to perform their work assignments and to communicate by speech. The responses to the questionnaire items were correlated with physical measurements of the noise. The currently used NC curves were a refinement of earlier speech communication (SC) criteria curves, and are now being modified to perferred noise criteria (PNC) curves.

Another auditory problem in buildings, especially homes, concerns privacy rather than noise. In multifamily buildings, lack of acoustical privacy is a major source of irritation. Acoustical privacy can be defined as the expectation that sounds generated within the household will not be broadcast to other households in the building. This problem deserves special attention because of the widespread use of lightweight construction materials and techniques in building.

Speech

A major consideration influencing the acceptability of the auditory environment is the ease or difficulty with which speech can be understood. The close relationship between auditory criteria and speech factors is evidenced by the work of Baranek in the development of NC criteria, where the ability to conduct conversations was an important determinant of the auditory quality of the spaces studied.

The evaluation of an environment's acceptability in terms of speech communication has been based on one or more of three factors:

1. A commonly accepted definition of an acceptable speech environment by speaker and listener.
2. The vocal sound level exerted by speakers as a function of frequency and time.
3. The degree of speech recognition measured in the presence of noise, that is, speech intelligibility tests. (Rubin and Elder 1980)

HUD GUIDELINE PROCEDURE

The Department of Housing and Urban Development (HUD) in its "Noise Assessment Guideline" suggests a procedure which may be employed to assess the overall noise level of a site. The technique proposed, known as the Walk-Away Test, is a simplified version of a speech intelligibility test. (The procedure is useful for rough estimation only and is one of several approaches described in the publication.)

The Walk-Away Test is an optional evaluation that may be performed during any visit to the site. However, when the site's exposure to more than one source of noise is found "Normally" rather than "Clearly Acceptable," the Walk-Away Test is strongly recommended as a means of assessing the cumulative effects of noise from various sources.

The Walk-Away Test has been designed to evaluate the overall noise condition at a site without reference to specific sources. Since noise may vary during a 24-hour period, this test should be performed at those hours when noise is apt to be most severe (during the peak morning and afternoon traffic periods) and at those hours when noise is apt to be most annoying (between 10:00 p.m. and midnight when people are trying to go to sleep).

Now that we have discussed the environment from the standpoint of speech communication, we will turn to the problem of annoyance and disturbance caused by noise. The section that follows traces the procedures used to measure the basic characteristics of sound (psychophysical procedures) and their evolution to methods used to assess the noises produced by major sources such as aircraft and motor vehicles. (Rubin and Elder 1980)

LOUDNESS LEVEL

The earliest attempts to quantify the subjective magnitude of sounds were made at the Bell Laboratories by H. Fletcher (psychoacoustician) and W. Munson. These studies were designed to define and measure loudness.

The loudness level of a tone was defined by Fletcher and Munson as the intensity level in dB of a tone when compared with a reference tone having the single frequency of 1000 Hz. The procedure employed in their data collection is known in psychophysics as the method of average error. The experimental subjects adjust the intensity level of the reference tone until it is judged as being equally as loud as the test tone. A compilation of many judgments, by a sample of subjects making these judgments with a variety of tones varying in intensity level, results in data that can be presented in the form of equal loudness contours.

These Fletcher-Munson curves are of special interest to both designers and acousticians, because the 30-phon level forms the basis for the dBA scale of sound level meters, the most commonly used measure of sound. (This curve measures the sensitivity of the average ear to broadband sound.)

Because of its importance as a noise source, a number of techniques have been developed especially to measure and evaluate aircraft noise. The man usually associated with the refinement of these measurement methods is K. Kryter (psychologist), who states that people's attitudes toward the un-wantedness of sounds are in part determined by their masking, loudness, star-

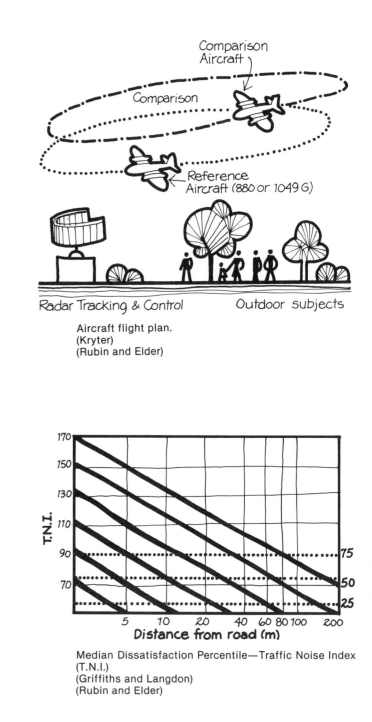

Aircraft flight plan.
(Kryter)
(Rubin and Elder)

Median Dissatisfaction Percentile—Traffic Noise Index (T.N.I.)
(Griffiths and Langdon)
(Rubin and Elder)

tle, distractive, and auditory fatigue effects. (Kryter 1970) Kryter indicates that these effects are also determined by the spectral characteristics.

A major advance in methodology was introduced by S. Stevens (psychophysicist) who, while retaining the concept of equal loudness contours, developed a new methodology in defining them. Instead of confining judgments to those of equality, he had subjects also estimate magnitude.

His basic procedure was as follows: A standard tone of 1000 Hz at 40 dB is given the arbitrary value of 1 sone. Subjects make adjustments of a comparison sound until, for example, it is twice as loud as the standard; this level is defined as 2 sones. Judgments are then made as to 1/2 the loudness of the standard; these are defined as 1/2 sone. Further comparisons can then be made in a similar manner for 1/4 sone and 4 sones, etc. Intermediate points are then computed on the basis of bisection between the empirically based data.

Perceived Noisiness

A scale was developed to express perceived noisiness (PN) based on occurrences of sounds of equal duration. The unit of perceived noisiness is the noy. A sound judged to be subjectively equal in noisiness to an octave band of random noise centered at 1000 Hz and a sound pressure level of 40 dB is given a value of 1 noy; a sound judged twice as noisy is 2 noy, etc.

The perceived noise level (PNL) was developed because loudness-based judgments on complex stimuli such as aircraft noise were inadequate. PNL measures were found to be deficient too, especially for jet aircraft noise. Investigators determined that certain tonal components within the broadband noise (i.e., pure tones which could be distinguished above the general noise) and flyover duration both had to be taken into account in any evaluation procedure. PNdB was the name of the unit given to the PNL calculated for a sound. The PNdB unit is the translation of the subjective noy scale to a dB-like scale; an increase of 10 PNdB in a sound is equivalent to a doubling of its noy value.

The judged PNL of a given sound is equal numerically to the maximum overall sound pressure level of a reference sound. Complex sounds designed to simulate jet aircraft noise (with pure tone high-frequency components) have been used in studies employing similar procedures. Kryter and K. Pearson (psychoacoustician) used a method of paired comparisons to determine the subjective noisiness of sounds consisting of a steady-state pure tone immersed in noise, and the same sound minus the pure tone. Stimuli of various frequencies, but at the same PNL, were used as standards. The comparison stimuli, similar to the standard in center frequency and bandwidth, were presented at a preselected number of levels above and below the standard. The sounds were recorded in pairs on magnetic tape. The subjects were then asked to indicate which of the two stimuli sounded noisier, or less acceptable to them. The researchers found that pure tone components in noise contributed significantly to judgments of annoyance. (Rubin and Elder 1980)

SOURCE NOISE—AIRCRAFT, TRAFFIC

Aircraft noise studies have also been conducted under semirealistic conditions. One of the most painstaking investigations of this type was performed for the National Aeronautic and Space Administration (NASA). In this experiment Kryter used sounds actually produced by aircraft as they passed directly overhead after takeoff. He measured the sounds by using an octave band analysis and then had subjects make "annoyance" judgments of them. Subjects were also asked to compare the two members of a pair of recorded sounds of aircraft. The subjects adjusted the level of the "comparison" sound until it was as equally acceptable as the sound which served as the standard. The investigation verified the complexity of evaluating aircraft sounds. The findings did not indicate that simplified noise rating procedures could be readily developed.

Kryter also conducted a study, using the same aircraft sounds, by the method of paired comparison. Subjects were presented with preselected pairs of sounds and were asked to judge which of the two sounds would be more disturbing if heard in the home.

The Kryter study is a good example of adapting traditional laboratory controls for use in an investigation conducted in a relatively realistic field setting (e.g., scheduled and controlled flyovers of houses, with judgments made live as well as by employing two different psychophysical methods). This approach permitted comparisons of findings using several different procedures. On the other hand, the study of Fidell et al. was designed to maximize the realism of a setting by recording and having people respond to sounds in their own environments. Unfortunately, the use of a tape recorder is such studies, while valuable from the viewpoint of a researcher, presents problems in terms of subject privacy: Recording instruments, being nonselective, provide records not only of noises, but of private conversations as well. Along with aircraft noise, automotive and truck traffic noise, and to a lesser extent railroad noise, have been determined by surveys to be major sources of disturbance in buildings.

I. Griffiths (physicist) and J. Langdon (psychologist) of the British Research Establishment developed a measure of the dissatisfaction caused by roadway noise. The technique, called the traffic noise index (TNI), is based on weighted physical measurements of noise for a 24-hour period and survey data that was correlated with the roadway noise data. Computations were made of the peak noise levels (defined as being levels exceeded 10% of the time) and the background noise (defined as the level exceeded 90% of the time). The TNI is based on a weighted combination of these values. The survey part of the study included 708 respondents from 12 sites around London, England. The locations were selected as representative of traffic flow throughout the country. The questionnaire dealt with the effect of noise on household practices such as putting children to bed and keeping windows open. Respondents were also asked to rate their dissatisfaction with noise on a 7-point scale.

The authors found that while average dissatisfaction scores from many people could be correlated with physical measures of sound levels, individual reactions could not be predicted. The TNI is proposed as a viable approach to dealing with traffic noise.

Hearing Impairment

Hearing impairment has been studied from the standpoint of anatomical structure as well as function.

Researchers, both in and outside the medical profession, have built up a substantial body of information based on deatiled physiological measures in animals as well as humans. A great deal is now understood about the permanent damage caused by intense noise that has specified characteristics.

Excessive noise exposure causes a loss of hearing acuity. A temporary hearing loss in the form of a temporary threshold shift (TTS) can result from short-term exposure to high-level noise. A permanent threshold shift (PTS) can result from either continued exposure to high-level noise or short exposure to very high-level noise. The permanent hearing damage risk associated with noise depends upon: (1) the intensity and frequency distribution of the noise, (2) the duration of each individual exposure, (3) the number of individual exposures per day, (4) the number of years over which the daily exposure is repeated, and (5) the individual susceptibility to this type of damage. Noise levels of this magnitude usually occur in industrial plants and airports where employees are constantly exposed to loud noises. The temporary threshold shift is used to estimate the possible permanent damage to the ear, the permanent threshold shift. (The relationship between TTS and PTS is a source of controversy, as are many criteria and procedures developed to clarify and quantify the effects of noise on people.)

SOUND—Research

While a city or neighborhood is usually thought of in visual terms, we also experience our surroundings by means of the sounds heard. The study that follows dealt with both visual and auditory perceptions of a city. The description is of the noise environment.

M. Southworth (urban planner) undertook a study which explored perception of Boston's 'soundscape.' The study explored two questions: (1) What is the perceived variety and character of city sounds, and (2) how do sounds influence perception of the visible city? Southworth hoped to identify areas which should receive further attention from researchers and urban planners.

To investigate changes in the 'soundscape' over time and under varied weather, the researchers took five subjects on wheelchair trips through various parts of the city. The subjects were blindfolded and the trips took place at different times on different days of the week. From this phase of the study the

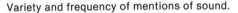

(chart after Southworth)

■■■■■■ MENTIONS BY VISUAL & AUDITORY SUBJECTS

●●●●●● MENTIONS BY AUDITORY SUBJECTS

Variety and frequency of mentions of sound.

researchers were able to determine: (1) the uniqueness of certain sounds in the urban environment, and (2) how well a sound conveyed the spatial form and activity of a particular location.

In the second phase of the study, Southworth studied the interactions between the auditory and visual environments. Three groups of subjects made the trip through the city on a Saturday. The groups were: (1) auditory subjects (could hear, but not see), (2) visual subjects (could see, but not hear), and (3) visual auditory subjects (had normal vision and hearing). A 2 3/4 mile (4.4 km) trip was mapped out which included settings with a variety of sonic characteristics, visual activities, and spatial forms. The subjects were given tape recorders so that they could record their impressions. At the conclusion of the trip the participants were asked to draw a map indicating the sequence of places visited and to describe the most and least liked settings.

An analysis of the interactions between the visual and auditory environments indicated that without sound, visual perception has less attention-demanding qualities and conveys less information. Southworth suggests two steps toward improving the city soundscape. The first would be to reduce and control noise; and the second would be to increase the amount of information provided by city sounds. (Rubin and Elder 1980, p. 73)

OLFACTORY SPACE

The anthropologist Robert Hall tells us that our sense of space, and the form of our arts, is due as much to our lack of a sense of smell as it is to our development of the senses of sight and hearing.

Man's evolution, Hall says, is marked by the development of the "distance receptors," which are sight and hearing. Therefore, humankind was able to develop the arts, which employ these two senses to the virtual exclusion of all others. Our lack of smell has given us poetry, painting, music, sculpture, architecture, and dance, all of which depend primarily, although not exclusively, on the eyes and ears, as do our communication systems. The different human cultures have placed different emphasis on sight, hearing, and smell, and have evolved differing perceptions of the relationships of individuals to space.

The present assumptions about the evolution of man, Hall tells us, are that he was originally a ground-dwelling animal. But competition forced our ancestors to take to the trees. Arboreal life demanded that keen vision and hearing be developed with less emphasis on smell, which is crucial for terrestial organisms. This is the reason our sense of smell ceased to develop and our powers of sight were enhanced.

As a consequence of this evolution an important medium of communication was diminished in human relationships. It may, Hall speculates, have endowed man with greater capacity to withstand crowding. If humans had noses like rats, they would be strongly influenced by the emotional shifts occurring in persons around them. One could smell other's anger. The emotional connotations of everything that took place in the home would be matters of public record as long as the smell persisted. The psychotic would begin to drive us all mad. The anxiety of one would be transferred to the other. To say the least, life would be much more involved, intense, and, perhaps, unbearable. It would be even less under our conscious control because the olfactory centers of the brain are older and more primitive than the visual centers.

The environmental pressures that dictated the shift from reliance on the nose to reliance on the eye have defined the human situation. Man's ability to plan has been made possible because the eye takes in a larger sweep; it codes vastly more complex data, and thus encourages thinking in the abstract. Smell, on the other hand, while deeply emotional and sensually satisfying pushes man in the opposite direction.

Even in an olfactory underdeveloped species, Americans stand out. Extensive use of deodorants and the suppression of odor in public places results in a land of olfactory blandness and sameness that cannot be duplicated anywhere else in the world, according to Hall's observations.

This blandness makes for undifferentiated spaces, and deprives Americans of richness and variety in their lives. Our memories also suffer for smells evoke

Olfactory space.

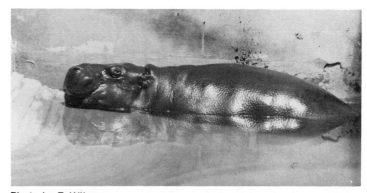

Photo by F. Wilson.

Photo by F. Wilson

memories much deeper than either vision or sound. Olfaction is biological. It must have served an important purpose in our past.

Chemical and natural odors are referred to as the chemical sense, which is an early and basic method of communication between organisms. Among its diverse functions is the differentiation of individuals. Odor also serves as a means of identifying emotional states in other organisms. It aids in the location of food, helps stragglers find or follow the herd or group, and provides means of marking territory. Smell betrays the presence of an enemy and may be used defensively, as the skunk has discovered. The powerful effect of sexual odors is known to all those living in the country where a bitch in heat draws males from much farther away than she can be seen or heard.

The silk moth can locate its mate at two or three miles. Smell operates better in dense than in thin mediums and is the method that salmon use to return over thousands of miles of ocean to the stream where they were spawned. Olfaction diminishes and gives way to sight when the medium thins as it does in the sky.

Chemical communication is the most suited to the releasing of highly selective responses, Hall observes. These, in the form of hormones, work on specific cells programmed to respond in advance while other cells in the immediate vicinity are unaffected. It would be impossible, Hall says, for advanced organisms to live at all if the highly developed chemical message systems of the body were not working 24 hours a day to balance performance with requirements.

Chemical messages can also act across time and act as a warning. When a deer comes to a place where another was frightened, it will have a flight reaction.

Although Americans are olfactorily deprived this is not true of many other people, as Hall has pointed out. In Mediterranean countries men use strong perfumes. The Arabs recognize relationship between disposition and smell. Intermediaries who arrange marriages may ask to smell the bride. This is not done on aesthetic grounds, but possibly because of a residual smell of anger or discontent. Bathing another person in one's own breath is a common practice in Arab countries. Americans are taught not to breathe on other people, and in a public gathering might find it so upsetting to be breathed upon that they cannot concentrate.

Americans have, Hall maintains, cut themselves off from a powerful communication channel, olfaction. ''Our cities lack both olfactory and visual variety. Anyone who has walked along the streets of almost any European village or town knows what is nearby. During WWII in France, I observed that the aroma of French bread removed from the oven at 4:00 AM could bring a speeding jeep to a screaming halt. What smells do we have in the U.S. that can achieve such results? In the typical French town, one may savor the smell of coffee, spices, vegetables, freshly plucked fowl, clean laundry, and the characteristic odor of

AN OLFACTORY ENVIRONMENT

Street smells—Hot Dog territory NYC.
Photo by F. Wilson.

188

Photo by F. Wilson.

outdoor cafes. Olfaction of this type can provide a sense of life; the shifts and the transitions not only help to locate one in space, but add zest to daily living.''

Activities are sometimes identified by means of characteristic odors. We can identify the kitchen of the house and amusement parks and fair grounds and certain parts of town are identified by the odors of fried food, candy, popcorn. A 'honky tonk' district can be smelled by the beer and liquor. The smell of garlic, oregano, and cooking oil from an Italian street fair may be remembered and recalled for years.

This smell attribute is both a source of enjoyment and a cause for complaint. Many people enjoy the smell of fresh coffee being brewed or the aroma of bread baking. We are all aware of perfumes, soaps, and candles developed primarily to satisfy our desires for pleasant odors. Similarly the food industry has been at the forefront of using odors to enhance the appeal of their products, especially of chemically derived foods. Household manufacturers have followed suit with scented and perfumed products from detergents to toilet paper. Although it is not admitted, out sense of smell has received a good deal of marketing analysis.

On the other hand, many environmental odors are undesired by-products of technology. Manufacturing processes and transportation systems contribute to poor air quality in our outdoor environments.

Although the nose is a sensitive detector, it is not totally reliable as a warning system. Many dangerous gasses are odorless. Miners recognized this a long time ago when they took birds such as canaries with them into the mines who would react or die from deadly coal gas before it was detected by the men. Today we find it difficult to detect carbon monoxide.

Although architectural consideration is given to some odors in buildings, such as in kitchens, conference rooms, and manufacturing processes, and it is generally agreed that certain building types such as hospitals, museums, libraries, schools, and homes have distinctive smells, there is not a great deal of research conducted in these areas.

When compared with the research and techniques developed to investigate the visual world, the state of odor investigation is best described as primitive. This study area has been largely neglected by many disciplines which would logically be expected to pursue it, namely, physiologists and experimental psychologists. Those few researchers active in the field have met with limited success, for the study of odor possesses unique problems for the researcher.

Odors call forth strong emotional reactions difficult to identify and measure. Many thousands of different odors can be discriminated, and different concentrations can be perceived. People also vary considerably in their ability to make reliable odor judgments. Yet olfaction is an alarm system with extraordinary sensitivity, and people possess the ability to distinguish among thousands of different odors. People can detect such minute concentrations of odor producing substances that chemists cannot accurately measure the concentrations.

Experimental apparatus and techniques to conduct studies have not been developed appreciably. Unlike auditory and visual studies, where sophisticated instrumentation is the rule, the working tools available to the odor researcher allow only crude measurements.

Uncertainty also exists in all phases of study, from defining the odor characteristics through measurement systems used to vary and transport it to the subject, as well as the means by which a person will receive and interpret the odor. Added to these problems is the lack of a classification and description system to reliably and accurately describe odors. Such a system is required to form a base of effective communication between scientists and laymen. The design olfaction experiments must be especially sensitive to olfactory fatigue. This phenomena is well known to anyone who has encountered a strong odor, which after a time appears to be unnoticeable.

CHARACTERISTICS OF ODORS

Odors, like other sensory stimuli, can be placed into one of two general categories: source and ambient.

Source odors are those existing at the point of origin or exit to the general atmosphere. Ambient odors are those existing in the general atmosphere. Odor sources can be categorized as either confined or unconfined. Confined sources can be characterized in terms of volumetric rate of discharge, temperature, moisture content, location, elevation, and area. Typical confined sources are stacks and fume vents. Unconfined sources consist of large sources such as sewage treatment plants and stockyards where the extent of the source precludes confinement.

Odors can be characterized by intensity, quality, acceptability, and pervasiveness. Odor intensity is defined as the numerical or verbal indication of the strength of an odor. Odor quality is the verbal description of an odor, accomplished within the vocabulary capabilities of the individual and normally expressed by comparison with common odors.

Acceptability is an absolute acceptance/rejection of the odor on the basis of intensity and/or quality. Pervasiveness is the ability of an odor to spread throughout a large volume of air and persist at perceptible levels.

The human nose is the ultimate standard against which the intensity of an odor must be evaluated. Nose response is bounded at the lower end by a smell threshold and marked near the upper by objectionable concentrations.

The threshold is defined as the concentration at which odor quality can be barely recognized. The detection threshold limit is used most commonly by researchers, although quality-recognition-sensation has resulted in more consistent research findings than detection sensation.

Individual response for detection of odors varies widely. As a result, a panel of people is normally used to determine odor threshold concentration and to

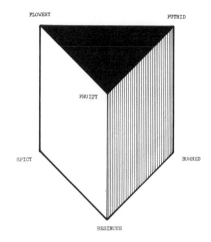

A drawing after Henning's 'smell prism.' It is supposed that every possible smell sensation can be located somewhere on the surface of this solid. It is a theoretical description of smell which implies that certain smells are impossible. For example, a putrid, flowery, burned, spicy smell should be possible because they all occur on the same plane. But a putrid, flowery, resinous smell cannot occur because they do not appear on the same plane.

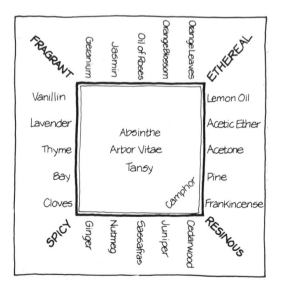

The Fers Odor Square (part of Henning's smell prism).

From *Building For People,* Rubin and Elder, 1980

Blast Injection Method

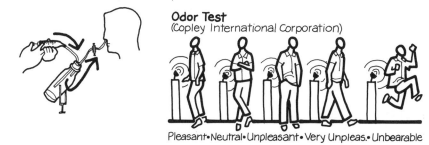

Odor Test
(Copley International Corporation)

Pleasant•Neutral•Unpleasant•Very Unpleas.•Unbearable

Methods of odor testing—from *Building For People,*
Rubin and Elder, 1980

Olfactometer

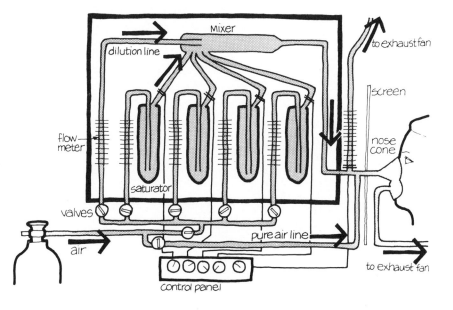

report threshold values as the "effective dosage" at which 50% of the panelists perceive the odor.

Reported threshold concentrations for the same odorant vary widely not only because of individual response variability, but also because of lack of standardization of techniques for managing samples and presenting them to observers.

HUMAN OLFACTORY RESPONSE

Olfactory sensitivity is known to be highly variable and is subject to physical as well as psychological influences. Some of the factors which have been reported to influence the olfactory sensitivity are:

- Odor sensitivity of the individual observer varies diurnally (according to the time of day), but is reasonably constant for a group of observers.
- The sense of smell is rapidly fatigued, though fatigue for one odor does not necessarily affect the perception of dissimilar odors.
- Responses to odors are not totally objective because psychological responses vary in different observers.
- The sensitivity of observers varies widely in that some persons are extremely sensitive while others are almost insensitive to odors; sensitivity decreases with age.

ODOR QUALITY

The characteristic of odor quality is normally defined in terms of commonly perceived odors, or by associating unfamiliar with familiar odors. Experimental subjects do not have the vocabulary to describe the thousands of odors distinguishable by most people. To make this problem more complex, the quality of an odor may change with dilution.

Description of Odors (Moskowitz and Gerbers)

1.	Sweet	10.	Goaty
2.	Pungent	11.	Putrid
3.	Heavy	12.	Camphor
4.	Flowery	13.	Fruity
5.	Solvent	14.	Spicy
6.	Fragrant	15.	Intensity
7.	Oily	16.	Pleasantness
8.	Minty	17.	Familiarity
9.	Burnt		

(Rubin and Elder 1980, p. 198)

191

TACTILE SPACE

The ability to respond to stimuli is the basic criteria of life. Hall has told us that sight was the last and most specialized sense to be developed in human ancestors. It became more important than smell when what were to eventually become humans left the ground and took to the trees. Stereoscopic vision is essential in arboreal life for without it jumping from branch to branch becomes a bit problematic. The other senses also underwent modification with this change of life.

To understand man one should know something of his receptor systems and how the information received from them is modified by environment and later by culture.

Man's sensory apparatus can be divided into two categories: the distance receptors—eyes, ears, and nose—concerned with examination of distant objects; and the immediate receptors to decipher the close-up world—the world of touch and the sensations we receive from the skin, membranes, and muscles.

The skin is the chief organ of touch. It is also sensitive to heat gain and loss. Radiant and conducted heat is detected by the skin and in this sense the skin becomes a distance receptor, as, for example, it responds to the heat of the sun.

The spatial experiences of vision and touch are so interwoven that they cannot be separated. Young children and infants reach, grasp, fondle, and mouth everything. Years are required to train children to subordinate the world of touch to the visual world.

The artist Braque distinguished visual and tactile space in that 'tactile' space separates the viewer from objects while 'visual' space separates objects from each other. Emphasizing the difference between these two classifications of space and their relations to experiencing space, he declared that 'scientific' perspective is nothing but a bad eye-fooling trick which makes it impossible for the artist to convey the full experience of space.

James Gibson (psychologist) also related vision to touch. He stated that if the two are conceived of as channels of information in which the subject is actively exploring (scanning) with both senses, the flow of sense impressions is reinforced. Gibson distinguished between active touch (tactile scanning) and passive touch (being touched). He reports that active touch enabled subjects to reproduce abstract objects that were screened from view with 95% accuracy. Only 49% accuracy was possible with passive touch.

Michael Balint, writing in the *International Journal of Psychoanalysis*, describes two different perceptual worlds, one sight oriented, the other touch oriented. Balint saw the touch oriented world as both more immediate and more friendly than that of sight in which space is friendly but filled with dangerous unpredictable objects (people).

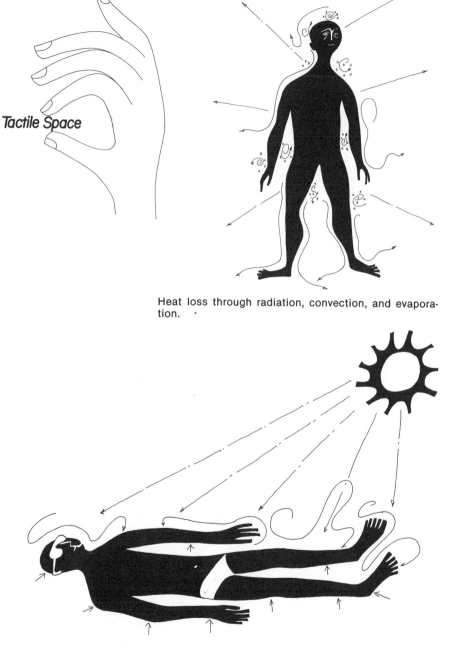

Tactile Space

Heat loss through radiation, convection, and evaporation.

Heat gain through radiation, convection, and conduction.

Hanging banners by Pamela Waters mediate between
marble walls, steel elevator doors, terrazzo floor, and
soft people.
Photo by and courtesy of Pamela Waters.

Despite all that is known about the skin as an information gathering device, designers and engineers seem to have failed in grasping the significance of touch, particularly active touch. There seems a lack of concern with the importance of touch in keeping the person related to the world in which he lives.

Texture is appraised and appreciated almost entirely by touch, even when it is visually presented. With a few exceptions, it is the memory of tactile experiences that enables us to appreciate textures.

The childhood experience of touch has been a popular research approach in this study area. The habit of holding and touching objects never leaves us, as indicated by the "don't touch" signs which appear in museums, zoos, and other places where novel objects (or species) can be found. Touch is an especially important source of information in the experiencing of form and texture, two attributes of special importance in buildings. (Rubin and Elder 1980, p. 212)

Information about form and texture is not obtained exclusively by touch. Rather, visual phenomena are also important information sources. For example, when we enter a building, within a short distance we often encounter several different surface characteristics. The street pavement, steps, doormats inside and outside of an entrance, the finished surface of the interior, and the carpets frequently have different and distinctive textural features which we become aware of by seeing and walking on them.

Cutaneous experience is therefore dependent on two sets of interrelated experiences—visual and tactual. In a sense, the information gained by each sensory system strengthens that obtained by the other, thereby making each perception more vivid than would otherwise be the case.

Although only form and texture have been mentioned so far, the skin senses provide a broad range of information concerning our environment and the objects around us. Studies have shown the skin to be sensitive to heat (cold), vibration, pain, and even light. The complexity and variety of problems addressed in this research area are indicated by the lack of a generally accepted name for the discipline. Among the terms used by researchers of the skin senses to describe the topic are "haptic," "cutaneous," and "tactile."

Our understanding of touch sensations is comparatively limited. The question of which nerve endings in the skin (and deeper-lying tissues) respond to common touches and pressures is still far from settled. It should therefore not be surprising that the phenomena experienced are even difficult to classify. A skin characteristic generally determined is that it is not uniformly sensitive. This characteristic has been noted by examining the surfaces of different parts of the body.

Three separate sets of responses have been classified under the skin senses: one for pressure reception, one for pain, and the last one dealing with temperature changes.

The problems typically addressed by researchers have dealt with determining the physiological basis of touch sensations and their sensory limits (and capabilities). Another research area has been to determine the relative importance of touch as compared with other senses as a function of age (especially in children). A limited number of studies have been conducted to determine the potential of touch as a means for communicating (braille, informational coding procedures).

We have been only partially successful in our attempt to find studies of direct application to building-related problems. However, the research methodologies employed in the investigations are sometimes applicable to building design problems.

Tactile Information

The skin senses have been looked upon as a potential means of communication under special circumstances. For example, doorknobs in public buildings are sometimes coded by having a rough surface to indicate that they are exits to a building. This coding device enables blind people to select the appropriate pathway to safety in emergency conditions.

In the design of aircraft controls and displays, researchers have examined the skin senses to determine how they might be used to augment the eye and the ear, which are sometimes overloaded with information. That is, more information is presented visually and aurally to pilots than can be handled efficiently by them. For many years, the skin senses have been employed as a means of conveying information to blind people. This general problem area has been explored in some depth to devise techniques which are more effective than braille writing for transmitting information.

Although various parts of the body have been used as sensing organs, the fingers and the hands have received the most research attention. T. Austin and R. Sleight wanted to determine how accurately familiar forms could be identified when touched with the index finger. They used numbers, letters, and geometric forms approximately 1/2 inch (1.3 cm) in size, which were cut from masonite. (Twenty-five of the forms were readily identified, but only when the subject was permitted to move his finger.)

The design of control equipment for aircraft was influenced by the ability of people to recognize different shapes.

The problem was studied by designing a variety of control knobs and having subjects identify them while blindfolded. The objective was to determine how many different shapes could be used, without too many confusion errors. Eleven shapes were found to be the maximum number which could be readily identified.

G. Hawkes (psychologist) conducted an investigation to determine the effectiveness of electrical stimulation to the finger and the hand as a means of communication. Electrodes were attached to the index finger and the palm. Several different levels of intensity were used, and the durations ranged from 50 to 1500 msec. Subjects could distinguish four intensity levels and four durations, but found it easier to distinguish among durations than intensities.

The memory of tactile experiences enables us to appreciate textures. Building Facade, Washington, D.C. Photo by Mike Crosbie.

Photo by F. Wilson (Mexico).

194

Photo by F. Wilson (Mexico).

Tactile experience—courtesy of Time Life, NYC.
Photo by F. Wilson.

J. Bliss et al. performed a number of studies to devise tactile means of communications. In one study, subjects had a series of airjet stimulators fastened to their fingers. The experiments consisted of the presentation of patterns of air stimulation on the fingers which were to be interpreted by subjects in accordance with instructions given to them beforehand. The subjects were able to perform the task this way as well as they did visually, but more training was required.

Another study by the same authors employed an array of vibrators to provide feedback information to subjects who remotely manipulated a set of tongs. By using this device, subjects successfully completed a number of simple tasks, e.g., lifting objects and opening latches.

A. Burrows and F. Cummings developed an aircraft column grip which was modified to house an electrically driven device. When an aircraft warning sensing system was activated, the device vibrated at 268 vibrations per minute. Subjects used this device and a visual warning signal in a study to determine their relative effectiveness. The tests showed that both methods of presenting danger signals gave comparable results.

Television scan signals have been used to switch an approximately one-foot-square array of tiny vibrators pressed against the soft skin on blind subjects' backs. After approximately 10 hours of training, they were able to recognize familiar objects viewed by the television camera. With additional experience the students could discriminate between people in a room, follow movements, and even discover visual effects, such as perspective and shadow.

The studies we have mentioned thus far fall into the applied research area. Now, we will examine the more fundamental work performed in this study area.

PRESSURE SENSITIVITY

Since the skin surface varies considerably with respect to sensitivity, one early approach was to develop sensitivity "maps." This was accomplished by using a rubber stamp in the form of a square (20 mm by 20 mm, containing 420 squares). The center of each square imprinted on a body surface was then stimulated. Because of the varied sensitivities of the skin surface, stimulation could be presented in many forms; mechanical, thermal, electrical, and chemical means have all been employed. Similarly, for the arousal of "touch," "contact," and "pressure" sensations, solids, liquids, and even air blasts are used.

The oldest and best known technique was developed by M. von Frey (physiologist). He used a series of straight (animal and human) hairs of different diameters, fastened to a wooden handle. The diameters of the hairs were measured and the force exerted computed. The threshold was then determined for a series of bodily regions, by determining the "weakest" hair which was noticeable to the subject by its touch.

195

S. Stevens (psychophysicist) collected judgments of the magnitude of vibration in three different ways: (1) a vibrating rod held between the fingers, (2) a vibrating button upon which the finger rested at a right angle to the direction of vibration, and (3) the vibrating button with the finger held parallel to the vibration.

He presented the subject with a vibration of moderate amplitude, and gave it an arbitrary value of 10. This number served as the standard for making futher estimates. For example, one which appeared to be twice as strong would be scored as 20; one half as strong, as 5.

Temperature Sensitivity

The temperature sensitivity of the skin has been examined by employing the grid technique mentioned earlier. The Dallenbach temperature stimulator has been a much used instrument in these studies. The instrument has a contact point which is limited to 1 mm, and whose temperature is controlled by a rapid flow of water. It has the added feature of controlling pressure by means of a spring mechanism at the bottom.

Shape vs. Texture

A number of studies have been designed to determine the relative importance of each of these attributes of materials. One such investigation, performed by C. Gliner, was designed to determine how well children in kindergarten and the third grade discriminate differences in shape and texture. In particular, Gliner was interested in finding out whether there was any identifiable trend in preferences with the passage of time. Gliner used a classical psychophysical procedure to collect her data. She describes her approach as follows:

"The conditions of the experiment were defined by the particular stimuli presented. . . . The texture stimuli were a series of sandpapers of different coarseness; the shape stimuli, a graded series of ellipses. The texture series consisted of 15 grits (24–500) of sandpaper. The particular grits were chosen because they represented the widest range and maximum number of values available in one kind of abrasive.

The shape series was composed of 15 ellipses which ranged from a circle 2 inches in diameter to an ellipse whose major axis was 3 3/4 inches and minor axis was 1/4 inches. The sum of the lengths of the major and minor axes remained constant at 4 inches for each shape throughout the series.

Both the shape and the texture series of 15 pairs were presented in two contexts. The texture pairs were presented side by side and either covered the entire perceptual field (Texture condition) or were confined to the top of a constant elliptical shape (Shaped-Texture condition).

Subject faced a 30 x 24 inch screen and reached his hand through a curtained 5 1/2 x 6 inch hole to feel two stimuli. The stimuli were mounted on a turntable 30 inches in diameter. Each standard was flanked by two different comparison stimuli, but a hand guide restricted the subject's movements such that he could feel only one pair of stimuli (the standard and one comparison) at a time. The subject was told that he would have to feel the two things and say if they were the same or different from each other. . ."

196

Man's Senses and the Energies That Stimulate Them
(Van Cott)

Sensation	Sense Organ	Stimulation	Origin
Sight	Eye	Some electromagnetic waves	External
Hearing	Ear	Some amplitude and frequency variations of pressure in surrounding media	External
Rotation	Semicircular canals	Change of fluid pressures in inner ear.	Internal
	Muscle receptors	Muscle stretching	Internal
Falling and rectilinear movement	Otoliths	Position changes of small, bony bodies in inner ear.	Internal
Taste	Specialized cells in tongue and mouth	Chemical substances	External on contact
Smell	Specialized cells in mucous membrane at top of nasal cavity	Vaporized chemical substances	External
Touch	Skin	Surface deformation	On contact
Pressure	Skin and underlying tissue	Surface deformation	On contact
Temperature	Skin and underlying tissue	Temperature changes of surrounding media or objects, friction, and some chemicals.	External on contact
Pain	Unknown, but thought to be free nerve endings	Intense pressure, heat, cold, shock, and some chemicals	External on contact.
Position and movement (kinesthesis)	Muscle nerve endings	Muscle stretching	Internal
	Tendon nerve endings	Muscle contraction	Internal
	Joints	Unknown	Internal
Mechanical vibration	No specific organ	Amplitude and frequency variations of pressure	External on contact

Chart from Rubin and Elder, *Building for People*, 1980.

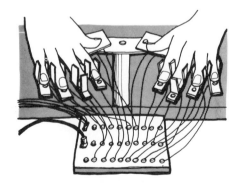

Array of airjets, connecting tubes, and hand holder used to present tactile dot patterns.

Tactile research using air stimulation (Bliss et al.),
from Rubin and Elder, *Building for People*, 1980.

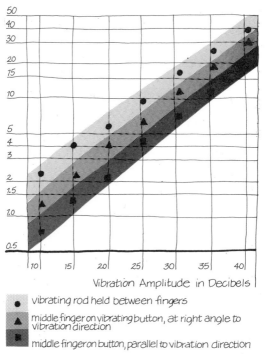

vibrating rod held between fingers

middle finger on vibrating button, at right angle to vibration direction

middle finger on button, parallel to vibration direction

Magnitude Functions for Apparent Intensity of Vibration (finger)

Magnitude Estimation

from Rubin and Elder, *Building For People,* 1980. National Bureau of Standards, Washington, D.C.

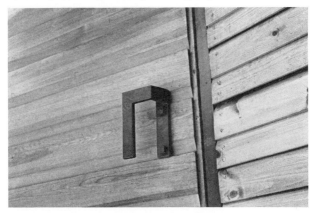

Texture is appraised and appreciated almost entirely by touch.
Door pull, Helsinki, Finland.
Photo by F. Wilson.

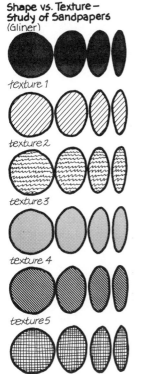

Shape vs. Texture—
Study of Sandpapers
(Gliner)

texture 1

texture 2

texture 3

texture 4

texture 5

texture 6

Gliner found that older children generally performed better than younger ones, but there was no evidence that either shape or texture changed in relative importance as environmental cues as a function of age. (Gliner 1967)

A. Siegel and B. Vance also studied children's preferences for touch and sight. The apparatus used in the study was a wooden tray with three wells. Inside the wells were spheres and cubes of different colors, sizes, and textures. The child had the opportunity to view and touch the samples; he then judged which two (of a group) were the "same." Texture ranked last, following the other attributes—color and shape.

Texture

D. Katz, the Gestalt psychologist, employed the same attributes to describe touch sensations that he did when examining color.

- Surface-discriminations are made by moving fingers against an object. Object is solid, oriented and located spatially.
- Something which fills a space—encountering a fluid material such as water or an air stream, which is not oriented or localized in space. Its resistance is elastic. Discriminations such as elasticity, stickiness, and viscosity can be made.
- Film-touching an object with thin rubber gloves or through a very thick film surface (0.0105 mm).

Katz then tried to determine how long it would take subjects to identify materials using only the sense of touch in their fingertips. He collected approximately 40 samples of material (15 cm x 15 cm) and mounted them on a wooden plate. Examples of the types of materials used are linens, velvet, blotting paper, sandpaper, woolen cloth, and leather. Subjects were asked to make two judgments: (1) when something was felt, and (2) when the material was recognized. (Katz hypothesized that every material has a "thermal Gestalt" which is used for recognition.)

M. Yoshida conducted a study which essentially followed up the earlier investigation by Katz. Yoshida employed 50 materials similar to those used by Katz, and had subjects rate the materials on a series of 7-point semantic differential scales. No particular instructions were given as to how the task should be performed. The subjects handled the material samples by stroking lightly on the surface, picking them up by the tip, or crumpling them in the hand at times.

Yoshida summarized his major findings as follows:

The results clearly indicate the opposition between fibers and materials. The most important physical dimension which differentiates these two groups is specific gravity (not weight).

Tactual impressions under colder conditions are nearly the same as those under warmer conditions. And tactual impressions without participation of vision are nearly the same as those in the main experiment with vision. (References from Rubin and Elder 1980)

THE THERMAL ENVIRONMENT

The recent serious interest taken in the thermal environment due to the shortage of energy has occasioned reexamination of both building practice and perceptions of thermal comfort.

Research concerned with the environmental conditions of survival has been going on for a number of years. The development of submarines and high altitude aircraft as well as the space program has required the examination of the human requirements to sustain life and perform tasks under acceptable thermal conditions.

Military and space research has focused on the environmental limits of man, the upper and lower limits of toleration in terms of (1) life safety, and (2) performance of activities.

Research has also been conducted examining less demanding thermal comfort conditions using relatively moderate ranges of temperatures to define the desirable thermal environment of buildings.

Early studies of thermal comfort were designed to obtain response measures which were subjective and physiologically based. Body and skin temperatures, pulse and sweat rate were among the physiological measurements taken. Subjects were also asked to evaluate the environment using verbal and numerical scales. While traditional investigations have been performed in laboratories, in recent years there has been an increasing emphasis on conducting research in actual buildings while typical activities are being performed. Still another approach has been to combine the features of laboratory and field investigations.

The goal for those studying the effects of the thermal environment on people is often stated in one of two ways. It is to describe environmental characteristics which produce:

- Thermal comfort, defined as that condition of mind which expresses satisfaction with the thermal environment, or
- Thermal neutrality, defined as the condition in which a person would prefer neither warmer nor cooler surroundings.

As with the auditory area of research, the approaches concentrate on preventing feelings of discomfort, rather than on producing positive responses—such as interesting, invigorating—to thermal conditions.

The classic studies of F. Houghton and C. Yagloglou (engineers), which started more than half a century ago, have provided the general framework for laboratory studies since that time. Their research rationale underlies most thermal comfort studies available today:

The bodily feeling of warmth is not due alone to the temperature indicated by the dry bulb thermometer, neither does it depend solely upon the wet bulb

Thermal Comfort, Oaxaca Mexico.
Photo by F. Wilson.

Radio City, NYC.
Photo by F. Wilson.

Hippo, Washington, D.C. Zoo on a hot summer day.
Photo by F. Wilson.

Taking the sun—NYC.
Photo by F. Wilson.

temperature. Dry air at a relatively high temperature may feel cooler than air of considerably lower temperature with high moisture content.

Human comfort or discomfort depend largely on the relation between the rate of heat production and dissipation. By the process of metabolism heat is constantly generated within the body, while on the other hand, loss of heat is constantly occurring from the surface of the body by radiation, convection, and evaporation. To maintain a constant body temperature, the loss of heat must equal the heat produced. It is therefore apparent that any interference with the elimination of heat from the body is accompanied by a rise in temperature and a feeling of discomfort.

There are three principal factors affecting loss of body heat:

1. Temperature.
2. Humidity.
3. Air motion.

As the temperature of the air and surrounding objects rises, the loss of heat by convection and radiation decreases. When the temperature reaches that of the body, the loss by radiation and convection ceases. Finally, as the air temperature exceeds that of the body, heat passes from the air to the body.

If, on the other hand, the relative humidity is increased, the heat loss by evaporation decreases. If while the dry bulb temperature increases, the wet bulb temperature decreases sufficiently, the increase in the loss of heat by evaporation may be made equal to the decrease in the loss of heat by radiation and convection, resulting in no change in the thermal state of the body temperature or comfort.

From the above, it is concluded that there must necessarily be certain combinations of temperatures and humidities that produce the same total body heat loss by radiation, convection, and evaporation, and, therefore, the same feeling of comfort or discomfort. Lines passing through such air conditions may be called equal comfort lines. The fact is further substantiated by the general experience of heating engineers in observing that the lower the humidity the higher the temperature required for the same degree of comfort. Determining these equal comfort lines for various temperatures, humidities, and air velocities is the object of important investigations being carried on at research laboratories. (Houghton 1923)

Later work by Houghton and Yagloglou and their successors in the following decades has also shown the importance of clothing and activity on thermal responses to building environments.

Laboratory Studies

The influence of the early work by Houghton and Yagloglou has been so great that the variables examined and the methods that they developed form the basis for most studies being performed today in this research area. Their investigations were designed to establish and define a comfort zone in terms of the variables comprising "effective temperature," namely air temperature, velocity, and relative humidity. In their studies, they used male subjects, sometimes fully clothed, in other instances stripped to the waist. The subjects entered the first of two adjoining rooms, which differed from one another in terms of one or more of the variables indicated above. They remained in the first room for either one-half or one full hour. Afterward they entered the second room. The conditions of wet-bulb and dry-bulb temperatures were adjusted in the second room until subjects reported that the rooms were equal in warmth or coolness. From these studies, they derived lines of equal comfort which still form the basis for accepted thermal performance of buildings in the United States-ASHRAE criteria. The investigators also made physiological measurements—pulse rate, weight loss, and increase of body temperature.

Possibly the most comprehensive investigation of thermal comfort was performed by F. Rohles (psychologist). The test subjects in the study consisted of 800 male and 800 female college students ranging in age from 18 to 24. A total of 160 experimental conditions were examined—8 relative humidities (15% to 85%) and 20 dry-bulb temperatures (60 to 98°F, or 16 to 37°C). Ten subjects, five men and five women, participated in each test condition. Different subjects were used for all conditions. (Rohles 1971)

The tests were conducted in an environmental test chamber consisting of: a main chamber 12 ft (3.7 m) wide, 24 ft (7.3 m) long with an 8 ft (2.4 m) ceiling; a pretest room 9 ft (2.7 m) wide and 18 ft (5.5 m) long; and a control room. All subjects wore cotton twill shirts and trousers.

Subjects reported to the pretest room where temperatures ranged from 75 to 78°F (24 to 26°C). They were read instructions about the study and told how to rate their thermal sensations. After approximately 30 minutes, the subjects entered the main test chamber. They sat at tables and were permitted to read, talk, or play cards. The study lasted 3 hours, and the environment was rated at 1.0, 1.5, 2.0, 2.5, and 3.0 hour intervals. The rating sheets were collected after each rating period.

The results of the study by Rohles led to an examination of the scale used to rate the environment, which combined thermal sensation (e.g., cool, warm) with a comfort rating (comfortable). Later ASHRAE studies employed two scales to obtain separate ratings of "sensation" and "comfort."

The ability to perform activities is generally important in thermal comfort work, this factor is especially significant. This is because activities require different levels of effort (i.e., the heat produced by a person performing an activity), which influence the balance of bodily heat production and dissipation—a major influence on feelings of thermal comfort. A goal of researchers has therefore been to develop a standardized procedure to define levels of activity, measured by heat production. P. McNall (engineer) et al. describe such a procedure in a study of temperature, humidity, and activity levels. The study was

ET °C	Temperature sensation	Discomfort	Regulation of body temp.	Health	ET °F
40	Very hot	Limited tolerance	Failure of free skin evaporation		100
		Very uncomfort.		Increasing danger of heat-stroke	
35	Hot	Uncomfortable			90
	Warm	Slightly uncomfortable	Increasing vasodilation sweating		
30	Slightly warm				80
25	Neutral	Comfortable	No registered sweating	Normal health	70
20	Slightly cool				
	Cool	Slightly uncomfortable	Behavioral changes	Complaints from dry mucosa	60
15	Cold		Shivering begins	Impairment peripheral circulation	
10	Very cold	Uncomfortable			50

Effective Temperature (ET).
(ASHRAE)
(Rubin and Elder 1980)

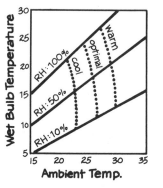

The line shows different combinations of ambient temperature and humidity which will provide optimal thermal comfort for sedentary persons.

Comfort line by Nevins.
(Fanger)
(Rubin and Elder 1980)

Representative Values for Heat Production at Various Activities
(From Canter)

Activity	Heat Production* W/m²
Basal metabolism	45
Seated at rest	60
Standing at rest	65
Office work	75
Walking on level ground	
at 3.2 km/h	115
at 8.0 km/h	340
Heavy manual work	250
Digging	320

*Metabolic Heat Production per unit surface area, W/m²

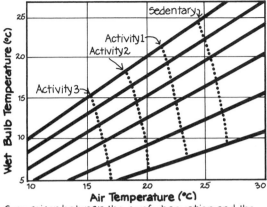

Comparison between the comfort equation and the results of Nevins and McNall. The curves are comfortlines corresponding to four different activities.
━━━ Nevins and McNall ••••••• Comfort equation

Comfort votes for four activities.
(Nevins and McNall)

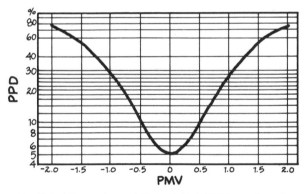

Predicted Percentage of Dissatisfied (PPD) as a function of Predicted Mean Vote (PMV).
(Fanger)
(Rubin and Elder 1980, p. 190)

performed in a way similar to that described in the Rohles study. The activity levels were achieved by having subjects walk up and down for 5-minute periods on two 4 in. (10 cm) steps. The rates of walking speed were varied to accomplish the three metabolic rates—600, 800, and 1000 Btu/h.

In contrast to the ASHRAE research approach, where several subjects participate simultaneously under environmental conditions specified by the researcher, P. Fanger (Danish engineer) conducted extensive laboratory studies in another way. Fanger's experimental technique is described in one such study by Fanger and B. Olesen concerned with skin temperature distribution for a resting person. Thirty-two subjects (16 males and 16 females) took part in the study, one at a time. Each subject wore a harness on which 14 heat measurement devices (thermistors) were attached. The thermistors were taped to the skin on the locations specified in the accompanying figure. A standard cotton twill uniform was worn in the environmental chamber.

At the start of the study, the temperature was set at 25.6°C, based on earlier studies by Fanger defining thermal comfort. The ambient temperature was then varied in accordance with the desire of the subject, who was asked at 10-minute intervals whether adjustments (warmer or cooler) should be made. The subject was encouraged to request very small changes if desired. Male and female subjects preferred similar temperatures. In addition, the only region where males and females differed significantly in their local skin temperature was on the feet, the feet temperatures of females being 2.10°C lower than that of males. (Fanger 1970)

Finally, in the case of one subject, a skin temperature distribution was obtained by means of thermography. This subject was tested and photographed in the nude.

Fanger later refined his method of obtaining thermographic records of subjects, which is described in the following way: Basically, the subject is photographed from many different directions. A fixed camera is used with mirrors mounted around the subject. A large number of photographs is then taken of each subject and each photograph is planimetered. Subjects are photographed seated and standing, nude and clothed. Each photograph then provides the projected area of the body for a given viewing angle. When the projected area of the body is known for an adequately large number of angles, the desired data for the human body is then calculated. (Fanger 1970)

PERFORMANCE MEASURES

The most direct way of finding out how temperature or other environmental conditions affect the ability to perform an activity is to vary the environment, e.g., room temperature, in an orderly way and determine the consequences, measured in terms of performance.

Studies of this type date from the time of the Hawthorne investigations performed in the 1920s and 1930s (see Chap. 19). More recently, human factors researchers since World War II have intensively examined task performance, primarily under extreme environmental conditions. At the same time, industrial psychologists have developed a multitude of standardized tasks and psychological tests for job selection and performance evaluation purposes.

D. Wyon (psychologist) has been a strong advocate of the need to include performance measures in M/E studies. In several studies, he has used measures of performance in conjunction with other methods of evaluating how subjects respond to thermal conditions. An illustration of his approach is an investigation carried out in a climatic chamber. Thirty-two subjects, 16 males and 16 females, participated separately in a 5-hour experiment, wearing standardized uniforms. Room temperatures were varied while several different types of measurements were made:

- physiological (body temperature, weight)
- subjective judgments (semantic differential)
- performance tests (numerical, word memory, typing).

One measure of performance was the score achieved on a task of adding sets of five 2-digit numbers. Subjects were paid on the basis of their accuracy. Another test was concerned with word memory. A list of 25 common words was shown to subjects. Later a list of 50 words as presented, and the task was to identify words from the earlier list of 25, which appeared on the test list. Wyon has found that the ability to perform several tasks was impaired at temperatures of 27°C and above.

Observational Studies

Since the thermal resistance of clothing has an important effect on thermal comfort, clothing cannot be ignored in such research. The traditional way of dealing with clothing has been to standardize it in laboratory studies. For example, all subjects participating in a study would wear a standard uniform, having known thermal resistance properties. Clothing would then be a "control" variable—one which would be fixed for all experimental conditions.

Clothing has also been used as a dependent variable or response measure in a field study of classroom behavior. M. Humphreys (British physicist) studied thermal comfort in a classroom, by keeping a record of the clothing worn by children aged 11 to 17, during the months of May through July. Boys and girls wore traditional uniforms to school, and were able to remove or add items of clothing at their discretion during the school day. Humphreys used a time-lapse camera to record the appearance of the children every 8 minutes. The time and temperature were recorded on each photograph as well. In general, he found a close relationship between room temperatures and the clothing worn by the children.

Checklist of Observations
(Wyon and Holmberg)

	Posture (−3 to +5)	Legs	apart	+1
			together	−1
		Arms	spread	+1
			held close	−1
		Hand	open	+1
			closed	−1
		Leaning	back	+1
			head in hand	+1
2	Clothing (0 to +5)	Collar	open	+1
		Jacket	open	+1
		Arms bare		+1
		Shoes off		+1
		Removal of item		+1
3	Appearance (0 to +6)	Sweating		+1
		Flushed		+1
		Mouth open		+1
		Fanning face		+1
		Wiping forehead or hands		+1
		Loosening clothing		+1

Index of perceptible response to heat (1 + 2 + 3) (−3 to +16)

4	Inattention (0 to +4)	Gazing around		+1
		Closing eyes		+1
		Playing		+1
		Yawning		+1
5	Restlessness (0 to +3)	Writhing about		+1
		Tipping chair		+1
		Fidgeting		+1
6	Disturbance (0 to +4)	Laughing aloud		+1
		Talking to neighbor		+1
		Standing up		+1
		Teasing neighbor		+1

Index of undesirable classroom behaviour (4 + 5 + 6) (0 to +11)

Another study dealing with the effects of thermal conditions on the behavior of school children was performed by I. Holmberg and Wyon. The investigation took part in an observational classroom, fitted with one-way mirrors to permit the children to be seen without disrupting their activities. Four researchers, using identical checklists, observed 50 individual children, aged 9 to 11, in a predetermined sequence whereby each child was observed for 1 minute in every 10-minute period. The behaviors recorded dealt with posture, clothing, appearance, concentration, restlessness, and conduct. These categories of observation were developed in a preliminary pilot study. Three room temperatures (20°C, 25°C, 30°C) were used to determine whether they affected the behavior of the children in an orderly way. The test sessions consisted of two 40-minute periods, separated by a 10-minute rest period.

We have discussed several procedures used to determine how thermal conditions may influence people. The earliest studies concentrated on physiological effects (e.g., skin temperature, sweat rate), and employed voting or rating procedures. Then, as we have seen, observational approaches were used, based on the judgments of trained researchers. In all of these approaches we still must determine the implications of the observations and measurements made. Can thermal conditions be related to the ability of people to perform desired and/or needed activities?

FIELD STUDIES

As far back as the 1920s, there was a realization among ASHRAE researchers that laboratory studies using college students were insufficient to define thermal conditions in buildings. Consequently, several field investigations were performed in office buildings. The subjects were male and female employees between 20 and 70 years of age. One such study was performed by A. Newton et al. in an air conditioned building in Minneapolis, Minnesota between May and July 1937. A questionnaire was given to the employees, to determine their responses to the environment. The questionnaires were filled out every day and collected the next day.

The building was divided into zones, and wet- and dry-bulb temperatures as well as relative humidity measurements were recorded in the morning, at midday, and at the end of the working day. The measures of thermal environmental conditions were then compared with the response data. The study did not demonstrate simple clearcut relationships between environmental attributes and the responses of subjects.

Another field investigation was performed in an office building by L. Anderson et al. In the study, humidity conditions were systematically modified, while temperatures were not altered. The conditions were as follows: (1) humidifier working always; (2) humidifier operating 1 hour in the afternoon; (3) humidifier working 2 hours AM, 2 hours PM; and (4) humidifier not working.

Wet- and dry-bulb temperatures were taken and workers (600+) were asked to fill out rating scales. Low humidity was cause for complaint, but temperature was a more critical factor when it exceeded 20–22°C, the recommended range in Sweden.

ASYMMETRICAL HEATING

The architect's involvement with thermal comfort is often indirect, since in most modern buildings this area is addressed by thermal engineers. The major exception concerns radiant heating primarily related to window areas and/or lighting systems. The relationship of building design features (e.g., room dimensions, window size, placement and orientation, shading materials, etc.) to thermal comfort was explored by F. Langdon and A. Loudon in a study of school buildings.

The school investigation was a follow-up of an earlier study dealing with office buildings. A questionnaire distributed to teachers dealt with questions about the use of the room, incidence of direct sunlight, and the efficiency of windows and blinds for ventilation and cooling. Thermal comfort was assessed on a 7-point scale ranging from comfortably cool to uncomfortably hot and by a question dealing with the frequency and intensity of discomfort. Teachers were also asked for observations about children (e.g., appearance) and opinions regarding the effects of overheating on their own performance and that of the children. Estimates of the thermal performance of the buildings (based on the building features cited above) were correlated with the thermal responses of occupants. The survey indicated the main factors which govern overheating in the summer, and (established) a general relationship between rise in calculated peak temperatures and increase in thermal discomfort. (Langdon 1970)

The problem of asymmetrical heating has also received considerable laboratory research attention in the past decade. For example, D. McIntyre (British physicist) conducted a series of experiments in a thermal environmental chamber where air was admitted through a permeable floor and was extracted through grills set at the top of the walls. Four subjects were run at one time. They sat in the chamber for 45 minutes, reading, talking, writing, or engaging in other sedentary activities and then rated the environment by means of a variety of rating scales. The results showed that uneven radiation was disliked by subjects.

The same author examined five levels of relative humidity (20% to 60%) with temperature held constant at 23°C for 5 hours. In this investigation, McIntyre used a questionnaire and a mood adjective checklist to obtain responses from subjects to the environment. Prior to the study, a personality test was administered to measure introversion and extroversion characteristics of the subjects. The differences in relative humidity had no apparent effect on the subjects. (McIntyre 1973)

Unlike other M/E problem areas (e.g., visual perception) where the features of the physical environment are sometimes not given sufficient attention (to correlate with human responses), thermal comfort research has always stressed this requirement. On the other hand, thermal comfort work still needs to: (1) cover extended time periods, (2) deal with the responses of individuals (rather than group averages), and (3) be conducted under realistic field conditions. (The latter criticism applies to most M/E research.)

A study designed to overcome some of these deficiencies was performed by Humphreys and J. Nicol. It took place at the then Building Research Station of the United Kingdom between April 1967 and July 1968 in a building housing offices and laboratories. The subjects were 18 members of the scientific and clerical staff who worked at their regular jobs while participating in the study. On the desk of each subject was an automatic environmental monitor which recorded globe temperature, air velocity, wet-bulb and dry-bulb temperature, and comfort votes. The monitors were connected to a central data logger. At hourly intervals an auditory signal (whistle) indicated when it was time to register a vote. Comparisons of simple measures of globe and air temperature were also good as complex indices for the conditions studied. (Humphreys 1971)

Fanger and I. Griffiths (British physicist) summarized requirements for better information dealing with the thermal environment:

"Research has concentrated on investigation of subjective warmth as a function of the four major physical variables, but work has (only) begun on other physical variables such as nonuniformity (with respect to space and time). The general picture that has emerged is that the work of the psychologist in this field has just begun." (Fanger, Griffiths 1970)

Finally, design for an energy efficient and acceptable thermal environment should include a degree of flexibility to enable occupants (or building operators) to control environmental conditions, e.g., by opening windows, having "local" thermostats, etc. (References from Rubin and Elder 1980)

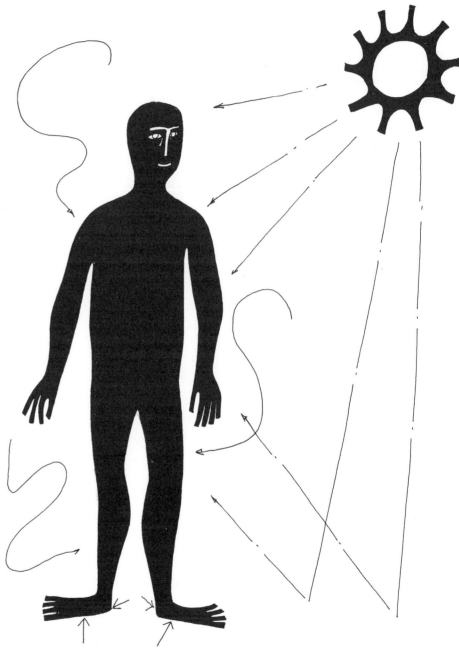

Heat gain through radiation, convection, and conduction.

THERMAL SPACE (Hall 1966, p. 52)

"The skin is a major sense organ. Without the ability to perceive heat and cold, organisms including man would soon perish. The subtle sensing and communicating qualities of the skin are commonly overlooked. These qualities also relate to man's perception of space.

Nerves called the proprioceptors keep man informed of what is taking place when he works his muscles, providing feedback which enables man to move his body smoothly. These nerves occupy a key position in kinesthetic space perception. Another set of nerves, the esterioceptors, located in his skin convey the sensations of heat, cold, touch, and pain to the central nervous system. Since two different systems of nerves are employed, kinesthetic space is qualitatively different from thermal space, but the two systems work together and are mutually reinforcing most of the time.

The capacity of the skin both to emit and detect radiant (infrared) heat is extraordinarily high. This capacity, since it is so highly developed, was most probably important to survival in the past and may still have a function. Man is well equipped both to send and to receive messages as to his emotional state by means of changes in the skin temperature in various parts of the body. Emotional states are also reflected in changes in the blood Isupply to different parts of the body. The blush is a visual sign; but dark skinned people also blush; it is apparent that the blush is not just a matter of change in skin coloration. Careful observation of people when they are embarrassed or angry reveals a swelling of the blood vessels in the region of the temples and the forehead. The additional blood raises the temperature in the flushed area."

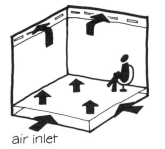

air inlet

Thermal Comfort Mood Adjective Check List
(McIntyre)

Time _____ Name _____

Each of the words in the following list describes feelings or mood. Please use the list to describe your feelings at this moment. Mark each word according to these instructions:

If the word definitely describes how you feel at the moment you read it, circle the double star (★★) to the right of the word. For example, if the word is *calm* and you are definitely feeling calm at the moment, circle the double star as follows:

Calm (★★) ★ ? no   (This means you definitely feel calm at this moment).

If the word only slightly applies to your feelings at the moment, circle the single star as follows:

Calm ★★ (★) ? no   (This means you feel slightly calm at the moment).

If the word is not clear to you or if you cannot decide whether or not it describes your feelings, circle the question mark as follows:

Calm ★★ ★ (?) no   (This means you cannot decide whether you are calm or not).

If you clearly decide that the word does not apply to your feelings at this moment, circle the no as follows:

Calm ★★ ★ ? (no)   (This means you are sure you are not calm at this moment).

Work rapidly. Your first reaction is the best. Work down the first column before going to the next. This should take only a few minutes.

worthless	★★ ★ ? no	sad	★★ ★ ? no	empty	★★ ★ ? no
angry	★★ ★ ? no	earnest	★★ ★ ? no	tired	★★ ★ ? no
concentrating	★★ ★ ? no	sluggish	★★ ★ ? no	kindly	★★ ★ ? no
drowsy	★★ ★ ? no	forgiving	★★ ★ ? no	fearful	★★ ★ ? no
affectionate	★★ ★ ? no	clutched up	★★ ★ ? no	regretful	★★ ★ ? no
apprehensive	★★ ★ ? no	lonely	★★ ★ ? no	egotistic	★★ ★ ? no
blue	★★ ★ ? no	cocky	★★ ★ ? no	overjoyed	★★ ★ ? no
boastful	★★ ★ ? no	lighthearted	★★ ★ ? no	vigorous	★★ ★ ? no
elated	★★ ★ ? no	energetic	★★ ★ ? no	witty	★★ ★ ? no
active	★★ ★ ? no	playful	★★ ★ ? no	rebellious	★★ ★ ? no
nonchalant	★★ ★ ? no	suspicious	★★ ★ ? no	serious	★★ ★ ? no
sceptical	★★ ★ ? no	startled	★★ ★ ? no	warmhearted	★★ ★ ? no
shocked	★★ ★ ? no	defiant	★★ ★ ? no	insecure	★★ ★ ? no
bold	★★ ★ ? no	thoughtful	★★ ★ ? no	self-centered	★★ ★ ? no
helpless	★★ ★ ? no	hopeless	★★ ★ ? no	pleased	★★ ★ ? no
miserable	★★ ★ ? no	tense	★★ ★ ? no	vulnerable	★★ ★ ? no

Diagram of test chamber.
(McIntyre)   Outlet
(Rubin and Elder 1980)

ENVIRONMENTAL STABILITY—MOVEMENTS

Movement in buildings typically results from wind, construction activities, mechanical devices, neighboring factories, and transportation systems (roadway, rail, and aircraft). Movement also occurs as a result of activities by building occupants, e.g., children's games. Until quite recently, architects have not demonstrated great concern about building deflections as a source of occupant dissatisfaction. The materials and techniques commonly used produced structures with few building movement problems. Newly developed methods, employing "light-weight" construction techniques, however, have altered the situation. While the engineers and designers have become highly sophisticated in producing buildings which are safe from a structural standpoint, the acceptability of buildings has assumed greater prominence, that is, the success of the structure in meeting the day-to-day needs of the occupants. Unfortunately, latter-day construction methods have introduced unwanted deflection. For example, floor deflections when walking across a room might be annoying in themselves but might also raise questions in the minds of occupants concerning the quality and safety of construction, regardless of the objective facts. High-rise structures have been prone to drift problems during storms and high winds. Vibrations have been another source of difficulty, sometimes associated with mechanical equipment, in other instances as a result of human related activities.

General Motors Manufacturing Plant circa 1908.
Photo courtesy of General Motors.

Since building movement has only recently been recognized as a problem area, most researchers dealing with the topic have been concerned with movements produced by vehicles, primarily to better understand the effects of vibration on people. While a few of these studies are mentioned, the reader should be aware that the experimental variables (usually vibrations) employed in them differ considerably from those encountered in buildings. As in many sensory research areas, an early study has made a profound impact upon later research.

The first of the more thorough research programs was carried out by H. Reiher and F. Meister. A total of 25 persons, between 25 and 40 years of age, either stood or lay down on a platform undergoing vertical or horizontal motion. After being exposed to one type of vibration for about 10 minutes, subjects were asked to make judgments on a 6-point scale (imperceptible, just perceptible, distinctly perceptible, strongly perceptible, unpleasant, or exceedingly unpleasant). The curves derived by these authors are in widespread use today and serve as the foundation for all following studies. (Reiher, Meister 1966)

Stimulation Studies—Building Movement

P. Chen and C. Robertson reviewed studies of movement in buldings and performed a series of investigations using a motion simulator. They indicated

Cadillac Assembly Line 1978.
Photo courtesy of General Motors.

Design for Museum of Modern Art Building, NYC by
Cesar Pelli.
Courtesy of Cesar Pelli and Associates.

The Cathedral at Lucca, Early 15th century. Photo
courtesy of the Italian Government Travel Office

that human reactions to vibration can be classified into six comfort zones. While describing their own investigations they further note that absolute thresholds (barely detectable) vary considerably from person to person and are influenced by several factors.

Chen and Robertson employed a motion simulator (HATS) consisting of a room mounted on a platform which could be moved simultaneously in two directions. The room had a door but no window (which might provide visual motion cues). Of particular interest are the instructions given to the subjects. This factor is an important one often neglected in research studies, and yet has an important influence on the results of behavioral studies. The same researchers systematically varied the information given to the subjects. The subjects in one instance were not told to expect the room to move. Instead, they were told that the study was a visual screening test, and later, tests of distance and height judgments. In a follow-up test, subjects were told the nature of the study, i.e., to determine when motion was perceived. (Chen and Robertson 1972)

M. Yamada (engineer) and T. Goto (engineer) designed a simulated house which enabled them to systematically vary a number of parameters associated with the perception of motion in buildings. The purpose of their experimental program was to develop criteria for motions in tall buildings. The researchers employed a variety of approaches in their work. The first procedure consisted of asking subjects to stand in the same direction to the longitudinal axis for fore and aft tests. When these tests were completed "side to side tests" followed. The simulator was operated in terms of a predetermined schedule. The experimental subjects indicated whenever the sensation of motion changed. This information was recorded together with a description of the characteristics and duration of the motion in physical terms.

The next series of studies described by Yamada and Goto was designed to determine the effects of motion on task performance. The task of the subject was to trace lines, squares, and circles while seated in a chair within the simulated house. The responses measured were the time taken to complete the tasks and the deviations from the base line, i.e., the degree of accuracy of tracing. The experimental conditions were similar to those employed in the earlier studies. (Yamada, Goto 1972)

The final study of the same authors was concerned with the movement of people in buildings—vertical and horizontal. In this investigation the researchers used a motion picture camera, focusing on the head and feet of the subjects. The camera was set on a platform above the house (the roof was removed). Vertical and horizontal lines spaced 200 mm apart were drawn on the ceiling and the walls of the house. The subject was brought into the house and marks were placed on the top of the head and toes. Then, with the house being moved in accordance with the experimental design, the subject "walks a line" back and forth between walls at a pace of 84 steps per minute (indicated by a

207

metronome). The subject is photographed while the tests are performed. A similar study was performed with subjects ascending and descending a stairway.

These studies demonstrate a highly innovative method of collecting building user responses to movement under controlled, yet semirealistic conditions.

FIELD STUDIES OF BUILDING MOVEMENT

Of the several causes of building movement, wind has perhaps the most widespread effect. J. Reed (engineer) investigated wind-induced motion in two office buildings. He instrumented the two buildings to measure the motions induced during severe storms. After storms lasting almost 24 hours, he conducted a survey of the building occupants to determine their reactions. He was especially interested in identifying the particular cues employed by occupants in making their assessments (auditory, visual). (Reed 1971)

D. Allen and J. Swallow (Canadian researchers) describe a study procedure recommended by them to determine whether a vibration problem exists in a building. It is based on a "heel impact" test, where a person standing on his toes drops suddenly to his heels. They suggest that the test be performed by a 170-lb. (77-kg) man, standing at the geometric center of a floor. Subjective impressions would be obtained from a subject also standing near the center of the floor. The authors further state that the test should be repeated at the 1/4 and 1/6 points on the centerline perpendicular to the direction of the stiffeners. (Allen, Swallow 1975)

At the Commonwealth Experimental Building Station, N.S.W., Australia, a vibrator was designed, built, and used. Research subjects performed their usual tasks unaware of the existence of the vibrator. The study consisted of enabling subjects to volunteer comments about their environment. The study authors noted that the lower values of the Reiher-Meister Scale did not elicit comments about vibration until the movements were brought to the attention of subjects, at which time the movements were noticed. They point out that the Reiher-Meister Scale was developed by subjecting people to vibration in a laboratory and asking them to state their reactions to movements. Under these circumstances, it is likely that subjects would be aware of vibrations that would not be noticed under everyday conditions.

STUDIES OF MOVEMENT—TRANSPORTATION

W. Helberg and E. Sperling had subjects sit on a wooden bench which was attached to a vibrating table. The bench was moved either horizontally or vertically, but not both ways simultaneously. Vibrations that were "very nearly" sinusoidal, at frequencies of between 1 and 12 Hz, were used. The amplitudes

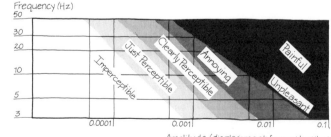

Human sensitivity to vibration (Reiher-Meister scale) (Australian study). (Rubin and Elder 1980)

Factors Influencing Vibration Thresholds

- Period of Isolation
- Body Orientation
- Body Movement
- Body Posture
- Expectancy of Sway
- Visual Cues
- Activity being performed

Motion Simulator
(Yamada & Goto)

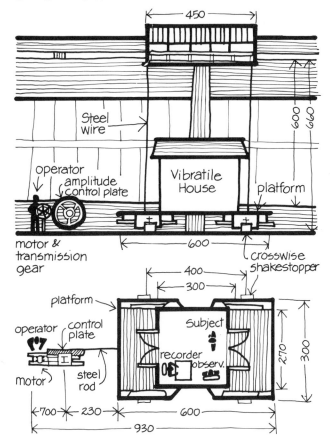

Motion simulator (Yamada and Goto).
(Rubin and Elder 1980)

employed were between 0.01 and 2.5 cm. Subjects were seated for periods ranging from 2 to 10 minutes. After this time, they were asked to make judgments on a 7-point scale (just perceptible to intolerable). (Helberg and Sperling 1966)

D. Parks and F. Snyder investigated human reaction to low frequency vibration. A hydraulically actuated shake table was used to provide vertical, sinusoidal vibrations at frequencies ranging from 1 to 23 hz. The vibration platform was mounted with a standard aircraft seat having felt covered plywood in place of a seat cushion. Four categories of subjective judgments were recorded along with electrocardiograms. The subjects were asked to identify four levels of vibration severity: (1) definitely perceptible, (2) mildly annoying, (3) extremely annoying, and (4) alarming. (Parks and Snyder 1961)

A study by A. Weisz et al. compared the effects of sinusoidal and random vibration. Actually three different vibration conditions were used: a simple sinusoid at 5 Hz; sinusoidal vibration at 5 Hz with random amplitude; and random vibration frequencies ranging from 4 to 12 Hz. Subjects were required to perform either visual or auditory monitoring tasks during exposure to the vibration.

C. Holland et al. used a simulator with an electrically controlled, hydraulically powered feedback system. The input to the system was a voltage supplied by an analog computer. Thirty-nine 'rides' (combinations of movement conditions) were made up of combinations of 8 or 32 sine-wave components. Frequency components were spaced at intervals of 0.25 Hz with a frequency range between 1 and 9 Hz. One 'ride,' at a gain setting of 1.50, was used as a standard for comparison. Subjects were told that the value of this standard was 10, and that other 'rides' were to be quantified in terms of "roughness" as compared with this value. Each 'ride' lasted 60 seconds, with the standard presented first. Background noises ranging between 90 and 94 dB were included under all experimental conditions.

H. Jacklin and G. Lidell followed up initial studies performed on a vibrating platform with tests in passenger vehicles. An accelerometer was placed on the rear seat of a conventional five-passenger automobile.

The subjects were tested under a variety of conditions (three roads, three loadings, three tire pressures) in order to determine when movement in the left rear seat was judged "disturbing" to the passenger. The test car was started slowly and accelerated gradually, until his condition was reported.

Van Deusen had subjects rate that "ride discomfort" of a truck moving on 21 different paved and unpaved road surfaces. The ratings were made by regulating the sound intensity of white noise until it "matched" the degree of discomfort associated with the ride. Physical measurements were made by means of pickup transducers located on the vehicle seats. Time records of vibration during acceleration were obtained for each vehicle in three mutually perpendicular directions for each noted condition.

PERFORMANCE STUDIES

The studies described have employed the procedure of having subjects make judgments concerning the noticeability and/or discomfort caused by motion. More recent studies performed for military and space missions have been designed to determine the effects of vibration primarily on the ability to perform tasks. A number of these investigations will be described to indicate the type of performance measures obtained.

A very common task is reading and it therefore has received considerable research attention. J. Dennis, for example had subjects read a series of 2-digit numbers (at a visual angle of 5 minutes of arc, distance 10 ft, 10 in. (3.3 m)) while seated on a vibration table. Subjects were exposed to "light" (5–27 Hz; amplitude 0.1 in. to 0.003 in. (2.5 mm to 0.076 mm)) and "heavy" (7–90 Hz; 0.1 in. to 0.003 in. (2.5 mm to 0.076 mm)) vibrations. Visual performance was significantly affected by all but one of the conditions. As expected, heavy vibrations were responsible for more errors than light ones.

M. Schmitz examined the effects of vibration on a number of tasks. In his study, 18 subjects were seated on a contour wooden chair, mounted on a shake table which was vibrated as follows: 0.15 g and 0.30 g at 3.5 Hz, and 0.18 g and 0.35 g at 2.5 Hz. Subjects first performed a driver simulation task for 15 minutes. Then the vibration conditions took place. Measurements taken were: visual acuity, using Landolt rings; a hand tremor test, which required the subject to keep his index finger steady; and a test to maintain constant foot pressure. The findings of this study were inconclusive—consistent effects were not apparent.

Since noise often accompanies vibration as an environmental problem, many studies have been conducted to determine their combined effects (as well as their individual ones) on task performance. R. Hornick examined the effects of noise and/or vibration on simple reaction time, responding to a simple signal as soon as possible. The experimental conditions were: control (no noise or vibration); noise alone (87 dB); vertical vibration alone (3.5 Hz at 0.30 g); and combined noise and vibration. The task of the subject was to press a button as soon as possible after the onset of a red signal light. This study also did not produce any systematic findings attributable to the experimental conditions.

The tasks most frequently examined in vibration studies have concerned tracking. Tracking involves following a target in two- or three-dimensional space with reference to an observer. The observer is required to make a continuously changing response to a continuously changing "error" signal which is fed back to him. Tracking tasks have been primarily designed for those responsible for monitoring and/or flying aircraft (and more recently, space vehicles). An example of a tracking task is as follows. A cathode-ray oscilloscope is used as a display device. The experimenter presents a signal (which moves in a manner preprogrammed to suit experimental purposes) on the display. The task of

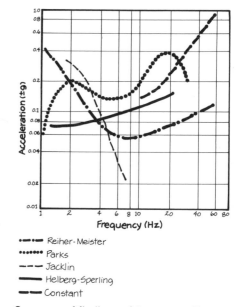

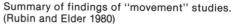

Summary of findings of "movement" studies. (Rubin and Elder 1980)

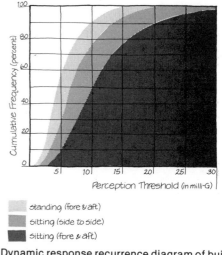

Dynamic response recurrence diagram of building movement (Chen, Robertson). (Rubin and Elder 1980)

Design for Museum of Modern Art Building, NYC by
Cesar Pelli.
Drawing by Jon Pickard.

the subject is to control the movement of the signal by means of a joystick (or other control) in accordance with experimental instructions, for example, center the target signal on a vertical line on the display. The complexity of tracking tasks can be varied readily (e.g., size, speed of movement, delay of feedback, number of other possible signals, etc.), thereby making them a very important and versatile research approach for many problems.

CONCLUSION

While comparatively few studies have been performed which deal with the effects of building movement on people, their quality has generally been high. Furthermore, the research approaches have been quite varied, ranging from performance to attitude measurements, under controlled laboratory and field conditions. (Rubin and Elder 1980)

Noticeability of Motion Cues
(MIT Survey)

Motion Cues	Building A			Building B		
	Total % (if noticed)	Most noticeable	Next most noticeable	Total % (if noticed)	Most noticeable	Next most noticeable
Movement of doors, fixtures, etc.	56.2	18.8	9.4	64.1	9.4	37.7
Creaking sounds	92.1	28.1	34.4	64.1	20.8	26.4
Feeling self moving (includes motion sickness symptoms)	62.5	28.1	17.2	69.9	51.0	15.1
Looking out window and sensing building moving	62.5	4.7	10.9	11.3	1.9	3.8
Comments from co-workers	37.5	12.5	7.8	17.0	11.3	
Other	46.9	4.7	12.5	34.0		1.9
No preference		3.1	7.8		5.6	15.1
Not knowing building was moving				5.6		
Total		100.0	100.0		100.0	100.0

(Rubin and Elder 1980, p. 206)

AGGRESSION AND DEFENSIBLE SPACE

Aggression is, according to psychologists, behavior intended to harm another person. There are a number of categories of explanation for the high level of abusive behavior between humans, some contend it is situational, others that it is learned, or biological. Some say it is an aberration of an otherwise cooperative, constructive, and peaceful organism.

Some researchers claim that physical and mental abnormalities explain the unique hot-tempered behavior of certain individuals. Violent behavior has been linked to chromosomal abnormalities and various types of brain damage. This theory, however, will not stand closer examination, for the majority of people with a history of violent behavior have no such abnormality or injury and the people with such damage or defects have not proven to be more aggressive than others.

Frustration and anonymity also appear to promote aggressive behavior, at least they have done so in laboratory experiments. Aggression can be provoked by frustration and anonymity can facilitate violence and other forms of antisocial behavior. However, here again, the outcome was not proven inevitable.

According to social learning theory, exposure to models of violent behavior and reinforcement for aggressive acts explain why people attack each other.

Apparently we learn how to perform specific aggressive acts and the general strategies for aggressive behavior by observing others. In our culture, two of the most influential models may be members of our families and the characters portrayed on television and film.

People do not behave aggressively unless such behavior elicits reinforcement, that is, unless aggression has rewarded them in the past or they expect it to reward them in the future, and this sad hope is all too often realized. Therefore aggression continues to be relied upon because it does work in acquiring or realizing the aims of the aggressor.

Freud believed that human beings were basically antagonistic towards each other and only achieved an uneasy balance between destructive and productive forces within themselves through sublimation of their natural tendencies.

A great many writers, from Freud to Lorenz, have suggested that aggression is an inescapable part of our basic animal inheritance. This view, however, is sharply contended. Not only is it contradicted because it promotes what its critics believe is an unnecessarily pessimistic view of human nature, but because it is not substantiated by the evidence they present.

It is known that human aggression can be modified to take many forms, some less destructive than others. We also know that just as cats appear to learn

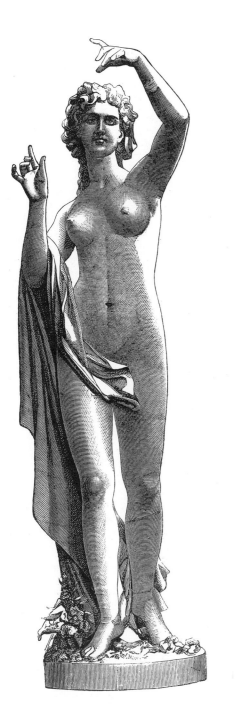

to control their species by controlling specific predatory behavior, humans can learn to suppress, control, and rechannel aggressive behavior. Or, for those that believe that humankind is basically good, it is contended that humans can refrain from aggression because it is in fact unnatural behavior.

Konrad Lorenz contends that aggression is instinctive and has adaptive benefits for humans as well as other animals. He feels that to block aggression by social sanctions may well be more dangerous than the aggression itself.

However many psychologists say this point of view will not bear closer scrutiny. Studies have shown that the emergence of "instinctive" aggressive behavior often depends on learning. Also, they state that the idea of a universal aggressive instinct make it difficult to explain variations in levels of human aggression within the same and between cultures.

Given these cautions and contentions against direct analogies between human and animal behavior, how is our understanding of ourselves to be enriched by the information gathered from observing other animals? One way is that some of the analytic tools borrowed from the studies of animals have proven valuable in clarifying the mysteries of human behavior, say a number of behavioral scientists.

For the designer, the benefit may lie in the realm of analogy and intuitive insight. Animal behavior may form a basis of insight as valid as Kandinsky's persuit of nonobjective form.

This idea was expressed by sculptor John Flannagan some years ago in speaking of his use of animals in his sculpture. He said that his intent was to create ". . .an abstract linear and cubical fantasy out of the fluctuating sequence of consciousness, expressing a vague general memory of many creatures, of human and animal life in its varied forms.

It partakes of the deep pantheistic urge of kinship with all living things and fundamental unity of all life, a unity so complete it can see a figure of dignity even in the form of a goat. Many of the humbler life forms are often more useful as design than the narcissistic human figure, because, humanly, we project ourselves into all art works using the human figure, identifying ourselves with the beauty, grace, or strength of the image as intense wish fulfillment; and any variant, even when necessitated by design, shocks as maimed, and produces some psychological pain. With an animal form, on the contrary, any liberty taken with the familiar forms is felt as amusing, strange cruelty.

To that instrument of the subconscious, the hand of a sculptor, there exists an image within every rock, the creative act of realization merely frees it."

We can extract this idea from the image in the rock that Flannagan saw and apply it to the image of animal behavior and humans in the design of architectural space. There may well exist within behavioral juxtapositions of other animals, an image of a suitable human environment.

The results of animal studies appear to apply to humans on other levels as well. Psychologists claim that in learning fundamental principles derived from the studies of lower animals they have been successful in applying them to the understanding of human learning.

The most basic concept to emerge from the studies of animals is that behavior is an expression of inherited as well as environmental factors working in unity.

The anthropologist Robert Hall notes that aggression normally leads to proper spacing of animals, lest they become so numerous as to destroy their environment, and themselves as well. Hall notes that when crowding becomes excessive, interactions intensify which lead to greater stress and aggression. As psychological and emotional stress builds, tempers wear thin and subtle but powerful changes occur in the body chemistry. Births decrease and deaths increase until a state known as population collapse occurs. Such cycles, he states, of buildup and collapse are now generally recognized as normal for warm-blooded vertebrates, and possibly for all life. Contrary to accepted belief the food supply is only marginally involved as a factor in these cycles.

As man has developed culture, Hall notes, and domesticated himself, he has created an entire new series of worlds each different from the other. Each of these worlds has its own set of sensory inputs, so that what crowds those in one culture may not necessarily crowd those in another. Similarly, an act that releases aggression and would therefore be stressful to one people may be neutral to another.

Hall also says that aggression is an essential component in the makeup of vertebrates, and that a strong, aggressive animal can and will eliminate weaker rivals. There is also a relationship between aggression and display. Aggression serves as a beneficial force in the process of natural selection. But to insure the survival of the species, aggression must be regulated. This is possible in two ways: by development of hierarchies, and by spacing. Ethologists seem to agree that spacing is the more primitive method, not only because it is the simplest, but because it is less flexible.

Konrad Lorenz agrees with Hall in that aggression forces a balanced distribution of animals of the same species over the available environment. It selects the strongest by rival fights and it is a means of defending the young. But the importance of aggression is not easy to understand and less easy to describe, he concedes.

We can, however, Lorenz says, describe the part played by aggression in the structure of society among highly developed animals. Though many individuals interact in a social system, its inner working are often easier to understand than the interaction of drives within the individual. This is perhaps so because the social aggregate draws behavior and action on a scale at which it can be recognized, such as the changing of the environment in the form of mankind's building.

One of these principles of organization without which advanced social life cannot develop in higher vertebrates, Lorenz contends, is the so-called ranking order. Under this rule every individual in the society knows who is stronger and who weaker than itself. Each social member can thus retreat from the stronger and expect submission from the weaker, thus avoiding overt conflicts. Lorenz pictures a condition in which every animal has the equivalent of military rank—from private to general. However, it seems to operate more efficiently in the animal kingdom than in the army, and perhaps the essential difference between man and animal is indeed that men do glory in their Good Soldier Schweiks and Kilroys, and animals do not.

Schjelderup-Ebbe, according to Lorenz was the first to examine the ranking order in the domestic fowl and to speak of the "pecking order," an expression used to this day. It seems a little odd, Lorenz muses, to speak of "a pecking order" even for large animals which certainly do not peck, but bite or ram. However he admits, with resignation, the wide distribution of the concept speaks for its survival value and therefore we must ask wherein this lies.

The most obvious answer is that the pecking order limits fighting between the members of a society. It could be asked if it would not be better if aggression were entirely inhibited. But if a wolf pack, a monkey herd or other grouping urgently needed aggressive behavior to be used for survival against another society of the same species it must be available to them and consequently developed.

Therefore aggression is only inhibited inside the horde. The society also may derive a beneficial firmness of structure from the state of tension arising inside the community from the aggressive drives and the resulting ranking order.

The Rats

There is one animal that seems to be both an exception to the actions of man and his closest imitator, the rat. It is among rats that some of the most interesting insights have been gleaned concerning human nature. Mickey Mouse, the rat writ small, may not be quite the innocent creature we take him to be.

Rats, like man, are omniverous. They eat anything that lets them, and, like man, will, under stress, devour their own kind. Rats breed in all seasons and again, like man, are the most amorous in the springtime. They hybridize easily, and, judging by the strained relationship between the brown and black rat, have developed social and racial prejudices against the practice. Like ourselves males are larger and females fatter. The rat adapts itself to all kinds of climates, carries almost all of man's diseases and suffers from them. It makes ferocious war upon its own kind. Rats fight bravely alone against weaker rivals for food or for love, and know how to organize armies and fight in hordes when necessary to avoid equal contests.

In their behavior toward members of their own community, rats, Lorenz maintains, are models of social virtue. But they change into horrible brutes as soon as they encounter members of any other society of their own species. Communities comprise too many individual animals for each to know individuals personally. In most cases membership in a society is identified by a common definite smell.

A similar condition exists with social insects whose societies comprise millions of members and are basically members of the same family consisting of the descendants of a single female or pair which founded the colony. The members of such a large clan recognize each other by characteristic, hive, nest, or anthill smell, like rats. Murder occurs if a member of a strange colony inadvertently enters the nest, and massacres ensue if a human experimenter tries to mix two colonies of either insects or rats.

Wild rats when put into a pen with each other in one experiment did not become aggressive until they began to settle and take possession of territories. Lorenz described such an experiment in a cage in which miscellaneous unrelated rats were placed. Two of the rats paired and then together methodically exterminated the remaining rats. Once they had triumphed and founded their own dynasty and raised their own brood they became forgiving and loving parents and were greatly respected by their numerous grandchildren through many generations.

THE ARCHITECTURAL FORMS OF AGGRESSION

As Edward Hall, the anthropologist, has pointed out, man is an organism unique in the development of extensions. Among these are weapons and buildings. Both are related, for much of man's history has been devoted to building buildings to withstand other men's weapons and building weapons to demolish other men's buildings.

During most of our history, until weapons became capable of destroying cities, nations, and continents, a defensive building form was an adequate response to weaponry. The building forms of city walls, machicolations designed to protect the base of the wall, spacing of towers to accomodate bow and crossbow fire and later to accomodate the range of muskets, and the eventual lowering of towers and digging of defenses into the earth all followed the advance of each new innovation in weaponry.

The design of fortresses, castles, and cities was as much planned to deter aggression by appearance as it was to withstand aggression when it occurred, much the same as a dog draws back its lips to bare its sharp incisor teeth to deter attack and be ready should an attack occur.

Man's desire and need for protection are as old as his aggressive impulses, and few of his occupations have absorbed as much of his attention, time, effort, and capital as the design and construction of defense against the transgressions of his human counterparts. The need for the protection of city walls and

the mutual aid of townsmen to man these walls resulted in a life style which eventually changed and abolished the feudalism city walls were designed to withstand.

As aggression forces a social ordering within the pack, the medieval city displayed aggression against potential enemies by the massiveness of its walls and inside them regulated the aggressions of its citizens with laws and established heirarchies or pecking orders. Spacing was a more difficult matter and medieval cities still bear marks of the constant contesting for space and position within them. Although the fortifying walls of earlier periods have been destroyed, cities formed during this period retain much of their original character.

So important were city walls that they were used as a symbol for 'city' in medieval times. When people built cities on an open plane it was a sign of their confidence in their ability to defend themselves. This location allowed them to build regular town plans. If they built upon a hillside the ability to resist aggression was increased, but regular streets were not possible and the possibility of expansion was limited. The regularity of streets and urban planning was also sacrificed in other ways by the necessity of defense, for military necessity and civic amenities did not always coincide. Very little in the design of medieval fortifications was accidental. Towers were placed at 30 meters or thereabout, which was the range of longbows and crossbows. Streets led straight to the defensive walls so that soldiers and townsmen could man them as quickly as possible and that forces could be shifted and redirected to meet the threat of attack.

Civic and military functions were in conflict like rival animals in a pack. Civic functions were preserved, but they were usually sublimated by the enclosing wall and the design of the streets. Fewer gates made the city easier to defend, but more difficult of access for its inhabitants. Hillsides that could be rendered inaccessible with minimum means and effort were effective militarily. If the slopes were steep enough to prevent the deployment of siege machinery, then relatively simple walls could be built, but civic functions were made more difficult by the terrain.

Most early medieval castles consisted of little more than high, strongly built walls surrounding a central tower or keep. The keep doubled as living quarters and the last refuge in repelling invaders. Many of these fortified strongholds became footholds for urban centers. The colonizing town from ancient times through the medieval period was planned symmetrically and founded for the colonizer to exert his aggressions on the surrounding countryside. Bastides were planned military towns.

The right to build town walls was treasured for they assured that other given rights could be protected. Walls became the symbol of a free society of citizens and because of this were considered beautiful. They were the object of civic pride. Walls defined the civitas, through which its inhabitants obtained and held their freedom and were protected from the dangers existing in the open country. The wall was a symbol of good for it detached the city from the countryside and converted it into a region of order and justice. The country or suburbs, unlike our day, were considered neither good nor beautiful. Pictures of paradise of the time depicted it surrounded by crenellated parapet walls. In expulsion scenes, Adam and Eve are driven out of Eden through a gate. In Giotto's allegories in the Arena Chapel in Padua, Justice is shown inside a city while Injustice is represented outside a city gate.

The 15th century marked the ascendency of firearms, a new class of weapons destined to revolutionize military tactics and render city walls obsolete.

Medieval military architecture had been refined to the point where it could offer successful resistance to all known offensive weapons. Stone missiles could damage but not break down well built walls. Battering rams were effective but hazardous to use since the advent of machicolation galleries increased the defender's ability to protect the base of the wall and thus neutralize the agressors siege machines.

The advantage evaporated when the cannon provided the attacker a breaching weapon that rendered the machicolation galleries useless by accomplishing the battering ram's purpose from a distance. The first cannon shot stone balls that shattered on impact. They were also used by the wall defenders, and the early efforts of military engineers were directed toward modifying protective enclosures to permit the cannon's efficient use.

The flat trajectory of cannonballs made sweeping, horizontal fire the most effective. High walls and towers lost most of their defensive advantages. Silhouettes of fortresses became lower and the traditional vertical defense shifted toward the horizontal. The cannon's first victim was the tower which was reduced in height until by the end of the 15th century it was cut off at wall top. Walls were now set in a deep ditch with only their upper parts exposed. Defensive batteries now sat a few feet above ground level and offered a smaller target to the enemy's guns. Early efforts to make walls resistant to cannon fire led to a battering of their lower surfaces and to backing them with earthern terraces.

Before the end of the 16th century it became evident that no masonry walls, no matter how strongly built or reinforced, could withstand the repeated impact of iron cannonballs. This fact was most forcefully impressed upon the Italians by Charles VIII's campaign in Italy to assert his claim to the throne of Naples in 1494. French artillery was able to reduce even the best and strongest medieval walls to rubble within a matter of hours. The disaster made it clear that only the most radical change in fortification design, and the complete abandonment of past approaches, could lead to a solution that might offer the defenders the hope of success.

The urgency with which the problem was viewed is indicated by the fact that not only military men, but artists, architects, and humanistic scholars eagerly applied themselves to the task of finding an answer to the threat of the cannon. The nimblest and most ingenious minds of the period, including Francesco di Giorgio, Leonardo da Vinci, and Michelangelo, set out to solve a problem that, to them, must have had the additional appeal of an intellectual challenge that might yield to rational analysis.

They did solve the problem with an entirely unique architectural form of defensible space that survived until aircraft made the city itself indefensible. (Horst 1972)

It was Oscar Newman, architect, who organized and directed a group of researchers and proved that the renaissance principles of geometry could be applied to modern building. Newman contended and proved that today's urban environment could be designed to withstand the onslaught of vandalism and crime, just as the architects of the Renaissance sought and found a satisfactory geometric solution to the threat of the iron cannonball.

Defensible space, as Newman described it, "is a model for residential environments which inhibits crime by creating the physical expression of a social fabric that defends itself. All the different elements which combine to make a defensible space have a common goal—an environment in which latent territoriality and sense of community in the inhabitants can be translated into responsibility for ensuring a safe, productive, and well-maintained living space." (Newman 1973)

Defensible space, Newman said, is a surrogate term for the range of mechanisms that are both real and symbolic barriers—strongly defined areas of influence and improved opportunities for surveillance that bring an environment under the control of its residents.

Newman contended that as building height increases so does crime. It is not the height alone that is the cause of the problem. It is the feelings of anonymity, isolation irresponsibility, and lack of identity with the surroundings. In high-rise buildings, a great proportion of the crime within the building takes place in the interior public spaces.

The New York City Housing Authority police found that of all recorded crime taking place, 79% occurs within the building proper. This includes all categories of serious crime—robbery, muggings, burglary, larceny, rape, and felonious assault. The buildings are less safe than the building grounds. The victim is the most vulnerable, and the possibility of being seen and apprehended is minimal. Twice as many criminals are apprehended on project grounds than within buildings.

Project grounds and building interiors are public in nature but hidden from public view. Three-story buildings have limited interior public spaces compared with six and seven story buildings and buildings thirteen stories and over. The

217

The ascension of firearms totally changed defensible space late in the 15th century. Charles VIII's campaigns in Italy to assert his claim to the throne of Naples in 1494 were the turning point. His French artillery was able to reduce even the best and strongest medieval walls to rubble within a matter of hours.

This disaster made it clear that only the most radical change in fortification design and the complete abandonment of past approaches could lead to a solution that might offer defenders the hope of successfully resisting a cannon led siege.

The urgency of the problem not only involved military men but artists, architects, and humanistic scholars. They all eagerly applied themselves to the task of finding an answer to the threat of the cannon. The nimblest and most ingenious minds of the period, including Francesco di Giorgio, Leonardo da Vinci, and Michelangelo set out to solve a problem that to them must have had the additional appeal of an intellectual challenge that might yield to rational analysis.
(De La Croix 1972)

The radial city plan made its first, tentative appearance in a treatise by Antonio Filarete around 1465. However he failed to integrate the rectangular units of his central piazza with the necessary radial street network. Francesco di Giorgio first produced practical designs some 20 years later when he adjusted the shape of his central piazza to that of the city's polygonal circumference as is shown here in Giorgio's ideal city plans from Codex Magliabechinus.

The central Piazza and the radiating avenues facilitate the movement of heavy artillery from bastion to bastion to meet attacks. Counterattacks can be launched from bastion flanks. Bastion forms became larger and pointed so that enfilading gunfire from the curtain walls protect them, and the star shaped Baroque city emerges.

The moat became the ditch ahead of the fortifications. The ditch became the trench and the city was left behind. The Maginot line was the last of the great defensive walls. The armies moved and confronted each other in their trenches. Projectiles were no longer limited by a charge of powder but were carried instead by airplanes and dropped. Defense moved from ground to air space over one's head and is now calculated in outer space. From the height of a tower to drop missiles on a foe's head to outer space to shoot down intercontinental ballistic missiles, man continues to carry his wars with him wherever he goes.

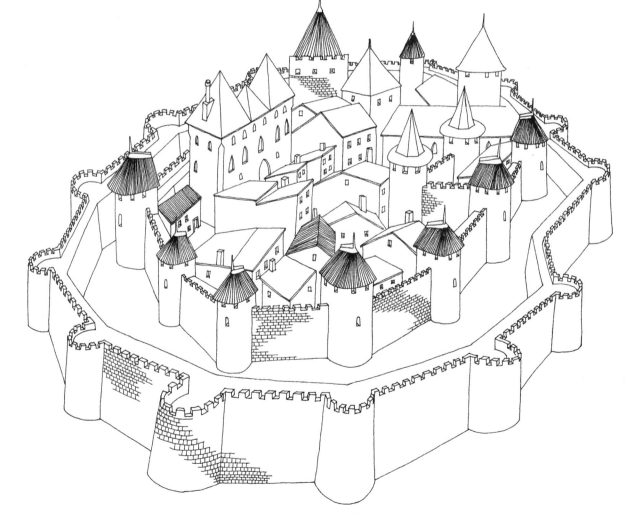

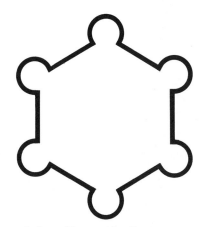

Hexagonal plan with round bastions.

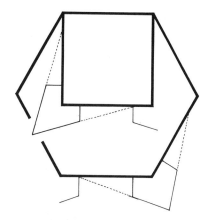

Comparison of bastions drawn for a square and a hexagon with equal sides. Dotted line indicates line of enfilading fire to protect bastion.
(after De La Croix 1972)

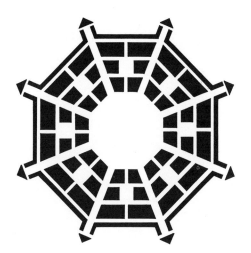

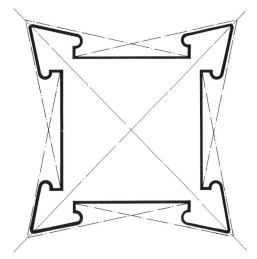

The flanks of rounded bastions cannot protect the shaded area with covering fire, therefore triangular bastions were designed.
(after De La Croix 1972, Fig. 60)

Diagram of the Nettuno, fortino, built from 1501–02, designed by Guilliano and Antonio da Sangalio the Elder, according to Horst De La Croix.

This small fortress built near the beach at Nettuno may be regarded as the military equivalent of Bramante's Tempietto in Rome, Horst tells us, for it ushered in a new era in the history of architecture. "The Nettuno fortress is the first military structure in which the possiblities of bastioned defenses have been fully explored and where on a small scale, a brand new theory of fortification found practical application."
(after De La Croix 1972)

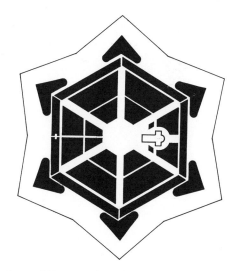

The form of the star-shaped 'ideal' city emerges as the result of enfilading lanes of fire and the requirement of moving heavy cannons from one bastion to another to counter attacks.
(drawing after Antonio Lupicini, ideal city, 1582)

most vulnerable space is the elevator where 31% of the crimes take place although the victim may be removed to other areas.

Newman outlined a language of symbols to define the boundaries of territory. These boundary definers are interruptions in the sequence of movement along access paths and serve to create perceptible zones of transition from public to private spaces. Some are real barriers, others are symbolic.

The symbolic barriers are identified by residents as boundary lines in defining areas of comparative safety. They force an outsider to the realization that he is intruding on semiprivate domain.

Symbolic barriers prove effective in restricting behavior within the defined space to that which residents find acceptable. For example, courtyards and stoops—windows to survey these spaces were necessary for both the resident and neighbors of the resident.

Newman proposed that inhabitants of multifamily dwellings have space with territorial definitions reflecting the areas of influence of the inhabitants in which adjacent residents easily adopt proprietary attitudes. He proposed the positioning of apartment windows to allow residents to naturally survey the exterior and interior public areas of their living environments, and the adoption of building forms and idioms that avoid the stigma of peculiarity that allows others to perceive the vulnerability and isolation of the inhabitants.

Safety is enhanced by locating residential developments in functionally sympathetic urban areas immediately adjacent to activities that do not provide continued threat.

New York City apartment facade.
Photo by F. Wilson.

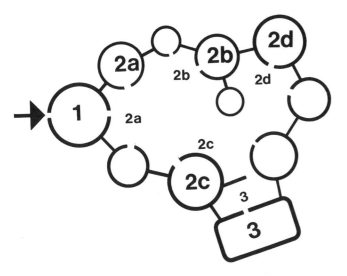

A Konkomba compound entered through an ante-chamber (1). 2a, 2b, 2c, 2d, mark the huts of the owner's four wives and the specifically assigned area of each wife and her children.
(After Prussin 1968, p. 44)

Older unmarried sons are quartered in the rectangular hut with its own courtyard (3).

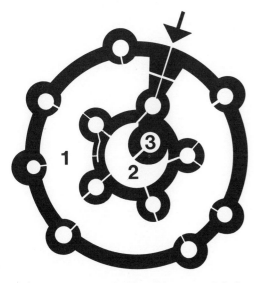

Concentric circles of defensible space; 1, 2, 3.

Drawing of a Sardinian fortress after Chermayeff and Alexander.
(After Chermayeff 1965, p. 122)

The most important single concern of low income residents is security, and lack of security for those without the power of choice is the most debilitating factor that leads to adopting negative and defeatist views of oneself and an expression of general impotence in a capacity to cope with the outside world.

Newman states that children who live in high-rise buildings seem to have a poorly developed perception of individual privacy and little understanding of territory. There may be evidence that the physical form of a residential environment plays a significant role in shaping the perception of children in making them cognizant of the existance of zones of influence and therefore the rights of others.

Newman proposed an architecture of surveillance. The building occupants survey the street and people in the street survey the entrance lobby. The participation of the people with their neighborhood and the neighborhood with the people is imperative, for withdrawal is not an option of high density urban dwelling.

Amost any type of behavior can occur on a city street Newman says—loitering, dancing to a transistor radio, leaning against cars, and begging. Within the confines of an area, defined if only by a change in surface texture or grade level, the range of possible behavior is greatly reduced. It is, in fact, limited to what residents have defined as the norm. All other behavior is incongruous and is so understood and dealt with. An intruder who does not know the rule system, or hesitates in making his intentions clear, is easily spotted as not belonging. He arouses suspicion which leads to the circumvention of his activities.

Real barriers differ from symbolic in that the intruders must possess a key, card, or other means of indicating belonging and enters by approval of the occupants only.

Fundamental to Newman's study is the proposition that through the manipulation of building and spatial configurations, one can create areas for which people will adopt concern. This may suggest that if our data and design methods were sufficiently sensitive, it would be possible to predict and control a wide range of behavior and social relationships through provision of particular architectural settings. This may or may not be true, Newman says, but it was not the focus of his research. His was a much smaller thesis, that it is possible through the provision of facilities in certain juxtapositions to release potential behavioral attitudes and positive social relationships.

Newman does not say that architectural design will have a direct casual effect on social interactions for architecture operates more in the area of "influence" than control. It can create a setting conducive to realizing the potential of mutual concern. It does not and cannot manipulate people toward these feelings but rather allows mutually benefitting attitudes to surface.

Newman and his group have conducted behavioral research and proposed architectural solutions that seem about as reasonable and as intelligent a basis for the integration of behavior into architecture as can be found, yet his findings and his attitude do not seem to have overly impressed either the behavioral or design communities. (Horst 1972, Newman 1973)

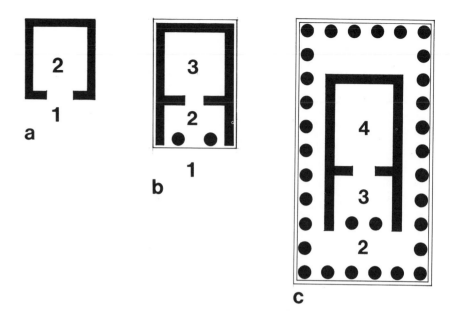

a, b, c Increasing levels of privacy and security 1, 2, 3, 4 as indicated in Greek temple plans—after Vitruvius. (After Vitruvius 1960, p. 115)

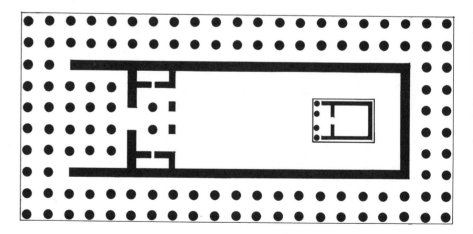

Plan of Temple of Apollo (Sanctuary at Didyma near Miletus, Turkey). Note the increasing levels of privacy, or sacredness, of the space from outside to the interior of the major temple and then to the temple within the temple. (After Millon 1965, p. 80)

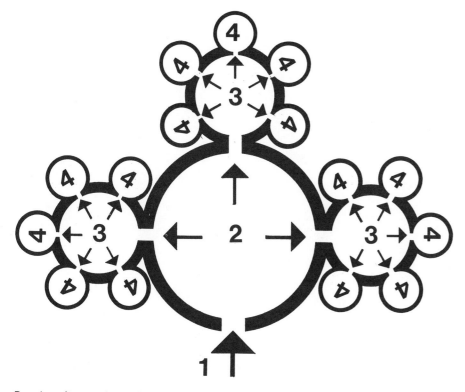

Drawing after a schematic diagram of Oscar Newman illustrating the evolving hierarchy of defensible space from public to private. Arrows indicate entries at different levels of the hierarchy:
1—Public (the street); 2—Semipublic; 3—Semiprivate; 4—Private.

Two F-15 aircraft make a low-level pass over a building complex, under reconstruction, dating from the Middle Ages (1977).
Photo courtesy of the U. S. Air Force.

CROWDING

The effects of crowding are perhaps the most difficult phenomena to understand in both animal and human behavior. There are cultural differences among humans in response to high density situations as extreme as differences in animal behavior exhibited by high contact species like the walrus and individual species like the swan.

In addition, most of the data used to establish criteria for crowding is extreme, drawn from knowledge of air raid shelters, prisons, hospitals, and slave ships, anthropologist Robert Hall notes. (Hall 1966, p. 58)

As more and more is learned about both men and animals, it becomes clearer that the skin itself is a very unsatisfactory boundary or measuring point for crowding. Like the moving molecules that make up all matter, living things move and therefore require more or less fixed amounts of space. Absolute zero, the bottom of the scale, is reached when people are so compressed that movement is no longer possible. Above this point the containers in which man finds himself either allow him to move about freely or else cause him to jostle, push, and shove. How he responds to this jostling, and hence to enclosed space, depends on how he feels about being touched by strangers.

Japanese and Arabs have much higher tolerance for crowding in public spaces and in conveyances than do Americans and northern Europeans. Although Arabs and Japanese are apparently more concerned about their own requirements for the spaces they live in than are Americans. The Japanese, in particular, devote much time and attention to the proper organization of their living space for perception by all their senses.

A society, Hall says, compensates for blurred social distinctions by clear spatial ones—physical barriers, keep-out signs, and property restrictions. Although there are signs that this sometimes happens, a rigid spatial order is not likely to endure in the face of rising population density. Research with animal societies in enclosures indicates that spatial as well as social orders crumble under the onslaught of crowding. The result is extreme social disorganization of the type described in rats and mice by Calhoun. Family structure disintegrated, mothers did not care for their young, and sexual perversion and cannibalism were frequent. Finally, the animals that survived became less aggressive and withdrew from social contact, cocooning as it were. An American biologist visiting a laboratory in England was asked in his welcoming note by his English host to "forgive us our seemingly cold indifference. This is a small and crowded island. We can exist only by ignoring each other."

De Jonge (de Jonge 1967) concludes that a person can live amidst a great multitude only by showing relative indifference toward the majority of them. Only by restricting personal contact to a limited number of people is a normal life possible. De Jonge hypothesizes a complementary relationship between

Mountainside Squatter Housing overlooking Rio De Janeiro.
Photo courtesy of Gilda and Vic Bonardi.

Festival of the Children—Mexico City.
Photo by F. Wilson.

family and societal organization. In urban areas, where population density is high, the family and home will be closed to the outsider but the larger society will be open. On the other hand, in sparsely populated rural areas, the number of people that one meets is limited and the inclination to greet them and know them is greater. Society tends to be closed, but the family remains relatively open. One is reminded here of the housewives who had moved from the city to the suburbs and were astonished at the way their suburban neighbors entered houses to gossip and borrow sugar without knocking. An exception to this pattern occurs in urban slums where the families are relatively open, but are isolated (closed off) from the larger society. (Sommer 1969, p. 23)

CROWDING AND HEALTH

The view that crowding due to increased population density has a hidden harmful effect on human health is widespread. It is believed that the harmful effects of crowding are not confined to increasing the spread of infectious diseases, but also increase the risk of noninfectious disease.

Higher death and morbidity rates are traditionally reported from more densely populated urban centers. A dramatic increase in death rates due to infectious diseases has followed industrialization and urbanism. There is also a higher rate of various diseases under crowded conditions such as military training camps, nurseries, and the like. Animal studies tend to confirm that crowding has the same hidden harmful effects upon them.

Careful review of recent data indicates important inconsistences in the relationship between crowding and health status. It appears that crowding and health status is a far more complex phenomenon than originally considered. Under certain conditions crowding is clearly associated with poor health status, but under others it may be neutral or even beneficial. (Gutman-John Cassel 1972, p. 250–251)

Of greater importance than the inadequacy or discrepancies of data is the failure of investigators to identify explicitly the processes through which increased social interaction leads to disease. The orthodox model espoused by the majority of authorities holds that crowding increases the risk of disease through increased opportunity for the spread of infection. Newer data and further examination of older data are making these views untenable. This view cannot, obviously, account for the increase in noninfectious disease that occurs under conditions of crowding. There is also a growing body of opinion that believes that even infectious diseases are spread only partially as an effect of crowding.

René Dubos, the pioneer microbiologist, has perhaps stated this view the most clearly when he says that the sciences concerned with the spread of microbial diseases concentrate almost exclusively on infections caused by outside sources but, "in contrast, the microbial diseases most common in our communities today arise from the activities of microorganisms that are ubiquitous in the environment, exist in the body without causing obvious harm under ordinary circumstances, and exert pathological stress. In such a type of microbial disease the event of infection is of less importance than the hidden manifestations of the smoldering infectious process and than the physiological disturbances that convert latent infection into overt symptoms and pathology.'' (Gutman, Cassel, p. 159)

What Dubos has said is that microbial disease is not necessarily acquired through exposure to new microorganisms. Disease occurs through factors which disturb the balance between the ubiquitous organisms and the host that is harboring them. It may well be that under conditions of crowding the balance may be disturbed, but this disturbance is then not a function of the physical crowding but of other processes.

The adaptability of people to new social environments, and the anxiety, fear, and uncertainty accompanying change may well be the agents that lower the body's resistance to the organisms causing disease.

Cassel concludes his article: "Finally, if the harmful effects on health of crowding are to be prevented and an orderly and healthful rate of population growth to be planned, the processes through which crowding is related to health need to be understood better than they are today. As indicated in this selection, the relatively simplistic notion that crowding exerts its deleterious effects solely through facilitating the interpersonal spread of disease agents is no longer adequate to explain the known phenomena. A more appropriate formulation would seem feasible if we recognize that increasing population density increases

Dining at Radio City, NYC.
Photo by F. Wilson.

New York City.
Photo by F. Wilson.

Facade of World Bank Building,
Washington, D.C.
Photo by F. Wilson.

the importance of the social environment as a determinant of physiological response to various stimuli, including potentially disease-producing agents; that within this social environment the quality of social interactions and position within the group seem to be important factors; and that adaption to these social changes can and does occur given time, but that the new comers to the situation will always be the segment of the population at highest risk."

The focus of attention on the decay of many large cities has led to speculation by urban planners and social scientists on the relationship of crowding and human behavior. While, not long ago, population density was thought by many to be synonymous with crowding, studies by Rapoport and D. Stokols have differentiated between these concepts. The major distinction is that while density is often defined objectively, i.e., "number of people per unit area," crowding is largely a subjective concept, which resists such a simple definition. These authors point to major cultural differences among people which affect their perception of being crowded. For example, although Japan is one of the most densely populated areas in the world, traditions and life styles have intensified the feelings of being crowded.

Most of the experimental work pertaining to crowding has been done in animal laboratories using small mammals. J. Calhoun's (biologist) work with rats is the most prominent research in this area.

Graduation ceremonies, Catholic University, 1981.
Photo by F. Wilson.

In his original experiment, Calhoun confined a population of rats in a 1/4-acre (1/10 hectare) enclosure. Within this enclosure there was an abundance of food and of places to live, predation was eliminated, and disease was minimized. The only factor remaining which could significantly influence the size of the population was the behavior of the animals toward one another. The population stabilized at 150 adults although the observed reproductive rate led researchers to postulate that the environment could support a population of 5,000. The researchers discovered an extremely high rate of infant mortality caused by a lack of appropriate maternal behavior. Apparently the population of 150 adults was so high that social interactions became very stressful.

Calhoun conducted other studies in which populations of rats were allowed to increase to twice the size that would normally occupy a given space. Through careful observations, the researchers were able to determine those changes in behavior which resulted from the increased population density. Many of the behavioral changes were observed among the females—litters were not carried to full term and proper maternal care was not given to those babies who did survive. Males displayed sexual abnormalities and behavioral disturbances ranging from overactivity to almost total withdrawal.

The work of Calhoun is thought by some planners and researchers to be applicable to human populations, while others are dubious about its relevance to urban problems. The opponents of this viewpoint stress that there are many other factors (e.g., economic, social) which affect behavior, while the supporters of the research point to the biological similarities between man and animals. In our view it is premature to either accept or reject the conclusions drawn from this work.

A limited number of research studies using human subjects has dealt with crowding behavior. A. Baum and G. Davis (psychologists) employed a simulation approach to study the phenomenon of crowding. They employed model figures made from clothespins, which were placed in scale model rooms to ar-

There is a connection between crowding of chickens and egg-laying, and the spacing of cows at the trough and food consumption. If a captive animal is given too little, too much, or the wrong kind of space, it is likely to become ill, lose its body sheen, fail to reproduce, and eventually die.
(Sommer 1969)

Delightful social environment were crowding is sought—Faneuil Hall Boston, designed by Ben Thompson Associates Architects, conceived and constructed by The Rouse Co.
(Photo courtesy of The Rouse Co.)

New York City subway.

As a rule of thumb, the closer strangers are forced together the less they become individual people. An indication of recognition of another person as a person is whether the invasion of personal space is mutually sought or forced because of conditions beyond the control of the participants.
(Sommer 1969)

Picnic, Aspen, Colorado.
Photo by F. Wilson.

rive at a definition for crowding. The researchers systematically varied the color and complexity of the rooms, as well as the activity being simulated.

Four scale model rooms were used in the study. Two rooms contained pictures to add to their visual complexity, while the other two rooms had walls which were covered only with paint. Two rooms were painted with dark colors, the other two with light pigments.

The research subjects were instructed in one of two social orientations: (1) Imagine that this room is a lounge where people are standing and talking at a cocktail party, and that you are there; (2) Imagine that this is a lounge area of an airport where people are standing and waiting between flights, and that you are there. (Baum 1976)

One clothespin figure was then designated to represent the participant, who was asked to place himself in the room, and then add additional figures until he began to feel crowded. The research findings were recorded by indicating the location of all figures on a scale drawing of the room. The most pronounced finding was that the lighter rooms contained more figures than the darker rooms, i.e., the lighter rooms appeared larger.

The concept of crowding is one which illustrates the interrelationship of psychological and physical factors. On the one hand, a person may have a feeling of being crowded, but is it the presence of "too many" people in a restricted space which promotes this feeling? As we noted earlier, this feeling might be attributed to the invasion of one's life space. However, another way of looking at the problem could be from the standpoint of purely physical factors, the requirement for a given volume of space to accomodate man and his activities.

The way of looking at the problem of crowding adopted by designers of the built environment is from the standpoint of purely physical factors. A given volume of space is allocated to each person and their activities. In view of the wide range of opinion, cultural differences, and attitudes of those using the space, this solution cannot help but be arbitrary. (Rubin and Elder 1980)

Bus Terminal, NYC.
Photo by F. Wilson.

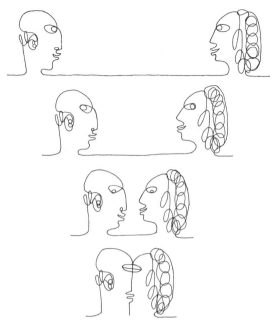

When people get very close together, they often close their eyes.

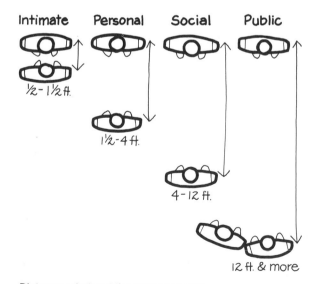

Intimate   Personal   Social   Public

½ – 1½ ft.

1½ – 4 ft.

4 – 12 ft.

12 ft. & more

Distance relationships among people
(Hall).
(Rubin and Elder 1980)

SOME THOUGHTS ON DOMINANT BEHAVIOR

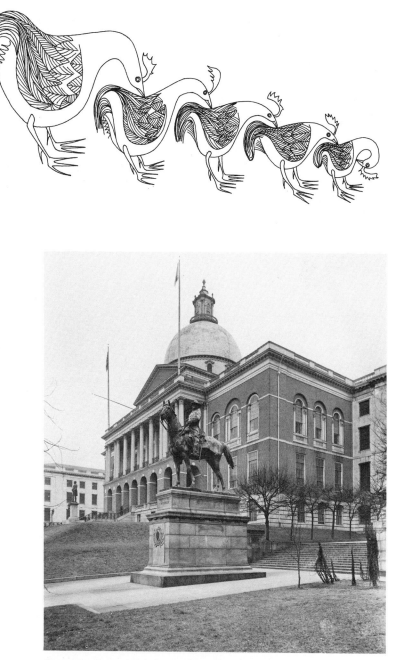

"A herd of deer whose natural food is scattered over fields will not fight over food as it grazes, but if the deer are fed grain in a small area so that the animals get in each other's way, they soon establish a dominance order in which the stronger animals have the readiest access to the food.

Dominance orders among penned chickens may be linear or these may be pecking triangles. In groups with males and females, the males usually show passive dominance over females with each sex having its own peck order. Among young chickens a peck order is formed between the tenth and twelfth weeks. Once a dominance order is formed a newcomer is at a disadvantage since he must engage in an encounter with each of the residents. In a comparison of flocks some of which have been together for a long time and others kept in flux by the regular rotation of birds, there was greater social stress and more overt aggression among the alternated birds. The stable group consumed more food, maintained or gained body weight and laid more eggs." (Sommer 1969, p. 13)

". . . within the city there will be neighborhood taverns that draw their clientele from the surrounding blocks and downtail cocktail lounges that draw people from all over the city and beyond. The neighborhood pub will encourage sociability among regular patrons, but the outsider will be looked upon with suspicion and hostility. . ." (Hall 1966, p. 124)

Mental patients when replaced increased the number of aggressive acts. (Sommers 1969, p. 13) Prisons with stable populations have less aggression than those where the prisoners are constantly changing.

People and animals have an idea of their place in the world and must assert and test it. Is there a parallel between human and animal studies that show that territoriality and dominance are means of maintaining a social order?
Dominance (Hall 1966, p. 9)

Territoriality offers protection from predators, and also exposes to predation the unfit who are too weak to establish and defend a territory. Thus, it reinforces dominance in selective breeding because the less dominant animals are less likely to establish territories. On the other hand territoriality facilitates breeding by providing a home base that is safe. It aids in protecting the nests and the young in them. In some species, it localizes waste disposal and inhibits or prevents parasites.

In addition to preservation of the species and the environment personal and social functions are associated with territoriality. C. R. Carpenter tested the relative roles of sexual vigor and dominance and found that even a desexed pigeon will in its own territory regularly win a test encounter with a normal

Massachusetts State House, Boston.
Photo courtesy of the Massachusetts Department of Commerce and Development, Divison of Tourism.

male, even though desexing usually results in loss of position in a social hierarchy. Thus, while dominant animals determine the general direction in which the species develops, the fact that the subordinate can win (and so breed) on his home grounds helps to preserve plasticity in the species by increasing variety and thus preventing the dominant animals from freezing the direction that evolution takes. (Sommer 1969, p. 13)

Dominant animals tend to have larger personal distances than those which occupy lower positions in the social hierarchy, while subordinate animals have been observed to yield room to dominant ones. Glen McBride, an Australian professor of animal husbandry, made detailed observations of the spacing of domestic fowl as a function of dominance.

With pairs incompatible in dominance, such as two highly dominant individuals, no stable order can be found, so aggression is limited by strict adherence to territorial rights.

Monkeys that are dominant in their own cages may become less dominant as guests in another monkey's cage or even lose their dominant position.

Baseball teams invariably do better in their hometown than as guests. It is not only the presence of the hometown fans, but their knowledge of the special environment.

Minnesota Fats said a man had to be an expert to travel from town to town and still win. Every table is different.

Animals that are dominant get more food and the choice of mates. In human society, they have larger homesites, more rooms per house, vacation homes, greater spatial mobility, and more opportunities to escape when they become tense, uncomfortable, or bored. (Sommer 1969, p. 17)

In many species the dominant animal has a territory which is larger and more desirable than that of other species members. The same pressures operate in social situations where there is competition for any item in short supply. The status of upper classmen in universities is reinforced by knowing the turf, long-term relationships, and more prestige. (Sommer 1969, p. 18)

Museum of Modern Art Bldg., NYC by Cesar Pelli.
Photo by Kenneth Champlin and J. Severtson.
Courtesy of Cesar Pelli Associates.

Dominance over waiting and office circulation.
Photo courtesy of Knoll International.

FURNITURE ARRANGEMENT

How, why, and where people arrange themselves in space with the aid of man-made objects has been the study of behavioral scientists and the design professions ever since rooms were assigned specific functions, from perhaps the middle of the 17th century onwards. The meaning of body language and furniture language has become somewhat of a commonplace, so much so that it was featured in an article in *the Wall Street Journal* entitled, "You Are Where You Sit." In it we find a staff writer quoting a Professor Hunsaker, a professor of Management and Organizational Development who has become an expert in the field of "proxemics," the term that Robert Sommer used to characterize the arrangements people assume in space.

The observations were obvious enough; bigger is better and juxtaposition is important. Those located closest to the most powerful men are conceived as being powerful. When people sit across the table from each other they are engaged in confrontation; sitting side by side indicates cooperation. Friends will usually use the corner of a table for intimate conversations. Round and oval tables tend to discourage power plays.

Robert Sommer in his book *Personal Space* observed: "The one that sits at the head of the table is usually elected chairman of the group since not to do so would be a personal rejection."

The selection of chairs in a room is seldom random. Those of higher economic class, proprietors, and managers select head chairs more often than would happen by chance.

In observations of pygmy behavior in the rain forest, it was noted that in a discussion when all are standing in a circle each one expresses themselves, but when a man steps to the center of the circle he expresses the ideas of the group as a whole.

Sommer also was highly critical of the way that furniture was commonly arranged in institutional settings. He said that it allowed the option of looking down at the new tile floor or up at the new fluorescent lights with chairs arranged side by side or back to back.

There is lack, Sommer claimed, of explicit principles in arranging furniture and its implications for human intercourse. Institutional furniture when not anchored to the floor has the feeling that it is anchored mentally and cannot be moved.

The therapeutic potential of furniture arrangement is not realized. Furniture as a tool of design of social interaction is neglected. More he says is known about furniture arrangement than of its social results. The customary becomes fixed and natural with people pointed at each other like projectiles to maximize conversation. But a change in any single element will change the parts, and this has been proven by a number of experiments.

Classroom seating, State University of New York at Buffalo.
Photo by F. Wilson.

Delightful use of minimal space—backyard of architectural critic Wolf Von Eckardt.
Photo by F. Wilson.

Some furniture arrangement is cultural, Edward Hall claims. For example, Americans will place their furniture around the edge of a room while the Japanese place it in the middle. As a result western rooms appear less cluttered to the Japanese than they do to us.

European and Japanese and our own concepts of space and how objects should be arranged within it differ markedly. In America, the conventional idea of the space required by office employees is restricted to the actual space required to do the job. Anything beyond the minimum requirement is usually regarded as a 'frill' Hall claims. The concept that there may be additional perceptual needs is resisted, at least in part, because of the American's mistrust of subjective feelings as a source of data. A person's ability to reach something can be measured by a tape, but we must bring to bear an entirely different set of standards if we are to judge the validity of an individual's feeling of being cramped.

Hall's investigations revealed that the single most important criterion was what people did in the course of their work without bumping into something. He based this on interviews with over one hundred people working in offices. There appeared to Hall to be three hidden zones in American offices.

1. The immediate work area of the desk top and chair.
2. A series of points within arm's reach outside the area mentioned above.
3. Spaces marked as the limit reached when one pushes away from the desk to achieve a little distance from the work without actually getting up.

An enclosure that permits only movement within the first area is experienced as cramped. An office the size of the second is considered 'small.' An office with Zone 3 space is considered adequate and in some cases ample.

Kinesthetic space, Hall states, is an important factor in day-to-day living in the buildings that architects and designers create. American hotels have rooms that are mostly too small, for the occupants cannot move around in them without bumping into things. If Americans are asked to compare two identical rooms, the one permitting the greater variety of free movement will usually be experienced as larger despite their actual size.

INSTITUTIONAL SETTINGS

The behavior of nurses on two different hospital wards was observed by K. Keleman (psychologist). The first ward was a single corridor design in an old hospital. The behavior of six nurses was observed and recorded in five major categories: interaction with people; interaction with objects; communication; posture; activity being performed. The same six nurses were then observed after they had moved to a new hospital with triangular-shaped wards. The differences between the two settings were fewer and smaller in magnitude than

Keleman had expected. One interesting finding was that walking increased on the triangular ward; the triangular ward had been designed to reduce the amount of walking required.

Another study noted changes in behavior after physical changes were made on a custodial care ward. B. Hartford and W. Kleeman (interior designer) first observed and coded the behavior of individuals on the ward, and found very little interaction. Several physical changes were then initiated such as curved continuous seating in conjunction with activity areas; tables used with the seating; a small kitchen and laundry area; and finally, a personal area where individuals could keep possessions. Observations after these changes showed that interaction more than doubled.

College dormitories or residence halls may also be considered institutional environments. The satisfaction of college students with their residences was explored by G. Davis and R. Roizen. The researchers designed a questionnaire which looked at overall satisfaction as well as satisfaction with 25 specific environmental variables. The questionnaire was given to students on eight campuses, occupying a variety of housing types. The housing types included conventional long corridor dorms, suites, apartments, and housing complexes. Particular environmental features had very little effect on overall student satisfaction. Instead, satisfaction was related to the general type of residence hall. Conventional long corridor dorms were the least liked, while apartments were rated as very satisfactory. (Rubin and Elder 1980)

ENVIRONMENTAL FEATURES

Another basic concern for the architect is to determine how particular environmental features affect building occupants. Although considerable Man/Environment research has addressed this issue, definitive findings are few.

OPEN SPACE PLANNING

The concept of open space or open office planning began in Germany in the 1960s. At that time, open office planning or office landscaping meant the absence of partitions, a scrambled furniture arrangement, and large plants located throughout the space. The purpose of this design was to facilitate communication among staff members. This concept, with variations, is now being used in offices throughout the world.

Most of the studies done to assess open office planning have employed questionnaires and, more specifically, the semantic differential. Few studies have used control or comparison groups so that the responses obtained in the open offices could be compared with responses obtained in traditional offices.

One study which did have a control group is reported by P. Boyce. In 1971, in Bristol, England, the South Western Electricity Board centralized its operations and moved staff from several buildings to a large new building in which almost all the office space was open-plan. Researchers were aware that past studies had indicated some disadvantages associated with open-plan offices such as distractions, loss of privacy and status, and loss of individual control. Questionnaires were designed to assess response to the new building.

The questionnaires were administered to the staff both prior to and after the move to the new building. Briefly, results indicated improved communications in the new building and satisfaction with lighting and windows. There was dissatisfaction with the heating and ventilating systems and complaints about noise although noise complaints were also evident in the older buildings. A literature survey indicated that responses to the new open-plan building were similar to responses to open-plan buildings in other parts of the world.

Another study of employee attitudes to old traditional office space and to a new open-plan space was conducted by M. Brookes. A semantic scale was given to each employee before the announcement of plans to move to a new space and nine months after the move to the redesigned space. Each employee was asked to respond to the semantic scale in three different ways. First, to describe the present office workspace; then, to describe an ideal office workspace; and, finally, to describe the way co-workers would want the office workspace. The open-plan office rated higher in aesthetic value, and lower in the areas of noise, visual distractions, and privacy.

Open space planning is also being applied in classrooms.

CLASSROOM DESIGN

As two researchers, C. Porteous (psychologist) and J. Porteous (geographer), note:

"Disillusionment with the traditional classroom has grown with the realization that during the lengthy learning day the child may require varying environmental conditions, whether of humidity, temperature, decor, or furniture arrangements. This recognition of learning as a dynamic process has led to attempts to manipulate the physical learning environment so that the child's learning advances with optimum speed and minimum stress. Since the 1950s there has been a concerted move toward open-plan classrooms, where the walls as well as the furniture are removable or capable of rearrangement in a variety of desired patterns." (Porteous and Porteous, 1975)

In a study concerned with open-plan classrooms, J. Durlak et al. observed students in traditional plan schools and open-plan schools. Four traditional plan schools and four open-plan schools were matched on the basis of geographical proximity, size of student body, and general demographic status of the neighborhood. The researchers made systematic observations and recorded information about the general structure of the area, the teacher's style, the activities of the students, and the dispersion of people in the spaces.

	Class Size		
	Small (6-20)	Medium (21-50)	Large (50 +)
Number of Classes	12	12	27
Above Median Participation	75%	50%	37%
Below Median Participation	25%	50%	63%
Average Total Time of Participation	5.8 Min.	2.4 Min.	2.6 Min.
Average Number of Different Students Participating Per Session	6.9	6.7	6.9

Study of classroom size and participation
(Sommer).
(Rubin and Elder 1980)

Modification of fixed-feature space as Sim Van der Ryn
and his group address the Aspen Conference sitting on
the stage instead of from behind a podium.
Photo by F. Wilson.

The results demonstrated that there were different general activity patterns in each type of school. It is now necessary to determine if these different patterns have different effects on learning.

The effect of environmental complexity on learning behavior was explored by Porteous and Porteous. The study took place in three different classrooms of high, medium, and low complexity levels; and at two grade levels, third and fifth. The children were required to learn a paired-associate task with both a time limitation and a number of trials limitation. There was a one-way mirror so that the children's attention or "looking behavior" could be observed. The dependent variables were, therefore, number of correct items on the learning task, and attention to the environment. (Porteous and Porteous 1975) Children at both grade levels performed better in the less complex environment.

Fixed Features—Interior Spaces

E. Hall (anthropologist) makes an important distinction between two different types of environmental characteristics. He describes environmental characteristics in terms of being fixed-feature space and semifixed-feature. A fixed-feature space is typified by specialized rooms, buildings, and towns which tend to shape behavior. The user has only a limited ability to modify its primary features (for example, a bathroom). In contrast, a semifixed-feature space is one where limited environmental modification is acceptable and possible (for example, the furniture arrangement in a living room). Hall emphasizes that in part the fixedness of features is culturally determined. (For example, in China, chairs are considered fixed features despite the fact that they are movable.)

The Swedish institute for Building Research has pioneered many M/E areas dealing with interior building spatial requirements. One such investigation, performed by M. Englund and G. Hallberg, was concerned with determining the size of the free space needed on each side of a door in order to freely open and close the door.

The study was conducted by having research subjects open a door, 90 cm wide (height not indicated), while the activity was recorded by a television camera. The floor was marked with a 20 cm grid, and the wall area near the door was marked off in 10 cm increments. Experimental subjects wore numbers to ensure identification during later analysis. (This procedure was required because the faces of the subjects were not always visible.) The research approach enabled the experimenters to specify the space requirements for door clearance for the conditions studied.

R. Blake (psychologist) et al. conducted a study in an Air Force barracks to determine the effect of room arrangement on the interactions of the occupants. Open and closed cubicle barracks were used in the study, and, in both types of barracks, bunks were segregated into units of six each. The only difference between the two types was that the closed cubicle barracks had walls which enclosed each unit of six bunks, with entrances from which doors were removed. The subjects were asked to indicate the degree (on a 4-point scale) to which they interacted with others and to identify the three men with whom each man preferred to "buddy." The open design fostered closer relationships in the barracks than the closed one. (Blake 1956)

The ceiling height of an experimental room was altered by J. Savinar in a study of personal space needs. The room was 16 ft by 12 ft (4.8 m by 3.6 m) on one wall. The ceiling was made of white translucent fiber glass and was adjusted to heights between 6 ft (1.8 m) and 9 ft (2.7 m) by means of a pulley system. Savinar asked subjects to determine their "comfort threshold," the point below which the ceiling space became inadequate. The ceiling was alternately lowered from 9 ft (2.7 m) and raised from a point below the preceding trial. The standing heights for all subjects (male and female) were recorded beforehand. The results indicated considerable variability from subject to subject (81 in. to 102 in. (205 cm to 259 cm)) not attributable to height or sex.

In a follow-up study, the same researcher examined the effects of two ceiling heights (6 ft., 9 ft. (1.8 m, 2.7 m)) on personal space needs. She positioned each subject in the room, and then approached the subject, who was instructed to say "stop" when personal space was perceived to be invaded. The floor was then marked to indicate how closely she had approached the subject. Ceiling height did not affect the invasion distance. (Savinar 1975)

Other building features receiving attention from M/E researchers are stairs and windows.

Stairs

Vertical movements by means of stairs pose a special challenge to the architect. Stairs, while essential to buildings, also are a threat to their users. They are a hazard because many accidents occur when people ascend and descend them; many severe accidents occur during descent.

A series of studies to verify the adequacy of current stair design practices was performed by J. Fitch (architect) et al. Current stair designs can be traced to the work of Francois Blondel, Director of the Royal Academy of Architecture in Paris (1672). Fitch and his colleagues indicate that Blondel:

"Concluded from personal observation that the normal pace in level walking (24 inches, he said) must be decreased by a regular and fixed amount to allow the foot to be raised in climbing stairs. Blondel derived a formula stating that the pace must be decreased by two inches for every inch of riser. Expressed mathematically, the formula specified that the depth of the tread should be 24 inches minus two times the height of the riser, or that the total of the tread and two times the height of the riser should be 24 inches."

The authors of the study note that Blondel's formula often leads to stair designs which are too wide or too narrow. They also indicate that, despite the fact the average person today is taller than his 17th century counterpart, many building and fire codes specify the stair dimensions recommended by Blondel. The research performed by Fitch and his colleagues was designed to improve the basis for recommended stair design.

Staircase, adjacent to the World Trade Center, NYC.
Photo by F. Wilson.

Stairs in underground passage, Helsinki, Finland.
Photo by F. Wilson.

Subway stairs descending from Grand Central to subway
(IRT), among the most dangerous in the city. The sister
collecting alms at the foot of the stairs reports frequent
accidents.
Photo by F. Wilson.

The Grand Staircase of the Paris Opera.
Photo courtesy of the French Government Tourist Office.

One study consisted of building replicas of four different stairways each one consisting of four steps. The angle of ascent ranged from 7.7 degrees to 36.8 degrees (New York City code). Men and women wearing ordinary clothing walked up and down the stairs and were photographed while doing so. Their next investigation employed a mechanical stairway, which permitted an increased number of variables to be studied. They examined three angles of pitch (25, 35, 45 degrees), three different riser-tread combinations, and three speeds of movement (controlled by the mechanical treadmill). Subjects wore special overshoes, equipped with pressure sensitive stitches which permitted measurements to be made of the length of time that the toes and heels were in contact with the stair treads. They found that: (1) more missteps occurred during descent, and (2) the safest stair configuration for descent was not the same as that for ascent. The stair design problem obviously needs further work.

J. Archea (psychologist) studied the relationship of stairs and accidents. A television camera was positioned at stairway locations to enable video recordings to be made of people as they ascended and descended. Data were collected at several sites, which differed primarily with respect to stairway design. In this way, many accidents and near-accidents (critical incidents) were recorded and later analyzed.

As energy conservation considerations have become more critical, designers and engineers have begun to pay more attention to the size, shape, and type of windows which are put into buildings. Investigators have attempted to define a range of acceptable window sizes and shapes through the use of scale models. A scale model allows a person to change the size, shape, and location of a window to suit his own particular preference. The model can even be equipped with miniature furniture to simulate either a home or an office environment. In addition, the experimenter can vary a large number of parameters including view, building orientation, and type of glazing.

In an investigation of minimum acceptable window size, E. Ne'eman (Israeli engineer) and R. Hopkinson (British researcher) employed a full-scale model and a 1/10-scale model. Three hundred and nineteen subjects determined minimum acceptable window size as a function of the dimensions of the room, the number of apertures, the outside view, the weather, external illumination levels, and two window heights. The results indicated that the subjects could identify a minimum acceptable window size both with the full-scale and with the 1/10-scale model. Type of view proved to be an important determinant of acceptable window size. (Ne'eman and Hopkinson 1970)

E. Keighley (British researcher) developed a scale model technique to investigate the visual requirements associated with windows. A 1/12-scale model was constructed and furnished to give a realistic impression of a landscaped office. The model was furnished with a window which could be controlled with respect to configuration by means of a pushbutton control panel, the total window area being fixed at 30% of the window wall. Beyond the window was a large translucent screen upon which a view was projected by means of eight color transparencies simulating different views as seen from different floors of a building.

Keighley had 30 subjects view the model as if it were their office. They were then asked to adjust the shape and location of the window to the most desirable dimensions. The subjects preferred a wide lateral scan and selected settings which produced wide rather than tall windows.

In another investigation employing the same general approach, Keighley used a series of templates to define window configuration. Subjects were asked to judge the acceptability of each arrangement on a 5-point scale (from "entirely satisfactory" to "very dissatisfactory"). Keighley found that, when total window area was restricted and the number of apertures varied, subjects were dissatisfied with a large number of apertures and with very narrow apertures. Satisfaction with window height was dependent upon the view. (Keighley 1973)

Window research studies have also examined the concept of spaciousness. M. Inui and T. Miyata (Japanese researchers) defined spaciousness as the feeling of openness or enclosure produced by an interior. Inui and Miyata used several models (1/20, 1/10, and 1/5-scale) and evaluated the impact of such variables as daylight, sunlight, window size, and room volume upon perceived spaciousness. Results indicated that window size had the greatest effect upon perceived spaciousness. The results did not vary with the size of the model used. (Inui and Miyata 1973)

Perceived spaciousness was also studied by V. Imamoglu (Turkish architect) and T. Markus (Scottish architect). They used both a full-scale and 1/10-scale model. Unlike Inui and Miyata, who had their subjects rate the spaciousness of different rooms, Imamoglu and Markus asked subjects to adjust each of two rectangular models to be equal to a fixed square model in spaciousness. The effects of window size, room proportion, and length of window wall upon spaciousness were assessed in this manner. Unlike the findings of Inui and Miyata, window size and perceived spaciousness were not found to be highly correlated.

Stately stairs to the great flatlands of the Seagrams Bldg. Plaza, NYC.
Photo by F. Wilson.

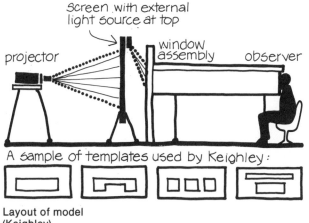

Screen with external
light source at top

projector

window
assembly

observer

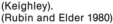

A sample of templates used by Keighley:

Layout of model
(Keighley).
(Rubin and Elder 1980)

Window configurations—Nettuno, Castello del San-
gallo.
Photo courtesy of the Italian Government Travel Office.

The results of these two studies indicate that subjects can define and use a concept termed "spaciousness" fairly consistently. This concept is related to, but not entirely dependent upon, the presence of windows within a room. Thus, a large windowless room, with a high ceiling, large volume, and bright lighting could be judged as spacious, although it probably would be judged as more spacious if a window were present. (Imamoglu and Markus 1973)

Movable Features

R. Sommer (psychologist) conducted several studies to determine how furniture arrangements in a classroom influenced participation by students.

In the first study, student observers recorded classroom interaction in 51 different classes. Results indicated that class size influenced student participation, but at the same time the actual number of students participating was similar for small, medium, and large classes. The observers then rearranged the chairs from straight rows to a circular pattern. This change was made before anyone arrived in the classroom. Results indicated that 20 of the 25 classes rearranged the chairs in straight rows prior to the start of class. Sommer interprets these rather discouraging results as an indication of how easily and unconsciously people adapt to traditional ways of doing things.

In a second study, observers recorded participation in laboratory settings—a more open arrangement than that found in the classroom settings. Both the total time of participation and the proportion of students participating were high (24% of class time compared with 12% found in the study of regular classrooms). (Sommer 1974) (Rubin and Elder 1980)

FIXED AND MOVABLE SPACE FEATURES

A. Maslow and N. Mintz (psychologists) conducted a study to determine the effects of room features on the task of evaluating facial photographs.

Three rooms were used by subjects who evaluated facial photographs on the amount of fatigue–energy and displeasure–well-being displayed by the individual in the photograph. The experimental rooms differed in terms of characteristics and furnishings. The rooms were evaluated as being "ugly," "average," and "beautiful."

"Ugly Room"   "Average Room"   "Beautiful Room"

Room evaluation study
(after Maslow and Mintz).
(Rubin and Elder 1980).

The "ugly" room was described by people as being horrible, disgusting, ugly, and repulsive. It was 7 ft × 12 ft × 10 ft (2.1 m × 3.6 m × 3.0 m) with two half-windows, battleship-gray walls, and one overhead bulb with a dirty, torn lampshade. The room contained two straight-backed chairs, a small table, and tin cans for ashtrays. The window shades were torn, the walls were bare, and refuse and cleaning implements were scattered around. The room had not been swept or dusted and the ashtrays were full.

The "average" room was a professor's office with three windows, battleship-gray walls, and an indirect overhead light. The room was 15 ft × 17 ft × 10 ft (4.5 m × 5.1 m × 3.0 m) and furnished with two mahogany desk and chair combinations, two straight-backed chairs, a metal filing cabinet, a metal bookcase, window shades, and a cot with a green bedspread. The general appearance was that of a clean, neat, and worked-in office.

People responded to the "beautiful" room as being attractive, pretty, comfortable, and pleasant. The room was 11 ft × 14 ft × 10 ft (3.3 m × 4.2 m × 3.0 m) with beige walls, an indirect overhead light, and two large windows. The furnishings gave the appearance of a comfortable and attractive study, and included a soft armchair, a mahogany desk and chair combination, a wooden bookcase, a small table, two straight-backed chairs, drapes for the windows, a large Navajo rug, paintings, and some art objects and sculpture on the desk and table. The beautiful room resulted in higher ratings in well-being and energy than did the others. (Maslow and Mintz 1972)

Mintz continued this study and demonstrated that these effects are not limited either to "laboratory" situations or to initial adjustments, but can be found under naturalistic circumstances of considerable duration. (Mintz 1972) Mintz instructed examiners to spend two hours per week for three weeks testing subjects on their reactions to facial photographs. The examiners were unaware of the purposes of the study and switched rooms on alternate weeks. The subjects in the beautiful room had ratings which were higher on the energy and well-being dimensions throughout the study. The examiners in the "ugly" room consistently finished testing in less time than the examiners in the "beautiful" room. These results indicate that the appearance of an individual's surroundings can have an effect on the individual and on the activities being performed. (Rubin and Elder 1980)

Public seating at 127 John Street, New York City by William Kaufman Organization.
Photo by Dirck Halstead. Courtesy of William Kaufman Organization.

Sitting at Faneuil Hall, Boston.
Architects: Ben Thompson Associates and The Rouse Co.
Photo courtesy of The Rouse Co.

Dole Pineapple Processing Plant, Honolulu, Hawaii.
Photo by F. Wilson.

POPULATION SIZES AND WEIGHTS

Knowing something about individual differences enables statements to be made about the distribution of responses of the population to design features; such as determining what proportion of a large group of people are likely to respond in particular ways to attributes of a building. As an illustration of this point, A. Rapoport (architect) and N. Watson conducted a review of physical standards used for building designs in a number of nations. They particularly noted the national standards governing the same aspects of the built environment (e.g., space, lighting, noise, etc.) often differ from country to country. They illustrate their point with the following example.

American standards recommend a minimum width of 5 ft. 4 in. for two people facing each other in a dining booth. This dining pattern is not shown at all in Indian data, but for two people facing each other across a dining table the American dimension is 6 ft. 2 in., while in India it is 5 ft. 6 in. (i.e., 8 in. less). The Indian data show additional requirements for eating in a squatting position (6 ft. 6 in.) and also distinguish between informal and formal situations with different dimensions, both for dining at a table and in a squatting position.

Rapoport deals extensively with cultural influences on house design in another work in which he hypothesizes that house form is the result of choice among existing possibilities, the greater the number of possibilities, the greater the choice, but there is never any inevitability, because man can live in many kinds of structures. For example, the degree of choice open to a builder in the United States is considerably greater than that available to someone building in the polar region. In this investigation, Rapoport attempted to find house features which seemed to be universal, to identify critical differences in house forms, and to try to relate both sets of characteristics to personal and cultural factors among populations. (Rubin and Elder 1980, p. 84) (Rapoport, Watson 1972)

SOCIAL DISTANCE

A method initially developed to study industrial and management problems is also useful for M/E research. It is called sociometry and provides one means for obtaining information dealing with the links between social interactions and environmental features.

Sociometry is a method of determining the structure of social relations among members of a given group. A sociometric test measures the preferences or rejections expressed toward members in a group.

Most sociometric tests are administered as questionnaires designing choice situations. These questionnaires have two characteristics:

- A specific criterion for the preferential choice is used, based on the functional activity of the group and the hypotheses being tested (such as, with whom do you like to eat, socialize, etc.).
- The number of choices allowed varies according to the size of the group.

The original method described by J. Moreno (sociologist) involves drawing a sociogram, a diagram which represents the choices made by the members of a group. The more frequently chosen individuals are located near the center and the isolates are placed on the periphery. Preferences or rejections are represented by lines between the individuals. Sociograms are used mainly with small groups for diagnostic purposes to analyze more complex interrelationships.

B. Wells examined the relationship of office design to interaction among employees in order to determine the cohesiveness of work groups in a large British insurance company. He compared friendship choices among workers in a large open area and among workers in smaller enclosed areas.

Wells administered a sociometric test to 285 general clerks by means of tape recorded instructions and slide projections, the responses to which were written in a booklet. Comparisons were made between the open areas and the small partitioned offices in: (1) the number of choices directed outside of each section, (2) the number of reciprocated choices within each office, and (3) the number of people who seldom interacted with others, i.e., isolates. The findings indicated that choices were directly related to the distances between employees and that group cohesion was greater in the smaller offices than in the open plan sections.

With the average life expectancy increases notable in recent years, and considering the already sizable group of elderly people, the question of the relationships between the aged and the population at large has been raised by many social scientists and planners. Two opposing viewpoints are apparent. One contends that old people prefer to be among those with similar interests and con-

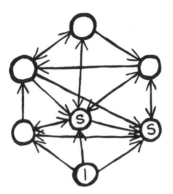

Simple Sociometric Diagram

7 Subjects
21 Preference Choices
6 Mutual Preferences
2 Stars
1 Isolate

Sociogram
(Moreno)
(Rubin and Elder 1980)

From *People and Crowds* by Jim Kalett, Dover Books, NY, 1978.

"The moment of truth." Old lady crossing street in Midtown Manhattan—apprehension as the light changes. Photo by F. Wilson.

Sitters on a swing before 777 3rd Avenue by the William Kaufman Organization.
Photo by Dirck Halstead. Courtesy of the William Kaufman Organization.

cerns and therefore should be housed in buildings suitable to their special requirements. The opposite viewpoint is that the aged should not be isolated, rather, they should be integrated into the community. Major design implications are associated with these or alternative approaches.

E. Steinfeld (architect) used three-dimensional scale models in conjuction with interviews to assess attitudes of older people toward increased contact with young children. Models were used which represented three different activity settings—a park (recreation), a community center (social meeting), and a neighborhood (housing).

The park was used to measure desirable proximity in terms of the physical distance to children. Three benches were positioned with identical surroundings (tree, walk) at three different distances from a playground for children. It was explained that each of the benches was exactly the same walking distance from the point at which the walk diverged. Respondents were then asked to indicate at which bench they would want to sit if they were walking into the park alone or with a friend.

The community center was used to measure desirable proximity in terms of accessible distance to children. It was explained that the three models represented three different ways in which a community center could be built to house a nursery school and a senior citizens' activity center. The differences in accessibility were also explained. In one model one group would have to go outside to visit the other. In another model they would both share a reception room and could visit without leaving. In the final model the groups had separate entrances but could choose to be together in the middle room if they so desired. Respondents made two choices and the pattern of their preferences was recorded. The pattern of choice as a whole was used as an indication of preference.

The neighborhood models were used to measure desirable proximity in terms of the degree of age-segregation of older people in the settlement pattern. Four cards were prepared with six plastic model houses on each, arranged on both sides of the street on individual lots. Each neighborhood or block had a different mix of senior adults and families with young children. Respondents were asked to choose the block on which they would like most to live and the block they would like least.

The findings indicated that on the whole the respondents preferred close physical distance to children in the recreation setting and neighborhoods with a high density of older people.

L. Pastaian (psychologist) reports a study that indicates the importance of keeping established relationships when individuals are relocated. He used two facilities in his study on the effects of relocation on nursing home patients. The control setting was a county medical facility that remained essentially unchanged for the duration of the study. One experimental setting was a county medical facility which was being closed down. Patients were moved to an existing facility. The existing building was totally different, the staff did not move, and the patients were integrated with the existing patient population. The second experimental setting was a facility that was moving from an old building to a new building on the same site. Patients and staff structures remained essentially the same.

An additional study was carried out in the second experimental facility. One group of patients was taken on five advance visits to the new building and in addition given problem solving tasks and spatial orientation sessions. A matched group of patients visited the new building once and were presented with slides of the new facility. They also had staff visits and group review sessions. In all cases the effects of relocation were measured by the patient mortality rate. Results indicated a significantly higher mortality rate for patients in the first experimental setting.

Social Distance (Hall 1966, p. 13) (Rubin and Elder 1980)

Social animals need to stay in touch with each other. Loss of contact with the group can be fatal for a variety of reasons including exposure to predators. Social distance is not simply the distance at which an animal will lose contact with his group, that is, the distance at which it can no longer see, hear, or smell the group. It is rather a psychological distance, one at which the animal apparently begins to feel anxious when he exceeds its limits. We can think of it as a hidden band that contains the group.

Social distance varies from species to species. It is only a few yards among flamingos, quite long among other birds. Male bowerbirds maintain contact over many thousands of feet by means of mighty whistles and harsh, rasping notes.

Social distance is not always rigidly fixed but is determined in part by the situation. When the young of apes and humans are mobile they are under the control of their mother's voice, social distance may be the length of her reach. Danger shrinks social distances.

Social distance in man has been extended by telephone, TV, and the walkie-talkie, making it possible to integrate the activities of groups over great

Social distance amid strangers at North Shore University Hospital Plaza.
Outside area design by Pamela Waters.
Photo by and courtesy of Pamela Waters.

Social Distance among pelicans in Puerta Valarta, Mexico.
Photo by F. Wilson.

Social distances with flamingos, Honolulu Zoo.
Photo by F. Wilson.

Academic procession.
Photo by F. Wilson.

distances. Increased social distance is now remaking social and political institutions in ways that have only recently begun to be studied.

The squatter housing in Zambia was built and spaced within the shouting distance that women could understand each other as they did their housework.

Crabs are solitary animals. They must locate each other by their sense of smell to mate. They also eat any of the soft shell stage which can also be smelled.

Notes on Interaction Within Social Distances

Physical Distance
Physical distance is a dimension of friendliness, talkativeness, intimacy, and equality. Increasing physical distance indicates less acquaintance. (Sommer 1969, p. 21)

Interaction Distance—Latin America
The interaction distance is much less in Latin America than it is in the United States. People cannot talk comfortably with one another unless they are very close to the distance that evokes either sexual or hostile feelings in the North American. The result is that when they move close, we withdraw and back away. As a consequence, they think we are distant or cold, withdrawn and unfriendly. We, on the other hand, are constantly accusing them of breathing down our necks, crowding us, and spraying our faces. (Hall 1959, p. 163)

Sociability—Designing for drinking
Soft lights and soft noise increase stay. Loud noise and high lighting levels shorten stay. (Sommer 1969, p. 122)

Hostility
Avoiding eye contact is hostility. Looking directly at their partners is trying to initiate action. (Sommer 1969, p. 22)

LEADERSHIP AND DOMINANCE

It is frequently necessary to distinguish between dominance—one individual intimidating or threatening another—and leadership—one individual directing the group. Among red deer, the dominance shown by males during the breeding season is vastly different from the leadership by the older females who are ahead of the group and determine its direction without the use of force. Describing a study of goats that showed that being dominant did not help an animal become a leader and vice versa, Scott hypothesized that leadership and dominance behavior are learned separately. Occasionally they may conflict since one depends upon punishment and the other on reward. However, for the most part, leadership and dominance are closely related.

Working with discussion groups in a cafeteria setting, Sommer showed that leaders tended to select the head position at a rectangular table and other people would arrange themselves so that they could see the leader. Visual contact with the leader seemed more important to the other people at the table than physical proximity. A similar finding was obtained by Stodtbeck and Hook who recorded the seating arrangements in experimental jury sessions carried out in Chicago which were not, however, actual court cases. The experimental jurors were accompanied by a bailiff into a jury room that contained a rectangular table with one chair at the head and one at the foot, and five chairs on either side. The jurors' first task was to elect a foreman, and there was a striking trend for the person seated at one of the head positions to be elected foreman. This was attributed to the "intrinsic propriety" of the chairman being at the head of the table as well as the likelihood that electing someone else would be taken as a personal rejection of the individual at the head position. It was also found that the initial choice of seats was not random. People from a higher economic class—proprietors and managers—selected the head chairs more than would have been expected by chance. In electing a foreman it appeared that the jurors looked at both occupants of the head chairs and selected the one with higher status. In view of the head chair's association with leadership as well as the fact that people of higher status occupied the head chair, it was not surprising that people in the head chair participated in the discussion more than people at the other positions. Subsequent ratings by all jury members showed that the people at the head chair were considered to have made the most significant contribution to the deliberations. (Sommer 1969, p. 20, 21)

Aerial photograph of the U. S. pavilion at Expo '70 in Osaka, Japan.

USSR Pavilion—A 109 meter high steel pipe structure. It was the largest of all the Expo '70 pavilions, covering a floor space of 90,200 sq. ft.
Photo courtesy of Expo '70 Corp.

Notes on Leadership

Leadership and dominant behavior are learned separately and may conflict. One depends upon punishment and the other on reward. For the most part leadership and dominance are closely related. (Sommer 1969, p. 20)

Arm position, body orientation, and standing above each other assert dominance as Charlie Chaplin demonstrated in the film *The Great Dictator*. The office size and locations and space assignments assert leadership and make it difficult for others to exercise leadership. In the army, housing difference of rank decreases contact with one's neighbors. (Sommer 1969, p. 22)

Aerial view contrasting the two structures on the 3,300,000 square meter Expo site.
Photo courtesy of Expo '70 Corp.

From *People and Crowds* by Jim Kalett, Dover Books, NY, 1978.

249

NOTES ON SPATIAL EDGES

Segregation As An Extreme Form of Territoriality

Chicago's Ashland Avenue—described by Gene Marine, free-lance journalist:

"Black people at Sixty-third from Justine to Ashland.

White people Ashland to Marchfield equally typical.

Not one white in the black district or one black in the white district. Group territoriality is expressed in national and local boundaries, a segregation into defined areas that reduces conflict."

Segregation forced on one group by another has unfortunate consequences but is one means of accommodation between two groups.

96th Street In New York City

"The street is nothing less, you say, then Manhattan's Berlin wall . . .You are staring into the Caribbean and Africa. You stand on wealthy ground staring at poverty, and wealth and poverty have this in common: the first sight of them is frightening.

Except on rare occasions, the white gangs stay on their side of the line, and the black gangs stay on theirs. There is no question but that this segregation, in the short run at least, reduces overt intergroup conflict. I do not condone residential segregation any more than death or poverty, but it has certain social consequences an one of these is the reduction of overt conflict between members of different groups. The worst race riots have not occurred in the rigidly segregated areas of the South, but in the border or fringe areas of the North. . .the only way to ensure future tranquility is to change the conditions that created the conflict." (Sommer 1969, pp. 16–17)

"Because social and spatial orders serve similar functions, it is not surprising to find spatial correlates of status levels and conversely, social correlates of spatial positions. In the barnyard, the top chickens have the greater freedom of space and can walk anywhere, whereas lower birds are restricted to small areas and can be pecked by other birds wherever they go." (Sommer 1969)

Social Distinctions—Blurred

"Society compensates for blurred social distinctions by clear spatial distinctions such as physical barriers, keep-out signs, and property restrictions. Such rigid spatial order does not endure with increasing population density. When social orders crumble under the onslaught of crowding the result is extreme social disorganization." (Sommer 1969, p. 23)

"England is a small crowded island. Englishmen exist by ignoring each other." (Sommer 1969, p. 23)

Segregation

"Segregation reduces overt conflict. The only way to prevent future conflict is to correct the conditions that created the conflict." (Sommer 1969, p. 16)

Pamela Water's manipulation of pavement forms and seating creates spatial edges of personal space melding community and privacy. People can be both 'in' and 'out' of 'the scene' as they choose.
Photos by and courtesy of Pamela Waters.

Spatial edges created by bollards—East Wing of the National Gallery, Washington, D.C. However the patterned cobblestone pavement continues on across a busy street (bus in background). A spatial edge is lacking where one is very sorely needed between the secure pedestrian area and the dangerous automobile territory of the street.
Photo by F. Wilson.

Squatters fill the spatial edges in the interstices between private development and public space. The squatting settlement marks the spatial edge.
Photo by and courtesy of Dhiru Thadani.

Spatial Edges
"Our concept (North American) of space makes use of the edges of things. If there aren't any edges, we make them by creating artificial lines. This is characterized by the way we give directions, such as five miles west and two miles north. Space is treated in terms of a coordinate system. (X marks the spot) in contrast, the Japanese and many other people work within areas. The y name "spaces" and distinguish between one space and the next or parts of space. . ." (Hall 1959, p. 159)

Space Centers
"Given a large enough room, Americans will distribute themselves around the walls, leaving the center open for group activities such as conferences. That is, the center belongs to the group and is often marked by a or some object placed there both to use and save the space. Lacking a form a "huddle" may be instituted in the center of the room. The pattern of moving from one's place to huddle is symbolized in our language by such expressions as, "I had to take a new position on this point," or, "The position of the office on this point is. . ." (Hall 1959, p. 157)

In a war, 'no man's land' is where the fighting takes place. In tenement living, the halls and entrance underneath the stairs is the space where most crimes take place for it is a 'no man's land' where the tenants do not have responsibility, the absentee landlord does not exercise responsibility, and the area is seldom visited by the police, whose usual rounds stop at the entrance door.

Blurring of spatial edges with lighting and reflective surfaces that fuse the hard edges of the building into a collage of buildings, people, and the activity of the street. Street paving leads into an animated facade.
Design by Pamela Waters. Photo by and courtesy of Pamela Waters.

PERSONAL SPACE

Personal distance and personal space proxemics both describe the relation of organisms and their spacing. Personal distance as used by Hediger refers to the normal spacing that noncontact animals maintain between themselves and their fellows. It is an invisible bubble surrounding an organism. Outside the bubble, two organisms are not as intimately involved with each other, no matter what the purpose of that involvement, as when the bubbles overlap.

Hall found that individually determined space factors play an important role in any study of distance relationships among people, and among animals as well. He was an early proponent of the need to consider cultural variability in the use of space, privacy, overcrowding, and other spatial concepts. Hall studied the problem of distance relationships by observing activities and developing a classification scheme to describe them.

His starting point was the individual who may be considered as being encased in Hediger's invisible bubble which defines his boundaries. The bubble serves as a reference point for the individual or group and distances may be described as they relate to the bubble.

Life space and the invisible bubble are theoretical models developed to describe requirements for individual privacy, and/or the need for freedom of the person, or group, from unwanted intrusion by others.

Hall described the bubble in his book, *The Hidden Dimension,* in his discussion of animals. Each animal is surrounded by a series of bubbles or irregularly shaped balloons that serve to maintain proper spacing between individuals.

Hediger's concept of flight distance and critical distance are used when individuals of different species meet. Personal distance and social distance can be observed during interaction between members of the same species.

Wild animals, Hall observed, allow potential enemies to approach only up to a given distance before fleeing. There is a positive correlation between the size of an animal and its flight distance. The larger the animal, the greater the distance it must keep between itself and an enemy. An antelope will flee at five hundred yards and a wall lizard at two.

The boundaries of the self extend beyond the body, as most now agree, and the realization of self, as we know it, is intimately associated with the process of making boundaries explicit.

There are critical distance zones present whenever there is a flight reaction. This encompasses the narrow zone separating flight distance from attack distance. The lion in a zoo will flee from approaching man until it meets an insurmountable barrier. If the man continues the cornered lion reverses the situation and begins to stalk the man who, if he is sensible, will precipitate his own flight reaction. This is the essence of the classic lion act in circuses. The trainer steps in and out of the lion's critical distance.

Public passageway, Helsinki, Finland.
Photo by F. Wilson.

Personal Space in an angular world.

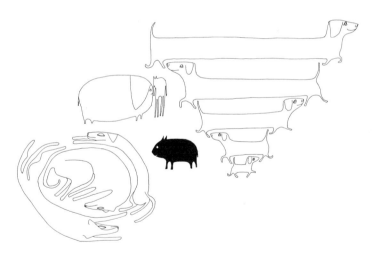

But there is an unexplained dichotomy among species of animals, as there is difference in reaction between people of different cultures in relation to the space around them. Some species of animals huddle together and require physical contact with each other. Other species completely avoid touching. No apparent logic exists in the division of species in this relation. The walrus, the hippopotamus, the pig, the brown bat, the parakeet, and the hedgehog, for example, are contact animals. The horse, dog, cat, rat, muskrat, and hawk are noncontact. For example, Hall points out that the Emperor penguin is a contact species and huddles to preserve bodily warmth and ranges over more territory than the smaller Adelie penguin, which is noncontact.

The term personal space was popularized by Sommer as referring to "an area which should be a volume of individual boundaries surrounding a person's body into which intruders may not come." This is the 'territory' that man carries around with him and regards as his. (Mercer 1975, p. 140)

It is an emotionally charged space that will evoke reactions if penetrated, as the lion reacts to the trainer. Sommer suggested that one of the best ways of studying this personal space bubble is to observe people's behavior when the bubble is violated. His investigators have sat too close to people as they studied in a library and very close to psychiatric patients on benches to see how close they could come before flight was precipitated. Variables that affect the size of the 'bubble' are situational: the physical context where the interaction is occurring, for example, open-air settings promote closer distances than contained settings; extroverts apparently tolerate physical closeness better than introverts; friends stand closer to one another than strangers; and when intrusion of another's bubble is unavoidable, females will intrude on another female's rather than on another male's. (Mercer 1975, p. 142)

Proof that the personal space and the body buffer zone perform a function as a spatial extension of self is given credence by the fact that when such space is violated without the accompanying desire for intimate exchange, people are either being treated as nonpersons—as in the head-to-feet, horizontal storage of slaves in the slave ships plying between Africa and America in the 19th century—or feel themselves to be nonpersons—as on crowded underground trains at rush hour.

Being a nonperson, or treating others as such, means simply refusing to recognize interchanges—tactile contact—that in other situations would be emotionally highly charged. The body buffer zone is acting as a flexible filter regulating the degree of intimacy that others are allowed. It would appear from Horowitz's and Kinzel's work that people who do have difficulty in relating to others have larger body buffer zones. Also interesting in this connection is that introverts' zones are larger than extroverts' (Williams, 1963) and introversion in this context means a person who is 'quiet, retiring . . . introspective, fond of books rather than people—reserved and distant except to intimate friends.' (Mercer 1975, p. 141)

Findings reported by Kinzel (1971) found that the body buffer zones of violent prisoners were almost all larger when compared to a group of nonviolent prisoners. Also their rear buffer zone was larger. (Mercer 1975, p. 140)

The personal space bubble can be conceived as an extension of 'self' that contracts and expands both according to circumstances and according to the person's own perception (conscious or unconscious) of how much protection the self requires.

The amount of protection will depend in turn on the degree of threat provided by other people or by the physical environment. Certain people, of course, find the environment and/or persons more threatening than others. Schizophrenics would appear to try to retain a larger 'extension of self' personal space than nonschizophrenics.

Hall divided and then described the expanding and contracting fields surrounding people and described their perceptual characteristics. It is this description that should prove most valuable to designers who tend to select interaction distances from sets of graphic standards and hardly bother their heads over the consequence that Hall describes here.

Humankind's sense of space has very little to do with the single viewpoint of linear perspective developed by Renaissance artists and still taught in contemporary schools of art and architecture.

Humans sense distance in a dynamic perception of space related to human action. What can be done in the given space is how it is perceived.

If we conceive man as surrounded by a series of expanding and contracting fields which provide information of many kinds, we shall begin to see him in an entirely different light, Hall contends. We can then begin to learn about human behavior. Not only are there introverts and extroverts, authoritarian and egalitarian, Apollonian and Dionysian types, and all the shades and personality gradations in between, but in addition each person assumes learned situational personalities.

The simplest form of the situational personality, Hall says, is that associated with responses to intimate, personal, social, and public transactions. Some never develop a public phase of their personalities and cannot fill public spaces. They make poor speakers or moderators, others have difficulty with intimate and personal zones and find closeness of others unendurable.

Because most of the distance-sensing process occurs outside awareness, we cannot always be sure what it is that enables us to characterize others. A great many things happen at once. It is difficult to sort out the cues on which we base our reactions. Was it voice, stance, or distance? The sorting process requires careful observation over a long period of time in a wide variety of situations noting each small shift in information.

Our perceptions are clues. The presence of warmth of the body, the smell of freshly washed hair, and the blurring of features are signs of close intimate contact. If one uses oneself as a control, Hall counsels, it is possible to identify structure points in the distance-sensing system.

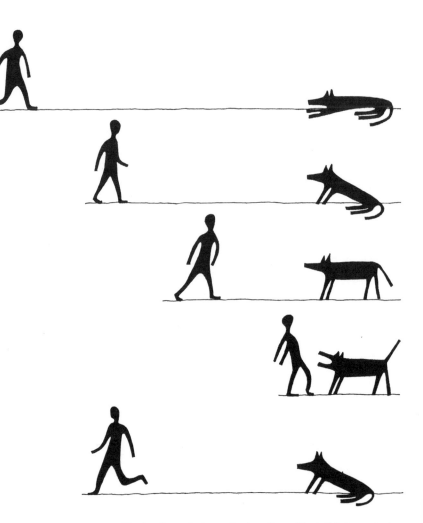

The best way to learn the location of invisible boundaries is to keep walking until somebody complains. Personal space refers to an area with invisible boundaries surrounding a person's body into which intruders may not venture. Like porcupines, people like to be close enough to obtain warmth and comradeship, but far enough away to avoid pricking one another.
(Sommer 1969)

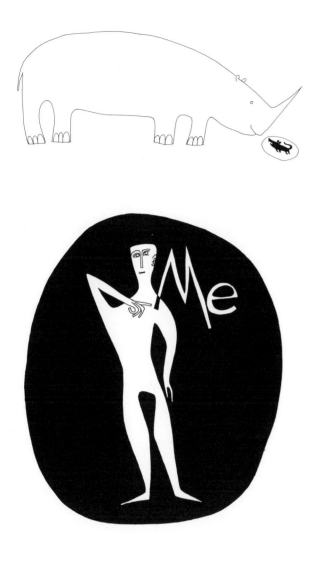

If the isolates can be identified one by one, as parts of the sets that constitute the intimate, personal, social, and public zones, then a basis of judgment is formulated.

Hall has identified the four distances that he has termed "proxemics." This is a term for personal distance originally used by Hediger to indicate the distance that consistently separates the members of noncontact species.

INTIMATE DISTANCE

Close Phase—The distance of lovemaking and wrestling, comforting and protecting. Physical contact or the high possibility of physical involvement is uppermost in the awareness of both persons. The use of distance receptors is greatly reduced except for olfaction and the sensation of radiant heat. Both are accelerated.

In the maximum contact phase, muscles and skin communicate. Pelvis, thigh, and head can be brought into play; arms can encircle. Except at the outer limits, sharp vision is blurred. When close vision is possible within the intimate range, as with children, the image is greatly enlarged and stimulates much if not all of the retina. An extraordinary amount of detail is visible. The detail plus the cross-eyed pull of eye muscles provide a visual experience that cannot be confused with any other distance. Vocalization plays a minor part in communication.

Far Phase—Intimate distance of six to eighteen inches. Heads, thighs, and pelvis not easily engaged. Hands can reach and grasp extremities. Head is seen enlarged in size, features are distorted. For Americans, Hall says that the ability to focus the eye easily is important. The iris of the other's eye seen at about six to nine inches is enlarged to more than life size. Small blood vessels are clearly perceived; pores are enlarged. Clear vision, to 15 degrees, includes the upper or lower portion of the face, perceived as enlarged to more than life size. The nose is seen as over large and may seem distorted, as may other features.

Peripheral vision of from 30 to 180 degrees includes outlines of head and shoulders and very often the hands.

Americans experience physical discomfort when foreigners come inappropriately inside this intimate sphere. Expressions such as, "get your face out of mine," "shook his fist in my face," and "breathing my air," express this discomfort.

At six to eighteen inches the voice is used but is normally held at a low level or whisper.

Heat and odor of the other person's breath may be detected, even though directed away from the other's face. The heat loss or gain from the other person's body may be noticeable.

Adult middle class Americans do not consider the use of the intimate distance proper although their young may be observed intimately involved with each other in automobiles or at beaches.

Crowding brings strangers into what would ordinarily be classed as intimate spatial relations, but subway riders have defensive devices which take the intimacy out of intimate space invasion in public conveyances.

A basic tactic, Hall observes, is to remain as immobile as possible, to withdraw when touched if possible, if not, muscles in affected areas are kept tense. It is taboo to relax and enjoy bodily contact with strangers. Hands are kept at the side or used to steady the body by grasping a railing. Eyes are fixed on infinity and are not brought to bear on anyone for more than a passing glance. These reactions differ in other cultures. (Hall 1966)

PERSONAL DISTANCE

Personal distance is a term originally used by Hediger to designate the distance consistently separating members of noncontact species like a small protective sphere or bubble that an organism maintains between itself and others.

Close Phase—Distance one and one-half to two and one-half feet. Sense of closeness derives in part from the possibilities present in regard to what each participant can do to the other with their extremities. One can hold or grasp the other person. Visual distortion of the other's features is no longer apparent. A visual angle of 15 degrees takes in another person's upper or lower face seen with exceptional clarity. The three-dimensional quality of objects is particularly pronounced. Surface textures are also prominent and clearly differentiated. Where people stand in relation to each other signals their relationship, or how they feel toward each other.

Far Phase—Keeping someone at arms' length expresses this phase of personal distance. It extends from a point just outside easy touching distance by one person to a point where two people can touch fingers if they extend both arms. This is the limit of physical domination in a very real sense. Beyond it, a person cannot easily 'get his hands on' someone else. Subjects of personal interest and involvement can be discussed at this distance. Head size is perceived as normal, and details of other person's features are clearly visible. These features are seen in fine detail, gray hair, stains on teeth, spots, wrinkles, or dirt. The gaze must wander, and where the eye is directed is a matter of cultural conditioning. Fifteen degree clear vision covers upper or lower face while 180 degree peripheral vision takes in the hands and the whole body of a seated person. Hand movement is detected but fingers cannot be counted. Voice level is moderate, no body heat is perceptible. (Hall 1966)

North Shore University Hospital Plaza. Pamela Waters.

SOCIAL DISTANCE

The intimate details of the face are now perceived, no touching or expectation of touching. Voice is normal and level with little change between the far and close phases.

Close Phase—Distance of four to seven feet. The head size is perceived as normal as one moves away from the subject. The foveal area of the eye can take in an ever-increasing amount of the other person. At four feet, a one degree visual angle covers an area of a little more than one eye. At seven feet the area of sharp focus extends to the nose and portions of either eye, or the whole mouth, one eye and the nose are seen clearly. Details of skin texture and hair are clearly perceived. At 60 degree visual angle and a distance of four feet, the head, shoulders, and upper trunk are perceived. At seven feet, the entire figure is seen.

Impersonal business occurs at this distance. In the close phase there is more involvement than in the distant phase. People who work together use close social distance. It is the common distance for people attending a casual social gathering. To stand and look down at a person at this distance has a domineering effect, as when a man talks to his secretary or receptionist.

Far Phase—Seven to twelve feet. This is the distance one moves when told to stand away, "so I can see you." Business and social discourse occurs at the far end of social distance and at this distance has a more formal character than if it occurs inside the close phase. The desks in the offices of 'important' people are sometimes large enough to hold visitors at the far phase of social distance. Chairs at the opposite side of standardized desks keep people eight or nine feet apart. At the far phase of social distance the finest details of the face such as the capillaries in the eyes are not seen. Skin texture, hair, and condition of teeth and clothes are readily visible. Heat and body odor are not detectable. The full figure, with surrounding space is encompassed in a 60-degree glance. At approximately 13 feet the eyes and the mouth of the other person are seen in the area of sharpest vision. It is not necessary to shift eyes to take in the entire face. During conversations of any significant length, it is more important to maintain visual contact at this distance than at closer ranges.

The proxemic behavior of the kind just described is culturally conditioned, Hall says, and is entirely arbitrary. However, it is binding on all concerned and failure to hold the other person's eye is to shut them out and bring the conversation to a halt. People can be observed craning their necks and turning their heads to maintain eye contact. A prolonged visual contact at less than ten feet with one person sitting and the other standing tires the neck muscles.

The voice level is noticeably louder for the far phase than for the close phase, and the voice can be heard readily in an adjoining room if the door is open. Raising the voice or shouting can have the effect of reducing social distance to personal distance.

The proxemic feature of social distance at the far phase is that it can be used to insulate or screen people from each other. It also makes it possible for them to work in the presence of another person without appearing to be rude.

Receptionists in offices are vulnerable, Hall notes, for most employers expect them to do several tasks, such as answering questions, being polite to callers, and typing. If the receptionist is less than ten feet from another person, even a stranger, she will be sufficiently involved to be virtually compelled to converse. More space will allow her to work quite freely without being required to entertain with conversation. A husband and wife sitting ten or twelve feet from each other can engage each other in spasmodic conversation. Back to back seating, Hall notes, is an appropriate solution to minimum space since it makes it possible for two people to stay uninvolved if this is their desire. (Hall 1966)

PUBLIC DISTANCE

Public distance is well outside the circle of involvement.

Close Phase—12 to 25 feet. At 12 feet it is possible to take evasive or defensive action if threatened. The voice is loud but not full volume. Careful choice of words and phrasing occur at this distance. Formal style demands advance planning, or the speaker may think on his feet.

Fine details of skin and eyes are no longer visible. At 16 feet the body begins to lose its roundness and begins to look flat. Only the whites of the eyes are visible. The head size is perceived as considerably under life size. A 15 degree area of clear vision covers the faces of two people at 12 feet. Thirty degree scanning includes the whole body with space around it. Other persons present can be seen peripherally.

Far Phase—25 feet or more. Thirty feet is the distance that is automatically set around important public figures. At 30 or more feet the subtle shades of meaning conveyed by the normal voice are lost as are the details of facial expression and movement. The voice and all actions must be exaggerated or magnified. The entire person is seen as quite small and can be perceived within the small circle of sharpest vision. When people appear as ants, contact with them as human beings fades rapidly. (Hall 1966)

NOTES ON PSYCHOSOMATIC FATIGUE

"A number of more or less spontaneous reactions to the physical environment are included among the causes of psychosomatic fatigue, an almost totally neglected phenomenon which may well be a factor of prime importance in determining the livability of a city or an interior. The clearest anecdotal examples of mentally induced weariness that come to my mind are not directly related to urban or institutional life, but their apparent simplicity may help to identify the general category of manifestations here referred to.

In my childhood and youth in Norway we were well acquainted with various situations likely to produce what I now think of as psychosomatic fatigue. Hiking in nature is always harder on the ones who walk behind then on those who lead. On a long walk the smallest members of the family, or group, were therefore commonly told to walk in front. Sometimes a system of rotation was used to prevent uneven strain on the flock, as the day wore on. We also knew that crossing a wide valley, or mountain plateau, with the far-off destination always in sight, is much more tiring than it is to walk the same distance across rolling terrain, seeing ahead only one lesser ridge, or bend, at a time. In both of these illustrations it is obvious that the least fatiguing performance demands fully as much, and in the second case even more, physical exertion than is required by the more exhausting alternative.

. . .In the complexities of an urban milieu particular causes of physically unwarranted fatigue are not so easily isolated. But every traveller knows that there are cities in which you can walk all day before weariness catches up with you, while there are others where the view from the window deflates your energies before the start. And this is not only tourist reactions. The walk to work can be invigorating or tiresome, depending to a large extent upon the physical surroundings through which it takes you." (Parr 1969, p. 5)

". . .the distance that becomes discouraging is undoubtedly more or less dependent upon the height and width of the channel through which it is seen. The height at which enclosing walls become oppressive is modified by their exposed length and the ogen span between them, and so onK Complications of shape beyond the simple rectangular forms also enter into the problem.

The idea of a sense of freedom bestowed upon us by the shape of our surroundings is an old concept often used through the centuries in praise of lofty interior of proportions that release, rather than overwhelm, the spirit by their dimensions. When we feel this liberation under the vault of some great cathedral, or in an exposition hall, it is clear that our spirit enjoys a freedom of perceptual penetrations through space, in which our bodies would be totally incapable of participating, since few of us are Batman. And, if freedoms we cannot use soothe and relax us, is it not also likely that obstacles we do not have to overcome may make us tense, as has been suggested before?" (Parr 1969, p. 7)

Walk through the woods to reach Calvert Road, College Park, Maryland.
Photo by F. Wilson.

Student Union at Dipoli in Otaniemi, Finland by architects
Raili Paatelainen and Reima Pietila.

A major building continually perceptually stimulating.

Entrance plaza, the Seagrams Bldg., NYC.
A formidable space not to be crossed without food and
water.
Photo by F. Wilson.

Desultory pedestrian traffic on a Leningrad street whose
proportions were specified by Peter the Great for
pageantry.
Photo by F. Wilson.

A walk through Carpenter Center (by Le Corbusier) at
Harvard University.
Photo courtesy of Harvard University.

TERRITORY

There is not a consistent agreement among those who observe and experiment with animals as to the value of extrapolating their actions to that of humans. At one time, the common practice was to interpret animal behavior anthropomorphically, that is to ascribe to it human values and motivations. Kipling's Rikki-Tikki-Tavi and Brer Rabbit were portrayed as thinking and acting like human beings. Recently, it has been popular to do the opposite. Human behavior is likened in simplistic ways to similar behavior in animals. Julian Edney (1974) has labeled this approach the 'beastopomorphic' interpretation. (Braun 1979, p. 65)

According to the 'beastopomorphic' view, said Edney, humans share with other animals the drive to claim, defend, and compete for territory. This drive is said to be inherited and irrevocable. But despite the similarities between animals and human beings, there are very significant differences, Edney points out.

According to Edney, in animals the use of space tends to follow stereotypical, fixed patterns, but among humans its use is highly variable, as an example, the contrasts between nomadic, sedentry, hunting, gathering, and farming peoples. The wide range of different ways of using space suggests that human territoriality is based largely on cultural traditions. Territoriality, for animals, serves primarily physiological needs such as providing food and shelter. For humans, territory serves a far greater range of needs, such as privacy, status, and ideology. This analogy, according to Edney, illustrates that animal analogies fall far short of accounting for human behavior.

But this is one of the virtues of animal studies, according to Edward Hall, for animals do not rationalize; they respond amazingly consistently. It is therefore, Hall says, possible to learn an amazing amount translatable to human terms.

The basic concept of territoriality in the study of animal behavior is defined as behavior by which an organism characteristically lays claim to an area and defends it against members of its own species.

Animals, Hall reminds us, contrary to romantic notions, are not free. They are often imprisoned in their own territories. Animal territory says H. Hediger, Zurich animal psychologist, insures the propagation of the species by regulating density. It is a frame in which things are done. It provides places to learn and play, and safe places to hide. The territory coordinates the activities of a group and holds the group together. It keeps animals within communicating distances of each other where the presence of food or of an enemy can be signaled. An animal with a territory of its own can develop an inventory of reflex responses to terrain features. When danger strikes, the animal in its own territory can respond automatically without requiring time to think about where to hide.

Art Students, San Carlos, Mexico City.
Photo by F. Wilson.

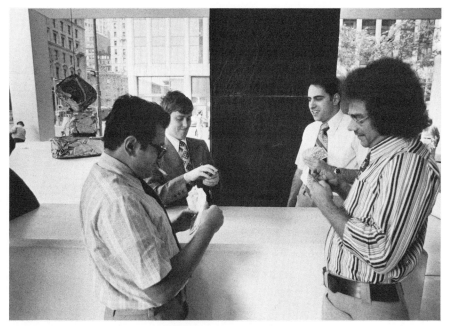

Social space created by card players at 77 Water Street.
Photo by Dirck Halstead. Courtesy of the William Kaufman Organization.

Salesman establishes vending territory at busy intersection in New York City.
Photo by F. Wilson.

C. R. Carpenter, who pioneered the study of monkeys in their native settings, listed thirty-two functions of territoriality. These included the important actions relating to the protection and evolution of the species. Differences in territories and territorial habits are now considered so important that they are used as a basis for distinguishing between species much as are the animals' anatomical features.

Territoriality offers protection from predators, and also exposes to predation the unfit who are too weak to establish and defend a territory, much as a landlord weeds out his tenants by raising the rent. One of the most important functions of territoriality is the proper spacing of the animals of a species. This protects against overexploitation of that part of the environment on which a species depends for its living.

The history of man's past, Hall reminds us, is largely an account of humankind's efforts to wrest space from others and to defend space from outsiders. (Hall 1966, p. 51) A quick review of the map of Europe since the turn of the century reflects this fact.

We need but look around us to see human territoriality on a small scale which on a large scale is reflected in the map of Europe. Beggars have beats as do the policemen who chase them. Prostitutes work their side of the street. Salesmen and distributors have their own territories, which they defend fiercely like any other living organism. The symbolism of the phrase, "to move in on someone," is ominous whether it be a gangster or a businessman and is accurate and appropriate. To have a territory is to have one of the essential components of life. To lack a territory is one of the most precarious of all human situations.

Space, or territoriality, as Hall, Sommer, and a host of other writers have repeatedly demonstrated meshes very subtly with the rest of culture in multitudinous different ways. For example, status is indicated by the distance one sits from the head of the table on formal occasions. We have seen how shifts take place in the voice as people increase the distances between them from whispering to shouting. There are areas, or territories, for work, play, education, and defense. There are also instruments such as rulers, chains, and range finders for measuring space; and boundaries for everything from a house to a nation.

Humankind has invented a great many ways of defending what it considers its own land or turf or spread, and these extend from atomic bombs to mental cruelty. The removal of boundary markers and trespass upon the property of another is a punishable act in most of the Western world. A man's home has been his castle in English common law for centuries, and it is protected by prohibitions on unlawful search and seizure even by officials of his own government. A distinction is carefully made between private property, the territory of an individual, and public property, the territory of the group. The distinction is made in areas of the house that strangers may enter and those in which only the intimate family is allowed. There are some areas that only the occupants themselves use, such as front porch, parlor, kitchen, playroom, living room, and bathroom.

Territory—Personal Space—Status—Dominance

Territoriality involves personal space, status, dominance, and a number of other biological and cultural actions and responses. This description of territoriality will therefore cross over into these other classifications.

The defense of territories hinges on visible boundaries and markers, but the defense of personal space, whose boundaries are invisible, is a matter of gesture, posture, and choosing a location that conveys clear meaning to others, Robert Sommer declares.

Many situations in the defense of personal space are so entangled with the defense of an immediate territory that they seem part of a single process which is the defense of privacy. This defense involves fundamental questions of space usage and property rights. An area that cannot be defended against intruders is not considered a private territory or domain. (Sommer 1969, p. 35)

Some birds use songs during the mating season to keep others away. A bear will claw the bark from tree trunks; a deer will secrete a smelly substance from a gland near its nostrils; and a wolf may urinate at the periphery of his territory.

The benefits bestowed by a territory can be known by examining the area to see what it supplies in the way of food, shelter, protection from predators, and the like. It has been found, for example, that animal territories generally become larger when food is in short supply and shrink when food is plentiful. If we can understand the functions of the space in relation to the organism using it we have a basis of hazarding how strongly it will be defended and the nature of the defense tactics to be used.

Sommer has listed four territorial types:

1. Public territories such as courtyards and parks provide the citizen with freedom of access but not necessarily of action.
2. Home territories that are public areas taken over by groups of individuals such as children's makeshift clubhouses, homosexual bars, coffeehouses that cater to habitues. Regular patrons have a sense of intimacy and control over the area.
3. Interactional territories that are areas where social gatherings may occur. They have clearly marked boundaries and rules of access and egress.
4. Body territories are territories encompassing the body that are most private and inviolate spaces belonging to the individual. (Sommer 1969, p. 44)

There are also some terms that Sommer uses for territorial encroachment.

Violation—Unwarranted use of territory.
Invasion—The physical presence of an intruder within the boundaries of the

Washington Zoo.
Photo by F. Wilson.

Washington, D.C. Zoo.
Photo by F. Wilson.

Washington, D.C. Zoo.
Photo by F. Wilson.

Political figure Scott Udall mixes informally at picnic at
design conference at Aspen, Colorado.
Photo by F. Wilson.

territory.

Contamination—Rendering the territory impure with respect to its definition and usage.

Territory—Threat and dominant position and posture. (Sommer 1969, p. 44)

Sommer also pointed out the significance of room position. A corner conveys a different meaning than that of a center of the room. A dominant position is also more vulnerable. Threats of aggressive attack serve to reduce overt physical combat by substituting ritualized approach, display of ritualized struggle and retreat. Avoidance works best in a room with many corners, alcoves, and side areas hidden from view.

Sommer quoted a London prostitute as stating that the fights always occurred in the center of the room. To be in the center is to invite the threat of being surrounded.

To sit in the middle of a long table will protect the entire table against timid invaders who will shrink away rather than risk the occupant's displeasure. An aggressive intruder on the other hand will be able to surround the occupant on all sides. A corner or alcove makes surrounding by aggressive invaders impossible. (Sommer 1969, p. 49) It is common practice when locating themselves in strange territories for those who are used to violence to sit against the wall close to means of retreat such as exit doors or windows.

Humans seem to adhere rigorously to preferences for a particular bed, table, or chair, which is an operational definition of territoriality paralleled to animal studies. Athletic teams demonstrate a preference for their home grounds. (Sommer 1969, p. 14)

SPACE MARKERS—RESERVED SPACE

People often use markers to state that a space is occupied. In libraries, books are left on the desk, and personal apparel or belongings are left when one leaves their table in a restaurant. Airplanes provide occupied seat signs. Placing a coat or books at a table before waiting in a cafeteria line sometimes proves to be an effective space marker and sometimes it is ignored. There are some space markers that are more effective than others. The principles of reserved space in public places are not explicit.

Staying in one place for a period of time gives people the feeling of a right to it. A man sitting in a seat for half an hour is less likely to move than one who has temporarily occupied the seat when he feels that his personal space is being encroached upon. Chairs are sometimes used to establish territoriality and reserve space.

The square footage per person used by architects and designers is an arbitrary computation. A design to sit six or eight people may appear occupied when there are only two or three. Territoriality produces waste space and not multiple use. Students who cannot find space which they feel adequate will not invade the space of others or ignore space markers but have a tendency to return to their rooms instead. (Sommer 1969, p. 57)

Group territories keep individual groups apart and thereby preserve the integrity of the group, whereas dominance is the basis for intergroup relationships. Nonwestern human societies where land is owned communally and a status order regulates social intercourse operate differently.

Western man uses a complex amalgam of individual ownership, communal ownership, and status relationships to maintain a social order. Perhaps the most unusual feature of human territories is the prevalence of 'rented space.' These are areas that belong to no one person, but are used by another for a prescribed period in return for a fee. (Sommer 1969, p. 15) While the people that rent them feel control over the space, they do not necessarily feel proprietary rites to it since it can be entered by the owner, often at will. The adjacent areas such as hallways become extensions of the street inside the building. The tenants do not feel responsible for them, and the landlord, if not an occupant of the building, neglects them. The result is that most crime and destructive behavior takes place in them. The ingestion of dope, mugging, rape, and assault occur much more frequently in the hallways and public corridors of tenement buildings than they do on the streets outside.

One of the most unique features of territoriality is that of the nonperson. For example, children are not expected to observe territorial boundaries. On the other hand, they defend their own turf by deciding that the adults and police that harass them are nonpersons.

Doctors and nurses in hospitals treat patients as nonpersons. They discuss the patient's illness and make social remarks to each other as if the patient were not in the room, much the same as patrons in a restaurant ignore the waitress or guests ignore maids in a hotel.

People can be driven from their places by refusing to show the proper deferential gestures normal to the local seating norms. Treating the occupant of the space as a nonperson lacking in humanity and territorial rights may drive the other person from the space or elicit an angry response, in which case the driver may become the driven.

An important consideration of defining spatial invasion is whether the parties involved perceive each other as persons. A nonperson cannot invade per-

Waiters at airport terminal in Helsinki, Finland align themselves along observation rail in formal territorial spacing.
Photo by F. Wilson.

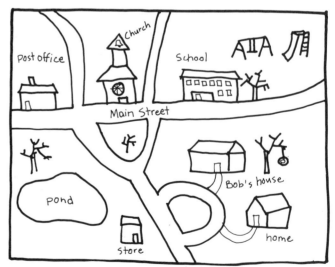

Example of "Turf Map."
(Anderson and Tindall)
(Rubin and Elder 1980)

Design by Pamela Waters.
Photo by and courtesy of Pamela Waters.

"My favorite rock."
Photo by and courtesy of Pamela Waters.

sonal space any more than a tree or a chair. It is common practice to react to another person as an object or part of the background, which is an effective social mechanism as our environment becomes more congested.

Nonpeople become people temporarily as they force recognition by excusing themselves treading on toes, or bumping. Shoving is permissable on crowded subways and buses. On an uncrowded street it is a personal violation of territory and an aggressive act which would be met by an act in kind.

TERRITORIALITY

The work of J. Crook (animal researcher) illustrates a research approach to better define the distance classifications developed by Hall. Crook recorded three types of spacing-arrival distance or how far from several birds a newcomer will land, settled distance or the resultant distance after adjustments, and distance after departure or how far apart birds remain after intermediate birds have left. Similarly, N. Russo (psychologist) noted that a number of flight reactions occurred when she maintained an arrival distance of about 6 inches (15 cm) (moved her chair when the subject did) and did not allow subjects to establish a comfortable settled distance.

J. Anderson (geographer) and M. Tindall studied territoriality in young adults. The participants were given the following instructions:

From memory draw a sketch map of your childhood (ages 6–12 yrs.) turf. By turf we mean that area or set of areas which you traversed, occupied, or used with sufficient regularity and assurance that you considered it for all practical purposes to be the proper domain of you and your friends and/or siblings. The sketch should show major and minor paths, activity models, and landmarks as well as "verboten" or danger areas, important barriers and boundaries, and include a legend. Scale and orientation shown may be relative and need not be precise. Then, write a two to four page analysis, exploring the nature of the patterns of movement and activity revealed by your sketch maps and their determinants.

The researchers view this approach as a tool for helping them to understand how people perceive and relate to their environments. Anderson and Tindall hope that an understanding of these concepts will lead to better planning and design of community facilities. (Rubin 1980, p. 86) (Anderson and Tindall 1972)

STATUS

Status, territoriality, and personal space mix and overlap, yet each seems to have definable characteristics although often it cannot be exemplified without overlapping. Status, Robert Sommer says, is expressed physically in ways of behaving as well as status symbols which are used to indicate status. Symbols are used to reinforce status and to insure the perpetuation of the existing status system. Status symbols permit the newcomer to know who is top dog at first glance. (Sommer 1969, p. 18)

The judge sitting above the jury indicates his status and reinforces it. Such symbols become codified into laws and customs that perpetuate status systems. We have house zoning in certain areas which require houses to be built of a given cost and design. In some restaurants admission is not permitted unless one wears symbols of the status of the middle class, a suit jacket and necktie.

Human status has been linked to animal hierarchies. Hall notes that years ago psychologists attracted considerable attention with their descriptions of the 'pecking order' of chickens. It will be remembered that in each flock there is always one chicken that pecks all the others but does not get pecked by any of the others. At the bottom there is one that gets pecked by all the rest and cannot peck back. Between the extremes the flock is arranged in an orderly progression of peckers ranging from the one that is second from the bottom and has only one chicken it can peck up to the number two bird, who is pecked only by the leader. As it happens, all living things arrange their lives in some sort of recognizable pattern of association, Hall claims. Chickens have a peck order, horses a 'kick-bite' order, and humans apparently arrange themselves in military, administrative, and educational levels of pecking and kick-biting.

However man's elaborations of the simpler mammalian base are so complex and varied that only the grosser outlines have been analyzed and described.

Our patterns of association are exemplified in language, in the tone of voice of a person when he is acting as a leader. It is reflected in the elaborate deference forms developed by the Japanese to fit their highly structured hierarchies. In our own society, the western, the deferential ways of talking to individuals who are ranked higher in work or other situations, such as the ways nurses talk to doctors, professors talk to students, privates talk to captains, and captains talk to generals, indicate status.

Hierarchies are quite obvious in the arrangement of offices and codified in large corporations into office size, the type of furniture, the height of partitions, floor covering, and office location. Chief executives generally are afforded the corner offices, the offices with the best views. Private toilets with keys are given to executives above certain ranks.

However status symbols do not remain constant. It was previously considered status to have a large house and a large automobile. As situations in

energy and size of family have changed, smaller cars and houses now have more status than the larger. The large houses of the Victorian aristocracy have become cheap rooming houses and run down tenements. The poorer people who cannot afford the smaller, trim, newer, energy efficient cars drive the large discarded 'gas guzzlers.' Status in clothing, automobiles, and buildings can become a matter of style. In some cultures status is associated with newness and in others with age.

Territoriality and status are also associated. A series of experiments by the British ornithologist A. D. Bain on the great tit altered and even reversed dominance relationships by shifting the position of feeding stations in relation to birds living in adjacent areas. As the feeding station was placed closer and closer to a bird's home range, the bird accrued territorial and status advantages it lacked when away from its home ground. This correlation of personal distance and status in one form or another, Hall notes, seems to occur throughout the vertebrate kingdom.

Yet status, dominance, and ranking order do not always result in what humans associate with bad aspects of behavior. Konrad Lorenz observed that in jackdaws and other social birds, ranking order leads directly to the protection of the weaker from the stronger. All social animals are 'status seekers,' Lorenz contends. There is always, therefore, particularly high tension between individuals who hold immediately adjoining positions in the ranking order. Conversely this tension diminishes the further apart the two animals are in rank. Since high-ranking jackdaws, particularly males, interfere in every quarrel between two inferiors, this graduation of social tension has the desirable effect that the higher-ranking birds always intervene in favor of the losing party. Redirection of attack is evolution's most ingenious expedient for guiding aggression into harmless channels, and it is not the only one, Lorenz comments.

Privacy is often a mark of status. The more important a person is in an institution the more difficult it is to see them. Their time is heavily scheduled and protected by one or two secretaries. A very important person may have both a business and a social secretary to guard his or her privacy and schedule his or her time.

Time itself is also a function of status. One cannot spend much time with important people. Newspaper accounts invariably report the amount of time a person spends with such people as the President of the United States as an indication of their importance or the importance of the matter under discussion.

In many species, the dominant animal has a territory which is larger and more desirable than that of other species' members. The same pressures operate in social situations where there is competition for any item in short supply. For example, when one college, Sommer noted, was confronted with overflow enrollments there were more students than available seats. The result was that the students of lower status, the freshmen and sophomores and those on probation, were dispossessed. A homeless aggregation of low-status students was created who wandered from English to History to Philosophy classes trying to gain admission.

An institutionalized status hierarchy, such as those found in armies or corporations, is accompanied by complex spatial norms. There are many places where a factory supervisor cannot go without the workers feeling he is spying on them. Officers in the army keep out of the enlisted men's quarters except on inspection. School administrators stay out of classrooms unless there is an emergency or a teacher invites them to visit.

Ordering is an important element in American behavioral patterns. As a general rule, whenever services are involved Americans feel that people should que up in order of arrival reflecting the basic equalitarianism of our culture. In cultures where class and status systems or their remnants exist such ordering does not take place. There will be crowding and a competition for the services among the commoners while those with status will either be served differently or have different entrances.

EXCEPTIONS

But status, dominance, and competitive behavior does not always result in an improvement of the species in either human or animal terms. The Argus pheasant is an example in which intraspecific selective breeding has led to the development of forms and behavior patterns which are not only nonadaptive, but have adverse effects on species preservation, Konrad Lorenz observed.

Family defense, a form of strife with the extraspecific environment has evolved the ritual fight which in turn developed the most powerful males and eliminated the weaker. If sexual rivalry, or any other form of intraspecific competition, exerts selection pressure which is not influenced by environmental exigencies, it can develop in a direction which is self-destructive and environmentally irrelevant. If the process does not prove positively detrimental to survival at best it gives rise to bizarre physical forms of little use to the species. In this area it would seem that humankind's development of styles often exhibits this characteristic.

Photo courtesy of Knoll International (comparison of office space).

(Comparison of office space).
Photo courtesy of Knoll International

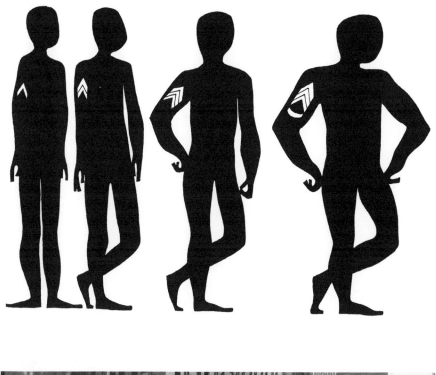

The antlers of stags, Lorenz notes, were developed in the service of rival fights and a stag without them has little hope of producing progeny. Antlers are 'sex objects' and otherwise useless, for male stags use their forehoofs when defending themselves against beasts of prey, never their antlers. Only the reindeer, Lorenz says, has based an invention on this necessity and 'learned' to shovel snow with the widened point of its antlers.

When the female makes the sexual selection, the result is the same as the rival fights. Whenever exaggerated development of colorful feathers or bizarre forms are discerned in the male, we may suspect that the males no longer fight for the females, but that the choice of the mate is made by the female and the male has no means of contesting this decision.

Birds of Paradise, the Ruff, the Mandarin Duck and the Argus Pheasant are examples of such behavior, Lorenz reminds us. The Argus hen pheasant reacts to the long secondary wing feathers of the cock. They are decorated with beautiful eye spots and the cock spreads them before her during courtship. In a well developed cock, these feathers are so huge that he can scarcely fly. The bigger they are the more the hen is stimulated. The number of progeny produced by a cock in a certain period of time is in direct proportion to the length of these feathers, even if the development of such extreme plumage is unfavorable in other ways, for it makes the bird unwieldly and easy prey for predators. A rival with less absurdly exaggerated wings may escape destruction but will nevertheless have many fewer descendents. The predisposition to huge wing feathers is preserved, encouraged, and continues quite against the well being of the species.

STATUS

John N. Hazard's description of furniture arrangements as symbols of judicial roles is an excellent analysis and description of the uses of furniture arrangement to emphasize the relative positions and importance of the actors in the plays of courtroom justice.

No comment.
Photo by F. Wilson.

269

A view of any empty courtroom will quickly reveal who has what authority by the arrangement of the furniture. And this is true in all countries, Hazard states.

Almost all countries seat their judges on a raised platform, and, if there are more than one, the presiding judge has a higher chair back which reaches a few inches above his neighbors. The judge's importance is further announced by the attendant's order for all to stand when he enters the courtroom. His position of respect may be further enhanced by the addition of a robe or wig, or, as is found in Poland, his neck is encircled with a great gold chain holding the seal of office.

There is a "bar" which is a barrier between the judge, jurors, lawyers, and court attendants, and the public in American courtrooms. On the judge's side of the bar to his left one will find a jury box and between it and the judge's platform there is a raised platform with a chair facing the audience in which the witness sits. There may also be a "bench" for the press and both the defense and prosecution lawyers sit at tables of equal size and equal height facing the judge.

In the assize court in Geneva the jury sits in two rows of chairs, to the judge's left behind the great semicircular bench that extends the width of the room. One needs not be told, Hazard remarks, that the judge retires with the jury and shares with them decisions of guilt and punishment.

In contrast to American courtrooms, the witness stand faces in toward the judge rather than out toward the courtroom. The audience sees nothing but the back of his or her head, and hears little of what they say unless they raise their voice. In Geneva, the press is placed along the right hand wall below the judge's bench forward of the public's seat. From this position they can hear and see everything that is done and said.

In contrast, in Eastern European courtrooms there are no special press galleries. Soviet concepts of "due process" do not require the participation of the press independent of the state. If the press is present, Hazard states, it is because the court has a case with a public message that the judges believe the public should hear.

The prosecutor's position varies widely in the different legal systems. In the American courtroom, there is no chair that can be quickly identified as his. The district, state's, or United States' attorney will sit in a chair inside the bar on the opposite of the aisle from the defense attorney. Neither sits higher than the other nor closer to the judge.

Hazard remarks that the setting is similar to that of an ancient tournament. Each attorney presents his strongest case, neither having any special advantage. The judge is the arbiter of the rules and the jury decides.

In contrast to this the prosecutor in the Geneva court sits at the left end of the great semicircular bench. The judge sits in the middle in frock coat, flanked by his jury at the other end. The prosecutor sits above the position of the council for the defense, the accused, and the witness stand, all of which are on the main floor. He carries by this location, Hazard says, a certain majesty. He is above the battle, and the procedural codes place a special responsibility upon him. He is required to be impartial, to be more than a state's attorney. In some countries, as in France, he is technically an arm of the magistracy.

The prosecutor's special position in continental Europe once created a struggle over furniture arrangement in Poland that illustrates the problem with exceptional clarity, Hazard says. The prosecutor sat at the left end of the judges before the Gomulka reforms of 1956 and thus had too much dignity, for he appeared as a fourth judge to untutored defendants. The solution was to cut a narrow slit in the bench so that the prosecutor is separated from the judges. But he still has special dignity since he wears a black robe as do the judges except that his is piped in red. (Hazard 1972, p. 291–298)

CONCLUSION—SUMMARY AND OPINION

The change of our environment and our perception of it during the past 50 years gives rise to the question: Have we passed through the age in which buildings can be defined as architecture? Have we entered another, yet to be defined, stage of humankind's building activity and perception of that activity?

The most recent generally accepted definition of architecture, that of 'the art of building,' was formulated 500 years ago during the Renaissance. But for most architects today, the art of building is a minor art.

Technical courses in architectural curriculums of most universities awarding architectural degrees involve only one third of the architect's education and courses devoted to actual building itself only a third of these. Most architects devote the least proportion of their time to the design and building of buildings. Technical responsibility is assigned to specialists, and 'design,' the actual arrangement of building elements, is another minor professional activity assigned to a separate and distinct department in the architectural corporation.

It may be argued that most architects work in small offices where these conditions do not prevail. But it cannot be contradicted that most building design is not done by such small offices. Large architectural offices, organized along corporate lines, do most of the design and building of buildings.

The users of buildings today perceive them quite differently then when buildings were termed architecture and architects were the designers and builders of buildings. Although the basic tools of human perception, eyes, ears, nose, mouth, and skin are much the same as they were when man was an aboreal creature, the context in which they are used has altered most drastically. The way humans think of their environment and the function of the architect in fashioning it today differ in almost every respect from the milieu in which architecture was defined as 'firmness, commodity, and delight.' Firmness and commodity are defined today by building codes and delight is an archaic experience seldom encountered amid frenetic activity in an urban context.

We do not know enough of how buildings influence our perception of the environment any more than we know how humans' perception of the environment affects buildings except in the simplistic stimulus/response models of the psychologist and the personal esoteric form determinants of the designer. Yet despite an almost unbelievable alteration of the world around us, the perceptual devices we humans bring to bear upon the man-made world remain basically unchanged. These are evolved and perfected over eons of time by trial and error sensing while what were to become humans were competing with other animals for survival. The senses we use to respond to strobe lights, the din of traffic, and the feel of plastic; the structure of the eye, the composition of the ear, how the nasal passages function, and the feel of textures all developed long before the beginning of recorded history and long, long before the idea of brick and mortar.

Under these peculiar circumstances it seems we know but a few things for certain. The first of these is that every organism must change its environment to live, and secondly that it in turn is changed by adapting to the environment it changes. This truth applies to the most elementary one celled life form that can only alter its ambience chemically to man who may have developed the awesome environmental capability of devastating the world and destroying the stuff of life itself, that is life as we know it. We can be certain that to be alive is to change our context and to be dead is to lose this ability and be changed by it.

We find ourselves in the strange position of having to change the world to live as a biological necessity and of being changed by the changes we bring about with very little sure knowledge of how either happens and what it means to us when it does.

Most discussions of the built environment are directed toward the conditions of architecture based on assumptions gleaned from the history of fine arts which have not, unfortunately, withstood, 'the shock of the new,' as Robert Hughes documented so well. (Hughes 1981)

The design of buildings in perspective perceived from the ground up is quite different than seeing them from the top down from an airplane or as one speck in a cluster from a rocket or as part of a blemish on the 'blue marble' from outer space. If the Eiffel tower heralded cubism, as Hughes linked the two, then, the jet and man on the moon predicted the succession of abstract expressionism, op and pop art, and happenings preceding our current displays of seasonal artistic enthusiasms and technological titulations. Art has evolved new forms to respond to radio, TV, radar, sonar, and the snorkel. The context of our perceptions has been fragmented. Architects responded to the machine world during the years designated as 'the modern movement' with simple minded geometries to still our flickering roving eyes. They may, incidentally, eventually prove the kindest solution for a humankind stunned by its sensual extensions, bombarded by auditory, olfactory, and visual environmental demands to focus on 'what's happening.'

We hear sounds never before heard at intensities previously unexperienced. Our senses tell us it is noise until we can detect order and call it 'rock.' Smells of carbon monoxide and noxious chemicals are added to the human smells of cooking and body odors. These are stinks, until we are persuaded to endure them as contextural norms which we must live with, if we wish to enjoy an ever higher standard of lower living. (M. Kaufman 1970). We deodorize ourselves and the smell of man vanishes as the smell of industrial processes and transportation devices dominate our olfactory apparatus.

We can no longer be sure which sounds, odors, sights, are fatal and which benign. We live with the unsettling suspicion that we are being bombarded by

"The Eiffel Tower topped out at 1,056 ft. This great attenuated vertical extension of a tiny patch of the earth's surface was designed by an engineer, not by an architect.

Hughes tells us that the tower was imagined as a benevolent colossus planted with spread legs in the middle of Paris. It could and can still be seen from every point in the city.

The effect of the Eiffel Tower on its mass audience comprising millions of people, the citizens of Paris, was mind shattering. The machine had meant the conquest of horizontal space, the Eiffel tower conquered the vertical.

The machine brought with it a succession and superimposition of views, unfolding landscapes, and flickering surfaces as the viewer was carried swiftly past. The machine gave us an exaggerated feeling of relative motion. The view from the train was not the view from the horse.

Seeing is the pivot of human consciousness. The sight of Paris from the Eiffel Tower in the first twenty years of its life was as significant in 1889 as the famous NASA photograph of the earth from the moon, floating like a vulnerable green bubble in the dark indifference of space, would be eighty years later." (Hughes 1980)

The Eiffel Tower, Paris.
Courtesy of the French Government Tourist Office.

Aerial view of Boston Harbor.
Photo courtesy of the Massachusetts Dept. of Commerce and Development, Division of Tourism.

A view of the earth from Apollo 17.
Photo courtesy of NASA.

sounds we cannot hear, odors we cannot smell, and rays we cannot see, and that all of these may be fatal. We begin to doubt our senses.

Building has become man's tempering of an incomprehensible environment, a refuge against poisionous odors, hazardous air, killing decibles, and also a utopian dream of an ideal world. It may be a bit more, or perhaps a bit less, depending on how one wishes to view them, than 'firmness, commodity, and delight.' Buildings are more akin to life support systems—health, safety, and welfare with emphasis on mental health.

But despite this constructed chaos, humans have inherited a remarkably keen, subtle, sensitive sensory apparatus which has assured our survival against enemies more fearful in their powers of destruction pitted against human's ability to withstand them then our present frenetic ambient technology. The difference is in the context. During the evolution of humankind's sensing apparatus our enemies varied in their capabilities of using talons, fangs, and claws and we developed our senses to outwit their various capabilities. Those birds, animals, fish that once ate man are now extinct or endangered species. The development of our sensory awareness, our survival techniques, to combat the major threats to our survival today demands other sensual awarenesses based on self-analysis. The study of human perception and behavior is vital to us for our major enemy today is man. A theory of design for the human context that is not based on a theory of man is somewhat foolish, even fatal.

An introductory survey of perception and behavior, such as this, has gathered together a sampling of what is known and understood of human sensual response to our environment. It is offered as grist to be ground by those that design and live in this context.

Today we live in an environment designed and built in response to our ideals of art and architecture.

What kind of environment will we fashion when we realize that the question is not art or architecture but humankind itself?

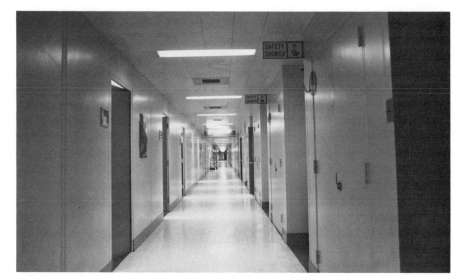

Corridor of the National Bureau of Standards, Gaithersburg, Maryland.
Photo by F. Wilson.

From *Optical Art* by Jean Larcher, Dover Books, NY, 1974.

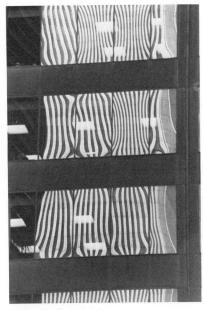

Nature imitates art.
Reflections of the World Trade Center, NYC.
Photo by F. Wilson.

Nature imitates art.
Reflections of the World Trade Center, NYC.
Photo by F. Wilson.

Sculpture group, St. Bartholamew Church garden, mid-town Manhattan.
Photo by F. Wilson.

Art imitates nature.
From *Optical Art* by Jean Larcher, Dover Books, NY, 1974.

World Trade Center reflected in the facade of Broadway Building, New York City.
Photo by F. Wilson.

GLOSSARY

Abacus—The flat top of the capital of a column, supporting an entablature.

Abutment—Solid masonry which resists the lateral pressure of an arch.

Acropolis—Most ancient Greek cities were on hills, the citadel on the summit being known as the Acropolis and containing the principal temples and treasure houses.

Agora—The Greek equivalent of the Roman forum, a place of open-air assembly or market.

Aisles—Lateral divisions parallel with the nave in a basiclica or church.

Ambulatory—The cloister or covered passage around the east end of a church, behind the altar.

Apse—The circular or multangular termination of a church sanctuary, first applied to a Roman basilica. The apse is a continental feature and contrasts with the square termination of English Gothic churches.

Arcade—A range of arches supported on piers or columns, attached to or detached from the wall.

Arch—An arch of a curve. A structure of wedge-shaped blocks over an opening, so disposed as to hold together when supported only from the sides.

Architect—From the Greek architekton, chief craftsman; hence the Latin architectus. In modern practice a person qualified to design buildings and to supervise their erection. In Greek and Roman times the architect's status was fully recognized, his duties being described in detail by Vitruvius. During the Middle Ages the title was seldom used, the architect was then described as 'master' in English (magister in Latin, maestro in Italian and Spanish, maistre in Old French, and baumeister in German). The Victorian contention that large medieval buildings were designed by bishops and monks rather than by lay architects has since been disproved by many competent authorities. Contemporary documents establish that the services of lay designers were utilized by ecclesiastical as well as by secular and royal employers.

The title of architect was revived during the 16th century and was used by Inigo Jones early in the seventeenth century. The status of the architect came to be more precisely defined during the seventeenth and eighteenth centuries and in 1934 the foundation of the Royal Institute of British Architects established a recognized standard of qualification in England. The American Institute of Architects was first organized in the mid-18th century, but did not become particularly active until around the 1880s.

Architectural Ideas—Concepts stated in architectural concerns like daylight, space, sequence of spaces, integration of structure and form, siting in the landscape, etc. A specific concern used as the basis for building design.

Architecture—The word 'architecture,' was first used about 1563, derived from the Latin architectura, and that in turn came from the Greek architekton, literally 'chief craftsman' or 'master builder.' Hence architecture refers to buildings designed by a competent person as distinct from buildings not so designed. This is admittedly not a very clear distinction. It is so difficult to clearly define architecture, that most of the attempts made in the past three or four centuries have proven unsatisfactory. An English writer in 1581 defined architecture as 'the science of building.' Ruskin in the 19th century wrote that it is 'nothing but ornament applied to buildings,' a dictum not universally accepted today when many stark and austere buildings devoid of ornament are accorded the distinction of architecture. It is something more than 'good building' in the sense of sound construction with good materials. An often quoted definition by Sir Henry Wotton, an amateur critic, in his book, *The Elements of Architecture* (1924), comes very near what is accepted as truth. He says that it must fulfill three conditions, 'commodity, firmness, and delight,' meaning that to constitute architecture a building must not only be conveniently planned for its purpose ('commodity'), and be soundly built of good materials ('firmness'), but must also give pleasure to the eye of a discriminating beholder ('delight'). It is this third quality, added to the other two essentials, that differentiates 'architecture' from 'building.'

Some very primitive buildings, such as rude huts or wigwams in all ages have not been counted as architecture under this definition. To these may be added primitive stone circles (such as Stonehenge), megaliths, and barrows; also, perhaps, the Egyptian pyramids; and, in modern times, bridges and other structures which are now commonly regarded as 'civil engineering' rather than architecture or even building.

The definition given in *Concise Encyclopedia of Architecture* by M.S. Briggs (1959) used here has been considerably widened in the two decades since the book's publication. Primitive building is now considered by some to be architecture; new building types such as pizza parlors and car washes were examined, extolled, and published in architectural magazines in the 1960s.

As licensed architects involve themselves less in actual building techniques and supervision, for a variety of reasons not the least of which is the increasingly onerous burden of liability claims, it is doubtful that the architect, architecture, or the practice of architecture can be said to conform to Wotton's definition, although it remains the romantic picture the public has of architects and a number of architects have of themselves.

Architrave—1. In any of the Greek and Roman 'orders' the lowest member of the entablature resting directly upon the capitals of the supporting columns. 2. A molding surrounding or framing a doorway or a window opening inside or outside a building.

Archivolt—The moldings on the face of an arch and following its contour.

Arcuated—Pertaining to a building, building system, or style of architecture, of which the principle constructive feature is the arch.

Arris—A sharp edge formed by the meeting of two surfaces.

Ashlar—Masonry of smooth squared stones in regular courses, in contradistinction to rubble work.

Atrium—An apartment in a Roman house, forming an entrance hall or court, with the roof open to the sky in the center.

Baroque—A term applied to design during the late Renaissance period (1600–1760 in Italy), when architecture reached a characteristic, non-Roman expression; rich, bold, and vital.

Barrel Vault—A continuous vault of semicircular section, used at most periods and in many countries from Roman times to the present.

Basilica—A hall for the administration of justice.

Bastide—One of the small fortified towns, laid out during the Middle Ages on a rectilinear or chess-board plan by the English in the parts of France occupied by them. Monpazier in Dordogne (1284) is a typical example.

Bastion—A gun platform projecting from fortress walls, consisting of two flanks behind a triangular head formed by two faces terminating in a salient angle.

Batter—A term applied to a wall with an inclined face.

Bays—Compartments into which the nave or roof of a building is divided. The term is also used for projecting windows.

Building Type—Classification of building by function, e.g., hospital, school, manufacturing, industrial, etc.

Capital—The molded or carved top of a column, serving to concentrate the superincumbent load onto the shaft of the column, and often treated with great ornamental richness.

Cella—The chief apartment of a temple, where the image of a god stood.

Chancel—The space for clergy and singers separated by a screen from the body of the church; more usually referred to as the choir.

Cheveron—A zigzag molding used in Norman architecture, and so called from a pair of rafters, which give this form.

Clear-story—An upper stage in a building with windows above adjacent roofs; especially applied to this feature in a church.

Colonnade—A row of columns supporting an entablature.

Column—1. A cylindrical and slightly tapered pillar, serving as a support to some portion of a building. 2. A similar pillar standing isolated as a monument, e.g., Trajan's Column at Rome, A.D. 112, and Nelson's Column in London.

Concepts—Ideas that integrate design elements into a whole. A specific combination of programmatic requirements, context, and beliefs.

Coping—The capping or cover to a wall.

Cornice—1. A projecting horizontal feature, usually molded, that crowns an external facade, or occurs internally at the junction of a wall and a ceiling. 2. In classical architecture, the topmost member of the entablature.

Corbel—A block of stone often elaborately carved or molded, projecting from a wall and supporting the beams of a roof, floor, vault, or other feature.

Cortile—The Italian name for the internal court, surrounded by an arcade, in a palace or other edifice.

Crenellation—Toothlike breastworks on wall tops, formed by alternating embrasures and merlons.

Curtain—In fortifications a stretch of wall connecting the towers or bastions of a fortified front.

Curtain Wall—The logical outcome of skeleton-frame construction, in which the external walls serve no load bearing purpose, but are suspended on the face of the building like a curtain. Not to be confused with the curtain wall of medieval military architecture, denoting a defensive outer wall linking towers and gatehouses.

Dormer—A window in a sloping roof, usually that of a sleeping-apartment, hence the name.

Enciente—A fortified enclosure

Eaves—The lower part of a roof projecting beyond the face of the wall.

Embrasure—A slit or opening in a parapet or wall through which defenders can shoot.

Entablature—Something laid upon a table; hence, something laid flat upon something else. In classical architecture, the arrangement of three horizontal members—architrave, frieze, and cornice—above the supporting columns in any of the classical orders.

Entasis—In classical architecture, the almost imperceptible and amazingly subtle convex tapering of a column, in order to correct the optical illusion of concavity created by simple tapering.

Escalade—To mount the ramparts of a fortress by means of ladders.

Escarp—The slope of the inner ditch walls and outer surfaces of curtains and bastions.

Esquisse—In Beaux Arts education, a design exercise in which the participants are required to conceive and design a given building project according to stated requirements.

Facade—The face or elevation of a building.

Fascia—A vertical face of little projection, usually found in the architrave of an order. Also a board or plate covering the end of roof rafters.

Flank—The side of a bastion which immediately adjoins the curtain.

Formwork—A temporary casing of woodwork within which concrete is molded.

Functionalism—A term coined in the twentieth century to express an idea held among rigid exponents of aesthetic puritanism, that every detail in the design of a building should be determined by its function, regardless of appearance. The argument may be extended to hold that the appearance of the entire building should proclaim its purpose—for example, that a railway station should look like a railway station, not like a Greek temple or a Flemish town hall; and that a church should look like a church, not a cinema or a factory. The real problem remains, however, what should a church or factory or station look like, intrinsically, apart from stylistic prejudices?

Gable—The triangular portion of a wall, between the enclosing lines of a sloping roof. In classical architecture it is called a pediment.

Groin—A curved arris formed by the intersection of vaulting surfaces.

Helix—One of the 16 small volutes (helices) under the abacus of a Corinthian capital.

Insula—A house not joined to another by a common wall. A block of apartments in a Roman Town.

Jugendstil—The movement in Germany comtemporary to 'Art Nouveau.' The name derives from the periodical *Jugend* ("youth").

Keep—A large tower in medieval strongholds serving as living quarters and last refuge.

Le Corbusier—Pseudonym of Charles-Edouard Jeanneret (born 1887), architect and writer on architecture and town planning. Trained in Vienna, Paris and Berlin under Behrens. Began independent practice in Paris about 1922.

Lintel—A piece of stone, timber steel, or concrete laid horizontally across a doorway or window opening, to carry superincumbent walling.

Lunette—Detached outwork placed outside ditch and in front of a bastion; usually consists of two faces forming a salient angle.

Machicolation—Opening in the floor of a gallery projecting outward from walltop (machicoulis gallery); designed for the vertical defense of walls and towers from above; derived from French macher, to crush.

Mannerism—A term coined to describe the characteristics of the output of Italian Renaissance architects of the period 1530–1600. Architecture of this character, which in fact is common to the European Renaissance as a whole, is distinguished as 'Proto-Baroque,' the Baroque being its ultimate outcome.

Megaron—The principal or men's hall in a Mycenaean palace or house.

Merlons—Solid sections of a crenlated parapet; they flank embrasures.

Metope—A square space between the triglyphs on the frieze of the Greek Doric Order.

Module—A measure of proportion, by which the parts of a classic order or building are regulated, being usually the semidiameter of a column immediately above its base, which is divided into thirty parts or minutes.

Moldings—The contours given to projecting members.

Mullions—Vertical members dividing windows into different numbers of lights.

Nave—The western limb of a church, as opposed to the choir; also the central aisle of a basilican, Medieval, or Romanesque church as opposed to the side aisle.

Necropolis—A burial ground.

Niche—A recess in a wall, hollowed like a shell, for a statue or ornament.

Norman—A style, also termed English Romanesque, of the 11th and 12th centuries.

Obelisk—A tall pillar of square section tapering upwards and ending in a pyramid.

Optimisation—The process of determining the optimum conditions, generally with the aid of a digital computer. The most common optimization is for cost, i.e., for finding the

Pediment—In classical architecture, the triangular end or gable of a building with a low-pitched roof; sometimes filled with sculpture, as is the Parthenon pediment in Athens.

Pendentive—The term applied to the triangular curved overhanging surface by means of which a circular dome is supported over a square or polygonal compartment.

Peristyle—A range of columns surrounding a court or temple.

Pier—A mass of masonry, as distinct from a column, from which an arch springs, in an arcade or bridge; also applied to the wall between doors and windows.

Pilaster—A rectangular feature in the shape of a pillar, but projecting only about one-sixth of its breadth from a wall, and the same design as the order with which it is used.

Pilotis—Posts on an unenclosed ground floor carrying a raised building.

design with the lowest cost. However, other factors can be optimised, such as construction time, weight, or maintenance.

Order—An order in architecture comprises a column with base (usually), shaft, and capital, with the whole supporting an entablature. The Greeks recognized three orders: Doric, Ionic, and Corinthian. The Romans added the Tuscan and the Composite (the latter also known as the Roman), while using the Greek orders in modified form.

Parapet—Breastworks atop walls and bastions, designed to protect defenders from enemy fire.

Ramparts—A defense or protective barrier.

Parti—A conceptual idea in architecture. Beaux Arts educational philosophy demanded that students develop a high level of conceptual skills. An initial parti (idea) was selected and held during the entire esquisse (design exercise).

Pavilion—A prominent structure, generally distinctive in character, marking the ends and center of the facade of a major building. A similarly distinctive building linked by a wing to a main block. An ornamental building in a garden.

Plinth—The lowest square member of the base of a column; also applied to the projecting stepped or molded base of any building.

Postern—A gate used for sorties; from Latin postera (back door).

Quadrangle—A broad enclosure or court defined by buildings.

Quadripartite Vaulting—A vault in which each bay is divided by intersecting diagonal ribs into four parts.

Quirk—A sharp V-shaped incision in a molding, such as that flanking the Norman bowtell.

Revetment—Facing of stone (or some other material) to sustain an embankment.

Rotunda—A round building.

Rustication—A method of forming stonework with roughened surfaces and recessed joints, principally employed in Renaissance buildings.

Sap—Originally to undermine; to dig a trench or gallery from the attacker's line to a point beneath the defender's works for the purpose of either destroying them or gaining entry into the stronghold.

Section—The representation of a building cut by a vertical plane, so as to show the construction.

Story—The space between two floors.

Stijl, de (Dutch, "the Style")—A short-lived geometric-abstract movement in Holland (1917–31), which had a lasting influence on the development of 'Modern' architecture and of industrial design.

Stylobate—A continuous basement or platform beneath a row of columns. Usually composed of three steps, in which case strictly speaking, only the top step is the stylobate and the three together constitute a crepidoma.

Superorganizing Idea—Geometric configurations or hierarchies that the parts of a project respect. In urban design and campus planning, an overall organizing pattern is established and the parts are designed to conform. If the pattern is strong the parts may vary considerably. For example, in Jefferson's campus at the University of Virginia the organizing is so strong that the parts can develop their own idiosyncrasies. The houses have their own design yet remain part of the overall pattern.

Theme—A particular idea or pattern that occurs throughout the design of a building. It may be a specific geometric pattern or, as in Kahn's Kimbel Gallery, a theme of light.

Triglyph—Thrice grooved (from the Greek). In the frieze of the Greek Doric Order, a slightly projecting block having three grooves or channels on its face.

Tudor—A term applied to English Late Gothic architecture of the period 1485–1558.

Vault—An arched covering in stone or brick over any building.

Vestibule—An anteroom to a larger apartment of a building.

Vitruvius, Marcus Pollio—First century B.C. Roman architect who during the reign of the Emperor Augustus composed and dedicated a manual of architecture and building construction to the emperor. De Re Architectura which has come to be known as "The Ten Books on Architecture" made Vitruvius famous and was apparently popular in its day and during the Renaissance and continues in use as a reference today.

Volute—The scroll or spiral occurring in Ionic, Corinthian, and Composite capitals.

Voussoirs—The truncated wedge-shaped blocks forming an arch.

Wagon or Wagonhead Vault—See Barrel Vault.

Weathering—The slope given to offsets to buttresses and the upper surface of cornices and moldings to throw off rain.

Ziggurat or Ziqqarat—A high pyramidal staged tower, of which the angles were oriented to the cardinal points, which formed an important element in ancient Mesopotamian temple complexes. The number of stages rose from one to seven in the course of time, and in the Assyrian version the stages were developed into a continuous inclined ramp, circulating the four sides in turn.

Zigzag—See Chevron.

GLOSSARY—BEHAVIOR

Absolute Threshold—The minimum amount of physical stimulus that is needed to produce a sensation; frequently interpreted as the level at which half (50%) of the stimuli presented are responded to. (psychophysics)

Achromatic—Lacking in hue and saturation. Achromatic colors vary only in brightness, from black to white, e.g., various shades of gray.

Acoustics—**1.** Acoustics is the science of sound, including its production, transmission, and effects. **2.** The acoustics of a room are those qualities that together determine its character with respect to distinct hearing.

Activity—Anything an organism does or that happens within an organism; anything requiring expenditure of energy by an organism.

Adaption—In general, adjustment to environmental conditions. Sensory adaption involves a change in the characteristics of experience as a result of prior experience. In design, becoming less sensitive to environmental attributes after prolonged experience.

Additive Mixture—A color formed by the combination of light or different colors, for example, the combination of blue and red light sources to produce violet.

Amplitude—The amount or value of a wave or a fluctuating quantity or variable.

Analytic Approach—An approach that assumes that a complex process can be understood by breaking it into its components, and that the complex can best be improved by improving its parts.

Analytical Survey—A survey designed to clarify associations and provide explanations. It presupposes a theoretical framework suggesting causality among variables, as contrasted with a descriptive survey, which enumerates but does not ask "why."

Anechoic Chamber—A chamber whose surfaces absorb effectively all the sound incident on them, thereby affording conditions where the effects of boundaries are essentially negligible. Hearing research is often conducted in anechoic chambers.

Anthropometry—The science of measuring the human body and its parts and functional capacities.

Architecture—**1.** The profession of designing buildings, open areas, communities, etc., usually with some regard to aesthetic effect. **2.** The result or product of architectural work, as a building. **3.** The character or style of a building.

Arrival Distance—The distance that a newcomer uses to separate himself from a person already occupying a space.

Articulation Index (AI)—A numerically calculated measure of the intelligibility of transmitted or processed speech. It takes into account the limitations of the transmission path and the background noise.

Articulation Test—A test for accuracy in pronouncing speech sounds, both singly and in connected speech.

Attenuation—A reduction in the degree or amount of anything. For example, the attenuation of noise produced by a barrier.

Audiogram—A graph showing hearing thresholds in terms of frequency and intensity.

Audiometer—An instrument for measuring hearing sensitivity.

Autonomic Response—Response by a division of the nervous system serving the endocrine glands and smooth muscles.

Average—Measure of central tendency. Three average scores are in common use—median, mode, and arithmetic mean.

A-Weighted Sound Pressure Level (A-Level, L^a)—A measurement of sound pressure level in which the sound has been filtered or weighted to quantitatively reduce the effect of the high and low frequency components. It was designed to approximate the response of the human ear to sound. A-level is measured in decibles with a standard sound level meter which contains the weighted network for "A."

Background Noise—The total of all noise in a system or situation, independent of the presence of the desired signal.

Behavior Setting—In ecological psychology, the bounded units (towns, schools, meetings, etc.) within which the behavior studied occurs.

Behavioral Mechanisms—Affective, gross motor, manipulation, verbal, and thinking mechanisms used in studying behavior settings.

Bimodal—Refers to a frequency distribution with two peaks.

Bounded Units—The behavior settings in which ecological behavior occurs. They are: 1) self-generated, 2) with specific time-space loci, and 3) with unbroken boundaries which separate them from differing external patterns.

Brightness—The subjective impression of the total amount of light reaching the eye from a visual stimulus.

Case Study—A collection of all relevant evidence—social, psychological, physiological, biographical, environmental, vocational—to illustrate a single social unit such as a family.

Cerebrum—In man, the largest portion of the brain occupying the entire upper part of the cranium and consisting of the right and left hemispheres.

Chance—In research, something that happens unpredictably without discernable human intention or observable cause.

Chroma—Synonym for color saturation.

Chroma Scale—A scale ranging from neutral (gray, black, or white) to the most saturated or nongray color. In the Munsell surface-color solid, the chroma scale is represented by distance from the central axis.

Chromaticity—The quality of a color stimulus determined by its dominant wavelength and its purity.

Chronocyclography—A photographic method of recording movements. A series of pictures of the sequence of movements is obtained by several exposures at known intervals on the same photograph.

Cine Camera—A camera used in interval photography with intervals that can be set from 2 exposures/second to 1 exposure/54 seconds.

Class Interval—In statistics, a small section of a scale, according to which frequency distributions are grouped, e.g., heights or weights.

Clo Value—A numerical value given to clothing in thermal comfort computations (O = no clothing).

Closed Message Set—Used in speech intelligibility studies in which the subject knows all of the possible messages.

Cochlea—A coiled structure of the inner ear which contains the receptors essential for hearing.

Coding—1. (Statistics) The process of transforming a set of scores into a more convenient set. 2. (Information theory) The transformation of messages into signals.

Cognitive Map—1. The ability to reorder and reconstruct parts of our experience to provide a complete picture of a situation. 2. The description of a place in terms of its location and psychological influences, from the standpoint of an individual.

Color—Visual sensation determined by the interaction of wavelength, intensity, and mixture of wavelengths of light.

Color Rendering—The effect of a light source on the color appearance of objects as compared with appearance under a standard light source.

Colorimeter—A device for measuring colors and specifying them in numerical or symbolic terms.

Comparison—The member of a stimulus pair which is varied by the subject until it matches the standard, or other stimulus in the pair. Also, the pair member upon which a judgment is made relative to the standard.

Conditioned Reflex—A reflex based on previous experience rather than inherited structure, such as dogs salivating at the sound of a bell. (Pavlov)

Cone—One of the cone-shaped cells of the retina used in color vision.

Confederate—A person working with an experimenter as a covert participant in a research study.

Confidence Level—The probability of the truth of a statement that a parametric value will be included in a confidence interval.

Constancy Phenomena—The tendency for brightness, color, size, or shape to remain relatively constant despite marked changes in stimulation.

Control Group—Similar in all respects to an experimental group, but not subject to changes in experimental conditions.

Control Setting—In laboratory research, control of the stimulus.

Control Variables—Those which are unchanged in an experiment, as distinguished from independent variables.

Correlation—A relationship between variables such that changes in one are accompanied by changes in the other, either positively (as when weight tends to increase with height) or negatively.

Critical Distance—The flight distance, or point at which encroachment into an animal's territory by another animal produces flight or attack. (Also called flight distance)

Critical Flicker Frequency (CFF)—The frequency of light flashes necessary to produce an uninterrupted experience of brightness, i.e., without flicker.

Cross-sectional Survey—A type of survey in which the data result from a time-ordered series of questions asked of a sample of a predefined population of subjects.

Cutaneous—Pertaining to the skin.

Dark Adaption—The process by which the daylight cone vision is taken over by night-time rod vision. Eyes are considerably more sensitive after dark adaption.

Data—Information obtained from a scientific study, or by other techniques.

Data Analysis—Analysis of information obtained from a scientific study, or other techniques.

dBA—A quantity in decibels that can be read from a standard sound level meter with an A-weighting network designed to approximate the sensitivity of the human ear at moderate sound levels.

Decible (dB)—The unit of sound intensity.

Deductive—The mode of reasoning that starts with premises or propositions and attempts to derive valid conclusions therefrom.

Defensible Space—A concept developed by Oscar Newman. It involves the idea that neighborhood security can be increased by specific architectural design features that allow surveillance by residents as a part of their everyday activities.

Dependent Variable—The variable whose value changes as a result of the experimenter's changes in the independent variable.

Descriptive Survey—A survey designed to answer questions about the distribution of some datum (e.g., income) in a population or among subgroups of a population.

Diary—A method used in man/environment (M/E) studies where people maintain records of activities performed. Duration times and frequencies are often critical.

Dichotomous Items—Survey questions which require the subject to make a forced choice between two explicit alternatives.

Difference Limen (threshold DL)—The smallest change in a physical variable that is detected by an observer; frequently interpreted as causing a response to 50% of the stimuli presented. (psychophysics)

Disability Glare—Glare resulting in reduced visual performance and visibility.

Discomfort Glare—Glare which results in a feeling of annoyance. It does not necessarily interfere with visibility or visual performance.

Discontinuous Photography—A technique for recording the behavior of subjects at discrete instants of time of interest to the researcher.

Display—Any means of presenting information to a person.

Distance After Departure—The distance which birds (or other organisms) will keep between each other after intermediate birds have left.

Drift—Movement of buildings, such as high rise structures, during storm conditions when high velocity winds are present.

Ecological Psychology—The study of organisms in reference to their physical environment; especially the study of their responses to stimuli which are environmental.

Effective Temperature—A combination of air temperature, wind velocity, and relative humidity used in investigations designed to establish and define a comfort zone for human subjects.

Electrocardiogram (EKG)—Graphic records produced by an electrocardiograph, a galvanometer device that detects and records the minute differences in potential between different parts of the body caused by heart action.

Electroencephalogram (EEG)—A graphic record of the wavelike changes in the electric potential observed when electrodes are placed on the surface of the head.

Electromyography (EMG)—A graphic recording of electrical activity of currents in a muscle.

Elements—Parts or constituents of a whole, especially those that cannot be reduced to simpler units.

Equal Loudness Contours—Curves which show sound pressure levels for different frequencies heard as having a fixed loudness level.

Ergograph—An instrument for studying fatigue in a restricted muscle group.

Ergonomics—The scientific study of the relationships between men and machines, particularly the psychological, biological, and cultural relationships, for the purpose of adapting machines and jobs to meet the needs of men and of choosing suitable persons for particular jobs or machines; biotechnology.

Error of the First Kind—If, as the result of a statistical test, a statistical hypothesis is rejected when it should be accepted.

Error of the Second Kind—If, as the result of a test, a statistical hypothesis is accepted when it is false, i.e., when it should have been rejected.

Experiment—Controlled arrangement and manipulation of conditions in order to systematically observe particular phenomena with the intention of defining the influences and relationships that affect those phenomena.

Experimental Design—Plan of an experiment structured to answer specific experimental questions. Design usually specifies: 1) choice of variables; 2) choice of subjects, species, age, sex, etc.; 3) apparatus used for stimulus presentation and response recording; 4) experimental procedure; 5) type of analysis of results.

Experimental Psychology—1. The investigation of psychological phenomena by experimental methods. 2. The methods of and the results obtained by psychological experiment, systematically set forth (often arbitrarily limited to the psychology of the laboratory).

Experimental Setting—The characteristics of a space where a study is being performed.

Experimental Subjects—Organisms to whom stimuli are applied for the purpose of evoking responses; or, more generally, the organisms whose reactions are observed.

Feedback—Knowledge of the results of an action; perception of a state of the body or the environment.

Field Study—Collection of data outside the laboratory, library, or clinic; the study of organisms in their usual habitats.

Figure-Ground—The principle that all perception and even awareness is fundamentally patterned into two parts or aspects that mutually influence each other: a) the figure, which has good contour and unity, and is perceived as being separate from the ground, and b) the ground, which is typically relatively homogeneous and whose parts are not clearly patterned.

Film Color—Hue seen as such without reference to its being a surface or other characteristic of an object.

Filter Question—A question, primarily factual in nature, which may be used in public opinion research to enable the interviewer to determine the extent of knowledge possessed by the respondent about the topic under study.

Fixed-Feature Space—Features of buildings that are not movable, e.g., windows and walls.

Flight Distance—A critical distance at which point further encroachment on an animal's territory by another animal causes flight or attack.

Focused Interview—An interview which uses an interview guide with a list of objectives and suggested questions. Using this technique, an interviewer can explore new topics as they are introduced and can follow up in detail when this appears to be a useful approach.

Fovea—The central part of the eye used for daytime vision.

Free Association—1. An unrestricted, random flow of words or ideas. 2. In psychoanalysis, a method in which the patient says whatever comes into his mind and speaks freely.

Frequency—1. The number of cycles per unit time in a periodic vibration. 2. The number of times a given event occurs; especially, the number of times the several values of a variable are found.

Galvanic Skin Response (GSR)—The changes in the electrical resistance of the skin measured by a galvanometer. It is used as an indicator of emotional arousal and tension.

Gaming—A research technique in which subjects' needs, activity patterns, preferences, etc., are determined by how they play certain games.

Gestalt—A configuration or figure whose integration sometimes differs from the totality obtained by summing the parts.

Glare—See disability glare, discomfort glare.

Gradient—Any regular change in a magnitude which slopes from high to low or vice versa.

Hard Architecture—A phrase used by R. Sommer to describe design features which hinder interaction and lead to feelings of isolation.

Hawthorne studies—A pioneering series of studies started in 1927 and continuing into the early 1930s done at the Western Electric Company by Elton May, F.J. Roethlisberger, W.J. Dickson, and their associates. The studies showed the importance of social variables, and demonstrated that work efficiency was not just the product of physical or economic conditions. They specifically demonstrated the stimulation to output or accomplishment that results from the mere fact of being under concerned observation (the Hawthorne effect).

Heel Impact Test—A test to determine whether there is a vibration problem in a building. A 170-lb (77-kg) man stands on his toes at the geometric center of a floor, then drops suddenly to his heels, while a subject standing near him gives subjective impressions of the vibration experienced.

Hertz (Hz)—Cycles per second; a specification of frequency in waves, commonly used in sensory research for auditory stimuli.

Hodometer—An instrument used to measure foot movement activity.

Holistic—Pertaining to the principle that an organism is not equal to the sum of its parts and must be considered as a whole.

Home Range—A series of linkages and settings traversed and occupied by an individual in his normal activities.

Homogeneous—Of the same or similar kind or nature.

Hue—The perceived dimension of color which corresponds to the wavelength of light which stimulates the retina. Hues may be grouped as reds, yellows, greens, and blues with their intermediates, the oranges, yellow-greens, blue-greens, and purples.

Hue Circle—Scale for constant visual hues represented by symmetrical color circle.

Human Factors—A discipline concerned with the optimization of the human component in man/machine systems. (Also referred to as human engineering or human factors engineering).

Hypnosis—An artificially induced sleeplike state characterized by increased suggestibility, decreased initiative and will to act on one's own, recollection of events not remembered in the normal state, and often amnesia for that which occurred while hypnotized.

Hypothesis—1. An assumption; a guess. 2. A tentative statement to be proven or disproven by evidence.

Illuminometer—An instrument which measures luminance, the objective correlate for brightness.

Illusion (Visual)—An incorrect visual perception usually affecting spatial relations.

Imageability—The degree to which characteristics of the environment lend themselves to the formation of a vivid image by the person experiencing them.

Incident Light—Light shining on a specified object.

Independent Variable—1. A variable that can be observed and assessed as a determinant of behavior. 2. The variable that is altered independently of any other variable, usually by the experimenter.

Individual Differences—Any psychological characteristic, quality, or trait by which an individual may be distinguished from others. Also, the differences characteristic of individuals in different categories.

Induction—The logical process by which principles or rules are derived from observed facts.

Industrial Design—A discipline concerned with improving the performance of products through better design.

Innate—present in the individual at birth.

Instructional Set—A preparatory adjustment or readiness for a particular kind of action or experience, as a result of instructions.

Intensity—1. (Physics) The magnitude of energy of force per given unit of space and/or time, as of a physical stimulus. 2. The strength of any behavior, emotion, or motivation.

Interval Photography—A technique for recording behavior on film during selected intervals of time. Interval photography is suitable for use with continuous sequences of events where it is sufficient to record only a sample of the process.

Interval Scale—A type of scale which does not have an absolute zero point but possesses equal intervals and differences.

Intimate Distance—The distance maintained between two people discussing matters of a personal nature.

Invisible Bubble—The space around a person which, when violated, is perceived as an intrusion of one's privacy.

Just Noticeable Difference (JND)—The minimum amount of difference detectable between two stimuli being compared.

Laboratory Study—A study performed in a place set aside for scientific research, especially, but not exclusively, for experiment. (Laboratory studies contrast with field studies and library research.)

Landolt Ring—An incomplete circle having a gap of varying size, used in the determination of visual acuity.

Learning Approach—A viewpoint which emphasizes the role of experience in behavior research.

Legibility—The quality of a visual symbol, usually of a printed or written symbol, that makes it easy to read or to distinguish from other symbols.

Level of Significance—Statistical term indicating the degree of confidence we can have that the result was not caused by chance alone. The level of significance is expressed as the number of times in 100 that the given result could be expected to occur by chance alone. Thus a level of 5% means that the result would be expected by chance alone only 5 times in 100.

Life Space (Lewin)—The entire set of phenomena in the environment and in the organism itself which influences present behavior or the possibility of behavior. Emphasis is placed on the interaction between the organism and its environment in an organized, unified field.

Lightness—An attribute of an object's color, or means by which it can be placed in the series between black and white.

Lightness Scale—A scale ranging from white to black with shades of gray in between. The lightness of a chromatic (nongray) color determines the gray to which it is equivalent in the lightness scale.

Loudness—The heard attribute of an auditory stimulus which corresponds to the physical attribute of intensity.

Luminance—Light energy transmitted, reflected, or emitted from a source; the actual strength of light in the whole of the space involved. It is the objective correlate of the subjective variable of brightness.

Macro—A combining form meaning "large" or "extended," in contrast to micro.

Mail Survey—A method of data collection in which self-administered questionnaires are mailed to subjects; typically, the response rate is low.

Masking—Interference with the perception of a stimulus caused by the simultaneous occurrence of another stimulus. In hearing, for example, a tone becomes harder to hear if it is accompanied by white noise. The noise is said to "mask" the tone.

Maslow's Need Hierarchy—A postulated hierarchy or order in which the individual must satisfy physiological needs first, followed by needs for safety, love, esteem, and self-actualization.

Matched Group—(Experimental research) One of the groups used in an experiment that is made equivalent to the other groups in as many respects as possible, to ensure experimental control.

Mean—The average score, the sum of the scores divided by the number of cases.

Median—The middlemost score in a series arranged in rank order.

Metabolic Rate—The rate at which certain vital physical and chemical and physiological reactions occur within an organism.

Metamerism—The phenomenon of color stimuli having different spectrophotometric characteristics, but appearing identical under favorable conditions of comparison.

Method of Average Error—One of three classic psychophysical procedures for measuring either the differential or the absolute threshold. The observer controls the independent stimulus dimension and set it according to experimental instructions, e.g., "just audible," "just noticeably different," etc. Also known as the method of adjustment.

Method of Constant Stimuli (Fechner)—A psychophysical technique used for determining absolute and differential thresholds by requiring the subject to compare various stimuli drawn from a preselected sample with a standard, or to state when a given stimulus is noticed.

Method of Limits—A psychophysical technique used for determining the smallest difference in a stimulus that can be discriminated by a subject. The distance between two nondiscriminable stimuli is increased, or the distance between two discriminable stimuli is decreased and the average point at which the former is first discerned or the later not discerned is recorded.

Methodology—1. The systematic and logical study and formulation of the principles and methods used in research. 2. The procedures actually used in a particular investigation.

Micro—A combining form meaning "small," "very small," or "diminished," in contrast to macro.

Milieu—A surround that provides the context of a setting and the behaviors which occur in it.

Mode—In statistics, the most frequent score of a series of scores.

Model—A system of principles or hypotheses or a representation that is postulated to explain relationships in data and is usually presented in mathematical terms.

Muller-Lyer Illusion—The distorted perception of length when a line has arrowheads, or reversed arrowheads. The former looks shorter, the latter longer than the line without arrowheads.

Multiple Choice Question—A question in which the subject is given several responses from which to choose.

Multiple Criterion Technique—A research technique in which the subject adjusts one parameter at a time out of a set of previously identified variables relevant to the behavior being studied.

Multivariate—In statistics, a technique of analysis designed to assess the existence and size of effect of many variables acting simultaneously. Also, characterizing a measure that reflects several variables.

Munsell System—A system for ordering surface colors by specifying hue (color), value (lightness), and chroma (saturation).

Nativists—A group of perceptual psychologists who place emphasis on the inherited factors determining perception rather than on experience.

Needs—1. Conditions of lacking, wanting, or requiring things, which if alleviated would benefit an organism by facilitating behavior or satisfying a tension. 2. Tensions induced in an organism by a lack, either internal or external.

Noise—1. The sensory effect of irregular sound waves; a sound that lacks tone, that is composed of conflicting pitches. 2. Undesired sound. 3. Anything that introduces extraneous variability into a communication process, or that reduces the information in it.

Noise Criteria (NC) Curves—Any of several versions (SC, NC, NCA, PNC), of criteria used for rating the acceptability of continuous indoor noise levels, such as those produced by air-handling systems.

Nominal Scale—A scale in which numbers are assigned to events or event classes for identification and with no reference to any property of the event class. Thus, the number does not represent any dimension of the event or class.

Nonsense Syllable—A syllable, usually of three letters (consonant-vowel-consonant), which has no meaning. Sometimes considered useful in eliminating the influence of meaning on memorization, but the evidence is that people memorize nonsense by giving it a meaning of their own.

Normal Distribution Curve—A symmetrical bell-shaped frequency curve with most of the measurements near the middle and tapering off at the sides.

Noy—A unit used in the calculation of perceived noise levels.

Null Hypothesis—(Statistics) A hypothesis stating that an experimental effect does not exist, that the mean of a group is equal to zero, or that there is no difference between means.

Objective Constancy—The fact that perceptual objects retain a certain standard appearance, in considerable independence of surrounding stimuli and also of the component stimuli making up the perceptual pattern.

Objective—Not depending on the judgment or accuracy of the individual observer; free from personal bias.

Observational Techniques—Techniques and procedures for assisting the observer to make more complete and accurate observations, included are mechanical aids to observation, charts and checklists for prompt and inclusive records, motion picture photography and sound recording, and special training of the observer.

Octave Band—A frequency interval including those frequencies between two tones whose frequencies are related by a ratio of 1:2.

Olfactometer—An instrument that regulates the degree of concentration of a substance used in odor research.

Open-ended Question—Any question which allows the person answering flexibility of form and substance in his response.

Open Message Set—A set of messages, all of which are unknown to a listener. These message units are presented under adverse conditions of communication in order to measure probability of reception.

Operational Definition—The definition of a scientific fact or concept in terms of the concrete operations through which it is produced.

Ordinal Scale—A type of scale which arranges objects with reference to their magnitude and assigns numbers accordingly—first, second, third, etc. It does not possess equal intervals or an absolute zero point.

Organism (O)—Any living entity which has the potential to maintain itself and exist independently as a self-contained system with functions such as respiration, digestion, etc. This includes all plants and animals.

Osmoscope—An instrument used in determining odor thresholds.

Paired Comparisons—The pairing of stimuli in all possible combinations, a technique often used in psychophysics and social psychology. The subject is asked to make comparisons for each pair formed.

Panel Study—A study in which one sample of people is interviewed recurrently over a long period of time to investigate the processes of response change, usually in reference to some variable.

Parallax—The apparent movement of objects when the viewpoint is shifted laterally in the field of vision.

Parametric—A research strategy which emphasizes difinition and understanding of basic variables usually in a laboratory setting.

Participant Observer—An observer who gathers observation data while taking part in a group or an activity being observed.

Passive Observer—An observer who gathers data by not intruding into the observed situation or altering the situation in any way.

Peak Noise—The maximum instantaneous sound pressure (a) for a transient or impulsive sound of short duration in time, or (b) in a specified time interval for a sound of long duration.

Pedometer—An instrument which measures distance walked by recording the number of steps taken.

Perceived Noisiness (PN)—The level of dB assigned to noise by means of a calculation procedure that is based on an approximation to subjective evaluations of "noisiness."

Perception—The process of obtaining information about the world through the senses.

Perceptual Constancy—A general term referring to the tendency of objects to be perceived in the same way despite wide variations in the manner of viewing them.

Performance Concept—An organized procedure or framework within which it is possible to state the desired attributes of a material component or system in order to fulfill the requirements of the intended user without regard to the specific means to be employed in achieving the results.

Permanent Threshold Shift (PTS)—A permanent increase in a hearing threshold level, e.g., the loss of hearing that results from exposure to noise.

Permissive—An attitude which grants freedom of choice and expression to another person out of respect for his personality.

Personal Space—The normal spacing between individual in their environments.

Phenomenologist—One who pursues the philosophical study of the progressive development of the mind.

Phonetically Balanced (PB) Words—A list of monosyllabic words that contains a distribution of speech sounds that approximates the distribution of the same sounds as they occur in conversational American English.

Phototropic—Tending to involuntarily look at the brightest spot.

Pilot Study—A limited preliminary study performed as a forerunner to an experiment, e.g., to test the adequacy of a research approach.

Pink Noise—Noise that when averaged over a period of time will show equal energy in each frequency interval (e.g., octave bands, 1/3-octave bands, etc.).

Population—In statistics, any collection or aggregation of individual units, e.g., buildings.

Preferred Noise Criterion (PNC)—A modification of the currently used Noise Criterion (NC) curves.

Proxemics—A formulation which describes relationships among people and animals in terms of distance, where physical distance may be described on the basis of cultural, behavioral, physiological, and social factors.

Psychoacoustics—A discipline that links physics and psychology in dealing with the physical phenomena of sound as related to audition, as well as with the physiology and psychology of sound receptor processes.

Psychoanalysis—A systematic approach to the study of human functioning, normal and abnormal, originated by Freud. The psychoanalytic method is designed to bring about accessibility to the unconscious process in the patient, and enable him to master those forces previously unknown to him that have seriously impaired his ability to function satisfactorily.

Psychology—A branch of science dealing with the behavior of organisms.

Psychophysics—The branch of psychology that investigates the relationships between physical stimulus magnitudes, or the differences between stimuli, and the corresponding sensory experiences.

Public Opinion Poll—A sampling of the general state of feeling, opinion, or attitude of some predefined segment of the population on an issue or group of issues.

Pulse Rate—The rate of the rhythmic rise and fall of pressure at a given point in the arteries resulting from heart action.

Pupillometer—An instrument which measures changes in eye pupil size; used in studying emotional responses and other phenomena related to eye pupil changes.

Qualitative—Concerned with characteristics, properties, or attributes not specified in numerical terms.

Quantitative—Pertaining to the description or measurement of anything in numerical terms.

Questionnaire—A set of questions, often elaborate, which is designed so as to investigate a given subject.

Questionnaire Items—Questions which make up a questionnaire survey.

Radiation—**1.** Diffusion in all directions from a source or center. **2.** The spreading of neural excitation to adjacent nerve elements. **3.** Emitted waves or particles, or the process of such emission.

Random—Occurring by chance, without voluntary control.

Random Noise—Noise that when averaged over a period of time will show equal energy at all frequencies in the audio range. (The magnitude of any specific frequency at any given point in time is random.)

Random Sample—A sample selected by using a random selection procedure.

Ratio Scale—A type of scale consisting of magnitudes with an absolute zero point, for which both intervals (differences) and ratios can be calculated. All statements of ratio must be based on this scale.

Reflection—The reversal or turning back of particles or waves which strike a surface.

Refraction—A change or bending in the direction of flow of a wave, especially of a light wave, caused by passage of the wave from one medium to another.

Relativity—The attitude or belief that the truth of anything is always dependent on the context, that standards of conduct are not absolute but relative to time, place, culture, and historical circumstances.

Relatoscope—An instrument used in assessing an individual's perception of an environment. The relatoscope is a long pencil-shaped tube with a lens; it extends from a mobile television camera down into a naturalistic model giving a view from eye level.

Reliability—The degree to which results are consistent upon repetition of an experiment, or test.

Requirements—Needs of the user (of a building), such as those of health, safety, and comfort.

Response (R)—**1.** Any overt or covert behavior. **2.** Any process in the body of an organism which results from stimulation.

Rhodopsin—A substance found in the rods of the dark adapted eye that bleaches on exposure to light.

Rods—Rod-shaped cells in the retina which are thought to be the specific structures for the reception of light for vision at the lower intensities. Rod vision is achromatic, i.e., in shades of gray.

Sample—A part of a larger or parent set, usually selected deliberately, used to investigate the properties of the parent population.

Sample Size—The number of sampling units included in a given sample.

Saturation—The degree to which any color possessing a hue differs from a gray of the same brightness.

Scale—Any series of items progressively arranged according to value or magnitude, into which an item can be placed according to its quantification.

Scale Model—A reduced-size physical representation of some aspect of the real world.

Scentometer—An instrument used in measuring odor intensities. A combination of critically sized holes admits ambient air to a mixing chamber, it then passes through two nosepieces on the way to the subjects lungs.

Scientific Approach—Principles and procedures for the systematic pursuit of knowledge involving the recognition and formulation of a problem, the collection of data through observation and experiment, and testing of hypotheses.

Semantic Differential—A method of measuring the subjective reaction to a concept or actual environment, in which the person rates the concept on one or more bipolar scales.

Semifixed Feature—A feature of building to which limited modification is acceptable and possible.

Sensation—Immediate elementary experience requiring no verbal, symbolic, or conceptual elaboration, and related primarily to sense organ activity such as occurring in an eye or ear and in the associated nervous system leading to the particular sensory area in the brain.

Settled Distance—The distance maintained between two individuals following adjustments after the arrival of one of them.

Signal-to-Noise (S/N) Ratio—The ratio of the signal intensity to noise intensity, usually expressed as the decibel difference between the signal level and the noise level.

Significant Difference—A difference in measured values which cannot reasonably be attributed to chance factors.

Silent Language—Nonverbal communication whereby the individual reacts to subtle influences such as gestures and other body and facial movements.

Simple Reaction Time—The time from the onset of a single stimulus until the organism responds.

Simulation—The imitation of certain environmental and other conditions for purposes of training or experimentation.

Sinusoidal—Characterized by simple harmonic, vibratory motions, such as those of the sine wave.

Snellen Eye Chart—A test of visual acuity consisting of a chart of printed letters ranging from very large to very small, which the subject is asked to read at a predetermined distance.

Social Distance—The relative accessibility of one person or group to association with another person or group; the degree of intimacy with which a person is willing to associate with another person or group.

Social Psychology—The branch of psychology concerned with the study of individuals in groups. It deals with the psychological processes and interpersonal interactions in groups and between groups.

Sociofugal—An arrangement of people maximizing interpersonal distance.

Sociogram (Moreno)—A diagram in which group interactions are analyzed on the basis of mutual attractions or antipathies between group members.

Sociology—The science of human societies, groups, organizations, and institutions.

Sociometry (Moreno)—A technique for the measurement of attraction and repulsion among people that uses the method of the sociogram, a diagram in which group interactions are analyzed on the basis of mutual attractions or antipathies between group members.

Sociopetal—An arrangement of people in small groups with little space between persons, as around two small tables in the middle of a large room.

Sone—The sone is a unit of loudness. By definition, a simple tone of frequency 1000 Hz, 40 dB above a listener's threshold, produces a loudness of 1 sone. The loudness of any sound that is judged by the listener to be n times that of the 1-sone tone is n sones.

Sound—1. An oscillation in pressure, stress, particle displacement, particle velocity, etc., in a medium. 2. An auditory sensation evoked by the oscillation described above.

Sound Insulation—The use of structures and materials designed to reduce the transmission of sound from one room or area to another or from the exterior to the interior of a building.

Sound Level (noise level)—Sound level is the frequency-weighted sound pressure level measured by the use of a sound level meter with A, B, or C weightings.

Sound Level Meter—An instrument, comprising a microphone, an amplifier, an output meter, and frequency-weighting networks, that is used for the measurement of noise and sound levels in a specified manner.

Sound Transmission Class (STC)—The preferred single figure rating system designed to give an estimate of the sound insulation properties of a partition or a rank ordering of a series of partitions. It is intended for use primarily when speech and office noise constitute the principle noise problem.

Spectrophotometer—An instrument used to measure the fraction of light transmitted through or reflected from an object, wavelength by wavelength, throughout the visible spectrum.

Speech Communication (SC) Criterion Curve—One of a family of curves generated to indicate different amounts of speech interference in auditory environments.

Speech Interference Levels (SIL)—Calculated quantities providing a guide to the interference effect of a noise on speech. The speech interference level is the arithmetic average of the sound pressure levels of noise in the most important part of the speech frequency range—commonly the three octave-frequency bands centered at 500, 1000, and 2000 Hz.

Speech Spectrogram—A graphic recording of speech used as a method of analyzing speech into its component frequencies.

Standard—In experimental psychology, a constant stimulus against which varying stimuli are compared.

Standard Deviation—A statistical measure of the variability of scores in a frequency distribution; provides a basis for expressing scores in terms of norms.

Standing Pattern—A discrete behavioral entity taking place at a given place at a particular time, e.g., worship service, piano lesson.

Statistical Probability—The likelihood of an occurrence, expressed by the ratio of the number of actual occurrences to that of possible occurrences; the relative frequency with which an event occurs or is likely to occur.

Statistical Significance—The degree of probability that, in an infinite series of measurements of the kind in question, the value or score obtained will not by chance alone occur with significant frequency, and hence can be attributed to something other than chance.

Stereophotography—A photographic method used for recording very detailed information about a bodily movement. The stereo camera consists of two interconnected cone cameras with synchronized exposures.

Stimulus (S)—Any action or situation that elicits response from an organism.

Stratified Sample—A sample selected from a population which has been divided into parts, a portion of the sample coming from each stratum.

Stress—A condition of physical or mental strain which produces changes in the autonomic nervous system.

Stroboscope—An instrument for determing speeds of rotation or frequencies of vibration of a revolving disk with holes around the edge through which an object is viewed.

Subject—The person or animal to whom stimuli are applied for the purpose of evoking response; or, more generally, the person or animal whose reactions are observed.

Subjective—1. Referring to experience available only to the person having the experience. **2.** Referring to judgments made without the use of independent devices or instruments.

Subsystem—A major functional part of a system, usually consisting of several components, such as equipment, activities performed by people, or a combination of the two.

Subtractive Mixture-Color formed by selective absorption, or subtraction of certain wavelengths from light.

Suprathreshold Task—A task which requires a judgment of how well an object can be seen.

Surface-Color Solid—A three-dimensional diagram, each point of which represents a unique color. In the Munsell surface–color solid, the central axis represents lightness, the distance from this axis is saturation, and the angle about the central axis is hue.

Survey—A method of collecting data by sampling a cross section of people, as distinguished from experimental methods.

System—An organized arrangement in which each component part responds in accordance with an overall design. It includes all equipment and personnel integrated in such a manner as to perform a function.

Tachistoscope—An apparatus used in experimental studies of perception, learning, etc., for exposure of visual stimuli (photos, digits) for brief intervals.

Task—A group of related job elements performed to accomplish work, e.g., discrimination, decisions, and motor actions related to one another.

Task Analysis—Task analysis is used to determine the psychological and physical factors essential to the adequate performance of a task. Its goal is to define the critical activities occurring in an operational or training situation in such a way as to provide a sound basis for performance evaluation.

Telephone Survey—Usually a questionnaire survey conducted over the telephone.

Temporary Threshold Shift (TTS)—A temporary increase in a hearing threshold level resulting from exposure to noise.

Territoriality—The perception of a person or group that they possess a given place and all others are intruders there.

Territory—The domain of an animal that is defended upon intrusion by another animal of the same or a different species.

Threshold—(Psychophysics) The minimum stimulus energy or energy change necessary for an experimental subject to indicate an awareness of the stimulus or stimulus change.

Time and Motion—A study involving the observation and analysis of movements in a task with an emphasis on the amount of time required to perform the task.

Time Budget Study—A record made of what a person has done during a specified period of time.

Trace Photography—A photographic method of recording behavior in which the most interesting points on the object or test subject are fitted with small lights. Light tracks of the subject are recorded by making a time exposure of his movements in a dark room.

Tracking Tasks—Tasks involving intermittent or continuous adjustment of an instrument or machine to maintain a desired or normal value, or to follow a moving reference marker.

Traffic Noise Index (TNI)—A measure of the noise environment created by highways; it is computed from measured values of the sound levels exceeded 10% and 90% of the time.

Transient Adaption—A brief variation in an observer's condition of visual adaption caused by momentary exposure to a stimulus differing from the more stable background (as by being brighter or dimmer).

Transmission Loss (TL)—A measure of sound insulation provided by a structural configuration. Expressed in decibels, it is 10 times the logarithm to the base 10 of the reciprocal of the sound transmission coefficient of the configuration. (The sound transmission coefficient is the fraction of incident sound energy transmitted through a structural configuration).

Transposition—1. The reaction to the relationships among stimuli rather than to the absolutes of the stimuli. **2.** The interchange of spatial, logical, or psychological relationships between two units of a system.

Trend Analysis—The statistical analysis of a series of measurements of a variable, taken at several points in time, in order to discover whether there is a basic direction of change.

Triangle Test—A method for selecting subjects for participation in odor tests. The person is presented with three odors, two of which are identical, and is asked to select the odd one. A series of such trials consitutes the triangle test.

Unobtrusive Measures—Methods of studying behavior which do not interfere with the normal environment in which the behavior occurs. The researcher observes without intruding into the scene.

User—An occupant of a building, i.e., anyone who uses or performs activities in a building.

Validity—The degree to which a research study or test can predict performance in a realistic situation, that is, where the problem investigated actually exists.

Value—The relative lightness or darkness of a color.

Vapor Dilution Method—A method of determining odor threshold levels by mixing various amounts of uncontaminated air with odorous air.

Variable—1. A factor the quantity of which can be increased or decreased either in discrete or continuous steps or along some continuum without any other concommitant change in that factor. **2.** Anything that can change or take on different characteristics appropriate to specified conditions.

White Noise—An acoustical stimulus composed of all audible frequencies at the same intensity with random phase relations between them; it sounds like "shhhhhhhhhhhhh."

Word Association Test—A projective technique consisting of a list of words which is presented to the subject one at a time. The subject is asked to respond with the first word that comes to mind.

BIBLIOGRAPHY

Aas, D. "Observing Environmental Behavior: The Behavior Setting." In: W. Michelson (ed.), *Behavioral Research Methods in Environmental Design*, Stroudsburg, PA: Dowden, Hutchinson, and Ross, 1975.

Alexander, C. *Notes on the Synthesis of Form,* Cambridge, MA: Harvard University Press, 1964.

Allen, D. L. and Swallow, J. L. "Annoying Floor Vibrations—Diagram and Therapy," *Journal of Sound and Vibration,* 1975.

Anderson, J. and Tindall, M. "The Concept of Home Range: New Data for the Study of Territorial Behavior. In: W. J. Mitchell (ed.), *Proceedings of EDRA3/AR 8 Conference,* Los Angeles, 1972.

Ardrey, Robert. *African Genesis,* NY: Delta, 1963.

Ardrey, Robert. *The Territorial Imperative,* NY: Atheneum, 1966.

Arnheim, Rudolf. *The Dynamics of Architectural Form,* Berkeley: U. of California Press, 1977.

Bacon, Edmund N. *Design of Cities,* NY: Penguin, 1974.

Barker, R. G. *Ecological Psychology: Concepts and Methods for Studying the Environment of Human Behavior,* Stanford: Stanford University Press, 1968.

Baum, A. and Davis, G. E. "Spatial and Social Aspects of Crowding Perception," *Environment and Behavior,* 8 (Dec. 1976).

Bender, E. K. and Collins, A. M. *Effects of Vibration on Human Performance: A Literature Review* (Bolt, Beranek, and Newman Report 1767), Boston: Bolt, Beranek, and Newman, Feb. 1969.

Blackwell, H. R. "Specification of Interior Illumination Levels," *Illuminating Engineering,* 1959.

Blackwell, H. R. "The Evaluation of Interior Lighting on the Basis of Visual Criteria," *Applied Optics,* 1967.

Blake, R. R. et al. "Housing, Architecture, and Social Interaction," *Sociometry,* 1956.

Bodmann, H. In: R. G. Hopkinson and J. B. Collins, *The Ergonomics of Lighting,* London: MacDonald, 1970.

Boyce, P. R. "Users' Assessments of a Landscaped Office, *Journal of Architectural Research,* 1974.

Boynton, R. M. "Some Visual Factors in Reducing Lighting Levels." In: D. K. Ross (ed.). *The Basis for Effective Management of Lighting,* Washington, D.C.: Federal Energy Administration, October 1975.

Braun, J. Jay; Linder, Darwyn E.; and Asimov, Isaac (eds.). *Psychology Today: An Introduction,* NY: Random House, 1979.

British Illuminating Engineering Society. "Artificial Lighting," *The Architects' Journal Information Library,* January 1967.

Brookes, M. J. "Changes in Employee Attitudes and Work Practices in an Office Landscape." In: W. J. Mitchell (ed.), *Environmental Design: Research and Practice, Proceedings of the EDRA 3/AR 8 Conference,* Los Angeles: U. of California Press, 1972.

Chen, P.W. and Robertson, F. "Human Perception Thresholds of Horizontal Motion," *Journal of Structural Division, Proceedings of ASCE,* Aug. 1972.

Chermayeff, Serge and Alexander, C. *Community and Privacy,* Garden City, NY: Doubleday Anchor, 1965.

Collins, B. *Windows and People: A Literature Survey* (Building Science Series Report no. 70), Washington, D.C.: NBS 1978.

Collins, J. In: R. G. Hopkinson and J. B. Collins, *The Ergonomics of Lighting,* London: MacDonald, 1970.

Conrads, Ulrich. Programs and Manifestoes on 20th Century Architecture. Cambridge, MA: M.I.T. Press, 1964.

Conway, D. J. *Human Response to Tall Buildings,* Stroudsburg, PA: Dowden, Hutchinson, and Ross, 1977.

Le Corbusier. *The Modulor,* Cambridge, MA: Harvard University Press, 1954.

Le Corbusier. *Modulor* 2, Cambridge, MA: MIT, 1955.

Dabbs, J. M., Jr.; Fuller, J.; and Carr, T. "Personal Space When 'Cornered': College Students and Prison Inmates," *81st Annual Convention of the American Psychological Association,* 1973.

Davis, G. and Roizen R. "Architectural Determinants of Student Satisfaction in College Residence Halls." In: J. Archea and C. Eastman (eds.), *EDRA 2: Proceedings of the 2nd Annual EDRA Conference 1970.*

De La Croix, Horst *Military Considerations in City Planning: Fortifications,* NY: Braziller, 1972.

Denis, J. In: E. K. Bender and A. M. Collins, *Effects of Vibration on Human Performance: A Literature Review* (Bolt, Beranek, and Newman Report 1767), Boston: Bolt, Beranek, and Newman, Feb. 1969.

Dubos, Rene *So Human an Animal,* NY: Scribners, 1968.

Duriak, J.T.; Beardsley, B. E.; and Murray, J.S. "Observations of User Activity Patterns in Open and Traditional Plan School Environments." In: W. J. Mitchell (ed.), *Environmental Design: Research and Practice, Proceedings EDRA Conference 1972.*

Egolf, B., and Herrenkohl, R. C. "The Influence of Familiarity and Age Factors on Responses to Residential Structures." In: D. J. Conway (ed.), *Human Response to Tall Buildings,* Stroudsburg, PA: Dowden, Hutchinson, and Ross, 1977.

Englund, M., and Hallberg, G. *Video Tape Techniques In Full-Scale Tests.* (National Swedish Building Research Document D3: 1973).

Fanger, P. O. *Thermal Comfort,* Copenhagen: Danish Technical Press, 1970.

Fanger, P. O., and Griffiths, I. In: P. O. Fanger, *Thermal Comfort,* Copenhagen: Danish Technical Press, 1970.

Farr, Lee E. "Medical Consequences of Environmental Home Noises." In: R. Gutman (ed.), *People and Buildings,* NY: Basic, 1972.

Faulkner, W. *Architecture and Color,* New York: John Wiley and Sons, 1972.

Festinger, L. "Architecture and Group Membership." In: R. Gutman (ed.), *People and Buildings,* NY: Basic, 1972.

Festinger, L.; Schachter, S.; and Black, K. *Social Pressures in Informal Groups: A Study of Human Factors in Housing.* Stanford: Stanford University Press, 1963.

Fitch, J.M. *The Architectural Manipulation of Space, Time, and Gravity,* NY: Columbia University, 1969.

Fitch, J. M.; Templer, J.; and Coercoran, P. "The Dimensions of Stairs," *Scientific American,* 1974.

Fletcher, Sir Banister. *A History of Architecture,* 18th Edition, NY: Scribners, 1975.

Flynn, J. E. and Segil W. A. *Architectural Interior Systems,* NY: Van Nostrand Reinhold, 1970.

Flynn, J. E. et al. "Interim Study of Procedures for Investigating the Effect of Light on Impression and Behavior, *Journal of IES,* October 1973.

Fried, M. and Glelcher, P. "Some Sources of Residential Satisfaction in an Urban Slum." In: H. M. Proshansky, W. H. Ittleson, and L. G. Rivlin (eds.), *Environmental Psychology: Man and His Physical Setting,* NY: Holt, Rinehart, and Winston, 1970.

Fryer, Douglas H.; Henry, Edwin R.; and Sparks, Charles P. (eds.). *General Psychology: Survey of Basic Principles,* NY: Barnes and Noble, 1965.

Gans, H.J. "Planning and Social Life: Friendship and Neighbor Relations in Suburban Communities." In: H. M. Proshansky, W. H. Ittleson, and L. G. Rivlin (eds.), *Environmental Psychology: Man and His Physical Setting,* NY: Holt, Rinehart, and Winston, 1970.

Gelb, P. M. "High Rise Impact on City and Neighborhood Livability." In: D. J. Conway (ed.), *Human Response to Tall Buildings,* Stroudsburg, PA: Dowden, Hutchinson, and Ross, 1977.

Geldard, F. A. *The Human Senses,* NY: John Wiley and Sons, 1972.

Gibson, J. J. *The Perception of the Visual World,* Cambridge, MA: Riverdale Press, 1950.

Giedion, Siegfried. *Architecture and the Phenomena of Transition.* Cambridge, MA: Harvard U. Press, 1971.

Giedion, Siegfried. *Mechanization Takes Command,* NY: Norton, 1969.

Gilbert, M. and Hopkinson, R. G. In: R. G. Hopkinson and J. B. Collins, *The Ergonomics of Lighting,* London: MacDonald, 1970.

Gliner, G. "Tactual Discrimination Thresholds for Shape and Texture in Young Children," *Journal of Experimental Child Psychology,* 5(1967).

Griffiths, I. D. and Langdon, F. J. "Subjective Response to Road Traffic Noise," *Journal of Sound Vibration,* 1968.

Gutman, Robert (ed.). *People and Buildings,* NY: Basic Books, 1972.

Hall, Edward T. *Beyond Culture,* Garden City, NY: Doubleday, 1977.

Hall, Edward T. "Environmental Communication." In: A.H. Esser (ed.), *International Symposium on the Use of Space by Animals and Men. Dallas, Texas 1968.*

Hall, Edward T. *The Hidden Dimension,* Garden City, NY: Doubleday, 1966.

Hall, Edward T. *The Silent Language,* Greenwich, CT: Fawcett, 1959.

Hartford, B. and Keleman, K. S. "Nurse Behavior and Nursing Unit Design." In: W. D. Bliss (ed.), *Proceedings of the Symposium on Environmental Effects on Behavior,* Bozeman: Montana State University, 1975.

Hazard, John N. "Furniture Arrangement as a Symbol of Judicial Roles." In: Robert Gutman (ed.), *People and Buildings,* NY: Basic Books, 1972, pp. 291-298.

Helberg, W., and Sperling, E. In: W. Bryce, *A Review and Assessment of Criteria for Human Comfort of Vibration* (N.G.T.E. R286), Pyestock, Hants, U.K.: Ministry of Aviation, National Gas Turbine Establishment, Dec. 1966.

Held, Richard (ed.). *Image, Object and Illusion: Readings from Scientific American,* San Francisco: Freeman, 1971.

Hitchcock, Henry-Russell, and Johnson, Philip. *The International Style,* NY: Norton, 1932.

Holland, C. et al. In: E. K. Bender and A. M. Collins, *Effects of Vibration on Human Performance: A Literature Review* (*Bolt, Beranek and Newman Report 1767*), Boston: Bolt, Beranek, and Newman, Feb. 1969.

Holmberg, I. and Wyon D. In Thermal Comfort and Modern Heat Stress (BRE Report 2). Garston, Watford, UK: HMSO, 1973.

Holmes, J. G. *Essays on Lighting,* New York: Crane Russak and Co., 1974.

Hopkinson, R. G. and Collins, J. B. *The Ergonomics of Lighting,* London: MacDonald, 1970.

Hornick, R. In: E. K. Bender and A. M. Collins, *Effects of Vibration on Human Performance: A Literature Review (Bolt, Beranek, and Newman Report 1767).* Boston: Bolt, Beranek, and Newman, Feb. 1969.

Houghton, F. C. and Yagloglou, C. P. "Determination of the Comfort Zone." *ASHVE Transactions,* 29 (1923).

Hughes, Robert. *The Shock of the New,* NY: Knopf, 1981.

Humphreys, M.A., and Nicol, J. F. *Theoretical and Practical Aspects of Thermal Comfort (BRS CP 14/71).* Garston, Watford, UK: Building Research Station, 1971.

IES Lighting Handbook (5th ed.), New York: Illuminating Engineering Society, 1972.

Imamoglu, V. and Markus, T. A. "The Effect of Window Size, Room Proportion, and Window Position on Spaciousness Evaluation of Rooms." In: *Proceedings of CIE Conference on Windows and Their Function in Architectural Design,* Istanbul, October 1973.

Inui, M. and Miyata, T. "Spaciousness in Interiors," *Lighting Research and Technology,* 1973.

Jacklin, H., and Lidell, G., In: E. K. Bender and A. M. Collins, *Effects of Vibration on Human Performance: A Literature Review (Bolt, Beranek, and Newman Report 1767),* Boston: Bolt, Beranek, and Newman, Feb. 1969.

Jencks, Charles. *Post-Modern Architecture,* NY: Rizzoli, 1977.

Jonge de, Derk. *Some Notes on Sociological Research in the Field of Housing,* Delft, mimeo 1967 (Sommer, *Personal Space,* pp. 23).

Kandinsky, Wassily. *Point and Line to Plane,* NY: Dover 1926.

Keighley, E. C. "Visual Requirements and Reduced Fenestration in Office Buildings: A Study of Window Shape," *Journal of Building Science, 1973.*

Kleeman, W. "Behavioral Change on Ward," In: W. D. Bliss (ed.), *Proceedings of the Symposium on Environmental Effects on Behavior,* Bozeman: Montana State University, 1975.

Kryter, K. *The Effects of Noise on Man,* NY: Academic Press, 1970.

Lam, W. M. C. "Lighting For Architecture," Reprinted from *Architectural Record,* undated.

Langdon, F. J. "Human Sciences and the Environment in Buildings," *Build International 6* (Jan–Feb 1973).

Langdon, F. J. and Loudon, A. "Discomfort in Schools from Overheating in Summer," *Journal of the Institution of Heating and Ventilating Engineers,* 37 (March 1970).

Lassaigne, Jacques. *KANDINSKY,* Geneva: Skira, 1964.

Leibman, M. "The Effects of Sex and Race Norms on Personal Space," *Environment and Behavior,* Dec. 1970.

Lorenz, Konrad. *King Solomons Ring,* NY: Signet, 1952.

Lorenz, Konrad. *On Aggression,* NY: Harcourt Brace, 1963.

Luckiesh, M. *Visual Illusions—Their Causes, Characteristics, and Applications,* NY: Dover, 1965.

Lynch, Kevin. *The Image of the City,* Cambridge, MA: MIT, 1960.

Lythgoe, R. In: R. G. Hopkinson and J. B. Collins, *The Ergonomics of Lighting,* London: MacDonald, 1970.

Maslow, A. H. *Motivation and Personality,* NY: Harper and Row, 1954.

Maslow, A. H. and Mintz, N. L. "Effects of Esthetic Surroundings: I. Initial Short-term Effects of Three Esthetic Conditions upon Perceiving 'Energy' and 'Well-being' in Faces." In: R. Gutman (ed.), *People and Buildings,* NY: Basic Books, 1972.

McIntyre, D. Thermal Comfort and Moderate Heat Stress (BRE Report 2), Garston, Watford, UK: HMSO, 1973.

McNall, P. "The Relative Effects of Convection and Radiation Heat Transfer on Thermal Comfort for Sedentary and Active Human Subjects," *ASHRAE Transactions* 1968 (Part II, pp. 131–143).

Mercer, Charles. *Living in Cities,* Baltimore: Penguin, 1975.

Millon, H. A. and Frazer, A. *Key Monuments of the History of Architecture,* NY: Abrams, 1965.

Mintz, N. L. "Effects of Esthetic Surroundings: II. Prolonged and Repeated Experience in a 'Beautiful' and an 'Ugly' Room." In: R. Gutman (ed.) *People and Buildings,* NY: Basic Books, 1972.

Moorehead, Alan. *Fatal Impact: The Invasion of the South Pacific,* NY: Harper and Row, 1966.

Moreno, J. L. Sociometry and the Science of Man, NY: Beacon House, 1956.

Ne'eman, E. and Hopkinson, R. G. "Critical Minimum Acceptable Window Size: A Study of Window Design and Provision of a View," *Lighting Research and Technology,* 1970.

Neenan, C. J. "Shadow Characteristics of Stage Lights for Theater, Television and Motion Pictures, *Illuminating Engineering 1968.*

Neumann, Eckhard. *Functional Graphic Design in the 20's,* NY: Van Nostrand Reinhold, 1967.

Newman, Oscar. *Defensible Space,* NY: Collier, 1973.

Ostberg, O. and Stone P. "Methods for Evaluating Discomfort Glare Aspects of Lighting," *Goteborg Psychological Reports,* Univ. of Goteborg, Sweden, 1974.

Overy, Paul. *De Stijl,* London: Studio Vista, 1969.

Parks, D. L. and Snyder, F. W. *Human Reaction to Low Frequency Vibration* (Tech. Rep. D3-3512-1), Wichita, Kansas: Boeing Co., July 1961.

Parr, A. E. "Problems of Reason, Feeling, and Habitat," *Architectural Association Quarterly,* London, Vol. 1, No. 3, July 1969, pp. 5–10.

Pastalan, L. A. and Carson, D. H. (eds.). *Spatial Behavior of Older People,* Ann Arbor: U. of Michigan, 1970.

Persig, Robert M. Zen and the Art of Motorcycle Maintenance, NY: Bantam, 1974.

Pile, John F. "The Open Office: Does It Work," *Progressive Architecture,* June 1977.

Porteous, C. W. and Porteous, J. D. "The Learning Environment Enrichment or Impoverishment?" In: W. D. Bliss (ed.), *Proceedings of the Symposium on Environmental Effects on Behavior,* Bozeman: Montana State University, 1975.

Proshansky, Ittelson, and Rivlin. *Environmental Psychology,* NY: Holt Rinehart, 1970.

Prussin, Labelle. *Architecture in Northern Ghana,* Berkeley: U. of C. Press, 1969.

Rapoport, A. and Watson, N. *Cultural Variability in Physical Standards.* In: R. Gutman (ed.), *People and Buildings,* NY: Basic, 1972.

Rasmussen, Steen Eiler. *Experiencing Architecture,* Cambridge, MA: MIT, 1959.

Read, Herbert. *The Meaning of Art,* Baltimore: Pelican, 1931.

Reed, J. W. *Wind-Induced Motion and Human Discomfort in Tall Buildings,* (Research Report R71-42), Cambridge, MA: MIT, Dept. of Civil Engineering, Nov. 1971.

Reiher, H. and Meister, F. In W. Bryce: *A Review and Assessment of Criteria for Human Comfort of Vibration* (N.G.T.E. R286) Pyestock, Hants, UK: Ministry of Aviation, National Gas Turbine Establishment, Dec. 1966.

Reimer, S. and Demerath N. J. "The Role of Social Research in Housing Design," *Land Economics,* 1952.

Ribiero, J. S.; Allen, W. A.; and Deamorium, M. "Lighting of the Calouste Gulbenkian Museum," *Lighting Research and Technology 1971.*

Rohles, F. H. "Psychological Aspects of Thermal Comfort," *ASHRAE Journal,* January 1971 (pp. 86–90).

Rubin, E. *Readings in Perception* (D.C. Beardslee and M. Wertheimer (eds.)), NY: Van Nostrand, 1958.

Rubin, Arthur, and Elder, J. (eds.). *Building for People,* Washington, D.C.: Nat. Bureau of Stds., 1980.

Sausmarez, Maurice de. *Basic Design: The Dynamics of Visual Form,* Reinhold, 1964.

Savinar, J. "The Effect of Ceiling Height on Personal Space," Man Environment Systems, Washington, D.C.: Nat. Bureau of Stds., 1975.

Schmitz, M. In: E. K. Bender and A. M. Collins, *Effects of Vibration on Human Performance: A Literature Review* (*Bolt, Baranek, and Newman Report 1767*), Boston: Bolt, Beranek, and Newman, Feb. 1969.

Schorr, L. *Slums and Social Insecurity* (Research Report No. 1), Washington, D.C.: U.S. Dept of HEW, Social Security Administration, 1966.

Siegel, Curt. *Structure and Form in Modern Architecture,* NY: Reinhold, 1962.

Sommer, R. Personal Space: The Behavioral Basis of Design, Englewood Cliffs, NJ: Prentice-Hall, 1974.

Sommer, R. *Tight Spaces: Hard Architecture and How to Humanize It,* Englewood Cliffs, NJ: Prentice-Hall, 1974.

Steinfeld, E. H. "Physical Planning for Increased Cross-Generation Contact," In: W.F.E. Preiser (ed.), *4th Annual EDRA Conference,* Stroudsburg, PA: Dowden, Hutchinson, and Ross, 1973.

Taylor, Joshua C. *Futurism,* NY: MOMA Doubleday, 1961.

Thompson, D'Arcy. *On Growth and Form,* Cambridge: Cambridge University Press, 1917.

Van Deusen. In: E. K. Bender and A. M. Collins, *Effects of Vibration on Human Performance: A Literature Review* (Bolt, Beranek, and Newman Report 1767), Boston: Bolt, Beranek, and Newman, Feb. 1969.

Venturi, Robert. *Complexity and Contradiction in Architecture,* NY: MOMA, 1966.

Vigier, F. C. "An Experimental Approach to Urban Design," *Journal of the American Institute of Planners,* Feb. 1965.

Vitruvius, Marcus Pollio. *The Ten Books on Architecture,* NY: Dover, 1960.

Weisz, A. et al. In: E. K. Bender and A. M. Collins, *Effects of Vibration on Human Performance: A Literature Review* (Bolt, Beranek, and Newman Report 1767), Boston: Bolt, Beranek, and Newman, Feb. 1969.

Wells, B. W. P. "The Psychosocial Influence of Building Environment: Sociometric Findings in Large and Small Office Spaces." In: R. Gutman (ed.), *People and Buildings,* NY: Basic Books, 1972.

Weston, M. In: R. G. Hopkinson and J. B. Collins, *The Ergonomics of Lighting,* London: MacDonald, 1970.

Williamson, P.; Le Resche, L.; and Geldzahler, M. "Space Use and Behavior in an Open Plan School: An Ethological Study." In: W. D. Bliss (ed.), *Proceedings of the Symposium on Environmental Effects on Behavior,* Bozeman: Montana State University, 1975.

Wittkower, Rudolf. *Architectural Principles: In the Age of Humanism,* NY: Random House, 1942.

Yamada, M., and Gato, T. "Human Response to Tall Building Motion." In: D. Conway (ed.), *Human Response to Tall Buildings,* Stroudsburg, PA: Dowden, Hutchinson, and Ross, 1977.

Yonemura, G. and Kohayakawa, Y. *A New Look at the Research Basis for Lighting Level Recommendations* (NBS Building Science Series 82), Washington, D.C.: National Bureau of Standards, March 1976.

Zevi, Bruno. *Architecture as Space,* NY: Horizon, 1974.

Zinsser, H. *Rats, Lice, and History,* NY: Bantam, 1935.

INDEX